INTERROGATING LESBIAN MODERNISM

INTERROGATING LESBIAN MODERNISM

HISTORIES, FORMS, GENRES

Edited by
Elizabeth English, Jana Funke
and Sarah Parker

EDINBURGH
University Press

Edinburgh University Press is one of the leading university presses in the UK. We publish academic books and journals in our selected subject areas across the humanities and social sciences, combining cutting-edge scholarship with high editorial and production values to produce academic works of lasting importance. For more information visit our website: edinburghuniversitypress.com

© editorial matter and organisation Elizabeth English, Jana Funke, Sarah Parker 2023, 2024
© the chapters their several authors 2023, 2024

Edinburgh University Press Ltd
13 Infirmary Street,
Edinburgh, EH1 1LT

First published in hardback by Edinburgh University Press 2023

Typeset in 10/12.5 Adobe Sabon by
IDSUK (DataConnection) Ltd

A CIP record for this book is available from the British Library

ISBN 978 1 4744 8605 7 (hardback)
ISBN 978 1 4744 8606 4 (paperback)
ISBN 978 1 4744 8607 1 (webready PDF)
ISBN 978 1 4744 8608 8 (epub)

The right of Elizabeth English, Jana Funke, Sarah Parker to be identified as the editors of this work has been asserted in accordance with the Copyright, Designs and Patents Act 1988, and the Copyright and Related Rights Regulations 2003 (SI No. 2498).

CONTENTS

List of Figures vii
Acknowledgements ix
Notes on Contributors xi

Introduction 1
   Elizabeth English, Jana Funke and Sarah Parker

Part I: Interrogating Lesbian/Queer/Trans Modernism
1 Loving/Hating/Loving Lesbian Modernism 31
   Jodie Medd
2 Lesbian-Trans-Feminist Modernism: Christopher St. John,
   Trans Masculinity and Celibate Friendship in *Hungerheart:
   The Story of a Soul* 56
   Jana Funke
3 The Ontology of the Pluri-Singular Body in Natalie Clifford
   Barney's *The One Who Is Legion or A.D.'s After-Life* 78
   Katharina Boeckenhoff

Part II: Genres and Forms
4 Imaginative Biography: Margaret Goldsmith, Vita Sackville-West
   and Lesbian Historical Life Writing 99
   Elizabeth English

CONTENTS

5 Modernism at the Margins: Mariette Lydis's Print Portfolio
   Lesbiennes 120
   Abbey Rees-Hales
6 Inverting the Gaze: Radclyffe Hall and Male Sexual Identities 145
   Steven Macnamara

Part III: Relationality, Networks and Kinship
7 Writing Widows of Lesbian Modernism 165
   Hannah Roche
8 Lesbianism in/and the Family: Eva Gore-Booth and the Making of
   Feminist Modernism 183
   Kathryn Holland
9 Lesbian Joyce 204
   Katherine Mullin

Part IV: Histories and Temporalities
10 Elizabethan Lovemaking: College Romance and Queer Anachronism
   in Edna St. Vincent Millay's *The Lamp and the Bell* 225
   Sarah Parker
11 The Lesbian Herstory Archives at Fifty 248
   Robin Hackett
12 Hidden in Plain Sight: The Reconstruction of Lesbian Modernist
   Sexual Histories 265
   Jo Winning

Index 285

FIGURES

5.1 Marc Vaux, Black and white photographic reproduction of hand-coloured etching from Mariette Lydis's *Lesbiennes* portfolio (1926), date of photograph unknown. Scan of original glass plate negative: © Centre Pompidou – MNAM/CCI – Bibliothèque Kandinsky – Fonds Marc Vaux　　121

5.2 Mariette Lydis, Untitled print from *Lesbiennes* [Lesbians], 1926. Hand-coloured etching, print size: 15 x 11 cm. Private collection; image courtesy of honesterotica.com　　121

5.3 Mariette Lydis, Two untitled prints from *Lesbiennes* [Lesbians], 1926. Hand-coloured etchings on paper, each print measures: 15 x 11 cm. Private collection; image courtesy of honesterotica.com　　122

5.4 Mariette Lydis, Untitled print from *Lesbiennes* [Lesbians], 1926. Hand-coloured etching, print size: 15 x 11 cm. Private collection; image courtesy of honesterotica.com　　123

5.5 Mariette Lydis, Untitled, 1937. Oil on canvas, size and current whereabouts of the original painting unknown. Scan of original glass plate negative: © Centre Pompidou – MNAM/CCI – Bibliothèque Kandinsky – Fonds Marc Vaux, photograph: Marc Vaux　　126

FIGURES

5.6 Mariette Lydis, Untitled (Virgin Mary holding the Holy Shroud), 1926. Gouache and graphite, size and whereabouts of the original artwork unknown. Scan of original glass plate negative: © Centre Pompidou – MNAM/CCI – Bibliothèque Kandinsky – Fonds Marc Vaux, photograph: Marc Vaux   128

5.7 Mariette Lydis, *La Pudeur* [Modesty], c. 1915. Watercolour and ink on paper. Private collection   128

5.8 Madame D'Ora, *Frau Bachhofen mit Reitkleid* [Mrs Bachhofen in riding dress] (Portrait of Mariette Lydis), 1921. Scan of original glass-plate negative, 18 x 24 cm. Vienna, Österreichische Nationalbibliothek   129

10.1 Margaret De Motte Brown, Beatrice (Clifford Sellers) and Bianca (Lois Duffie) in performance of *The Lamp and the Bell*, reproduced in *Vassar Quarterly* 6, no. 4 (1 August 1921), n.p.   240

12.1 Kay Dick's 'Dorothy Richardson' notebook, Series 1 Works, Kay Dick Papers, Harry Ransom Center, University of Texas at Austin   273

12.2 Thomas Lowry's editorial memo to William A. Koshland about the 'March Moonlight' manuscript   281

ACKNOWLEDGEMENTS

This volume originated in the 2018 *Queer Modernisms II: Intersectional Identities* conference at the University of Oxford, which was organised by Lloyd (Meadbh) Houston, Rio Matchett and Séan Richardson. Our two panels on lesbian modernism allowed us to begin the conversations that resulted in this book. We continued these discussions at the *Radclyffe Hall: 90 Years Since the Well of Loneliness* Symposium in the summer of 2018, which we organised together, and for which we gratefully received funding from the British Society for Literature and Science. Special thanks to Jo Winning for delivering an outstanding keynote at the Radclyffe Hall symposium. We are thankful to everyone else who participated in these events whether as a speaker or audience member. Your thoughtful comments and feedback have been invaluable in shaping this book.

We are immensely grateful to Jackie Jones at Edinburgh University Press for supporting this project from the very start. We also extend our gratitude to Susannah Butler at Edinburgh University Press, who provided excellent support throughout the publication process, and to everyone else involved in making this volume a reality. We also want to thank Holly James Johnston and Henri T. for allowing us to use the *Orlando in 'A Well of Loneliness'* portrait from the *Orlando in Lockdown* series as our cover image.

Our main thanks are due to the contributors to this volume, who remained committed to the project throughout the pandemic and the many challenges it held for all of us. We are grateful for the care and insight with which you interrogated, probed and questioned the uses, meanings and boundaries of lesbian modernism. We are thrilled to be part of such a supportive and inspiring network of scholars working within and across lesbian, queer, trans and feminist modernist studies.

On a personal note, Elizabeth would like to thank her English and Creative Writing colleagues at Cardiff Metropolitan University, particularly Carmen Casaliggi and Nick Taylor-Collins who provided thoughtful feedback on her chapter and vital encouragement as it took shape. Thanks also go, of course, to her co-editors Jana and Sarah who made this project a pleasure to work on. Jana would like to thank her friends and family. She is grateful to colleagues in the University of Exeter's Department of English and Creative Writing, and LGBTQ+ Staff Network. Jana credits her numerous collaborators on the Rethinking Sexology and Adventures in Time and Gender projects for profoundly shaping her understanding of lesbian modernism. Thanks are also due to her fellow co-convenors of the IHR History of Sexuality seminar series for continuously expanding her understanding of the histories of sexuality and gender. She is also grateful to Elizabeth and Sarah for being such insightful and good-humoured co-editors. Sarah would like to thank her colleagues at Loughborough University, particularly members of the Cultural Currents: 1870–1930 research group for numerous interesting discussions of nineteenth- and twentieth-century crossovers and continuities. Thank you to Fraser Riddell for providing thoughtful feedback on her chapter in development. Sarah is especially grateful to staff at Vassar College Special Collections for providing access to materials that she was unable to see in person due to the pandemic.

NOTES ON CONTRIBUTORS

Katharina Boeckenhoff holds a PhD from the University of Manchester and currently works as an independent researcher and language teacher based in São Paulo. Her research interests include literary modernism, gender politics and sexuality. She has also published on the German filmmaker Lotte Reiniger.

Elizabeth English is a Senior Lecturer in English Literature at Cardiff Metropolitan University. Her research focuses on modernism and early twentieth-century popular fiction, with a particular interest in gender and sexuality. She is the author of *Lesbian Modernism: Censorship, Sexuality and Genre Fiction* (Edinburgh University Press, 2015) as well as essays and articles in such publications as *The Female Fantastic: Gendering the Supernatural in the 1890s and 1920s* (2018) and *Women: A Cultural Review*.

Jana Funke is Associate Professor of English and Sexuality Studies at the University of Exeter. Her research focuses on modernist literature, the history of sexology and queer feminist theory. Books include *Sex, Gender and Time in Fiction and Culture* (2011, co-edited with Ben Davies), *The World and Other Unpublished Works by Radclyffe Hall* (2016), *Sculpture, Sexuality and History: Encounters in Literature, Culture and the Arts* (2018, co-edited with Jen Grove) and the first Oxford World's Classics edition of Radclyffe Hall's *The Well of Loneliness* (2023, co-edited with Hannah Roche). Forthcoming books include *Sexological Modernism: Queer Feminism and Sexual Science* and *Sexperts: A History of Sexology*.

Robin Hackett is an Associate Professor of English and Women's Studies at the University of New Hampshire. She writes and teaches about literary modernism, and feminist and queer studies.

Kathryn Holland teaches English and Gender Studies at MacEwan University and she is Associate Director of the Orlando Project, a long-running experiment in the integration of feminist literary history and digital humanities. She has published in such collections as *Bodies of Information: Intersectional Feminism and Digital Humanities* (2018) and journals including *Tulsa Studies in Women's Literature*.

Steven Macnamara is an independent researcher with an interest in Radclyffe Hall, modernism and queer theory. His PhD explored masculinity in Radclyffe Hall's work. He has published an essay on Joan of Arc and Hall in *Reimagining Masculinities: Beyond Masculinist Epistemology* (2014) and an article on the silent novel in *The Well of Loneliness* for the *Ransom Center Magazine* (2017).

Jodie Medd is Associate Professor of English Literature and Women's and Gender Studies at Carleton University, on unceded Anishinaabe land in Ottawa, Canada. She is the author of *Lesbian Scandal and the Culture of Modernism* (2012) and the editor of *The Cambridge Companion to Lesbian Literature* (2015).

Katherine Mullin teaches Victorian and modernist literature in the School of English at the University of Leeds. Her publications include *James Joyce, Sexuality and Social Purity* (2003; paperback 2007) and *Working Girls: Fiction, Sexuality, and Modernity* (2016). She is currently completing her third monograph about the complex and strangely productive relationship between literature and censorship during the Victorian and Modernist periods, *Provocateurs: Censorship, Backlash, and the Invention of Modernism*.

Sarah Parker is a Senior Lecturer in English at Loughborough University. She is the author of *The Lesbian Muse and Poetic Identity, 1889–1930* (2013), *Michael Field: Decadent Moderns* (with Ana Parejo Vadillo, 2019) and *Michael Field: 'For That Moment Only' and Other Prose Works* (with Alex Murray, 2022). She has published several articles on poets including Edna St. Vincent Millay, H.D., Amy Levy, Olive Custance and Iris Tree.

Abbey Rees-Hales is a final-year AHRC Midlands4Cities-funded doctoral researcher in the Department of Art History, Curating and Visual Studies at the University of Birmingham. Her thesis examines the contribution made by women artists to the lesboerotic visual cultures of interwar Germany and France. Previous publications include essays on the erotic graphic works of Charlotte Berend-Corinth and Lene Schneider-Kainer.

Hannah Roche is Senior Lecturer in Twentieth-Century Literature and Culture at the University of York. She is the author of *The Outside Thing: Modernist Lesbian Romance* (2019) along with articles in *Essays in Criticism*, *Modernist Cultures* and *Textual Practice*. Hannah is co-editor, with Jana Funke, of the first Oxford World's Classics edition of Radclyffe Hall's *The Well of Loneliness*, forthcoming.

Jo Winning is Professor of Modern Literature and Critical Theory in the Department of English, Theatre and Creative Writing at Birkbeck, University of London. She has published extensively on the practitioners and practices of lesbian modernism. She is one of the editorial team of the Dorothy Richardson Scholarly Editions Project and is currently editing the first volume of Richardson's letters with Professor Scott McCracken.

INTRODUCTION

Elizabeth English, Jana Funke and Sarah Parker[1]

In April 2018, we organised two panels on lesbian modernism as part of a conference at the University of Oxford entitled *Queer Modernism(s) II: Intersectional Identities*.[2] During our panel sessions, we asked several questions with the aim of interrogating lesbian modernism from various angles, including in the context of queer modernist scholarship and in relation to the potential inclusions and exclusions of this term. What do scholars mean when we use the term 'lesbian modernism'? What is the relationship between lesbian modernism and queer modernism? Are these overlapping, mutually informative categories, or does one effectively displace the other? Have we, for example, moved on from lesbian modernism, into the era of queer modernism? If so, what might we lose and what might we gain in leaving lesbian modernism behind? What are our personal and affective investments in lesbian modernism as a field and how do they shape our work? As these discussions provoked lively debate between our panels and our audiences, we realised that our enquiries into lesbian modernism extended beyond the confines of a conference programme and required space for further consideration in a volume. We also understood how timely these interrogations were, both within modernist studies as an ever-evolving field and within our present-day cultural and political contexts, in which terms like 'lesbian,' 'queer' and 'transgender' are often contested. In writing about lesbian modernism, we wanted to keep these discussions, disjunctions, affinities and intersections in play; to avoid taking either 'lesbian' or 'modernism' for granted, to probe and examine these categories, both in tandem and apart.

Interrogating Lesbian Modernism: Histories, Forms, Genres is the result of this endeavour, presenting twelve chapters that address and challenge lesbian modernism from a variety of perspectives.

WHAT IS LESBIAN MODERNISM?

Makiko Minow is often credited with coining the phrase 'lesbian modernism' in a review article on 'Versions of Female Modernism' in 1989.[3] Minow was responding to a wave of feminist scholarship in the 1970s and 1980s that had significantly expanded the predominantly male modernist canon and drawn attention to the important contributions lesbian, bisexual and queer women had made to the formation and development of modernist literature and culture. As Mary Loeffelholz remarks in a 1991 review of Karla Jay and Joanne Glasgow's landmark edited volume *Lesbian Texts and Contexts: Radical Revisions*, 'if there is any period to which lesbian writers and writing about lesbianism have been utterly central, yet for the most part critically evaded or silenced until the advent of feminist criticism, it is modernism.'[4] Over the last three decades, scholars working in the field of lesbian modernism have built on these earlier feminist, and lesbian feminist, interventions to critique and expand the modernist canon.

Instead of seeking to define what constitutes a lesbian modernist text or determining who counts as a lesbian modernist author, scholars have frequently drawn attention to the indeterminate and capacious nature of lesbian modernism.[5] Lesbian modernism has often been positioned as part of a wider interest in female autonomy (sexual and otherwise) within modernist culture. In *Writing for Their Lives: The Modernist Women, 1910–1940*, Gillian Hanscombe and Virginia L. Smyers argue that the attempt to challenge conventional notions of heterosexuality and articulate more autonomous understandings of female sexuality, including expressions of same-sex desire, contributed to modernist women's literary creativity and production.[6] Similarly, Robin Hackett's influential *Sapphic Primitivism: Productions of Race, Class, and Sexuality in Key Works of Modern Fiction* sees modernist articulations of 'homoerotics' as part of wider 'fictional representations of female sexual autonomy.'[7] This means that a lesbian modernist interest in articulating forms of same-sex desire is inevitably entangled with an investigation of the ways in which other expressions of intimacy and relationality can open up forms of freedom and autonomy for women and for people more broadly.

If lesbian modernism is part of a wider feminist project concerned with challenging restrictive constructions of sexualities, it also exists in close dialogue with queer modernism.[8] Scholarship on lesbian and queer modernism tends to share a commitment to challenging stable identity categories and binary sexual and gendered divisions. For instance, Jo Winning, in her influential work on Dorothy Richardson, adopts an open-ended definition of lesbian modernism, arguing that it is not possible to limit the field to authors or artists who either identified as or wrote about lesbianism or bisexuality.[9] On the contrary, lesbian modernist writing is concerned with 'breaking the binary terms of language and representation' to engage in 'the search for new forms of language.'[10] This commitment to non-identitarian approaches and to thinking critically about binary constructions of gender and sexuality, including categories like 'woman' and 'lesbian,' can and does coexist with scholarly and personal investments in foregrounding and appreciating the importance of desire, kinship and solidarity between women.

In addition, since lesbian modernist writers and artists interrogated sexuality and gender in tandem, there are important intersections between lesbian modernist and trans modernist studies. As we explain further below, there are many historical and political reasons why both trans masculinity and trans femininity need to be seen as constitutive elements of lesbian modernist culture. Emma Heaney's important work on modernist appropriations of trans femininity, for instance, demonstrates that trans feminine characters – like Doctor Matthew O'Connor in Djuna Barnes's *Nightwood* (1936) – were central to some key works in the lesbian modernist canon.[11] Modernist scholars have also repeatedly shown that trans masculinity is an integral element within the lives and works of authors and artists firmly associated with lesbian modernism.[12] This scholarship has begun to demonstrate that the rich conceptual lenses provided by the flourishing interdisciplinary field of trans studies have much to offer lesbian modernist studies. The reason for this is that lesbian and trans modernism are already intertwined, not only through forms of intimacy and kinship between cis and trans women, but also because the lesbian modernist interest in female sexual autonomy was inseparable from interrogations of the meanings of the sexed body and gendered ideals. As a result, in this volume, we approach lesbian modernism as a field that is inseparable from other fields, including feminist, queer and trans studies.

What Is a Lesbian Modernist Text?

In attempting to feel our way around, interrogate and consider the borders of lesbian modernism, we must also address the slippery question of what constitutes a lesbian text. Is it defined by the themes and content of a cultural text, or by the creator's own identity, their life and relationships? Perhaps it is a combination of the two? Must 'lesbian texts' directly explore lesbian passion and identity; should this representation be largely affirmative; and must its author be a woman whose primary romantic and/or sexual relationships were formed with other women? Considering late twentieth-century literature, Bonnie Zimmerman believes that the answer to this last question is 'yes,' because 'the nature of lesbian fiction makes it impossible to separate the text from the imagination that engenders it.'[13] Lillian Faderman, however, offers a more flexible approach:

> perhaps literature need not confront the matter of same-sex sexuality head on to be 'lesbian.' Can we identify a lesbian sensibility in literature that may not be concerned specifically with lesbian sexuality and attendant matters? For example, if a work criticizes [. . .] heterosexual institutions, focuses on women apart from their erotic connection with men, and presents romantic friendships between women (which fall short of genital sexuality), is it lesbian? [. . .] Conversely, if an author is ostensibly nonlesbian, can we nevertheless consider her work as lesbian if it concerns sexual love between women?[14]

Faderman's more capacious definition of lesbian writing has much in common with Tirza True Latimer's use of the term 'lesbian' as not 'a singular, historically or culturally transcendent erotic or affective orientation but the various alternatives to normative (patriarchal) relational and social models imagined by women together and apart.'[15] Our collection both embraces the openness and inclusivity of these understandings of the lesbian text and takes them a step further. For example, Steven Macnamara's chapter directly challenges readings of lesbian modernism which are limited to representations of women. To make this point, Macnamara examines Radclyffe Hall's depiction of heterosexual and cisgender male characters and what he calls their 'ambiguous masculinity.' Interrogating male sexuality and gender identity, Macnamara argues, was an important element of Hall's lesbian modernist project. In a related manner, Katherine Mullin's chapter on James Joyce offers new ways of understanding this canonical male writer's involvement in lesbian modernism. Joyce's work, Mullin argues, was enabled by lesbian women, and, in turn, his writing pays tribute to them through its representation of lesbian passion and identity. Sarah Parker's chapter, which proposes that Edna St. Vincent Millay's play *The Lamp and the Bell* (1921) should be considered an overlooked lesbian modernist work, suggests that Millay's bisexuality has, in part, served to exclude her from studies of the field. Jana Funke's chapter draws on trans studies to consider representations of trans masculinity in texts that have previously been associated with lesbian identity. While masculinity has often been understood as a way of encoding lesbian desire, Funke concentrates on the work and life of Christopher St. John to argue that lesbian and trans masculine experiences and forms of representation intersect.

As we hope is apparent, these and other chapters in *Interrogating Lesbian Modernism* are not constrained by either the gender or sexual identification of the author, or the subject matter of the text. Instead, they collectively embrace a more expansive vision of lesbian modernism which reflects the ever-shifting boundaries of the field as well as the historical fluidity of the term 'lesbian,' thus offering a range of understandings of what constitutes a 'lesbian' text. As Colleen Lamos states,

> there is not, on the one hand, a 'homosexual' modernism and, on the other hand, a 'heterosexual' modernism, but a single literary corpus that is torn in various ways by the scission between these (supposedly) incongruent longings. 'Queer' describes this uneasy conjunction.[16]

This collection resists the artificial boundaries that Lamos refers to here by examining texts and cultural artefacts which interrogate, expose and challenge the dominance of heteronormative and cisnormative values and ideals, representing a diverse range of identifications, experiences and desires. At the same time, we continue to centre artists and texts that engage with or emerge out of an interest in lesbian erotics, kinship and politics. It is this, we argue, that categorises these texts as 'lesbian.'

Key Historical Contexts

Our volume deals with a number of key historical contexts of the late nineteenth and early twentieth centuries through which authors and creators understood their desires and identities. Chief among these is sexual science or sexology, which occupies a prominent if ambivalent place within scholarship on lesbian modernism. For some scholars, the sexological fascination with perversion and pathology, especially in relation to the figure of the 'mannish lesbian,' provided a highly stigmatising and reductive framework for understanding female same-sex desire and women who did not conform to socially sanctioned models of femininity.[17] Moreover, the sexological investment in classification and categorisation is often seen to run counter to the (lesbian) modernist desire to challenge and expand fixed notions of the gendered, sexed and desiring subject. Yet, sexology was also less rigid and more unstable than many scholars have assumed.[18] As Martha Vicinus argues in relation to Havelock Ellis's work on female sexual inversion, for instance, sexology often failed to provide any consistent or coherent models for understanding lesbian desire: 'He [Ellis] attempts to include all possibilities and can settle on no defining characteristic [of the female sexual invert]. Never afraid of inconsistency, he frames lesbianism as an emotion, a sexual act, a general reversal, and either situational or innate.'[19]

As scholars like Jack Halberstam and Jay Prosser note, the category of the 'female sexual invert' also conflated what would later come to be teased apart as trans masculinity and female homosexuality, thus adding to the definitional instability Vicinus foregrounds.[20] This means that a novel like *The Well of Loneliness* (1928), which engages directly with sexological knowledge and whose protagonist, Stephen Gordon, famously identifies as a 'sexual invert,' should be read as part of both lesbian and trans modernism. The same can be said about the novel's author, Radclyffe Hall, who came to identify as a sexual invert.[21] More broadly, this definitional capaciousness and openness of sexological frameworks allowed literary writers and artists to engage with sexological models in highly idiosyncratic ways, which is one reason why sexual science was such an important discourse for many lesbian, queer and trans individuals.[22]

At the same time, the significance of sexology within lesbian modernism has often been overstated. As Laura Doan stresses, sexology was a fairly elite discourse that was not widely accessible in the first decades of the twentieth century, and it is vital to ask 'who knew what when.'[23] In addition, even for authors who had access to sexological knowledge, sexology did not always provide the primary lens through which they chose to understand sexuality and gender. Scholars have, at times, assumed that a writer like Hall, for instance, was very strongly indebted to sexological frameworks when writing about gender and sexuality, which can obscure the many other forms of knowledge that shaped her work, including spiritual and religious frameworks ranging from Catholicism to spiritualism and theosophy.[24] Feminist journal *Urania*, founded in 1916 and co-edited by cis lesbian couple Esther Roper and Eva Gore-Booth and trans feminine lawyer Irene Clyde, amongst others, offers another interesting example.[25] *Urania* worked with a feminist interpretation of theosophical frameworks to articulate a utopian feminist project that sought to abolish the very notion of sexual difference and the gender binary. Each copy of the journal was published with an opening declaration stating that '*Urania* denotes the company of those who are firmly determined to ignore the dual organisation of humanity in all its manifestations. [. . .] There are no "men" or "women" in *Urania*.'[26] As Alison Oram has shown, the editors drew on theosophical ideas to argue that reincarnation offered one means through which individuals could inhabit differently sexed bodies over several lifetimes.[27] These theosophical accounts sat alongside sexological ideas, which inspired the name of the journal but were also discussed critically.[28] The 1929 review of *The Well of Loneliness* in *Urania*, for instance, possibly written by Clyde, praises Hall's engagement with same-sex desire between women but challenges her reliance on sexological ideas of 'perversion' in the novel.[29]

As *Urania* and several of the other texts mentioned so far demonstrate, lesbian modernist writing was often concerned with unsettling, questioning and expanding understandings of 'lesbian' and/or 'woman' rather than offering a singular or coherent definition of these categories. This is evident when considering works published in and around 1928, which has been seen as a key year within lesbian and Sapphic modernism.[30] Despite radical differences in approach and style, works like *The Well of Loneliness* by Hall, *Ladies Almanack* (1928) by Djuna Barnes, and *Orlando* (1928) by Virginia Woolf illuminate various ways in which lesbian modernist writing intersects with feminist, queer and trans modernisms. As already mentioned above, *The Well of Loneliness* reveals the unstable boundaries between lesbian and trans modernism. Moreover, in placing Stephen Gordon as a sexual invert alongside other characters like Mary Llewellyn and Valerie Seymour, who adopt radically different explanatory models to understand their own queer desires, the book resists any singular or coherent framework for making sense of gender and sexuality.[31] Although written in part as a mock hagiography of Natalie Clifford Barney and her lesbian networks in Paris, *Ladies Almanack* explodes all classificatory attempts at understanding and labelling desires, experiences and bodies that may be read as 'lesbians' or 'women.'[32] *Orlando* has similarly been read as a lesbian homage to Vita Sackville-West, while also refusing definitional stability in relation to its protagonist's sex, gender and sexuality.[33] Nella Larsen's *Passing* (1929) encodes queer desire between the novel's married protagonists, Irene and Clare, thus calling into question their heterosexuality without making them clearly legible as lesbian or bisexual subjects.[34] Moreover, as Sami Schalk argues, Clare's ability to 'move between identity categories [. . .] challenges the eugenic notion that race, class, gender, and sexuality are natural and knowable categories.'[35] Natalie Barney's *The One Who Is Legion or A.D.'s After-Life* (1930) also has a conceptually unstable protagonist at its centre and, according to Katharina Boeckenhoff's chapter, this mutability is used to interrogate the very notion of static and dualistic identities.

Beyond sexology and spirituality, turning to history was also a way of sourcing alternative understandings of queer desire and identity. By discovering precedents for their desire in the past or recovering historical ancestors, writers and artists were able to find more empowering understandings of same-sex love compared with the often pathologising discourses forwarded by science or the law. Some of the writers and artists discussed in this volume found the early modern period particularly inspiring, in line with what Valerie Traub refers to as a 'Renaissance of Lesbianism.'[36] Another cultural discourse that offered a more enabling understanding of same-sex desire was the classical or Hellenic model, rooted in Ancient Greek history, art and culture. As the nineteenth century drew to a close, Ancient Greece increasingly came to represent a historical period in which homoerotic or 'Uranian' love was celebrated rather than condemned, based on the ideal of 'Platonic,' spiritually enriching love between an older and younger man. Most famously, Oscar Wilde gestured to this love at a key moment of his 1895 trial. When asked to describe the 'love that dare not speak its name' which featured in his lover Lord Alfred Douglas's poem 'Two Loves,' Wilde responded:

> 'The Love that dare not speak its name' in this century is such a great affection of an elder for a younger man [. . .] such as Plato made the very

basis of his philosophy, and such as you find in the sonnets of Michelangelo and Shakespeare. It is that deep, spiritual affection that is as pure as it is perfect. [. . .] There is nothing unnatural about it. It is intellectual, and it repeatedly exists between an elder and a younger man, when the elder man has intellect, and the younger man has all the joy, hope and glamour of life before him.[37]

Although Wilde was perhaps its most famous exponent, the model of 'Greek love' provided inspiration for a wide range of nineteenth-century figures, including Walter Pater, Walt Whitman and John Addington Symonds, who wrote about it in his *A Problem in Greek Ethics* (1883). Symonds's work makes clear the link between historical scholarship on Ancient Greece and the possibilities for a recognition of homosexual identity and desire in the present, using Hellenic culture to establish a noble historical precedent for same-sex desire.

Though largely associated with male homosexuality, Ancient Greece was no less significant for women defining lesbian desire. The figure of Sappho of Lesbos, in particular, fostered the inspiring vision of a female-centred, artistic community founded on relationships between women, even if this image was largely based on myth and conjecture rather than proven historical fact.[38] Though Sappho had long been celebrated as the greatest of the classical lyric poets, by the fin de siècle she was also a figure that represented queer desire. The discovery of several new Sappho fragments throughout the nineteenth century, combined with the publication of accessible translations in English, such as Henry Thorton Wharton's *Sappho: Memoir, Text, and Selected Renderings* (1885), made clear that Sappho had addressed love poems to women as well as men (previous translations had changed female addressees to male). Prior to this, only those with classical training would have been able to discern the gender of Sappho's beloveds, though hints of her sexuality featured in the notorious works of Charles Baudelaire, Algernon Charles Swinburne and Honoré de Balzac, among others. As several critics have observed, these writers represented Sappho as a femme fatale figure, associating her with 'perversity' of other kinds, such as the sadomasochism expressed in Swinburne's dramatic monologue 'Anactoria' (1866) in which Sappho declares, 'Would I not hurt thee perfectly? [. . .] / Take thy limbs living and new-mould with these / A lyre of many faultless agonies?'[39]

However, Wharton's translations proved inspiring to women writers and artists too, who offered alternatives to these decadent and obscene portrayals. For example, Michael Field (Katharine Bradley and Edith Cooper) endeavoured to recreate Sappho's voice in their collection *Long Ago* (1889), while Renée Vivien translated Sappho in 1903. This impetus to reimagine Sappho continued into the early twentieth century. The Imagist poet H.D. was deeply inspired by Sappho's lyrics, eulogising her in the experimental essay 'The Wise

Sappho' (written ca. 1916–1918) and employing a Sapphic aesthetic for her own Imagist poems and Greek translations.[40] In 1925, fellow Imagist poet Amy Lowell counted Sappho among her poetic 'sisters' (alongside Elizabeth Barrett Browning and Emily Dickinson), declaring, 'we're a queer lot / We women who write poetry.'[41] As Elizabeth English makes clear in her chapter in this volume, some writers sought not only to uncover but to reshape and correct narratives of the past, in order to recover queer historical figures as enabling models for future generations. Margaret Goldsmith, for example, addressed Sappho's legacy in the biographical study, *Sappho: A Psychological Reconstruction of Her Life* (1936). Sappho also played a key if indirect role in novels such as Barnes's *Ladies Almanack* and Compton Mackenzie's *Extraordinary Women* (1928).[42]

Lesbian modernist uses of the past also intersected with modernist primitivism, a self-representational mode central to different strands of European and North American modernism. Modernist primitivism built on racist, colonialist and classist depictions of people and cultures that were constructed as alien and located within a pre-modern and pre-civilised time that was associated with the past.[43] Although predominantly white and middle- or upper-class, Euro-American modernist writers and artists often sought to valorise these allegedly 'primitive' cultures, associating them with sensuality, regeneration or liberation, their work usually reinforced damaging and reductive clichés. As Robin Hackett shows, 'Sapphic primitivism' – 'a mode of writing in which figurations of blackness and working-class culture appear as constitutive elements of white-authored fictional representations of female sexual autonomy including homoerotics' – was central to lesbian modernism.[44] One specific effect of Sapphic primitivism was to enable white women writers like Sylvia Townsend Warner and Virginia Woolf, to name only two, 'to identify a powerful and benevolent un-raced white self' positioned at the heart of the lesbian modernist project these artists began to create.[45] On a wider level, Sapphic primitivism offers one example of the many different ways in which understandings of sexuality and gender in anglophone and European modernist culture intersected with constructions of race and class.[46]

Another important historical context that shaped the emergence of lesbian modernism is censorship. 1928 is often considered a landmark year for lesbian modernism, not only due to the number of works published but also for the notorious backlash that one of these works garnered. The cultural legacy surrounding Hall's *The Well of Loneliness* plays a central role in the production of lesbian modernism and lesbian texts more widely. Hall's novel was published at the tail-end of a period which witnessed a crack-down by British authorities on texts deemed to be obscene. As Celia Marshik notes, '[b]etween 1888 and the late 1930s, purity organizations and government censors pressured writers through visits and surveillance, public proclamations and warnings, and threatening letters as well as trials for obscene libel.'[47] Other casualties of the drive to 'clean' or purify literary expression were James Joyce's *Ulysses* (1922) and D. H. Lawrence's *Lady Chatterley's Lover* (1928), both banned in Britain for their representation of sexual acts, though many other, more obscure, texts also fell victim to this period of literary policing.[48] Similarly, other novels with which we are more familiar, like Woolf's *Orlando*, were reported for indecency or for suppression though censorship was ultimately not pursued.[49] Lesbianism was merely one subject which provoked the ire of the censors. Others included birth control, masturbation, abortion, adultery, prostitution and male homosexuality – subjects which challenged or undermined the heteronormative status quo. Censorship operated in various guises ranging from more obvious mechanisms (legal prosecution, the ban and destruction of 'obscene' works) to more implicit tactics (bookshops and libraries refusing to stock titles or pressure exerted on publishers to self-police their publications). For, of course, it was the booksellers, printers and publishers, rather than the authors, who were vulnerable to prosecution.

This is the reason why publishers were not eager to take a chance on Hall's novel. Jonathan Cape agreed to publish the novel only on the condition that Hall share liability in the event of a prosecution.[50] After James Douglas's review of the novel entitled 'A Book That Must Be Suppressed,' in which Douglas infamously compared the novel to poison, Cape was prosecuted for obscene libel and the novel was banned on 16 November 1928.[51] Hall suffered, arguably, because of the earnestness of the novel. As Hall wrote to Ellis on 2 December 1928, 'the book is a cry for better understanding, for a wider and more merciful toleration, for acceptance of these people as God has made them.'[52] This motivation was clearly appalling in the eyes of the censors. As Sir Chartres Biron, the chief magistrate on the case, writes in his judgment on Hall's novel,

> There is not a single word from beginning to end of this book which suggests that anyone with these horrible tendencies is in the least blameworthy or that they should in any way resist them. Everybody, all the characters in this book, who indulge in these horrible vices are presented to us as attractive people and put forward for our admiration.[53]

Of course, in defending lesbian love and sexuality, Hall was also writing a defence of her own life, and this was precisely the problem for the censors, as is obvious from the Home Office archives. In a file on Compton Mackenzie's *Extraordinary Women*, a satire of a community of lesbian women on the island of Capri, the Director of Public Prosecutions, Sir Archibald Bodkin, wrote that

> It is disturbing to think that the books were produced independently, as two books on the same subject so produced indicate the extent to which Miss Hall knew, and Compton Mackenzie supposed, abnormal

sexual relations had developed, and these two books are not the only ones which have been brought to the attention of the Home Office dealing with or at least referring to this most unsavoury subject.[54]

Perhaps unsurprisingly, Mackenzie's work was not banned. Hall's knowledge and personal experience of lesbianism was clearly a deciding factor in her text's 'guilt.' We are reminded here of the 1918 court case in which the dancer Maud Allan accused right-wing MP Noel Pemberton Billing of libel. Pemberton Billing had published a newspaper article reporting Allan's performance in Oscar Wilde's *Salome* (1891), but the use of the heading 'The Cult of the Clitoris,' Allan's lawyer argued, implied 'some connection with that nameless vice between women and the performance.'[55] As scholars such as Laura Doan and Lucy Bland suggest, much rested on proving that Allan simply understood the word 'clitoris,' which deemed her indecent because, as Bland argues, 'a woman's knowledge of sexual terms carried different implications from a man's.'[56]

Yet despite these attempts to quash lesbian voices and negate their experiences and 'knowledge,' scholars have consistently commented on the way in which censorship stimulated modernist production, what Marshik calls the 'censorship dialectic.'[57] Adam Parkes similarly believes that censorship provided the conditions ripe for aesthetic experimentation.[58] More specifically, it is important to recognise how Hall's novel and its prosecution, as well as Hall's visibility as its author, became a reference point for other lesbian writers and those wanting to write – or sell – lesbian fiction. We might look to other examples of lesbian modernism published in the same year. Woolf's *Orlando* and Barnes's *Ladies Almanack*, for instance, are often seen as succeeding where Hall failed, writing joyfully of lesbian passion, all the while cleverly escaping the censor's grasp.[59] Hall's novel might not be part of the narrative of canonical modernism, it might even be derided in some quarters for being dull and unexperimental, but its publication and its place in cultural history are undeniably pivotal to the production of lesbian modernism as well as to the emergence of a recognisable body of 'lesbian literature.'[60]

Lesbian Modernism: Inclusions and Exclusions

As a result of *The Well of Loneliness* censorship trials, Hall became internationally recognisable as a sexual invert and was, over time, associated with the archetype of what Esther Newton has called the 'mythic mannish lesbian.'[61] Like Hall herself, this archetype was typically racialised as white and associated with economic status and class privilege. In general, many of the writers and artistic networks at the heart of the movements that have come to be known as lesbian modernism tend to be white and middle- or upper-class. Several chapters in this volume acknowledge the resulting constitutive exclusions of lesbian modernism.[62] With regard to race, whiteness needs to be recognised as a racialised category that played a key role in shaping the aesthetic and political projects associated with lesbian modernism. As scholars like Hackett and Jean Walton have shown, racist, colonialist and classist ideologies played an important role in enabling lesbian and queer modernism more broadly.[63]

The Well of Loneliness, for instance, presents the plight of sexual inverts as analogous to (rather than intersecting with) the liberation of Black people, thus reinforcing the idea that sexual inversion is in itself associated with whiteness. Analogy functions here to create a connection via comparison, but it also maintains a clear separation, suggesting that sexual inverts are in some ways similar to Black people, but they cannot themselves be conceived as Black.[64] This is evident in the scene featuring two Black American singers who are invited to give a concert for Stephen Gordon and other white inverts. As Walton has shown, the purpose these two brothers and their performance serve in the context of the novel is that they offer a biologised model of kinship that Hall mobilises for white sexual inverts.[65] Hall presents Blackness as a biological category and argues that, by virtue of analogy, sexual inverts, too, share a biological difference and are therefore constituted as a community of 'brethren,' which is the religious term Hall uses to suggest that sexual inversion is a god-given and allegedly biological form of difference.[66]

This scene in the novel was based on a real concert that Hall and Troubridge had organised in London. In 1927, the year before *The Well of Loneliness* was published, Troubridge and Hall invited the singers Taylor Gordon and J. Rosamond Johnson to perform for them and their other white middle- and upper-class friends in their London home in Chelsea. Gordon and Johnson were important artists associated with the Harlem Renaissance and internationally famous singers touring Europe at the time. Gordon wrote about the performance at Hall and Troubridge's home in his memoir *Born to Be* (1929), commenting that Hall and Troubridge presented an image of complete Englishness.[67] This episode indicates that, unsurprisingly, white lesbian modernist artists were deeply familiar with contemporary Black artistic movements, like the Harlem Renaissance, but often chose to exclude them from the lesbian modernist tradition they began to create.

The POOL Group's film *Borderline* (1930), directed by Kenneth Macpherson and starring Paul and Eslanda Robeson alongside H.D. and Bryher, provides another example of the damaging ways in which white queer artists appropriated Blackness in the modernist period. As Walton argues, the film presents the characters of Pete and Adah (played by Paul and Eslanda Robeson) as a natural and primitivist heterosexual couple and explicitly contrasts them with an overcivilised and neurotic white heterosexual couple made up of Astrid and Thorne (played by H.D. and Gavin Arthur).[68] The white owners of the bar and hotel in which much of the film takes place, played by Bryher and Charlotte Arthur, are queer-coded and perform a mediating role between the predominantly heterosexual white and Black characters. As Walton explains:

> Arguably, *Borderline* transgresses the heterocentric cinematic conventions of the period, and attempts to present an antiracist politics that is inextricable from a 'queered' modernist aesthetic. But in the process, it reserves psychological depth and complexity only for its white characters, constructing its black characters as the primitivized others, the prehistorical background against which the white psyche may be laid bare through its own artistry.[69]

This highly ambivalent assessment of the POOL Group's ostensibly antiracist ambitions is also reflected in Eslanda Robeson's account of her experiences on the set of *Borderline*. According to Robeson, 'Kenneth and H.D. used to make us so shriek with laughter with their naïve ideas of Negroes that Paul and I often completely ruined our makeup with tears of laughter. We never once felt colored with them.'[70] In different ways, these examples from *The Well of Loneliness* and *Borderline* demonstrate the rich connections between Black artistic movements, like the Harlem Renaissance, and the white lesbian and queer modernism that has come to be canonised. They also make it obvious that white lesbian and queer artists drew inspiration from Black artists while often reinforcing racist divisions and hierarchies that contributed to a predominantly white modernist canon.

Black queer artists associated with the Harlem Renaissance responded favourably to *The Well of Loneliness*. Richard Bruce Nugent and Alain Locke praised the book, and Gladys Bentley repeatedly engaged with the novel in her work.[71] Bentley was beginning to develop her career as a blues singer and entertainer in Harlem in the late 1920s when the novel was published. Although the American censorship trial was unsuccessful, it nevertheless served to increase the book's notoriety and popularity in the US, and Bentley strategically marshalled its appeal. Bentley performed a number called 'In My Well of Loneliness' as part of the 1937 musical revue *Brevities in Bronze* at a time when she was carving out her public persona as an artist who was more open about her desire for women than other lesbian, bisexual and queer blues singers of the time.[72] Although Bentley engaged with Hall's novel, her work was far more radical than *The Well of Loneliness* in terms of opposing respectability politics. As Saidiya Hartman explains:

> Bentley's queer masculinity ran roughshod over the righteous propaganda that resided at the heart of every racial melodrama. Bentley trashed the gendered norms and family ideals central to the project of racial uplift – self-regulation, monogamy, fidelity, wedlock, and reproduction – and scoffed at the moralism of the latter-day Victorians, the aristocrats of uplift.[73]

The Well of Loneliness served a very different purpose in Bentley's 1952 autobiographical article for *Ebony* magazine.[74] In the essay, entitled 'I Am a Woman Again,' Bentley draws on plot elements from *The Well of Loneliness* to tell her life story and concludes by outlining her 'conversion' to heterosexual femininity, which allowed her to leave behind the 'well of loneliness' of her past transgressions.[75] This shows that Bentley skilfully referenced Hall's novel both in her music and autobiographical writing to construct very different public personae.

Future scholarship is required to expand or abolish a predominantly white lesbian modernism, which this collection continues to centre even as it begins to acknowledge its incoherencies and exclusions.[76] Equally, the class exclusions of lesbian modernism need to be addressed, as the artists and writers included in this collection continue to be predominantly middle- and upper-class. As Jodie Medd observes in a highly ambivalent and powerful chapter that opens this volume, lesbian modernism has a long association with unacknowledged class privilege. Bertha Harris states in the foundational essay 'The More Profound Nationality of Their Lesbianism' that the majority of lesbian modernists appear as 'rich; sophisticated, cool; longlimbed' with 'huge hunks of papa's fortune stuffed in their pockets – fortunes made for the most part by the usual grinding-the-noses-of the-poor.'[77] While our volume reveals that the class backgrounds and wealth of individuals who engaged with lesbian modernism are somewhat more diverse than this image suggests – Goldsmith found employment in numerous professions including as a journalist, translator and literary agent; Millay spent her youth in poverty in Maine; Richardson wrote for money and was reliant on patronage from Bryher; even Woolf had to earn money by her pen – the fact that class privilege and whiteness remain constitutive elements in the formation of lesbian modernism is undeniable and evident across this book. The fact of lesbian modernism's various exclusions provokes a series of challenging questions for the future of the field: to what extent can lesbian modernism expand? Are there fundamental limitations to the term? Does the expansion of lesbian modernism ultimately entail entirely new concepts, or is lesbian modernism capable (and deserving) of wholesale transformation? In other words, do we want to keep the term 'lesbian modernism,' or start over?

One potential response to these challenges is the repurposing or reimagining of lesbian modernism to new, politically efficacious and liberatory ends. As Hackett's chapter explores, the Lesbian Herstory Archives, co-founded by the working-class Jewish lesbian Joan Nestle in 1974, offers one illuminating model of such practice. According to Hackett, this archive, founded on collaborative, intersectional principles drawn from lesbian feminist, including Black lesbian feminist, traditions, acknowledges rather than glosses over the white supremacy evident in lesbian modernism and offers the possibility of connection and reparation across lines of race, class and gender. A different critical and liberatory response to the silences and exclusions of lesbian modernism and its archives can be found in Cheryl Dunye's film *The Watermelon Woman* (1996), in which the protagonist, Cheryl, tracks down the submerged history of Fae Richards, a Black lesbian actress who remains uncredited and hidden from history. As the final frame states, 'Sometimes you have to create your own history. *The Watermelon Woman* is fiction.'[78] This call has also been taken up in recent novels that reimagine or 'fabulate' queer and trans Black modernist pasts for the present, including Shola von Reinhold's *LOTE* (2020).[79]

Genre/Form/Style

Just as our volume interrogates the term 'lesbian' and the inclusions and exclusions shaping 'lesbian modernism,' several of our chapters are simultaneously engaged in testing the boundaries of 'modernism' more broadly as an aesthetic and historical category. A number of the authors and texts included in our volume fulfil stylistic expectations regarding experimentation, abstraction, fragmentation and nonlinear narrative associated with modernism (Richardson and Joyce, for instance, are considered in Winning's and Mullin's chapters respectively). However, many of our chapters feature authors and works that lie outside the bounds of modernism as it is conventionally defined. In spite of the considerable achievements of the New Modernist Studies in diversifying the canon, the present-day reader may still be surprised to find the likes of Gore-Booth, Goldsmith, Millay and St. John taking centre stage in a volume published under the 'modernist' banner, with less substantial attention given to authors such as Barnes, Gertrude Stein and Woolf. This partly results from our aim to amplify alternative voices in our collection and shed light on those less-discussed individuals and institutions who were crucial to the shaping of lesbian modernism in the early twentieth century. In Hannah Roche's chapter, for instance, Stein's overshadowed partner Alice B. Toklas steps forward as a key creator of the Stein myth, directing and shaping a vital narrative of avant-garde modernism. In Kathryn Holland's chapter, the journal *Urania* (co-edited by Gore-Booth) emerges as equally crucial to discussions of sexuality and modernity compared with better-known modernist periodicals such as *BLAST* or *The Egoist*. In bringing these significant players shaping modernism out of the shadows, we hope to continue and extend the New Modernist project of redefining 'modernism' both as historical movement and as a set of aesthetic interventions.

In relation to the latter, beyond our desire to shed light on overlooked players and institutions shaping lesbian modernism, our emphasis on writers and artists who engaged with traditional forms and popular styles reflects our aim to challenge the continuing dominance of the aesthetically 'experimental' as a non-negotiable qualification for modernism. While critics such as Winning convincingly argue that 'female writers of this period may be seen to subvert censure by inscribing lesbian desire within the remit of modernist aesthetics of fragmentation and dislocation,' other, more mainstream forms and styles also offered opportunities to the lesbian modernist.[80] As several critics have shown, women writers and artists occupy a rather different relationship both to traditional forms and to the avant-garde compared with their male counterparts. As Celeste M. Schenck demonstrates in relation to twentieth-century women's poetry, the decision to write in conventional poetic forms rather than experimental free verse does not necessarily reflect conservative politics on the part of the writer. Schenck raises the possibility that 'in privileging those female poets who broke form with the boys,' feminist modernist critics have inadvertently 'reproduced the preferences of dominant critical discourse and extended the hegemony of an exclusive, in this case antigeneric, prejudice,' as well as overlooking the fact that the 'seemingly genteel, conservative poetics of women poets [. . .] might pitch a more radical politics than we had considered possible.'[81] Marsha Meskimmon makes a similar argument regarding art history in *We Weren't Modern Enough: Women Artists and the Limits of German Modernism*, suggesting that women's modernist art engages in representation on different terms to male modernism by continuing to employ realism to reflect on and redefine womanhood within modernity. As Schenck's and Meskimmon's work shows, the decision to 'break' form, to abandon narrative, or to reject representational art, comes with distinct, and sometimes limiting or damaging, implications for creators who already occupy a different relationship to established traditions. After a hard-won struggle to gain access to aesthetic institutions and have their work recognised within them, for some women writers and artists to claim a place within tradition, and to reshape it from within, was a more powerful and radical choice than the breaking of form and narrative.

The assumed association between aesthetic innovation and progressive politics therefore needs to be interrogated, especially when one considers that some of the most radical avant-garde modernists were also aligned with right-wing and fascist politics.[82] Equally, the decision to create art in a traditional, popular and/or accessible form may align with left-leaning political ideals, as can be seen in the work of writers like Sylvia Townsend Warner and Katharine Burdekin. Several of the authors in our collection drew on traditional forms precisely because of their popularity and affective power. For example, as Abbey Rees-Hales recounts in her chapter, the artist Mariette Lydis rejected abstraction in favour of figurative realism, as a way of making lesbian invisibility present and tangible. The use of these forms was also a way of gaining public notice, of alerting a wide readership to the plight of the sexual invert (as in Hall's case), and of marshalling the 'sentimental' in favour of their cause. With their subject matter – lesbian desire and subversive gender identities – already considered new and controversial, the decision to address these themes in established, familiar, even popular forms was a political and bold one. As the illustrative comparison of the reception of Hall's *The Well of Loneliness* and

Woolf's *Orlando* shows, to write a novel drawing on, rather than rejecting, the aesthetics of nineteenth-century realism was a decision riven with its own risks and rewards.[83] Indeed, Norah James, the author of banned novel *Sleeveless Errand* (1929), understood the dangers of what she called 'frankness' when she stated that 'you cannot write a really sincere book in Britain without having the police down on you.'[84] For writers less willing to risk exposure, condemnation and potentially censorship, generic and middlebrow forms of writing arguably offered a somewhat protected alternative to the dissemblance of modernism. We might look to Burdekin's speculative fiction, for instance, for an example of a writer influenced by the same discourses as other modernists (sexology, theosophy, psychoanalysis, etc.), engaging with the same contexts (the rise of European fascism, for instance), and writing about lesbian women and gay men but almost always against a fantastical backdrop.[85] Yet despite these similarities, Burdekin is not generally considered a lesbian modernist. In response to cases such as Burdekin's, this collection recognises that lesbian modernism can take place in/through diverse literary forms and styles, and that aesthetic experimentation is merely one avenue lesbian modernist artists could take.[86]

Thus, the conceptual instability or indeterminacy we have been tracing so far is also a key component of a broader modernist project in terms of aesthetics and style. In her discussion of Richardson's *Pilgrimage* (1915–1938), Winning usefully links modernist textual fragmentation, plurality and resistance to closure to sexuality itself: 'Here, the modernist text – itself characterized as fragmented, plural, resisting closure – may be seen as a site parallel to that of sexuality, with the aim of breaking the binary terms of language and representation.'[87] Another way of embracing plurality is to expand the notion of what constitutes a lesbian modernist 'text.' Although our collection is largely rooted in literary manifestations of lesbian modernism, we also attend to visual and material cultures throughout the volume, as these were crucial to how lesbian modernism emerged and circulated in the early decades of the twentieth century. Rees-Hales's chapter on Lydis is primarily focused on fine art and the inclusions and exclusions of art history, while other chapters incorporate discussions of photography, theatre, book production and fashion. From a discussion of Cecil Beaton's portraits of Stein and Toklas (Roche), to the costumed pageants of Vassar College that inspired Millay's plays (Parker), to the ephemera, fliers, and posters found in the Lesbian Herstory Archive (Hackett), our chapters show that lesbian modernism circulated in myriad ways, manifesting in self-fashioning, visual codes, and performance, as well as on the printed page. This gestures to another fruitful direction in which lesbian modernist studies continues to expand and develop, moving beyond written texts to consider other media and art forms from an interdisciplinary perspective.

Beyond their popular and affective potential, these forms, styles and genres also offered a way of engaging with history and with past iterations of lesbian subjectivity. As already mentioned, the importance of history, of past identities rediscovered in the present, recurs across several chapters in our volume. Whether Millay's use of Elizabethan pastiche to represent romantic attachments in women's colleges, Sackville-West's and Goldsmith's biographical research as a way of recovering the lives of queer women, or, in more recent years, the archival reclamation mission undertaken by the Lesbian Herstory Archive, the desire to uncover the past and engage with it in the present appears as a recurrent impulse within lesbian modernism. Though this desire to return to the past might appear at odds with modernism's emphasis on 'making it new' or looking to the future, it is worth remembering that modernism in fact has a complex relationship to history. As T. S. Eliot famously writes in *The Waste Land* (1922), 'These fragments I have shored against my ruins.'[88] In a parallel manner, the writers and artists included in this volume sought to 'shore' the fragments of lesbian existence against the destructions and distortions wrought by time and prejudice.

Summary of Chapters

Our volume is structured thematically and is divided into four parts. The first part, 'Interrogating Lesbian/Queer/Trans Modernism,' presents three chapters that grapple explicitly with the limitations of lesbian modernism. It considers alternative approaches to identity, gender and sexuality emerging out of queer and trans modernist studies, which put pressure on lesbian modernism, asking: how useful is it to organise an entire field around the definitionally unstable and potentially limiting term 'lesbian'? In 'Loving/Hating/Loving Lesbian Modernism,' Medd explores their own 'love–hate' relationship with lesbian modernist studies in the form of an ambivalent love letter to the field itself. Tracing the term's (nonlinear) emergence, submergence and resurgence, Medd explores how we can productively navigate our own personal and professional investments in lesbian modernism. In doing so, Medd reveals that definitions of 'lesbian modernism' are as much about the shifting affiliations and (dis)identifications of our own times as they are about the desires, identities, communities, epistemologies and texts of the past. Funke's chapter 'Lesbian-Trans-Feminist Modernism: Christopher St. John, Trans Masculinity and Celibate Friendship in *Hungerheart: The Story of a Soul*' examines the foundational intersections between lesbian and trans modernism. In contrast to other scholars who have read *Hungerheart* as a book about lesbian failure, Funke considers how the text engages with models of ascetic masculinity and celibate friendship to open up rich possibilities for intimate connection and spiritual fulfilment for its trans masculine protagonist. Funke suggests that there are far-reaching individual and relational uses and meanings of masculinity, which may include, but are not limited to lesbian eroticism. Finally, Boeckenhoff's chapter 'The Ontology of the Pluri-Singular Body in Natalie Clifford Barney's *The One Who Is Legion or A.D.'s After-Life*' probes the links between lesbian and queer modernism by presenting a new reading of a rarely studied novel by Barney. The novel scrutinises identity's relation to sexual desire and the gendered body through a series of inquiries into philosophical theories of matter. Boeckenhoff uses *The One Who Is Legion* to explore critically how the re-reading of a text frequently identified as 'lesbian' through the lens of queer theory enhances our understanding of modernism's multi-faceted engagement with theories of sexual identity and, more generally, with modalities of existence.

Part II of our volume focuses on the 'Genres and Forms' of lesbian modernism, exploring how lesbian modernism often makes space for forms and genres that are not overtly 'experimental,' while simultaneously reinventing these established artistic and literary modes. In 'Imaginative Biography: Margaret Goldsmith, Vita Sackville-West and Lesbian Historical Life Writing,' English examines the work of Sackville-West alongside that of her sometime lover and somewhat neglected writer, Goldsmith, to position the two women as writers of lesbian historical biography. While the historical biography is not a genre we typically associate with modernism, English argues that Goldsmith and Sackville-West use it to contribute to the discursive formation of modern sexual identity and to craft a narrative of queer lineage that challenges masculine concepts of historical truth and accuracy. Rees-Hales's chapter 'Modernism at the Margins: Mariette Lydis's Print Portfolio *Lesbiennes*' focuses on the visual cultures of Sapphic modernism. Rees-Hales challenges the boundaries of the modernist artistic canon by arguing for the inclusion of Lydis, who makes the modern lesbian subject central to her art. Rees-Hales proposes that Lydis has been overlooked by both art historians and lesbian modernist scholarship precisely because her art is representational (rather than abstract), while her portrayal of Sapphic spectatorship further complicates theories of the gendered gaze. Macnamara similarly challenges expectations regarding the content and focus of lesbian modernist writing in his chapter 'Inverting the Gaze: Radclyffe Hall and Male Sexual Identities.' Macnamara focuses on (often overlooked) cis male protagonists in Hall's well-known and lesser-known fiction. The chapter provocatively argues that the lesbian modernist qualities of Hall's writings may not only lie in her well-known depictions of lesbianism but also extend to Hall's careful interrogation of cisgender and heterosexual masculinities. As Macnamara shows, Hall manipulated the generic and stylistic conventions of the traditional novel to complicate cisnormative and heteronormative representations of masculinity.

The third part on 'Relationality, Networks and Kinship' expands our understanding of lesbian modernism by shifting away from a primary focus on lesbian desire and identity towards an exploration of the relational networks and forms of kinship that emerged in and around lesbian modernist writings. In so doing, the contributors present frameworks that allow for new voices to be included within the lesbian modernist project. Roche's chapter 'Writing Widows of Lesbian Modernism' focuses on the autobiographical writings of Toklas and Una Troubridge. Through turning the spotlight onto these overlooked spouses, Roche challenges established readings of their relationships with Stein and Hall, and reveals alternative ways of interpreting their roles as 'lesbian modernist wives.' Continuing the focus on overlooked figures, Holland's chapter 'Lesbianism in/and the Family: Eva Gore-Booth and the Making of Feminist Modernism' uses the neglected writer Gore-Booth to reconsider the relationship between lesbian modernism and kinship systems. Holland demonstrates how, far from representing oppression and ostracism, the intergenerational feminist family for Gore-Booth and others represented an important site of collaboration and intertextual exchange that facilitated the articulation of dissident views of gender and sexuality. Finally, Mullin's chapter 'Lesbian Joyce' proposes a new lesbian modernist reading of Joyce's work, by exploring his friendships with lesbian women whose support and networks fostered his career and facilitated the publication of his writings. Mullin traces a distinctively Sapphic strain through *Ulysses*, placing lesbian desire at the very heart of canonical modernism.

The fourth and final part of the book, 'Histories and Temporalities,' interrogates the shifting temporal boundaries and historically unstable definitions of lesbian modernism. The chapters in this section make visible the ways in which periodisation, retrospection and affect have shaped historical constructions of lesbian modernism. In 'Elizabethan Lovemaking: College Romance and Queer Anachronism in Edna St. Vincent Millay's *The Lamp and the Bell*,' Parker analyses Millay's little-known play of 1921, written for Vassar's Fiftieth Anniversary, which celebrates relationships between women. Asking why Millay uses an apparently anachronistic form – the Elizabethan verse drama – to uphold and defend same-sex desire, Parker proposes that Millay employs 'temporal drag' to both elevate lesbian love in the present and forge inspiring connections to its historical past. Bringing us forward in time, Hackett's 'The Lesbian Herstory Archives at Fifty' examines how lesbian modernist writings were collected, framed and interpreted as part of the broader collections of lesbiana that constitute the Lesbian Herstory Archives, founded in New York in 1974. Hackett argues that the founding of the Archives exposes an essential feature of modernity: the opening of opportunities for cultural affiliation apart from heteronormative ties of geography, nation or family. Remaining in the archives, Winning's chapter 'Hidden in Plain Sight: The Reconstruction of Lesbian Modernist Sexual Histories' considers how biographers, critics and scholars that have approached the lesbian subject have often wilfully misread dissident sexualities in the past, reducing them to a 'ghost note' or something hidden in plain sight. Through the example of recent archival work on the Dorothy Richardson Scholarly Editions Project, Winning discusses the demands that new textual materials and narratives of lived experience place on our understanding of the relationship between textual production and sexual history. Using the Richardson project as a test case, the chapter explores the politics of visibility alongside the validity (or otherwise) of notions of lesbian modernism in our contemporary moment.

As a whole, *Interrogating Lesbian Modernism* demonstrates both the enduring uses and persistent limitations of the field of lesbian modernism. As the contributions to the book show, lesbian modernism is capacious and ever-expanding, existing in ongoing dialogue with adjacent fields like trans, queer and feminist modernism. The commitment to centring erotics, collaboration and kinship between women alongside the embrace of indeterminacy and the refusal to shut down debate about definitions of key terms like 'lesbian' or 'woman' are among the most vital lines of current inquiry in lesbian modernist studies. At the same time, lesbian modernism remains a restrictive and exclusionary field that produces scholarship which often continues to centre the predominantly white middle- or upper-class voices of largely anglophone writers, even if scholars are aware and critical of these choices. As this Introduction and several chapters in the book show, these exclusions are deeply rooted in broader Euro-American modernist cultures and constructions of gender and sexuality that continue to shape scholarship in modernist – and lesbian modernist – studies to this day. Readers of *Interrogating Lesbian Modernism* will share the ambivalence that we and many other contributors to the volume feel about lesbian modernism. They will draw different conclusions as to the future of the field, which may require further expansion or which may need to be abolished in favour of new and different ways of mapping, understanding and valorising the lesbian artistic, intellectual and political contributions and networks at the heart of modernist culture.

NOTES

1. The Introduction is equally and jointly written by the authors.
2. The conference was organised by Lloyd (Meadhbh) Houston, Rio Matchett and Séan Richardson.
3. Makiko Minow, 'Versions of Female Modernism: Review Article,' *News from Nowhere* 7 (1989): 64–9.
4. Mary Loeffelholz, 'Voices in a Conversation: *Radical Revisions* by Karla Jay and Joanne Glasgow,' *The Women's Review of Books* 8, no. 5 (1991): 7–8.
5. See, for example, Laura Doan and Jane Garrity, 'Introduction,' in *Sapphic Modernities: Sexuality, Women and National Culture*, ed. Laura Doan and Jane Garrity (Basingstoke: Palgrave Macmillan, 2006), 1–13; Joanne Winning, 'Lesbian Sexuality in the Story of Modernism,' in *The Oxford Handbook of Modernisms*, ed. Peter Brooker, Andrzej Gąsiorek, Deborah Longworth and Andrew Thacker (Oxford: Oxford University Press, 2016), 224–8; Susan Lanser, '1928: Sapphic Modernity and the Sexuality of History,' *Modernism/modernity Print Plus* 1, no. 3 (October 2016),

accessed 10 March 2020, https://doi.org/10.26597/mod.0016; Karla Jay, 'Lesbian Modernism: (Trans)Forming the (C)Anon,' in *Professions of Desire: Lesbian and Gay Studies in Literature*, ed. George E. Haggerty and Bonnie Zimmerman (New York: Modern Language Association of America, 1995), 72–83, 79; and Shari Benstock, 'Expatriate Sapphic Modernism: Entering Literary History,' in *Lesbian Texts and Contexts: Radical Revisions*, ed. Karla Jay and Joanne Glasgow (New York: New York University Press, 1990), 183–203, 185.
6. Gillian Hanscombe and Virginia L. Smyers, *Writing for Their Lives: The Modernist Women, 1910–1940* (London: The Women's Press, 1987).
7. Robin Hackett, *Sapphic Primitivism: Productions of Race, Class, and Sexuality in Key Works of Modern Fiction* (New Brunswick, NJ: Rutgers University Press, 2004), 3.
8. This is unsurprising given the fact that important strands of queer theory emerged out of feminist and, specifically, lesbian feminist scholarship. For instance, Judith Butler's early work was explicitly presented as a contribution to feminist scholarship and engaged carefully with earlier lesbian feminist writers like Monique Wittig, e.g. Judith Butler, *Gender Trouble* (New York: Routledge, 1990). Cherríe Moraga and Gloria Anzaldúa's feminist scholarship is an equally important influence on queer studies, e.g. Cherríe Moraga and Gloria Anzaldúa, eds, *This Bridge Called My Back: Writings by Radical Women of Color* (New York: Kitchen Table Press, 1983). For more on queer modernism, see Benjamin Kahan, 'Queer Modernism,' in *A Handbook of Modernism Studies*, ed. Jean-Michel Rabaté (Chichester: Wiley-Blackwell, 2013), 347–61.
9. Joanne Winning, *The Pilgrimage of Dorothy Richardson* (Madison: University of Wisconsin Press, 2000), 7–8.
10. Ibid., 13, 8.
11. Emma Heaney, *The New Woman: Literary Modernism, Queer Theory, and the Trans Feminine Allegory* (Evanston, IL: Northwestern University Press, 2017), 143–51.
12. See, for instance, Jana Funke, 'Intersexions: Dandyism, Cross-Dressing, Transgender,' in *Late Victorian into Modern*, ed. Laura Marcus, Michèle Mendelssohn and Kirsten E. Shepherd-Barr (Oxford: Oxford University Press, 2016), 414–28; K. Allison Hammer, 'Epic Stone Butch: Transmasculinity in the Work of Willa Cather,' *TSQ: Transgender Studies Quarterly* 7, no. 1 (2020): 77–98; Jay Prosser, *Second Skins: The Body Narratives of Transsexuality* (New York: Columbia University Press, 1998), 135–70; and Chris Coffman, *Gertrude Stein's Transmasculinity* (Edinburgh: Edinburgh University Press, 2018).
13. Bonnie Zimmerman, *The Safe Sea of Women: Lesbian Fiction 1969–1989* (Boston: Beacon Press, 1990), 15.
14. Lillian Faderman, 'What Is Lesbian Literature? Forming a Historical Canon,' in Haggerty and Zimmerman, *Professions of Desire*, 49–59, 51-2
15. Tirza True Latimer, *Women Together/Women Apart: Portraits of Lesbian Paris* (New Brunswick, NJ: Rutgers University Press, 2005), 3.
16. Colleen Lamos, 'Queer Conjunctions in Modernism,' in *Gender in Modernism: New Geographies Complex Intersections*, ed. Bonnie Kime Scott (Urbana and Chicago: University of Illinois Press, 2007), 336–43, 336–7.

17. See, for instance, Lillian Faderman, 'The Morbidification of Love between Women by 19th-Century Sexologists,' *Journal of Homosexuality* 4, no. 1 (1978): 73–90; George Chauncey, 'From Sexual Inversion to Homosexuality: Medicine and the Changing Conceptualization of Female Deviance,' *Salmagundi* no. 58/59 (1983): 114–46; Carroll Smith-Rosenberg, *Disorderly Conduct: Visions of Gender in Victorian America* (Oxford: Oxford University Press, 1985), 265–78; and Ann Heilmann, *New Woman Fiction: Women Writing First-Wave Feminism* (Basingstoke: Palgrave, 2000), 128.
18. On this, see also Jana Funke, *Sexological Modernism: Queer Feminism and Sexual Science* (Edinburgh: Edinburgh University Press, forthcoming).
19. Martha Vicinus, 'The History of Lesbian History,' *Feminist Studies* 38, no. 3 (2012): 566–96, 566.
20. Jack Halberstam, 'Butch/FTM Border Wars and the Masculine Continuum,' *GLQ: A Journal of Lesbian and Gay Studies* 4, no. 2 (1998): 287–310; Prosser, *Second Skins*.
21. In a letter to Evguenia Souline, written on 24 October 1934, Radclyffe Hall declares, 'I am a born invert,' in *Your John: The Love Letters of Radclyffe Hall*, ed. Joanne Glasgow (New York: New York University Press, 1997), 78. It is important to note that *The Well of Loneliness* should not be considered autobiographical, and there were many different ways in which individuals could situate themselves within sexological categories like 'the sexual invert.'
22. See, for instance, Laura Doan, *Fashioning Sapphism: The Origins of a Modern English Lesbian Culture* (New York: Columbia University Press, 2001), 126–63. For feminist and queer engagements with sexology in early twentieth-century Germany, see Kirsten Leng, *Sexual Politics and Feminist Science: Women Sexologists in Germany, 1900–1933* (Ithaca, NY: Cornell University Press, 2018).
23. Doan, *Fashioning Sapphism*, 130.
24. We are using she/her pronouns for Hall to acknowledge the fact that Hall and those closest to her used these pronouns even in private and personal writings. This is not to suggest that Hall's life and work cannot or should not be read as part of trans history and culture. The use of other pronouns can equally be justified.
25. Clyde also published legal scholarship and an autobiography under the name Thomas Baty. See Alison Oram, 'Feminism, Androgyny and Love between Women in *Urania*, 1916–1940,' *Media History* 7, no. 1 (June 2001): 57–70.
26. For instance, 'Anonymous, Urania: To Our Friends,' *Urania* 75 and 76 (August 1929): n.p.
27. Oram, 'Feminism, Androgyny,' 58.
28. 'Uranian' was the English translation of Karl Heinrich Ulrich's term 'Urning' for 'homosexual.' The term 'Uranian' was used in English by Edward Carpenter. See Oram, 'Feminism, Androgyny,' 67.
29. Anonymous, '"The Well of Loneliness" Or "Cut by the County,"' *Urania* 75 and 76 (August 1929): 1–2, 1. Oram, 'Feminism, Androgyny,' 66, argues that the review was probably written by Clyde.
30. See Lanser, '1928.'
31. Clare Hemmings, '"All My Life I've Been Waiting for Something . . .": Theorizing Femme Narrative in *The Well of Loneliness*,' in *Palatable Poison: Critical Perspectives*

on *The Well of Loneliness*, ed. Laura Doan and Jay Prosser (New York: Columbia University Press, 2002), 179–96.
32. Christine Berni, '"A Nose-Length into the Matter": Sexology and Lesbian Desire in Djuna Barnes's *Ladies Almanack*,' *Frontiers: A Journal of Women Studies* 20, no. 3 (1999): 83–107; Daniela Caselli, 'Novitiates, Saints and Priestesses: The Unreadable Pleasures of *Ladies Almanack*,' *Textual Practice* 20, no. 3 (2006): 463–89.
33. On *Orlando* as a trans narrative, see, for instance, Pamela L. Caughie, 'The Temporality of Modernist Life Writing in the Era of Transsexualism: Virginia Woolf's *Orlando* and Einar Wegener's *Man into Woman*,' *Modern Fiction Studies* 59, no. 3 (2013): 501–25.
34. Deborah E. McDowell is often credited with acknowledging the queer dimensions of *Passing* for the first time. See Deborah E. McDowell, 'Introduction to Quicksand and Passing,' in Nella Larsen, *Quicksand and Passing*, ed. Deborah E. McDowell (New Brunswick, NJ: Rutgers University Press, 1986), ix–xxxv; and Deborah E. McDowell, '"That Nameless . . . Shameful Impulse": Sexuality in Nella Larsen's *Quicksand* and *Passing*,' in *Black Feminist Criticism and Critical Theory*, ed. Joe Weixlmann and Houston A. Baker Jr. (Greenwood, FL: Penkevill, 1988), 139–67.
35. Sami Schalk, 'Transing: Resistance to Eugenic Ideology in Nella Larsen's *Passing*,' *Journal of Modern Literature* 38, no. 3 (2015): 148–61, 148.
36. See Valerie Traub, 'The Renaissance of Lesbianism,' *GLQ* 7, no. 2 (2001): 245–63; and Valerie Traub, *The Renaissance of Lesbianism* (Cambridge: Cambridge University Press, 2002).
37. Oscar Wilde, 'Testimony of Oscar Wilde,' *Famous Trials*, accessed 16 July 2022, https://famous-trials.com/wilde/342-wildetestimony; see Lord Alfred Douglas, 'Two Loves,' *The Chameleon* 1, no. 1 (December 1894): 26–8, 28.
38. This discussion of Sappho's legacy raises the question: why not use the term 'Sapphic modernism' rather than 'lesbian modernism' in the title of this book? In earlier scholarship, 'Sapphic modernism' has frequently been favoured to designate a queer subset of 'female modernism,' starting with Shari Benstock's 1990 essay 'Expatriate Sapphic Modernism: Entering Literary History.' The term was then used in the titles of important studies including Erin G. Carlston's *Thinking Fascism: Sapphic Modernism and Fascist Modernity* (Stanford, CA: Stanford University Press, 1998) and Diana Collecott's *H.D. and Sapphic Modernism 1910–1950* (Cambridge: Cambridge University Press, 1999). More recently, Laura Doan and Jane Garrity offered a new inflection on the term in the title of their collection *Sapphic Modernities: Sexuality, Women and National Culture*. As Latimer explains, 'sapphist' and Sapphic 'articulates a cultural heritage as well as an explicit cultural practice.' See Latimer, *Women Together/Women Apart*, 3. As a result, the term retains a certain air of cultural elitism, implying a classical education, or at least an awareness of antique precedents for female same-sex desire. As a term that crosses both sexological and artistic understandings of desire between women, the term 'lesbian' is preferred by us, particularly as it continues to have contemporary meaning and currency. Nonetheless, in this collection, we aim to keep both terms, 'Sapphic' and 'lesbian' modernism, in play and in dialogue, interrogating the meaning of both, including their exclusions and intersections with other alternative designations, such as queer modernism and trans modernism.

39. Algernon Charles Swinburne, 'Anactoria,' in *Poems and Ballads* (London: J. C. Hotten, 1866), 65–76, 70.
40. See Eileen Gregory, *H.D. and Hellenism: Classic Lines* (Cambridge: Cambridge University Press, 1997); and Collecott, *H.D. and Sapphic Modernism*.
41. Amy Lowell, 'The Sisters,' in *The Complete Poetical Works of Amy Lowell* (Boston: Houghton Mifflin, 1955), 459–61, 459.
42. Virginia Woolf also refers obliquely to Sappho in her work. 'Sapphism' was her favoured term to describe women who loved women. For example, she writes of Vita Sackville-West on 21 December 1925, 'These Sapphists love women; friendship is never untinged with amorosity,' quoted in *The Diary of Virginia Woolf, Volume 3: 1925–1930*, ed. Anne Olivier Bell and Andrew McNeillie (New York: Harcourt Brace Jovanovich, 1980), 51.
43. On modernism and primitivism, see, for instance, Elazar Barkan and Ronald Bush, eds, *Prehistories of the Future: The Primitivist Project and the Culture of Modernism* (Stanford, CA: Stanford University Press, 1995); and Ruth B. Phillips, 'Aesthetic Primitivism Revisited: The Global Diaspora of "Primitive Art" and the Rise of Indigenous Modernisms,' *Journal of Art Historiography* 12 (2015): 1–25. On wider constructions of the 'primitive' in the modern period, see Johannes Fabian, *Time and the Other: How Anthropology Makes Its Object* (New York: Columbia University Press, 1983).
44. Hackett, *Sapphic Primitivism*, 3.
45. Ibid., 7.
46. See also Valerie Rohy, *Anachronism and Its Others: Sexuality, Race, Temporality* (Albany: State University of New York Press, 2009).
47. Celia Marshik, *British Modernism and Censorship* (Cambridge: Cambridge University Press, 2006), 3.
48. On the censorship of Joyce's and Lawrence's work, see ibid.; Katherine Mullin, *James Joyce, Sexuality and Social Purity* (Cambridge: Cambridge University Press, 2003); Adam Parkes, *Modernism and the Theater of Censorship* (New York and Oxford: Oxford University Press, 1996); and Paul Vanderham, *James Joyce and Censorship: The Trials of Ulysses* (Basingstoke: Macmillan, 1998).
49. Marshik notes that the Home Office received a complaint demanding *Orlando*'s censorship in October 1928. Marshik, *British Modernism*, 118.
50. Diana Souhami, *The Trials of Radclyffe Hall* (London: Virago, 1999), 168.
51. For Douglas's review, see Doan and Prosser, *Palatable Poison*, 36–8.
52. Letter from Hall to Ellis, 2 December 1928, quoted in Parkes, *Theater of Censorship*, 144.
53. Sir Chartres Biron, Chief Magistrate, 'Judgement,' 16 November 1928, in Doan and Prosser, *Palatable Poison*, 39–49, 42–3.
54. See London, The National Archives, HO 45/15727.
55. Quoted in Doan, *Fashioning Sapphism*, 31.
56. Lucy Bland, 'Trial by Sexology? Maud Allan, *Salome*, and the "Cult of the Clitoris" Case,' in *Sexology in Culture: Labelling Bodies and Desires*, ed. Lucy Bland and Laura Doan (Chicago: University of Chicago Press, 1998), 183–98, 192. On the trial, see also Doan, *Fashioning Sapphism*.
57. Marshik, *British Modernism*, 205.

58. Parkes, *Theater of Censorship*, 19.
59. Susan Sniader Lanser states that the *Ladies Almanack* was 'shrouded in obscurity' to avoid attention from the censors. Susan Sniader Lanser, 'Speaking in Tongues: *Ladies Almanack* and the Language of Celebration,' *Frontiers: A Journal of Women Studies* 4, no. 3 (Autumn 1979): 39–46, 40. Although published a few years later, *Nightwood* was also protected, Leigh Gilmore argues, by T. S. Eliot's preface, which confirmed its status as experimental text: 'His relatively vague literary/critical judgement, in effect, preempted a legal judgement.' Leigh Gilmore, 'Obscenity, Modernity, Identity: Legalizing *The Well of Loneliness* and *Nightwood*,' *Journal of the History of Sexuality* 4, no. 4 (1994): 603–24, 618.
60. In a letter to Vita Sackville-West on 30 August 1928, Woolf relays her efforts to support *The Well of Loneliness* despite Hall's insistence that 'she won't have any letter written about her book unless it mentions the fact that it is a work of artistic merit—even genius.' Woolf complains that 'no one has read her book; or can read it,' adding that 'instead of offering to reprint the masterpiece, we are already beginning to wish it unwritten.' Virginia Woolf, *The Letters of Virginia Woolf Volume 3: 1923–1928*, ed. Nigel Nicolson and Joanna Trautmann (London: Harcourt Brace Jovanovich, 1978), 520.
61. Esther Newton, 'The Mythic Mannish Lesbian: Radclyffe Hall and the New Woman,' *Signs* 9, no. 4 (Summer 1984): 557–75. See also Doan, *Fashioning Sapphism*.
62. See also Lanser, '1928.'
63. Hackett, *Sapphic Primitivism*; Jean Walton, 'White Neurotics, Black Primitives, and the Queer Matrix of Borderline,' in *Out Takes: Essays on Queer Theory and Film*, ed. Ellie Hanson (Durham, NC and London: Duke University Press, 1999), 243–70; Jean Walton, *Fair Sex, Savage Dreams: Race, Psychoanalysis, Sexual Difference* (Durham, NC: Duke University Press, 2001); Jean Walton, '"I Want to Cross Over into Camp Ground": Race and Inversion in *The Well of Loneliness*,' in Doan and Prosser, *Palatable Poison*, 277–99.
64. Walton, 'Race and Inversion,' 277–99.
65. Ibid.
66. Radclyffe Hall, *The Well of Loneliness* (London: Virago, [1928] 1982), 356, 367.
67. Taylor Gordon, *Born to Be* (Lincoln: University of Nebraska Press, 1995), 214. For a more detailed discussion of this encounter, see Walton, 'Race and Inversion,' 282.
68. Walton, 'White Neurotics, Black Primitives.' For more on race and primitivism in *Borderline*, see Carolyn A. Kelley, 'Aubrey Beardsley and H.D.'s "Astrid": The Ghost and Mrs. Pugh of Decadent Aestheticism and Modernity,' *Modernism/Modernity* 15, no. 3 (2008): 447–75.
69. Walton, 'White Neurotics, Black Primitives,' 267.
70. Eslanda Robeson's diary, quoted in Walton, *Fair Sex, Savage Dreams*, 62.
71. James F. Wilson, *Bulldaggers, Pansies, and Chocolate Babies: Performance, Race, and Sexuality in the Harlem Renaissance* (Ann Arbor: University of Michigan Press, 2010), 158.
72. Scholars have written about Bentley as a 'bulldagger,' a term used in non-pejorative ways within early twentieth-century Black culture to describe masculine and otherwise gender non-conforming and queer people who were assigned female at birth.

See, for instance, Regina V., 'How Does a Bulldagger Get Out of the Footnotes? Or Gladys Bentley's Blues,' *Ninepatch: A Creative Journal for Women and Gender Studies* 1, no. 1 (July 2012): n.p. For more on the blues tradition in relation to female sexual politics, see Angela Y. Davis, *Blues Legacies and Black Feminism: Gertrude 'Ma' Rainey, Bessie Smith, and Billie Holiday* (New York: Vintage, 1998); and Hazel V. Carby, *Cultures in Babylon: Black Britain and African America* (London: Verso, 1999).

73. Saidiya Hartman, *Wayward Lives, Beautiful Experiments: Intimate Histories of Social Upheaval* (London: Serpent's Tail, 2019), 200.
74. Gladys Bentley, 'I Am a Woman Again,' *Ebony* (August 1952): 92–8.
75. For a detailed discussion of the essay, see Wilson, *Bulldaggers, Pansies, and Chocolate Babies*, 158–63.
76. Lesbian modernism, and modernism more widely, has historically focused on English-language texts. The exclusion of literature on the basis of language and frequently, by implication, nationality, race and ethnicity, needs to be addressed by scholars of modernism. Boeckenhoff's chapter, for instance, notes the fact that Barney wrote in French as a significant factor in her neglect.
77. Bertha Harris, 'The More Profound Nationality of Their Lesbianism: Lesbian Society in Paris in the 1920s,' in *Amazon Expedition: A Lesbian Feminist Anthology*, ed. Phyllis Birkby, Bertha Harris, Esther Newton, Jill Johnston and Jane O'Wyatt (New York: Times Change Press, 1973), 77–88, 78–9.
78. *The Watermelon Woman*, directed by Cheryl Dunye (New York: First Run/Icarus Films, 1997). For more on this film in relation to Black lesbian visibility, see Kara Keeling, '"Joining the Lesbians": Cinematic Regimes of Black Lesbian Visibility,' in *Black Queer Studies: A Critical Anthology*, ed. E. Patrick Johnson and Mae G. Henderson (Durham, NC: Duke University Press, 2005), 213–27.
79. Von Reinhold uses the term 'critical fabulation' to describe their approach in *LOTE*. See 'Interview with Shola von Reinhold,' Lucy Writers Platform, June 2021, accessed 1 August 2022, https://lucywritersplatform.com/2021/06/01/interview-with-shola-von-reinhold-it-felt-like-hermia-fabulated-herself-out-of-the-archive/. The methodology of 'critical fabulation' was developed by Hartman. See, for instance, Saidiya Hartman, 'Venus in Two Acts,' *Small Axe* 12, no. 2 (2008): 1–14.
80. Winning, *Pilgrimage*, 112.
81. Celeste M. Schenck, 'Exiled by Genre: Modernism, Canonicity, and the Politics of Exclusion,' in *Women's Writing in Exile*, ed. Mary Lynn Broe and Angela Ingram (Chapel Hill: University of North Carolina Press, 1989), 226–50, 230.
82. See Andrew Hewitt, *Fascist Modernism: Aesthetics, Politics, and the Avant-Garde* (Stanford, CA: Stanford University Press, 1993); Carlston, *Thinking Fascism*; and Hackett, *Sapphic Primitivism*.
83. See Jodie Medd, *Lesbian Scandal and the Culture of Modernism* (Cambridge: Cambridge University Press, 2012), 151–91.
84. Norah James, quoted in Angela Ingram, '"Unutterable Putrefaction" and "Foul Stuff": Two "Obscene" Novels of the 1920s,' *Women's Studies International Forum* 9, no. 4 (1986): 341–54, 347.
85. This point draws upon Winning's argument that *The Well of Loneliness* 'operate[s] upon the same sets of discourses' as modernist texts such as *Ladies Almanack*.

Joanne Winning, 'Writing by the Light of *The Well*: Radclyffe Hall and the Lesbian Modernists,' in Doan and Prosser, *Palatable Poison*, 372–93, 374.
86. On Burdekin's speculative fiction and, in particular, its representation of lesbian and gay identities, see, for instance, Elizabeth English, *Lesbian Modernism: Censorship, Sexuality and Genre Fiction* (Edinburgh: Edinburgh University Press, 2015); Alexis Lothian, 'A Speculative History of No Future: Feminist Negativity and the Queer Dystopian Impulses of Katharine Burdekin's *Swastika Night*,' *Poetics Today* 37, no. 3 (2016): 443–72; and Glyn Salton-Cox, *Queer Communism and the Ministry of Love: Sexual Revolution in British Writing of the 1930s* (Edinburgh: Edinburgh University Press, 2018).
87. Winning, *Pilgrimage*, 8.
88. T. S. Eliot, *The Waste Land*, in *The Annotated Waste Land with Eliot's Contemporary Prose*, ed. Lawrence Rainey (New Haven, CT: Yale University Press, 2005), 70.

PART I
INTERROGATING LESBIAN/ QUEER/TRANS MODERNISM

1

LOVING/HATING/LOVING LESBIAN MODERNISM

Jodie Medd

I. Alluvion

The time between signing on to this collection and finalising the chapter has been the time of 2019–22. The unpredictable cascade of changes flooding this interval has rerouted my ideas of *life, work, meaning, reading, writing, care* again and again. Just like you.

Consequently, my ambivalence towards *Interrogating Lesbian Modernism* has grown heavier, soggier, deeper than ever. Rather than getting dragged to the bottom, I allow the detritus that floats upon the frangible surface of an uncertain now to flow through this writing.

May you be reading this in a now that can hold you.

II. Lesbian Modernism?: It's Complicated

*Now to delight my women friends
I'll make a beautiful song of this affair.*[1]

I have been contemplating a break-up with Lesbian Modernism for a long time.

She's my first love. And yet, we all know, that's rarely enough.

Years ago, I was ready to abandon our relationship – How to define it? How to understand it? How, even, to understand her?

(I was, frankly, not that interested in her identity crises: no terms, no definitions can capture her complexity, her inconstancy, her caprice.[2] Lesbian Modernism, Sapphic Modernism, Queer Feminist Modernism – *it is not a matter of any importance. Let us choose LM* as *a convenient term for something that has no real being.*[3])

I was fed up.

And yet. How to let her go? She was all I had. And even as our affair dwindled, I still wanted it to be known. Published. Then, I could end it.

My ambivalence and publishers' indifference stalled us. My attentions wandered, straying into other flirtations.

Time passed.

She gained more recognition. The gatekeepers nodded and I went public with a warmed-over account of our beleaguered *histoire d'amour*.

Now, I thought, time to let her go, start over with someone else, something else.

And yet. As my way in, she was now in my way: What I *knew*. How I knew. *All I knew*. Still holding her appeal and my loyal heart.

And yet. Life and loving beyond the page divaricated along unexpected pathways, attracting suspicion from her more categorically possessive devotees.

(My FtM transpartner in life, the parent of my kids, would gladly wear the T-shirt declaring, 'I'm not a lesbian, but my girlfriend is.')

(Or, I might say, 'I'm not not a lesbian. I just love Nick.')

'Queer' landed as my best fit. Because it did not require me to fit.

And yet: Hasn't LM *always* been queer?

But, oh, such territorial and terminological wranglings. The problems. The posturings.

The age-old *prancing and squatting on the academic stage.*[4]

And yet. LM is not the sort to prance or squat. She's more ... demure? One earlier admirer praised her as a 'literary transvestite, a saucy trompe l'oeil.'[5] Another appreciated how she 'wore many necessary and elaborate disguises, making it almost impossible for the literary historian to categorise and group' her 'various occurrences.'[6]

Certainly, she seduced generations of paramours, with her *splendour*, her *candle lit radiance*. Even now, still attracting the young and passionate. You, too, perhaps, dear reader? Under this enduring, *vinous, amorous light*, she *glows* again with that *secret glamour* that first drew me in.[7]

And yet, intimacy with her is always a bit of an embarrassment, isn't it? That unreflective elitism; that presumptuous privilege, access, and wealth; that jet-setting mobility re-branded as 'exile.' Her ever-present discomforting ways, rippling on the surface, flowing in her depths.

What first lit my attraction, anyway?

Certainly, I am not the only one whose unfurling literary critical passions queerly coincided with self-understandings. *Let us admit in the privacy of our own society that these things sometimes happen.*[8]

As a Canadian undergraduate in a 'traditional' English department in the early 1990s, I learned to seek out feminist faculty outliers. I knew to pay attention when Prof V, adjunct instructor, feminist bookstore owner, dry-witted greying dyke, wryly observed, 'Everyone talks about the importance of *Ulysses*'s obscenity trials, but no one talks about *The Well of Loneliness*.' Bemused pause: 'Surprising, isn't it?'

Indignant, I vowed to redress the omission.

But that wasn't all. Turned on to literary modernism and sensing its sexy undersides, I chased my new bookish crushes across the US border just as 'queer' was gaining currency in graduate programmes, and Hall's neglected trials were inspiring an imminent deluge of academic publishing.

Ostensibly researching the story of modern/ist lesbian emergence in the English-speaking West, I was also – unknowingly – seeking my own de-pathologising identity origins story.[9] A story of art and literature, community and history, a claim to historical (be)longing both exhilarating and reassuring.

And yet. Other alliances beckoned. As English graduate students during the last half of the 1990s, we were besotted by the brash charisma of queer theory, whose anti-identitarian and un-disciplined glamour often cast 'lesbian' – especially when coupled with 'modernism' – in the shade: *outré*, behind the times, out of step, a bit of a drag, inconsequent, anachronistic.[10]

And yet. LM suited my conventionally (cons)trained disciplinary sensibilities, granting safe passage to the cachet of modernist literature, while smuggling in queer, feminist variation. Dodging the dead straight white male canon, I ventured only so far as the adjacent, emerging canon of dead queer mostly white privileged women+.[11] As Madelyn Detloff observes, the 'queer feminist modernist' cultural worker is as *metic* as the writers she studies.[12]

Certainly, modernism alone was not the attraction. It was Rhoda crushing on Miss Lambert, Chloe liking Olivia, Sally kissing Clarissa, Stein *Lifting Belly*, the allure of Robin Vote, Clare Kendry, Lily Briscoe, and Miss La Trobe. Not to mention those who wrote, published, defended, promoted, and paid for it all: Margaret and Jane, Sylvia and Adrienne, Gertrude and Alice, Vita and Virginia, Sylvia and Valentine, Natalie and Renée, H.D. and Bryher, Harriet and Dora ... Keeping literary company with smart, sexy, mysterious, often expatriate and gender-confounding queer people 'who might be identified as female,'[13] I could contemplate the arts of gender and sexuality, desire and identity, without directly contemplating myself.

I know I am not alone in this. We all have our stories of the stories that are ours.

Nor am I alone in my squirming unease with LM's often unchecked entitlements. Cultural access, white imperial privilege, education, cosmopolitan mobility, relative financial ease: such were the conditions and adherent violences that enabled LM to live, to write, to persist – even flourish – queerly.[14] They imparted forms of freedom to create 'modern' art, a liveable life, and a durable record: texts composed, published, archived, documented, remembered.

As such, LM's combination of literary prestige and edgy marginality afforded an unexpected advantage on a millennial Canadian academic marketplace awakening to the kinds of queerness that could impart 'diversity' without disrupting the status quo. LM helped me secure a job and a repatriation home, just before George W. won the election and the US government lost its mind.

And yet. I remain a perennial colonial misfit among LM's American and British suitors. Our relationship continuously founders and stalls. Why not just end the whole affair?

(Meanwhile, fresh, young, more daring and unabashed LM admirers come calling, reviving her pleasures, seeing her anew.

A twinge of jealousy? Or finally time to turn my back?)

III. Invitation Hesitation

I don't know what to do. I have two thoughts.[15]

The invitation for this collection arrives; I try to resist. Send an abstract anyway.

Time passes.

[2020 shatters in, taking hold and not letting go.][16]

Do I even care about LM any more? Does anyone?

Like many others, I read Saidiya Hartman's *Wayward Lives, Beautiful Experiments*.[17] Exhilarating and heart-rending by turns, it is what Jennifer Nash theorises as 'beautiful black feminist writing.'[18] These are the 1920s queer feminist stories that need at/tending to. This is how they must be told.

I read Melanie Micir's *The Passion Projects*.[19] It rewarms my affections, lifts my heart.

Reading about pandemic reading reminds me that Woolf will always be of value, teaching lessons for our times.[20]

And yet.

Is this how best to orchestrate my attention, my care, my labour, now?[21]

It's hard to come to terms with my writing when the world's on fire and here I am, obsessing over a handful of paper.[22]

And you, dear reader: Is this how best to spend our waning time together?

And yet.

Isn't LM always out of (step in) time?

Isn't that why we love her so?

IV. THE QUEER TIME OF LESBIAN MODERNISM

Oh, these *Impossible Women*. 'That seemingly defunct figure,' behind the times, *out of place*, such a *drag*: *Feeling Backward. Inconsequence. Sapphic Primitivism. Palimpsestic.*[23] Long before there was *No Future*, LM was annihilating the future with her 'self-exterminating ... ultra-civilisation.'[24] Her temporal dislocation suspended in a perennial time warp: erotohistory, anachronism, present future.[25] LM itself is a scholarly backformation, borne from the feminist historical recovery work that, as Makiko Minow put it in 1989, first taught us 'what we may have to learn to call "lesbian modernism."'[26]

Such queer becoming has always been in temporal suspension: at once drawing on Sapphic fictions of the past and knowingly forecasting itself as and into an anticipatory (often posthumous) future.[27] From Pierre Louÿs's dedication of *Les chansons de Bilitis 'aux jeunes filles de la société future'*[28] to the archived and recalled words of Stein, Sackville-West, Townsend Warner, and many more who planned and projected the public afterlives of their biographies, archives, and unpublished writings, LM dwells in the queerest of temporalities: of her time, before her time, behind the times, belated, beleaguered, intimate with/as the dead,[29] foretelling her posthumous time to (be)come.

My own timeworn troubled intimacy with her, dallying on for a quarter century.

And her other lovers? Who else has sought her, when, and why?

What have 'we' wanted from LM and offered to her, as we have learned to call her by her – by our – name(s)?

And how to clock the time(s) of (our) desiring?

V. OUR TIMELINES, OURSELVES

It might well be to honour the creature slowly, that you may afford it.[30]

Suzanne Raitt's 2003 *GLQ* review article 'Lesbian Modernism?' opens:

> It is now a truism in sexuality studies that contemporary versions of lesbian, gay, bisexual, transgendered [*sic*], or queer identity for women can trace their variously hyphenated being back to a moment in the early twentieth century when the modern lesbian first became visible.[31]

Reviewing five monographs that 'engage the received wisdom about how early-twentieth-century modern and postmodern lesbian identities were consolidated as well as the relationship between lesbianism and modernity itself,' Raitt observes that 'critical investment in finding ourselves in the past, and in establishing ourselves as politically and socially radical – "modern" – from the outset, is intense' (112).[32]

Here Raitt diagnoses – in order to deflate – 'our' longing to pair lesbian with modernism as an unruly passion that risks breeding critically unaware scholarship impaired by the 'politics of identification' (118).[33] Heeding Laura Doan's historical correctives to certain enduring mythologies, Raitt cautions, 'It may be that we have wanted to believe ourselves more central than we are to the coming of a modernity we have been, perhaps, too eager to embrace' (115). Such scholarship, Raitt concludes, raises 'complicated and disturbing questions': 'Is there an inevitable link between lesbianism and modernity? Or have we imagined such a link – or at least exaggerated it – as a way of rescuing our sense of our own radicalism in a rapidly reconfiguring postmodern world?' Admonishing the 'mythologizing' (120) hazards of such 'intense' 'investment[s]' (112), Raitt advises the familiar caution of tempered disinterestedness and sceptical critique: we must not muddle literary-historical accounts with our own messy longings, attachments, and projections. We are chastened to know our place and to place our knowing.

Beware of schwärmerei.[34]

And yet. Raitt's own hermeneutics of suspicion constitutes just one posture within a half-century-long series of affective-academic orientations towards LM.

Notwithstanding:

- the pitfalls of chronology as a 'normalizing practice'[35]
- the insights of queer temporalities, historicisms, and asynchronies, which eschew linear, progressive, developmental narrativising
- the inadequacies of oceanic metaphors to figure activist or intellectual movements, particularly feminism
- the myriad problems with supersessionist paradigms, particularly when applied to sexual epistemes, structured as they are by 'the unrationalized coexistence of different models'[36]

I hazard here a highly selective chronological foray into early post-Stonewall LM criticism, storied with semi-arbitrary 'waves.'[37] Plunging into the earlier decades, my account dives down for hidden treasures – pearls? – in their depths, while sculling brusquely over more recent currents and eddies.

Like any love affair, we tell our stories after the fact, feeling backward to chart a history of our unstable, heartbroken, and heartopening present.

First Wave: Stalking the Ancestress

In 1973, Bertha Harris (1937–2005) published 'The More Profound Nationality of Their Lesbianism: Lesbian Society in Paris in the 1920s' in *Amazon Expedition: A Lesbian Feminist Anthology*. Described by Jaime Harker as 'one of the earliest artifacts of lesbian feminism,'[38] this scrappy anthology was issued by a small, independent press whose advocation 'for a world socialist society, free of sexual, racist, ageist, and class oppression – free of all forms of domination' exemplifies what Roderick Ferguson identifies as the oft-forgotten multi-dimensional aspirations of early gay liberation movements.[39]

Harris's contribution recalls a summer job in New York 1959, when she spent her leisure time 'hanging out on the corner of Patchin Place [in Greenwich Village] [. . .] waiting for Djuna Barnes to take her afternoon walk':

> As often as I could (and with discretion) I followed her and, trailing her, received the silent messages about my past that I needed and she could give; and never once during our exchange did I encroach upon her lordly solitude to give her my name. [. . .] [I]n my fantasy, she would stop and take my hand to thank me for all the flowers I daily stuffed into her mailbox in Patchin Place and then tell me how it was to be a dyke in Paris, in the Twenties.
>
> [. . .]
>
> It never happened.[40]

Instead, Harris masqueraded as a Cambridge professor (in 'a dumpy tweed skirt, a starched white shirt, black neck tie') and infiltrated the New York Public Library rare book room to access Barnes's publications a decade before their mass reprinting (78).

Further discovering Colette, Stein, Toklas, Beach, Hall, Troubridge, Brooks, Barney, and Vivien, Harris notes:

> we Englit majors had never heard a word of any of them. Our teachers had never heard a word of any of them – or, if they had, had dismissed the word as inconsequential compared to those of the real makers and breakers and shakers of modern literature: those men with the paperback book names. (78)

Harris claims *The Autobiography of Alice B. Toklas* as her 'book of ancestors,' but also declaims a foundling disparity from her newfound kin:[41]

> But I was poor and grubby; naïve, emotional, sweaty with lower class need. I was short and peasantmade – and my ancestors, I learned, as I read my censored history, were rich or nearly rich; sophisticated, cool;

longlimbed; and our family bloodline, the common identity among us [...] will always be my acknowledgement of these women, despite all the material difference between us, as my first ancestors. (78–9)

Holding her 'ancestors' accountable for their unreflective class privilege and capitalist collusion, Harris identifies the majority as ex-pats who 'escaped the American Gothic with huge hunks of papa's fortune stuffed in their pockets – fortunes made for the most part by the usual grinding-the-noses-of-the-poor and fortunes spent by these women solely on themselves and on each other' (79). Harris directly calls out 'their elitism, their decadence, their snobbery,' but also calls in *Ladies Almanack*'s satire of this 'intensely exclusive milieu,' as 'in its way and for its time, a document of lesbian revolution' (81). Indeed, by Harris's reckoning, '[b]etween Sappho and Gertrude Stein [...] these women represent practically the only available expressions of lesbian culture we have in the modern western world' (87). Or, to invoke Raitt's terms, these found/l/ing ancestors may not be sufficiently 'politically and socially radical' for Harris, but they are all she has.

The next year, in 1974, Gayle Rubin (b. 1949) opens a carefully typed letter addressed to Djuna Barnes with the same wish that Harris longed to whisper: 'I would like to come and meet you and talk with you.'[42] Introducing herself as an anthropology grad student, Rubin explains how, four years prior when she was a 'new born' lesbian 'madly in love, dreadfully unhappy, and utterly intoxicated with passion and pain,' a 'literate' friend prescribed *Nightwood*. 'I took to the book as if it were a lover,' Rubin confesses, 'I wrote lines from it all over the walls of my room, and responded in my typical fashion by starting a research project' (1).

(Who among us has not traversed that surprisingly short but covert path between taking 'to a book as if it were a lover' and 'starting a research project'?)

Deciphering that *Ladies Almanack*'s characters were 'modeled on a living group,'[43] Rubin celebrates them as '"gay liberationists" long before the term was coined,' whose conversations 'were just the sort of thing I wanted to hear about' (1). Consequently, Rubin declares, while in Paris purportedly to research French anthropology, 'I set out in search of my ancestresses': exploring the Bibliothèque Nationale; 'scouring the city for tracks and traces left by Barney, Vivien, and the others'; tracking down Parisian bookstore owners and ageing literati who remembered Barney and Barnes (1). Conducting this 'dogged research' to find literature to support her 'new born' lesbian identity, Rubin laments, 'It is an artifact of what this culture does to certain passions that it should take so much effort to find out about other people's experiences of them' (2). 'Yet there is a record,' she continues, 'and I have spent a lot of time excavating it. [...] the Paris group around Barney stands out as one of the most significant landmarks' (2). Hailing Barnes as 'one of the major contributors to the pool of lesbian experience,' Rubin proposes:

'I would like to know what you might have to say to us, the young. [. . .] You are a living ancestress. I want you to speak' (2).

Barnes, as we might predict, did not answer this letter.

But she did *keep* it.

This is not lost on me.

As easy as it might be to ascribe this epistolary failure to the incommensurable gulf between Rubin's post-Stonewall lesbian community-identifications and Barnes's identity-dodging prickliness, such a dismissal would belie the letter's delicate and affective complexity. And, although Barnes refused to speak, Rubin *did* continue to speak, functioning as 'a vehicle of tradition' (2), and absorbing paradigm-shifting lessons from her 'ancestresses.' In the introduction to *Deviations* (2011), Rubin considers how these early discoveries prompted her own 'turning point' towards the 'social construction of sex.' In researching and relating to 1920s Sapphic Parisian communities, Rubin did not posit a transhistorical essentialism, but rather gleaned 'that "lesbianism" was a historically specific concatenation of same-sex desires, gender variability, forms of identity, and institutional repertoires. [. . .] [W]hat might be called "modern" lesbianism was a distinctive [historical] development.'[44] In other words, to recall (or anticipate) Raitt's terms, Rubin was formulating – with other sexuality studies forerunners – what eventually became 'our' mythology of 'a moment in the early twentieth century when the modern lesbian first became visible.'[45]

Nor do I interpret as naïve Harris's and Rubin's emotional, political, historical, and aesthetic investments in their pursuit of Barnes. Theirs is a consciously formulated, strategic, self-reflective identification that knows what it seeks and why.[46] Harris owns her critical ambivalence; Rubin retrospectively acknowledges her 'tunnel vision' that 'characterized so much of that era of lesbian feminist scholarship.'[47] These 1920s Parisian lesbians did not constitute an unproblematic model of identification, but, as Rubin tells Barnes, they offered the only available writing on female same-sex desire 'outside of the literature of clinical psychology' (2). Whether infiltrating restricted reading rooms or haunting the streets, archives, and bookstores of New York and Paris, Harris and Rubin intrepidly assembled a queer feminist imagined community of the past. Wise to the historical, class, and political disjunctions of their quest, they were equally undaunted by Barnes's refusal to acknowledge the letters and roses thrust in her mailbox and the quiet desperation of the 1970s lesbians who tread in her path.

By 1979, historian Blanche Wiesen Cook (b. 1941) crests the first LM wave in which Harris and Rubin swim with her *Signs* article '"Women Alone Stir

My Imagination": Lesbianism and the Cultural Tradition.' Cook's scholarly approach and publication venue index the early field formation of politicised women's and feminist studies; indeed, her prophetic opening attests to the cultural scarcity that a half-century of queer-minded feminist intellectual labour has since worked to correct: 'In literary history, were all things equal, 1928 might be remembered as a banner year for lesbian publishing.' (Herein we may sing the now-familiar litany: Woolf's *Orlando*, Hall's *The Well*, Barnes's *Ladies Almanack*.[48]) 'But,' Cook continues, 'all things were not equal': with Woolf's and Barnes's texts largely ignored or unavailable, only *The Well*'s scandalous infamy kept it known and in print. Consequently, 'most of us lesbians in the 1950s grew up knowing nothing about lesbianism except Stephen Gordon's swagger [. . .] breeches, and [. . .] wonderful way with horses.'[49]

'Now suppose,' Cook muses, 'we had read [. . .] *Orlando* instead,' or known about Woolf's affair with Sackville-West, or read Woolf's then unpublished letters to women. 'Alternatively, imagine: to have read the *Ladies Almanack* in 1956! [. . .] No self-loathing; just the joyous play' of Barnes's raunchy prose and characters. Like Harris, Cook acknowledges that all three 1928 novels 'dealt with the rarefied and privileged existence of lesbians of aristocratic mien and means,' while pointing out that the only one readily available to generations of readers was also the only one that 'denied joy in the positive choice to live with and love women' (719).

Cook, much like Rubin, observes, 'History tends to bury what it seeks to reject,' compounding the foundling ache of her generation: 'Many women thought they were the only lesbians in their communities, maybe even in all human history' (720). Even with emerging historical recovery work, Cook warns of anti-feminist accounts and their 'continued denials and invalidation of lesbian experience' (724). Indeed, Cook takes Woolf's literary biography as a case in point. Equipped with the first freshly published volumes of Woolf's letters and diaries, Cook counters the 'marred' standard Woolf biographies by the 'sons of Bloomsbury' – Quentin Bell, John Lehmann, and Nigel Nicholson – with Woolf's own voice (725). On Woolf's affair with Sackville-West, Cook notes, 'For almost every interpretation of Quentin Bell we have a possible alternative in Virginia Woolf's own words' (726). With a nod to Jane Marcus's forthcoming edited collection *New Feminist Essays on Virginia Woolf*, Cook proposes that 'feminists may want to read every newly available letter and journal entry to decide for themselves such questions as whether or not Woolf was an elitist aristocrat or a socialist, asexual or woman-loving' (726).

Aligning Woolf's life-work with second-wave feminism in which 'the public and private worlds are inseparably connected,'[50] Cook endorses Woolf's relevance given her understanding 'that the freedom – personal, economic, and political – to which we aspire connects our work with passion to all our human relations' (730). Cook's insistent counter-memory here sails upon the historical tidal turn, whereby Woolf (re)surfaces as a social justice minded feminist/queer/lesbian icon and inspiration.

By such measures, Stein does not fare so well. Critiquing Stein's partnership with Toklas as heteroconventional, Cook derides Stein's cultural, gender, racial, and economic politics as 'simply impoverished' (731).[51] Even here, Cook rescues Stein from history's amnesia: 'however we may interpret the Stein–Toklas relationship, "in the old days" we knew nothing about their affection and their joy' (731). Reiterating that '[o]ur only picture of lesbian love' was Hall's 'joyless' version (731), Cook also notes that insightful 1928 feminist critiques of *The Well* were 'obscured' by its legal scandals (732), and Hall was disserved by Lovat Dickson's 'puerile and hateful' biography (733).[52]

Turning to the 'far more self-affirming environment' offered by 'the rediscovery' of the 1920s Parisian milieu (733), Cook distinguishes 'our' historical interests from heterosexist and voyeuristic accounts:

> We are searching the past because there are to be found there a great variety of models to alter, enhance, intensify our own visions, our own options, as we move from the male dominance of patriarchy to more equalitarian relations and the full range of choices available [. . .] in a fully creative and unconfined society. (736)

Here, Cook's aspirational 'we' mingles with twenty-first-century queer voices and visions:

> *My approach to hope as a critical methodology can be best described as a backward glance that enacts a future vision.*
>
> *I think of queerness as a temporal arrangement in which the past is a field of possibility in which subjects can act in the present in the service of a new futurity.*[53]

Enumerating contemporary (lesbian) feminist efforts 'in the service of a new futurity,' Cook's peroration aligns the (still-so-relevant) insights from her lifetime friend and colleague, Audre Lorde, on 'the erotic as power' with what Cook identifies as Woolf's aspirations for a 'future both feminist and classless' (739).[54] Indeed, Harris, Rubin, and Cook all unapologetically reach out (and feel backward)[55] for what they want from LM – ancestors who offer art, models, alternatives, and sustaining potentialities for a future horizon – as a means of historical be/longing 'best described as a backward glance that enacts a future vision.' Reciprocally, they tender their devotional and reparative labour of research, reinterpretation, and recovery, to rescue LM writers from the historical tides that have wilfully washed over, forgotten, casually dismissed, or blithely (mis)interpreted their life/work.[56]

Ask not (only) what LM can do for you – ask what you (also) can do for LM.

And so. Admitting the folly of equating a decennial turn with a politico-epistemic one, I propose to let Cook carry us from 1970s feminist and lesbian movements towards 1980s academic feminist field formations. Cook channels the energy of Harris's and Rubin's personal and political cathexes into the emergent field of women's studies as a scholarship of liberation and world-building. Indeed, Cook's attention to Woolf and her critically under-served 1928 contemporaries along with Harris's and Rubin's personal researches demonstrate how early politically minded white (lesbian) feminists fuelled modernist field (re)formations.[57] Meanwhile, let us heed Cook's call to perennially (re-)read available and emerging primary texts for ourselves, to form provisional understandings attuned to how past texts and lives are perpetually made and remade by the shifting communities, methodologies, and histories of our present(s) and tenuous futures. As Woolf instructed a group of schoolgirls in 1926, 'you cannot get other people to do your reading for you. Each generation must read everything over again for itself.'[58]

Drawing together Harris's, Rubin's and Cook's unabashed attachments to LM, I want to reiterate that as much as their shared demand for literary historical (be)longing is laid bare, it is also consciously, thoughtfully, and reflectively considered. I wonder, now: What have we done with our own longing? How have we submerged, disavowed, secluded, camouflaged, sacrificed, or neutralised it, to comply with industry standards of critique? How have we emptied it out, poured it out, hidden it, or nursed it furtively, quietly, slightly ashamed? How might our primal found(l)ing demand, sublimated into scholarly desire, become in our field 'The Love that dare not speak its name'?

Second Wave: Field Work

In the spirit of Minow's prescient 'Versions of Female Modernism: Review Article' (1989), I pair together the monographs *Women of the Left Bank: Paris, 1900–1940* (1986) by Shari Benstock (1944–2015) with *Writing for Their Lives: The Modernist Women, 1910–1940* (1987) by Gillian Hanscombe (b. 1945) and Virginia L. Smyers (b. ?) as LM game-changers.[59] Both books compile extensive recovery work on female cultural producers who were central to the making of modernism, while also offering feminist reconsiderations of modernism attentive to queer sexuality. Insisting on modernism's 'highly individualistic and diverse, even divisive' and often 'anarchic' practices, Benstock recognises how limited male-dominated accounts have shaped modernist studies.⁶⁰ In turn, she is careful not to over-generalise about 'women's modernism' or 'force the delicate network of female relationships and individual achievements of expatriate women into preconceived patterns,' while appreciating how these women 'participate in the Modernist enterprise often seeking to subvert and invert its cultural and aesthetic premises' (32, 34). *Writing for Their Lives*, meanwhile, directly posits 'what appears to be a clear connection between literary endeavour and the shunning of conventionally heterosexual lives'⁶¹ and ultimately celebrates how modernist women's experiments in intimate, domestic, and social relationships correlate with their experiments in literature and publishing.⁶² As such, both monographs also mapped the social relations and cultural formations supporting modernist literary production – what Minow presciently identified as 'modernist *institutional* innovation' – a decade before Lawrence Rainey's *Institutions of Modernism*.⁶³

Let us further consider that Benstock's 'Expatriate Sapphic Modernism: Entering Literary History' first appeared in Karla Jay and Joanne Glasgow's landmark collection *Lesbian Texts and Contexts: Radical Revisions* (1990), as academic publishing sanctioned self-declared lesbian literary criticism and the queer nineties rolled in. Here, Benstock (citing Cook) turns from cataloguing the variety of modernist women's lives and texts towards a general theory of 'Sapphic Modernism': 'were the critics who confer canonization to take seriously Cook's claim that Woolf's imagination was fueled by Sapphic erotic power, they would be forced to redefine modernism in ways that acknowledge its Sapphic elements.'⁶⁴ Admitting that '[w]e are saddled with inadequate definitions of modernism and restrictive notions of lesbianism' (185), Benstock nevertheless reifies 'Sapphic modernism' as endowed with a deconstructive-Lacanian semiotic magic whereby 'revolution' is enacted through 'grammatical-rhetorical "deviation"' (192) vaguely linked to 'Sapphic' identities and desires: 'The Sapphic is a structure of the unconscious; it is not a language, but it structures language; [. . .] and when it finds a medium through which to speak, it radically restructures the rules of the cultural game' (193–4).

Contra Cook, Benstock anoints (redeems?) Stein as Sapphic modernism's 'philosopher-theorist' whose 'breakthrough' disruption to 'structures of representation [. . .] could only have been made in the wake of her own crisis of identity as a woman, specifically as a Sapphic woman' (194–5). Designating 'disruptive' and 'avant-garde' aesthetic practices as the measure of Sapphic revolutionary potential – more so than the communities, networks, and lived relationships of the practitioners – Benstock secures 'the Sapphic's' right to claim 'modernism' and thereby *enter into literary history*.

That 'Expatriate Sapphic Modernism' migrates from *Lesbian Texts and Contexts* to *Rereading Modernism: New Directions in Feminist Criticism* in 1994 – a collection that centralises *Women of the Left Bank* as a landmark in modernist studies' feminist turn – further signals LM's own migration from women's studies and lesbian criticism towards the emerging field of feminist modernist studies. There is much to debate about this political and disciplinary travel and its implications. It is a conversation in which all of us – generations of readers, scholars, past, present, and yet to come – might take part. *For which reasons we leave a great blank here, which must be taken to indicate that the space is filled to repletion.*[65]

And yet. Having splashed ahead to 1994, let us drift back a little – not fussing too much over where we are in the current – for *the truth is that when we write about LM, everything is out of place.*[66]

Julie Abraham identifies Sherron E. Knopp's 1988 '"If I Saw You Would You Kiss Me?": Sapphism and the Subversiveness of Virginia Woolf's *Orlando*' as '*PMLA*'s first foray into lesbian criticism,'[67] another index of LM's field (re)formation. Working to resuscitate critical interest in *Orlando*, Knopp defends both the novel and Woolf's affair with Sackville-West as worthy of 'serious' scholarly consideration.[68] Following Cook's methodology, Knopp references Woolf's and Sackville-West's life writing, along with *Orlando* itself, to correct accounts that minimise the novel, the relationship, and their combined significance to Woolf studies, in a bid to advance the wave of LM's scholarly credibility with *PMLA*'s readership.

Floating temporally back upstream, we find Karla Jay's (b. 1947) 'Lesbian Modernism: (Trans)Forming the (C)Anon' in George Haggerty and Bonnie Zimmerman's *Professions of Desire: Lesbian and Gay Studies in Literature* (1995). Lest we forget, 'lesbian and gay studies in literature' had its moment – with these editors at the forefront – and, as we've seen, was the early home for queer modernist scholarship and field-formations. Jay, a grassroots organiser, activist, editor, and scholar since the 1970s, forwards a bold proposition that now reads as axiomatic: 'I interpret literary modernism [. . .] as a movement fueled to a great extent by lesbian writers,'[69] to which we would now add editors, patrons, promoters, publishers, and booksellers.

Decrying the failures and exclusions of traditional modernist canon formation, Jay nevertheless relies on industry-standard conceptualisations in her claim that 'lesbian modernists [. . .] quietly undermined and re(de)fined generally accepted modernist principles' (73–4), a formulation that posits such principles as inherent to (what we have learned to call) modernism rather than retroactively installed by modernist studies. Broadly celebrating 'lesbian modernists' as 'revolutionary literary thinkers' engaged in 'subvert[ing] [. . .] the power system' (80, 79), Jay concludes by glimpsing the mounting wave on the horizon: 'Queer theory and lesbian feminist scholarship are suggesting new ways to read literary modernism, ways that foreground texts and writers marginal to the grand récit of Western culture. What was once deviant is now central to the concerns of readers' (81).

Third Wave: Title Surge

Herein we might catalogue the onrush of publications and notable moments in the field-formation of LMS (Lesbian+ Modernist Studies), developing alongside and within 'feminist and sexuality-aware studies of modernist writers' and contexts.[70] We would observe the accumulating torrent of titles from the mid-1990s through the millennial-turn, settling into a modest but steady stream flowing up to the present moment. We would nod approvingly at the imprimatur of academic presses and scholarly societies. We would chart field-formation bell buoys, beginning seventy years after 1928's banner year and bobbing up every subsequent decade: 1998 (founding of the Modernist Studies Association), 2008 (declaration of the 'New Modernist Studies'), 2018 (founding of Feminist Modernist Studies) and debate LM's presence or absence at each turn. We might note a refreshing upswell of inspiring and inspiriting reconsiderations within and around LM at our latest decennial turn – whether we call it *Lesbian Modernism*, *Misfit Modernism*, *The Outside Thing*, or *The Passion Projects*, we are in an era rife with *Disturbing Practices*, *Shattered Objects*, and *Wayward Lives and Beautiful Experiments*.[71] You might chime in about all the paradigm-shifting conferences and conversations I've missed, and the American-academic-imperialism pervading my account. Together, we might applaud – or question – the successes that have established, legitimated, and reinforced LMS as a field of scholarly inquiry of central importance to modernist and literary studies.

And yet.

In the privacy of our own society, I might whisper: At what cost, such success? In the quest to gain ground in Western academic field formation, how have we learned to discipline our desires, downplay our subjectivities, and disavow our affinities? In the name of scholarly *rigour*, how have we betrayed our own *vigour*, subduing our thinking and writing against the presumably distorting effects of our own messy identifications, attachments, and longings?[72] Conditioned to retreat from the secret object(s) of our desire, how – and why? – have we continued to reproduce the very same forms and methods of modernist scholarship that betrayed our beloved in the first place?

And yet, we know how, we know why. Intellectual production that centralises lived experiences that are not white cis male have been perpetually dismissed as 'too personal' or 'too emotional.' Layer upon this the age-old move of marginalising queer-identified utterances as 'special interest pleading' and we learn quickly to please a culture of legitimacy that was always meant to foreclose us. We love and study texts, lives, and socialities that refused, reimagined, and revolutionised social and literary forms, and yet we deform our own work to serve a culture that was never meant to serve us.

Of course we decry such epistemic failures: queer feminist decolonising materialist epistemology knows that thinking is loving; learning is feeling;[73] lived experience and embodiment are legitimate bases for knowledge; observer and observed intra-act; being and knowing are relational practices; form matters and matter forms; the entire hierarchical dualistic pretence upon which Western metaphysics is founded is as ill-conceived and oppressive as it is pervasive and persistent. *Nevertheless, we go on, perseveringly, conscientiously, constructing our peer-reviewed performances after a design which more and more ceases to resemble the visions in our feeling-mind-bodies. . . . But sometimes, more and more often as time goes by, we suspect a momentary doubt, a spasm of rebellion, as the pages fill themselves in the customary way. Is knowledge like this? Must scholarship be like this?*[74]

Fourth Wave: Not Waving but (Not Yet?) Drowning?

So, what happens now – with LMS having set sail from women's studies, then paddling through the streams of 'lesbian and gay' studies and floating along the tributaries of gender, sexuality, queer and trans studies, all the while mastering the codes of scholarly legitimacy required by both the 'new' and 'old' modernist studies?

What happens, apparently, is exhaustion. And a lot of negative affect.

Isn't it telling that the inaugural issue of the *Journal of Feminist Modernist Studies* (May 2018) included Madelyn Detloff's 'Strong-Armed Sisyphe: Feminist Queer Modernism Again . . . Again,' detailing 'the difficult, unfortunately repetitive, seemingly unwinnable task before the queer feminist cultural worker who is faced with rolling a giant boulder (call it fascism, call it misogyny, racism, ablism, heterosexism, anti-intellectualism, militarism, xenophobia . . .) up a hill so that it does not careen down and crush the things one values'?[75] Detloff comes to the beautiful if heartaching understanding of 'Sisyphe as a cultural worker who performs willful rebellion *regardless of the prospects for success or failure* [. . .] [H]er effort [. . .] is ongoing because justice is not an end to be achieved, but a mode [. . .] of doing life,' a mode that Detloff explains, via José Esteban Muñoz, 'originates from a state of distress, even rage. Rage, rebellion, wilfulness all keep Sisyphe moving' but in a 'form of reparation grounded in love for the object' (40; emphasis in the original).

Indeed, perhaps it is the likes of *Feminist Modernist Studies* – in a North American context, anyway – that has held space for modernist scholarship energised by that rage, frustration, rebellion – and love for the object – with special clusters on #MeToo and on the inadequacies of modernist studies as failing 'to keep pace with its claims to newness in part because of its refusal to excavate old inequities.'[76] As an antidote to this 'state of distress,' Erica Gene Delsandro introduces her edited collection *Women Making Modernism* (2020) as motivated by 'discovery, empathy, and excitement.'[77] Welcoming such an 'orientation of openness' aligned with an intersectional inclusive feminism,[78] I might go so far as to scavenge inspiration from adrienne maree brown's exhilarating *Pleasure Activism* – whose liberatory vision begins with Lorde's 'Uses of the Erotic' – to propose a practice of 'Pleasure Scholarship.' Pleasure Scholarship might originate from, rather than repress; be nourished by, rather than ashamed of; and further promote, rather than disavow, all the seductive, sustaining, and transformative pleasures and attachments that literary scholarship, particularly LMS, has to offer.

VI. Loving/Hating/Loving Lesbian Modernism

And yet. I am left clutching a loosely gathered bouquet of questions:

How has what we have learned to call lesbian modernism been shaped by what we have needed it to be, according to our own – once declared, now often unclaimed or repressed – wanting and feeling? What if such attachments were not denied in the name of scholarly impersonality, but cultivated as paths to knowing? How might integrating affective self-awareness transform how, what, and why we read, research, and write? How might we ask, 'What do we want from and for LM?' from a place of listening, even loving, curiosity? How have our stories of LM/S served 'our' own becomings and unbecomings, whether as readers, students, academics, activists, queer feminists, uncomfortably privileged, or comfortably marginal? How will it – how might 'we'? – change with the present un/becoming times and those yet to come?

What of the institutionalisation of LMS? How has LM's celebrated variegated modes of writing and living pressed up against its homogeneity of shared time, place, and racial, social, and financial privilege to render it a figure of disruptive white queer feminist resistance and possibility that still safely dwells within the conservative terms of a conventional literary field? What might this say about, and to, those of us who support and are supported by such institutions of academic legitimacy?[79]

How might 'interrogating' LM/S function – productively? narcissistically? – as a proxy for interrogating with vigour our own identities, biases, access, history, and knowledge systems? Insofar as LM's 'ancestral' models of community once inspired feminist and queer world-building, how might our re-turn to LM – as now an established formation open to critical 'interrogation' – inspire our own self-interrogation, including attending care-fully to our own inherited metic privileges and limitations, obligations and constraints, possibilities and exclusions?

Is 'interrogating' even the affective position we want to assume, now?

How is LMS, a field founded in white feminist recovery work, haunted by those unvoiced modern women+ whose livingness may not reside in an artistic milieu or movement,[80] but whose *wayward lives and beautiful experiments* in trying to live freely constitute fugitive artistic acts of creativity and resistance? How might attending care-fully to these hauntings transform (our relationship to) LMS?

How and why do we care about and for LM(S)?

How and why, at times, might we – should we – *just not care*?

And yet.

Notes

1. Sappho, *The Poetry of Sappho*, trans. Jim Powell (Oxford: Oxford University Press, 2007), LP 160. My citational practice will at times incorporate and adopt intertextual voices, signalled by italics rather than quotation marks.
2. On such terminological debates, see for example, Laura Doan and Jane Garrity, 'Introduction,' in *Sapphic Modernities: Sexuality, Women and National Culture*, ed. Laura Doan and Jane Garrity (Basingstoke: Palgrave Macmillan, 2006), 1–13; Joanne Winning, 'Lesbian Sexuality in the Story of Modernism,' in *The Oxford Handbook of Modernisms*, ed. Peter Brooker, Andrzej Gąsiorek, Deborah Longworth and Andrew Thacker (Oxford: Oxford University Press, 2016), 224–8; and Susan Lanser, '1928: Sapphic Modernity and the Sexuality of History,' *Modernism/modernity Print Plus* 1, no. 3 (October 2016), accessed 10 March 2020, https://doi.org/10.26597/mod.0016.
3. Adapted from Virginia Woolf, *A Room of One's Own* (Peterborough: Broadview Press, [1929] 2001), 7.
4. Lauren Berlant and Michael Warner, 'What Does Queer Theory Teach Us about X?,' *PMLA* 110, no. 3 (May 1995): 343–9, 348.
5. Karla Jay, 'Lesbian Modernism: (Trans)Forming the (C)Anon,' in *Professions of Desire: Lesbian and Gay Studies in Literature*, ed. George E. Haggerty and Bonnie Zimmerman (New York: Modern Language Association of America, 1995), 72–83, 79.

6. Shari Benstock, 'Expatriate Sapphic Modernism: Entering Literary History,' in *Lesbian Texts and Contexts: Radical Revisions*, ed. Karla Jay and Joanne Glasgow (New York: New York University Press, 1990), 183–203, 185.
7. Adapted from Woolf's description of Vita Sackville-West in Virginia Woolf, *The Diary of Virginia Woolf, Volume 3: 1925–1930*, ed. Anne Olivier Bell and Andrew McNeillie (New York: Harcourt Brace Jovanovich, 1980), 52, and from Rhoda's description of Miss Lambert's ring in Virginia Woolf, *The Waves* (Oxford: Oxford University Press, [1931] 1998), 25.
8. Woolf, *Room*, 97.
9. I prefer not to capitalise west/western, but I am following the press's style guide.
10. See the work of Robyn Wiegman, Elizabeth Freeman, Annamarie Jagose and Valerie Rohy cited later in this essay.
11. My use of women+ and lesbian+ takes inspiration from Rachel Ricketts, who credits Bear Herbert's practice. See Rachel Ricketts, *Do Better: Spiritual Activism for Fighting and Healing from White Supremacy* (New York: Atria Books, 2021), 338.
12. Madelyn Detloff, 'Strong-Armed Sisyphe: Feminist Queer Modernism Again . . . Again,' *Feminist Modernist Studies* 1, no. 1–2 (May 2018): 36–43, 36; Madelyn Detloff, 'Iconic Shade . . . and Other Professional Hazards of Woolf Scholarship,' in *Women Making Modernism*, ed. Erica Gene Delsandro (Gainesville: University Press of Florida, 2020), 203–20, 215. For a full discussion of Detloff's concept of white feminist modernist writers as *metics*, see Madelyn Detloff, *The Persistence of Modernism: Loss and Mourning in the Twentieth Century* (Cambridge: Cambridge University Press, 2009).
13. Madelyn Detloff, 'Modern Times, Modernist Writing, Modern Sexualities,' in *The Cambridge Companion to Lesbian Literature*, ed. Jodie Medd (New York: Cambridge University Press, 2015), 139–53, 139.
14. On 'flourishing,' see Madelyn Detloff, *The Value of Virginia Woolf* (Cambridge: Cambridge University Press, 2016), 14–28.
15. Sappho, *Poetry of Sappho*, LP 51.
16. With a nod to 'Time Passes' in Virginia Woolf's *To the Lighthouse*.
17. Saidiya Hartman, *Wayward Lives, Beautiful Experiments: Intimate Histories of Riotous Black Girls, Troublesome Women, and Queer Radicals* (New York: W. W. Norton, 2019).
18. Jennifer C. Nash, 'Writing Black Beauty,' *Signs* 45, no. 1 (2019): 101–22, 108.
19. Melanie Micir, *The Passion Projects: Modernist Women, Intimate Archives, Unfinished Lives* (Princeton, NJ: Princeton University Press, 2019).
20. Detloff's *The Value of Virginia Woolf* makes a case for the ongoing value of Woolf's work. There are many 2020 articles about Woolf and the pandemic. See, for example, 'Why Anxious Readers Under Quarantine Turn to "Mrs Dalloway,"' *The New Yorker*, 10 April 2020, accessed 23 June 2022, https://www.newyorker.com/books/page-turner/why-anxious-readers-under-quarantine-turn-to-virginia-woolfs-mrs-dalloway; Jennifer Spitzer, 'Me and Mrs Dalloway: On Losing My Mother to COVID-19,' *Avidly: LA Review of Books*, 19 July 2020, accessed 23 June 2022, https://avidly.lareviewofbooks.org/2020/07/19/me-and-mrs-dalloway-on-losing-my-mother-to-covid-19/; and Kabe Wilson, 'On Being Still,' *The Modernist Review*

25, 9 November 2020, accessed 23 June 2022, https://modernistreviewcouk.wordpress.com/2020/11/09/on-being-still/.
21. 'Orchestrate attention' is a term from Ezra Klein's interview with Jenny Odell, in reference to her book *How to Do Nothing: Resisting the Attention Economy* (Brooklyn: Melville House, 2019). See 'Jenny Odell and the Art of Attention,' *Vox*, 23 May 2019, accessed 23 June 2022, https://www.vox.com/ezra-klein-show-podcast/2019/5/23/18636332/jenny-odell-how-to-do-nothing.
22. Ocean Vuong, interview in *The Well and Often Reader*, quoted in Bahar Orang, *Where Things Touch: A Meditation on Beauty* (Toronto: Book Hug Press, 2020), 60.
23. Valerie Rohy, *Impossible Women: Lesbian Figures and American Literature* (Ithaca, NY: Cornell University Press, 2000); Robyn Wiegman, *Object Lessons* (Durham, NC: Duke University Press, 2021), 102; Gillian Whitlock, 'Everything Is Out of Place: Radclyffe Hall and the Lesbian Literary Tradition,' *Feminist Studies* 13, no. 3 (Autumn 1987): 554–82; Elizabeth Freeman, *Time Binds* (Durham, NC: Duke University Press, 2010); Heather Love, *Feeling Backward: Loss and the Politics of Queer History* (Cambridge, MA: Harvard University Press, 2007); Annamarie Jagose, *Inconsequence* (Ithaca, NY: Cornell University Press: 2002); Robin Hackett, *Sapphic Primitivism: Productions of Race, Class, and Sexuality in Key Works of Modern Fiction* (New Brunswick, NJ: Rutgers University Press, 2004). 'Palimpsest' is a concept associated with both Sappho and H.D.
24. Lee Edelman, *No Future: Queer Theory and the Death Drive* (Durham, NC: Duke University Press, 2004); *Hansard Official Reports*, 5th Series, Parliamentary Debates, House of Commons, vol. 46 (4 August 1921), 1800, 1802.
25. Freeman, *Time Binds*; Valerie Rohy, *Anachronism and Its Others: Sexuality, Race, Temporality* (Albany: State University of New York Press, 2009); Valerie Traub, *Thinking Sex with the Early Moderns* (Philadelphia: University of Pennsylvania Press, 2015), 82–3.
26. Makiko Minow, 'Versions of Female Modernism: Review Article,' *News from Nowhere* 7 (1989): 64–9, 67.
27. See Jodie Medd, 'Posthumous Queer Modernism,' in *The Routledge Companion to Queer Theory and Modernism*, ed. Melanie Micir (New York: Routledge, forthcoming). On the ways in which modernist women themselves created archives that would support feminist recovery reconsiderations of modernism, see Micir, *Passion Projects*.
28. Pierre Louÿs, *Les chansons de Bilitis* (Paris: Modern-Bibliotheque, 1894), title page.
29. See Kate Thomas, 'Lesbian Postmodern at the Fin de Siècle,' in Medd, *Cambridge Companion to Lesbian Literature*, 122–35.
30. Djuna Barnes, 'Foreword' (1972), *Ladies Almanack* (1928; repr., New York: New York University Press, 1992), 4.
31. Suzanne Raitt, 'Lesbian Modernism?,' *GLQ* 10, no. 1 (2003): 111–21, 112. Subsequent references will cite page numbers in-text.
32. Raitt reviews Laura Doan, *Fashioning Sapphism: The Origins of a Modern English Lesbian Culture* (New York: Columbia University Press, 2001); Gay Wachman, *Lesbian Empire: Radical Crosswriting in the Twenties* (New Brunswick, NJ: Rutgers University Press, 2001); Lisa Walker, *Looking Like What You Are: Sexual*

Style, Race, and Lesbian Identity (New York: New York University Press, 2001); Jean Walton, *Fair Sex, Savage Dreams: Race, Psychoanalysis, Sexual Difference* (Durham, NC: Duke University Press, 2001).

33. I agree that certain scholarship Raitt reviews is critically unaware of its own investments; however, I propose that self-aware identifications with our subjects of study are possible and generative. From here on, I will release the quotation marks around 'us/our,' intending this troublesome pronoun to read as both appropriately ironic and invitingly cosy. As if 'we' know who we are and how we do/do not belong to such interpellations. Not to mention Sylvia Wynter's theorisation of the *referent-we*. See Sylvia Wynter and Katherine McKittrick, 'Unparalleled Catastrophe for Our Species?,' in *Sylvia Wynter: On Being Human as Praxis*, ed. Katherine McKittrick (Durham, NC: Duke University Press, 2015), 9–89.
34. In *The Passion Projects*, Micir beautifully discusses schwärmerei, in the context of Hope Mirrlees's use of the term in relation to Jane Harrison, to evoke 'a zealous, passionate, possibly erotic, yet somewhat illegitimate or immature attachment. Schwärmerei occurs between women; even more often, schwärmerei is what happens between immature women or girls' (71). Micir considers how this term of excessive attachment may apply not only to the projects of 'intimate biography' (72) she examines but also to any scholarly work, 'perhaps especially in identity-based recovery projects' (72).
35. Erin Grogan and Siobhan Somerville, 'Chronology,' in *The Cambridge Companion to Queer Studies*, ed. Siobhan Somerville (Cambridge: Cambridge University Press, 2020), xiv–xxiv, xiv.
36. Eve Kosofsky Sedgwick, *Epistemology of the Closet* (Berkeley: University of California Press, 1990), 47.
37. Not only are my reference choices here highly selective, but I have also had to ruthlessly abbreviate citations and summaries.
38. Jaime Harker, 'Paris Was a Lesbian: Women's Liberation and the Re-Queering of Modernism,' in *The Routledge Companion to Queer Theory and Modernism*, ed. Melanie Micir (New York: Routledge, forthcoming). Many thanks to Jaime for sharing this MS before its publication.
39. The press's self-description is from the inner cover of *Hip Culture: 6 Essays on Its Revolutionary Potential* (New York: Times Change Press, 1970). On the multi-dimensionality of the early gay liberation movement, see Roderick A. Ferguson, *One-Dimensional Queer* (Cambridge: Polity Press, 2019).
40. Bertha Harris, 'The More Profound Nationality of Their Lesbianism: Lesbian Society in Paris in the 1920s,' in *Amazon Expedition: A Lesbian Feminist Anthology*, ed. Phyllis Birkby, Bertha Harris, Esther Newton, Jill Johnston and Jane O'Wyatt (New York: Times Change Press, 1973), 77–88, 77–8. Subsequent references will cite page numbers in-text.
41. See Christopher Nealon, *Foundlings: Lesbian and Gay Historical Emotion before Stonewall* (Durham, NC: Duke University Press, 2001). Nealon's theorising of the 'foundling' as a mid-twentieth-century figure that 'allegorises a movement between solitary exile and collective experience' (8) applies beautifully to the accounts by Harris and Rubin I discuss. Nealon calls it 'becoming historical' (180) or a desire to 'feel historical' (18); I call it 'queer historical (be)longing.'

42. Rubin letter to Barnes, Series II: Correspondence, Box 14, Folder 36, Djuna Barnes Papers, University of Maryland, 1. All subsequent citations from Rubin's letter to Barnes are from this correspondence. The letter has two (unnumbered) pages, which I reference by page. Subsequent references will cite page numbers in-text. I am grateful to Matthew Clarke for introducing me to this letter in his PhD dissertation, *Unanswered: Letter Writing and the Queer History of Modernism* (University of Sydney, 2019) and for providing me with a copy of the letter. I am deeply thankful to Gayle Rubin for her permission to quote from this letter and for her generous and lively email correspondence about it.
43. This may be common LM knowledge now, but only because of the obsessive recovery work of readers like Rubin.
44. Gayle Rubin, 'Introduction,' in *Deviations: A Gayle Rubin Reader* (Durham, NC: Duke University Press, 2011), 1–32, 18.
45. Raitt, 'Lesbian Modernism?,' 112.
46. For another, more sustained discussion of 1970s lesbian feminist attachments to 1920s queer female modernism, see Harker, 'Paris Was a Lesbian.'
47. Rubin, 'Introduction,' 17, reconfirmed in her email correspondence with me in 2021.
48. Cook does not include Compton Mackenzie's *Extraordinary Women*, which might not qualify as 'lesbian' publishing if Cook intended the adjective to apply to both author and content and may not have been as well known in 1979.
49. Blanche Wiesen Cook, '"Women Alone Stir My Imagination": Lesbianism and the Cultural Tradition,' *Signs: Journal of Women in Culture and Society* 4, no. 4 (1979): 718–39, 718, 719. Subsequent references will cite page numbers in-text.
50. Ibid., 730, citing Woolf, *Three Guineas*.
51. For a recent debunking of this standard narrative, see Hannah Roche, *The Outside Thing: Modernist Lesbian Romance* (New York: Columbia University Press, 2019).
52. Esther Newton countered this not uncommon anti-*Well* lesbian feminist approach with 'The Mythic Mannish Lesbian: Radclyffe Hall and the New Woman,' *Signs* 9, no. 4 (Summer 1984): 557–75. Dickson's would have been the only biography of Hall, save for Una Troubridge's, available at the time.
53. José Esteban Muñoz, *Cruising Utopia: The Then and There of Queer Futurity* (New York: New York University Press, 2009), 4, 16.
54. For a recent engagement with 'Uses of the Erotic: The Erotic as Power,' see adrienne maree brown, *Pleasure Activism: The Politics of Feeling Good* (Chico, CA: AK Press, 2019). On Lorde's ongoing legacy, see Pauline Alexis Gumbs, *The Eternal Life of Audre Lorde: Biography as Ceremony* (New York: Farrar, Straus and Giroux, forthcoming).
55. Heather Love's *Feeling Backward* inhabits my thinking and language in this discussion.
56. Here my insistent repetition of the 're' prefix takes inspiration from Rita Felski, *The Limits of Critique* (Chicago: University of Chicago Press, 2015), 17, also discussed by Delsandro, 'Introduction: Making a Feminist Modernist Studies,' in *Women Making Modernism*, 1–18, 3.
57. A point aligned with Harker's 'Paris Was a Lesbian.'

58. Virginia Woolf in Beth Rigel Daugherty, 'Virginia Woolf's "How Should One Read a Book?,"' *Woolf Studies Annual* 4 (1998): 123–85, 147–8.
59. For a more extensive discussion of not just the importance of these two monographs and Minow's review but also the history of lesbian modernist criticism that follows, see Winning, 'Lesbian Sexuality,' 218–34.
60. Shari Benstock, *Women of the Left Bank: Paris, 1900–1940* (Austin: University of Texas Press, 1986), 33, 32. Subsequent references will cite page numbers in-text.
61. Gillian Hanscombe, 'Preface I,' in Gillian Hanscombe and Virginia L. Smyers, *Writing for Their Lives: The Modernist Women, 1910–1940* (London: The Women's Press, 1987), xiii–xv, xv.
62. See the inspired and impassioned conclusion in Hanscombe and Smyers, *Writing for Their Lives*, 248.
63. Minow, 'Versions of Female Modernism,' 66.
64. Benstock, 'Expatriate Sapphic Modernism,' 183. Subsequent references will cite page numbers in-text.
65. Virginia Woolf, *Orlando: A Biography* (Oxford: Oxford University Press, [1928] 2015), 147.
66. Ibid., 180. With a nod to Whitlock, 'Everything Is Out of Place.'
67. Julie Abraham, *Are Girls Necessary?* (Minneapolis: University of Minnesota Press, 1996), xii.
68. Sherron E. Knopp, '"If I Saw You Would You Kiss Me?": Sapphism and the Subversiveness of Virginia Woolf's *Orlando*,' *PMLA* 103, no. 1 (January 1988): 24–34. The term 'serious' circulates throughout Knopp's essay.
69. Jay, 'Lesbian Modernism,' 73. Subsequent references will cite page numbers in-text. See now, Diana Souhami, *No Modernism Without Lesbians* (London: Head of Zeus, 2020).
70. Detloff, 'Strong-Armed Sisyphe,' 37. See also Detloff for a brief listing of major queer feminist cultural workers.
71. Elizabeth English, *Lesbian Modernism: Censorship, Sexuality and Genre Fiction* (Edinburgh: Edinburgh University Press, 2015); Octavio R. González, *Misfit Modernism: Queer Forms of Double Exile in the Twentieth-Century Novel* (University Park: Penn State University Press, 2020); Roche, *The Outside Thing*; Laura Doan, *Disturbing Practices: History, Sexuality, and Women's Experience of Modern War* (Chicago: University of Chicago Press, 2013); Elizabeth Pender and Cathryn Setz, eds, *Shattered Objects: Djuna Barnes's Modernism* (University Park: Penn State University Press, 2019); Micir, *Passion Projects*; Hartman, *Wayward Lives*.
72. Stephen Murphy-Shigematsu juxtaposes academic rigour with vigour in conversation with Angel Acosta. See NYC Healing Collective podcast, *Listen Notes*, 9 February 2020, accessed 10 April 2022, https://www.listennotes.com/podcasts/nyc-healing/ep-3-healing-through-xQ9yl5MWCGV/.
73. Madelyn Detloff reminds us of Woolf's insight in 'How Should One Read a Book?' that 'we learn through feeling.' Detloff, 'Iconic Shade,' 214.
74. Adapted from Virginia Woolf, 'Modern Fiction,' in *The Essays of Virginia Woolf, Volume 4: 1925–1928*, ed. Andrew McNeillie (San Diego: Harcourt, 1994), 160.

75. Detloff, 'Strong-Armed Sisyphe,' 36. Subsequent references will cite page numbers in-text.
76. Erica Gene Delsandro, Laurel Harris, Jennifer Mitchell and Lauren M. Rosenblum, 'Inadequate: A New Feminist Manifesto,' *Feminist Modernist Studies* 3, no. 3 (2020): 267–76, 271.
77. Delsandro, 'Introduction,' 3.
78. Ibid., 3. While heeding Jennifer Nash's critique of intersectional feminism in *Black Feminism Reimagined: After Intersectionality* (Durham, NC: Duke University Press, 2019).
79. There is a long and ongoing history of purportedly 'well-meaning' white feminists perpetuating unacknowledged systemic racist harm against Black, Indigenous and women of colour; for recent discussions of the problems of white feminism both past and present, see, for example, Ricketts, *Do Better*; Ruby Hamad, *White Tears/Brown Scars: How White Feminism Betrays Women of Color* (New York: Catapult, 2020); Koa Beck, *White Feminism: From the Suffragettes to Influencers and Who They Leave Behind* (New York: Atria, 2021); Mikki Kendall, *Hood Feminism: Notes from the Women That a Movement Forgot* (New York: Viking, 2020); and Kyla Schuller, *The Trouble with White Women: A Counterhistory of Feminism* (New York: Bold Type Books, 2021). On academia's structural alignment with racism, colonialism and systemic oppressions, Katherine McKittrick notes powerfully and succinctly, 'The institution will not save us.' Katherine McKittrick, '"My Heart Makes My Head Swim": A Conversation with Katherine McKittrick,' Florence Bird Lecture, Carleton University, 22 March 2022.
80. On Black livingness, see Katherine McKittrick, *Dear Science and Other Stories* (Durham, NC: Duke University Press, 2021).

2

LESBIAN-TRANS-FEMINIST MODERNISM: CHRISTOPHER ST. JOHN, TRANS MASCULINITY AND CELIBATE FRIENDSHIP IN *HUNGERHEART: THE STORY OF A SOUL*

Jana Funke

INTRODUCTION

In 1909, the dramatist and actor Cicely Hamilton completed the script for *A Pageant of Great Women*, which would become one of the most successful plays of the British women's suffrage movement. Between 1909 and 1912, the spectacular performance was staged across Britain under the direction of costume designer and stage director Edith Craig, attracting large audiences and garnering significant press attention.[1] Featuring a parade of great women from history, including Sappho, Hypatia, Joan of Arc, Jane Austen, the Rani of Jhansi and Florence Nightingale, *A Pageant of Great Women* aimed to counter anti-suffrage arguments by foregrounding the important contributions women had made to politics, the arts, warfare, science, religion and faith.

Unsurprisingly, given its feminist ambition to celebrate historical figures who challenged restrictive gender roles, *A Pageant of Great Women* includes several individuals who 'move[d] away from the gender they were assigned at birth.'[2] Some of the performances featured Craig's life-long partner, Christopher St. John (1871–1960), in the role of eighteenth-century soldier Hannah Snell/James Gray. Snell/Gray, who was assigned female at birth, enlisted in the British armed forces to pursue life as a male soldier, later becoming a sailor. They fought and were wounded in battle. The 1910 edition of the play, issued by The Suffrage Shop, includes a striking photograph of St. John dressed as Snell/Gray.[3] Katherine Cockin, author of pioneering scholarship on Craig and St. John, describes Snell/Gray and St. John as 'soul mates.'[4] Like other individuals who have, for a long time, been read as cross-dressing women, Snell/Gray has more recently been situated within trans history.[5] Jen Manion, for example, reads Snell/Gray as a person who 'trans[ed] gender' in order 'to carve out a social and cultural place for themself as a gender in-between.'[6]

As her fascination with Snell/Gray in the context of suffrage politics indicates, St. John's life and work give insight into the deep entanglements of feminist, lesbian and trans culture that were central to many creative networks in the modernist period. St. John is a marginal figure in modernist scholarship and best known for her involvement in suffrage theatre as a member of the Actresses' Franchise League and the Women Writers' Suffrage League, and as a co-founder of the Pioneer Players theatre society. Scholars have also recognised her as the life partner of Edith or Edy Craig, who has herself been overshadowed by her brother, the theatre practitioner Edward Gordon Craig, and her mother, the famous Shakespeare actor Ellen Terry. St. John and Craig met in 1899 and stayed together until the latter's death in 1947. In 1916, they were joined by the painter Tony Atwood, living and working together in a ménage-à-trois in London and at Smallhythe Place in Kent.[7]

In 1915, St. John published her second novel *Hungerheart: The Story of a Soul* anonymously.[8] The Bildungsroman charts the life story of its protagonist, John-Baptist Montolivet.[9] Assigned female at birth and adopted into a middle-class family, John-Baptist rejects expectations around heterosexual femininity and motherhood. Although equally critical of cisnormative and heteronormative constructions of masculinity, John-Baptist identifies and is frequently recognised by others as masculine. From childhood, they are driven by an indeterminate hunger for connection that initially expresses itself in strong attractions to and intimate friendships with older women and men. After studying history at Oxford on a scholarship, they become a writer and eventually meet the famous actress Louise Canning and her daughter Sally (modelled on Ellen Terry and Edith Craig). John-Baptist and Sally fall in love and move in together, but their relationship is interrupted when a male suitor proposes to Sally, and she briefly considers the offer. After an attempt to take their own life, John-Baptist continues to live with Sally while also having intimate relationships with other women. These fleeting encounters prove to be unsatisfying for John-Baptist, and it is only when they convert to Catholicism and develop a deep spiritual friendship with a nun that their hunger begins to be satiated.

Much of the existing scholarship on *Hungerheart* presents the book as a failed lesbian narrative that adopts a rhetoric of suffering, shame and martyrdom to close down the possibility of embodied lesbian sexual expression.[10] This chapter proposes a different reading of the novel by arguing that the models of ascetic masculinity and celibate friendship John-Baptist inhabits open up rich alternative possibilities for intimate connection and spiritual fulfilment. My reading draws on scholarship in trans studies to expand the ways in which we read expressions of masculinity in works by writers who have (not always correctly) been read as female and lesbian. Although masculinity often can and does signal same-sex desire, it has other individual and relational uses and meanings that need to be recognised, as *Hungerheart* demonstrates.[11] Furthermore, I seek to expand queer approaches that insist on 'reading the "absence" of sex as itself a sign of [repressed or failed] homosexuality,' acknowledging that John-Baptist's ascetic and celibate masculinity creates numerous possibilities of intimacy and kinship that include but are not limited to lesbian eroticism.[12] In line with other work in queer and trans studies, the chapter also shifts away from identitarian approaches that seek to make firm judgements about an individual's identity. The deliberate blurring of the autobiographical and fictional in *Hungerheart* encourages readings that acknowledge the fact that gender and sexuality are understood and lived in idiosyncratic and relational ways that may exceed those explanatory models or definitive ways of knowing available to us.

Lesbian-Trans-Feminist Modernism

This chapter begins from the starting point that there is no lesbian or feminist modernism without trans modernism.[13] In other words, trans masculinity and trans femininity need to be recognised as constitutive elements of lesbian and feminist modernism.[14] With regard to trans masculinity, central figures within the lesbian modernist canon, including Bryher, Willa Cather, Radclyffe Hall and Gertrude Stein, transed gender in different ways both in their personal lives and in their writing, as recent work has begun to acknowledge.[15] This scholarship offers an important corrective to existing readings of masculinity as experienced, claimed and represented by people assigned female at birth, especially those who desired and were in relationships with women. Feminist and lesbian scholarship has often assumed that masculinity in people assigned female at birth either served to access forms of privilege and power usually reserved for white middle- and upper-class men, or to express same-sex attraction.[16] This is evident in scholarship on St. John, which has repeatedly acknowledged her masculinity while reading it primarily as a means of encoding lesbian desire, for instance, via the appropriation of homophobic and heterosexist stereotypes of the 'mannish lesbian' derived from Western sexology.[17] In so doing, scholarship has limited our understanding of the individual and relational meanings and uses of masculinity in St. John's life and work.

In response to this wider tendency within lesbian studies, and lesbian modernist studies in particular, Jack Halberstam and Jay Prosser have stressed the importance of acknowledging that some authors and characters who have typically been read as lesbian women should be understood as trans men instead.[18] Halberstam also highlights that there are cases in which the distinction between these identity designations is unclear: 'While it is true that transgender and transsexual men have been wrongly folded into lesbian history, it is also true that the distinctions between some transsexuals and lesbians may at times become quite blurry.'[19] The point here is not to take meaning away from or undermine the difference between these categories in the past and certainly not in the present, but to acknowledge that there are entanglements that can make clear-cut designations undesirable or unhelpful. In fact, claiming a lesbian identity and experiencing lesbian forms of relationality can serve to expand and exceed notions of femininity and make it possible (and desirable) to trans gender. Certainly, as this chapter demonstrates in relation to Christopher St. John and *Hungerheart*, lesbian and trans masculine experiences and forms of representation intersect, and both play an important role within a wider feminist project.[20]

Recent work in trans studies has placed emphasis on the need to move beyond identitarian approaches to trans history and culture, and this shift is central to my reading of trans masculinity in this chapter. As Susan Stryker and Paisley Currah remind us, '[t]he work of the field [of trans studies] is not confined to identitarian concerns any more than queer theoretical manoeuvres were confined to the study of gay and lesbian identities.'[21] Similarly, Manion uses the term 'trans' as 'a verb, [. . .] a process or practice without claiming to understand what it meant to that person or asserting any kind of fixed identity onto them', and without imposing linear and teleological transition narratives that assume individuals are 'simply shifting between two unchanging binaries.'[22] In these articulations, trans becomes an analytical and heuristic category that makes it possible to interrogate how gender is constituted, embraced and negotiated in shifting historical and cultural contexts and as part of wider political systems.

This is a particularly useful stance to take within historical and literary scholarship, allowing us to move beyond the (often unhelpful) question of whether or not an author or fictional character in the past should be read as, for instance, either cis lesbian or trans masculine. Frequently, imposing these labels on individuals in the past who did not claim them to describe themselves obscures intersections and forms of solidarity across identity categories that cannot always be teased apart easily. This is all the more important when talking about cultural contexts and historical moments, like early twentieth-century Britain, in which these conceptual divisions did not apply in any straightforward sense. As other scholars have noted, sexological taxonomies that may have been available to St. John in the 1910s, for example, did not clearly differentiate between gender and sexuality, and there were many other ways of knowing and articulating gender and sexuality in tandem, as discussed further below.[23] Using 'trans' in a non-identitarian sense offers us a valuable critical framework to begin to capture these processes of knowledge formation and forms of experience. This approach also makes it possible to explore the ways in which feminist, lesbian and trans engagements with masculinity intersect. While it can be crucial to differentiate between gender and sexuality, as this chapter does on many occasions, it is equally important to acknowledge their inseparability, something Kadji Amin signals by introducing the term 'gender-sexuality.'[24]

Lesbian culture, in particular, has often served to interrogate gender and sexuality as part of wider lesbian, feminist and trans projects, and St. John's life and work offer rich examples of these convergences. St. John was deeply embedded in feminist and lesbian creative and political networks of her time. In addition to her sustained engagement with suffrage theatre and politics, Smallhythe Place was a social and creative hub for queer, lesbian and bisexual women and people assigned female at birth. Frequent visitors included Radclyffe Hall and Una Troubridge, who lived in nearby Rye and planned to build a house next to the home of St. John, Craig and Atwood. The trio staunchly supported Hall and Troubridge during and after the English and American censorship trials of *The Well of Loneliness* in 1928 and 1929.[25] Smallhythe Place was also close to Sissinghurst Castle, and St. John had a short-lived affair with its owner, Vita Sackville-West, in the early 1930s. After their first meeting, Sackville-West wrote to her friend and lover, Virginia Woolf, describing St. John uncharitably as 'the most tearing old Lesbian – not unlike your friend Radclyffe Hall.'[26] Despite this initial reaction, Sackville-West and St. John spent a single night together in late 1932.[27] St. John's subsequent heartbreak did not prevent her from remaining friends with Sackville-West.

These lesbian and queer networks provided forms of community, friendship and erotic attachment that made it possible for many people to trans gender. For Stryker and Aren Z. Aizura, transgender studies 'compels attention to emergent forms of relationality,' highlighting that gender is an outcome of relational practices and forms of recognition.[28] Similarly, Amin stresses that 'gender categories – including trans, cis, nonbinary, and binary – are social and interpersonal, not individual.'[29] St. John was friends with trans masculine people like Hall, and she acknowledged, affirmed and desired other people's gender nonconformity.[30] In November 1932, for example, she wrote to Sackville-West:

> Orlando de-breeched, allow me to tell you that you are as dear to me thus, as breeched. [. . .] I know you must be a woman – evidence your husband and your sons. But I don't think of you as a woman, or as a man either. Perhaps as someone who is both, the complete human being who transcends both.[31]

In addition, although St. John is usually remembered primarily as Craig's partner, it is equally important to recognise her intimate relationship with Atwood. Friends like Troubridge nicknamed St. John and Atwood 'the Boys,' affectionately acknowledging the masculinity that connected these two partners within the ménage-à-trois.[32]

Although St. John's life offers vital opportunities to explore trans masculinity within lesbian, bisexual and queer networks, it is not my goal in this chapter to speculate further about her personal identity. Even if additional archival work might allow future critics and biographers to arrive at different conclusions, it is important to note that St. John was deliberately self-effacing in her own writing and in the choices she made regarding the preservation of personal papers. Biographers have speculated that St. John destroyed Craig's personal correspondence and memoirs after her death, although it is also possible that Craig sorted through the papers herself.[33] While St. John wrote several biographies, she actively obscured her own family history and life story and was overshadowed by other, more famous people in her life. As a result, there are very few autobiographical sources that might offer access to St. John's private or personal sense of self.[34]

Scholarship on St. John needs to address this desire for obscurity rather than try to overcome it. Ellen Ricketts, who has published important work on St. John, reminds us that this 'unknowability' needs to be recognised as 'meaningful' in relation to St. John's understanding of sexuality and, I would add, gender.[35] Although *Hungerheart*, in particular, has been read as an autobiographical roman-à-clef, scholars have also pointed out that the novel self-consciously troubles this generic designation through the use of John-Baptist as an unreliable narrator and through the deliberate falsification of St. John's own history.[36] As a result, the book does not offer any straightforward insights into St. John's own identity, but rather prompts readers to question how we relate to and read others. Even with regard to the fictional character of John-Baptist, my goal is not to label them as trans and/or lesbian, but to examine how and to what effect their character transes gender in the narrative. This chapter argues that masculinity in *Hungerheart* is deeply entangled with, but not exhausted by, lesbian uses. It demonstrates that masculinity in the novel serves to open up radical relational possibilities that are not premised on singular or stable understandings of identity.

'I HAD A FAMINE IN MY HEART': HUNGER AND THE SEXUAL INSTINCT

The idiosyncratic understanding of gender and sexuality presented in *Hungerheart* has often confounded critics. Even though scholars have argued that 'the protagonist of *Hungerheart* is the victim of "sexological" theorizing, a self-diagnosed invert,' the book does not, in fact, map easily onto this specific sexological framework.[37] 'Sexual inversion' was a term introduced to English audiences by sex psychologist Havelock Ellis and his co-author, the classicist and poet John Addington Symonds, in their 1897 book of the same title. In *Sexual Inversion*, Ellis and Symonds suggest that congenital sexual inverts, who are the main focus of the text, are born with 'inverted' sexual instincts, that is to say, instincts which are 'turned by inborn constitutional abnormality toward persons of the same sex.'[38] Gender and sexuality are inextricably linked within the concept of sexual inversion: sexual instincts for women are constructed as masculine whereas sexual instincts for men are assumed to be feminine. Reading *Hungerheart* carefully, John-Baptist is not, by their own account, born with a masculine sexual instinct that is congenitally turned towards women; rather, they understand themself to be born without any sexual instinct whatsoever. John-Baptist explicitly states that they are 'entirely free from sexual instincts' (88). Reflecting on their adolescence, they write, 'I had no morbid curiosity about sex. I reached a certain age without feelings of any kind' (57). In presenting John-Baptist as free from sexual instincts, St. John moves beyond the sexological model of sexual inversion and carves out an alternative configuration of gender-sexuality.

The fact that John-Baptist does not experience sexual instincts places *Hungerheart* in dialogue with scholarship on asexuality and its histories. Although asexuality as a politicised and fully articulated sexual identity linked to activist movements has a relatively short history beginning in the 2000s, scholars have demonstrated that it has far longer genealogies.[39] As Megan Milks and Karli June Carnkowski highlight, there are 'multiple iterations of sexual non-practice and non-desire that have come before' and anticipate more recent conceptualisations and experiences of asexuality.[40] For instance, Benjamin Kahan has charted the complex relationship between present-day understandings of asexuality and late nineteenth- and early twentieth-century constructions of celibacy, suggesting that celibacy occupies a place 'between sexuality and asexuality' within modernist culture.[41] In line with later conceptualisations of asexuality, celibacy challenges assumptions about the importance and centrality of sexuality to an individual's life and interpersonal relationships. Yet, according to Kahan, celibacy also differs from (some articulations of) asexuality in that it does not necessarily signal the absence of alloerotic desire. Rather, celibacy can be understood as a different 'organization of pleasure' and alternative form of non-genital sexuality that may include attraction to other people.[42] This model of celibacy offers one productive framework for reading John-Baptist's gender-sexuality. While John-Baptist describes themself as free from sexual instincts, they feel desire and attraction for other people, which is articulated through recurrent references to hunger. *Hungerheart* continues to present sexuality within a highly gendered economy of drives and instincts, but uses hunger to expand sexuality beyond a focus on reproduction, genitality and the romantic couple.

The instinct of hunger featured prominently in late nineteenth- and early twentieth-century constructions of sexuality. Hunger was often understood as the most primal instinct that provided the template for other instincts, including the sexual instinct, that emerged later in the process of individual development. According to Kathleen Frederickson, 'hunger lay at the root of sexual difference because [. . .] it provided the formal model in reference to which more exclusively sexuating instincts took shape.'[43] Ellis stressed in the preface to his *Studies in the Psychology of Sex* (1897–1928) that the sexual instinct was directly modelled on the nutritive instinct.[44] The implication was that instincts of hunger and sexuality were similar in that they were natural and purposeful, aiding self-preservation and the reproduction of the species.

These understandings of instincts were highly gendered. As Nancy Cott has shown, nineteenth-century religious and scientific accounts presented 'passionlessness' as an ideal for white middle- and upper-class women, which set them apart from the allegedly more lustful and egotistical sexual behaviours of men.[45] Although highly contested, these gendered, racialised and classed constructions of the sexual instinct were mobilised within feminist debates, and 'the idea that women could be defined as morally pure by virtue of gender-giving instincts [. . .] remained a widely popular normative middle-class ideal among feminists and nonfeminists alike.'[46] Within the British context, the suggestion that white middle- and upper-class women were less governed by sexual instincts than men played a central role in the feminist fight against the Contagious Diseases Acts in the 1870s and 1880s and had continued to feed into suffrage rhetoric in the 1900s and 1910s.[47] The notion of female passionlessness could also be linked to an allegedly instinctive orientation towards altruistic motherhood, which suggested that women's sexual instincts were primarily aimed at reproduction and child rearing rather than pleasure.[48] Some leaders of the suffrage movement went further in distancing themselves from the sexual instinct, taking vows of celibacy to signal 'a being toward independence, a being toward reform.'[49] The widely publicised hunger strikes of suffragette campaigners in the late 1900s and early 1910s, in particular, served to demonstrate women's superior ability to control their instincts. Being able to resist the instinct of hunger was a way of rejecting the notion of 'natural and instinctive womanhood' and demonstrating a capacity for rational thought, as Frederickson has argued.[50] At the same time, women were seen to be capable of resisting hunger precisely because they were allegedly less strongly governed by their instincts to begin with.

Hungerheart engages critically with these gendered frameworks, which St. John confronted as part of her suffrage activism. To a certain degree, John-Baptist's declaration that they are free from sexual instincts is aligned with the feminist logic of the vows of celibacy and hunger strikes mentioned above. John-Baptist is not defined by an impulsive sexual nature that inevitably orients them towards heterosexual marriage and motherhood. They emphasise that the instinctive hunger they feel is not that of a woman who desires men and reproduction: 'There was no hunger for maternity in me, any more than there was a desire to be loved as men love women' (192). This makes it possible for John-Baptist to begin to imagine new possibilities for themself, which are not limited to heterosexual desire, marriage and motherhood, and which exceed the imagination of what they call 'natural' men and women:

> Sexual love [. . .] is the promised land for every girl born into the world, and those who see it only, and never enter in, are the despised and rejected ones, the loveless ones whose heart-hunger excites pity or contempt. The idea that there may be women, neither wives nor mothers, nor mistresses, who are yet fulfilling themselves completely, who are not poor or starved in their singleness, but rich and fed with angels' food, is one which the natural man rejects as incredible, and the natural woman entertains perhaps for a moment in a lifetime, and dismisses for ever as the folly of dreams. (90)

As this quote demonstrates, *Hungerheart* – as a feminist, lesbian and trans narrative – is dedicated to expanding gendered constructions of allegedly feminine instincts to carve out alternative ways in which people assigned female at birth can exist in the world, relate to others and find fulfilment.

The text goes further in distancing John-Baptist from the constructed category of womanhood, however. In contrast to the figure of the naturally passionless and celibate woman, John-Baptist is compelled by an urgent and seemingly undirected instinct of hunger that drives their development: 'I had a famine in my heart, and did not know for what food I longed.'[51] This powerful instinct of hunger comes to connote their desire for love and intimacy: 'The hunger I had to find some one [sic] to love burnt me more with every inch that was added to my stature' (88). John-Baptist's hunger initially finds expression in their erotic attachments with women and intimate friendships with men. They experience a hedonistic phase, acting as a 'wild, undisciplined creature, whose utter carelessness of anything but the pleasure of the moment would end one day in disgrace and shame' (197). In this regard, St. John challenges the rhetoric of purity that often fed into feminist appropriations of instinct and distances themself from the construction of womanhood on which they are based. Indeed, the way in which John-Baptist experiences desire is explicitly presented as one of the reasons why they are not a woman:

> I did not understand women, I thought, because they loved to attract love. They desired *to be loved*. I felt in myself a burning desire to *love*, to be the active one who gave, who held the world's record for giving. To be content to receive, to be passive, to be the loved, was not my aim. I saw myself always as the lover. (184–5; emphasis in the original)

Here, John-Baptist's masculinity is associated with the active desire to love rather than to receive love passively.

Hungerheart also troubles this conventional model of masculine gender-sexuality through its engagement with celibacy. As Kahan has argued, 'celibacy itself is a crucial modality of gender-bending,' and figures like the celibate male bachelor, for instance, have often expanded cisnormative and heteronormative understandings of masculinity.[52] Towards the end of the book, John-Baptist learns to satisfy their hunger through spiritual love and friendship, which exceeds the physical desire and worldly pleasures they have previously enjoyed. As argued in the next section, it is by transing gender and inhabiting ascetic masculinity that John-Baptist eventually learns to satisfy their hunger. The ascetic renunciation of desire does not result in a denial of intimacy and connection, but rather reveals that desire can be organised in celibate ways to make multiple attachments and alternative forms of kinship possible.

'ALL THE VIRILITY IN ME RESPONDED TO HIM': ASCETIC MASCULINITY

John-Baptist's estranged father names them after his favourite saint in the hope that the male name might 'give her a man's strength to fight her way in this brutal world' (6). John-Baptist reflects critically on the privilege and power held by men in society, who enjoy access to 'a fairer field for the development of those noble qualities which I did not believe to be essentially masculine' (245). Here and elsewhere, John-Baptist challenges the notion that any trait or characteristic is essentially masculine or feminine, arguing that 'the [human] soul [. . .] has no sex, and differs in every human being born into the world' (195). John-Baptist is aware that their resistance to femininity and occasional misogynistic thoughts are a response to restrictive social definitions of femininity rather than a rejection of women themselves. They admit, for instance, that their younger self went through a phase of being a 'girl-hater. I was sorry to have been born a girl because for a girl apparently there was no human life, only a girl's life' (58). The text thus exposes how social expectations around femininity and masculinity limit individual opportunities for development and connection.

The way in which John-Baptist transes gender and inhabits masculinity is not presented as a means of accessing stereotypically masculine forms of privilege and power. Their masculinity is tied to an ascetic ideal of masculinity that also challenges dominant feminist constructions of men as naturally lustful and driven by overwhelming sexual instincts.[53] The emphasis on ascetic masculinity is already implied in John-Baptist's name. Within biblical and artistic traditions, St John the Baptist is typically presented as an ascetic living in the wilderness, clothed in camel hair and subsisting on locusts and honey alone. St. John, who named herself after the Saint following her conversion to Catholicism, is also building on fin-de-siècle representations of the minor biblical character of Salome.[54] These include Oscar Wilde's 1894 play *Salomé: A Tragedy in One Act* in which Iokanaan (St John the Baptist) is beheaded after rejecting Salome's persistent advances. The play focuses on the relationship between Salome and

Iokanaan, highlighting the latter's 'sexual innocence' and refusal to be touched or kissed by the sexually active Salome, thus reversing conventional gendered understandings of the sexual instinct.[55]

Wilde himself provides an important model for John-Baptist, who remembers their sleepless nights during the Wilde trial, which took place while they were studying at Oxford: 'Often I had lain awake at nights thinking of Oscar Wilde's *débacle*, and wishing that I could serve a few days of his sentence in his stead [. . .]' (141; italics in the original).[56] Later on, John-Baptist returns to Wilde to foreshadow their own transition from a lifestyle of hedonistic pleasure and indulgence towards spiritual conversion and renunciation (244).[57] John-Baptist is inspired by the following passage from Wilde's *De Profundis* (1905), written during his imprisonment at Reading Gaol:

> I don't regret for a single moment having lived for pleasure. I did it to the full, as one should do everything that one does. There was no pleasure I did not experience. I threw the pearl of my soul into a cup of wine. I went down the primrose path to the sound of flutes. I lived on honeycomb. But to have continued the same life would have been wrong because it would have been limiting. I had to pass on. The other half of the garden had its secrets for me also.[58]

In response, John-Baptist reflects that:

> There was never a moment when my downward path did not wound my feet. Instead of sweet instruments of music, the sound that accompanied my mad pursuit of pleasure was a lamentation faintly chanted by the pure and austere spirit of my guardian angel. (244)

In contrast to Wilde, John-Baptist maintains that hedonism and pleasure were always alien to their nature; yet, they also feel an affinity with Wilde, believing that his life demonstrates how even 'the commonest sinner' can alter their past and change (142). For John-Baptist, this possibility of transformation entails their eventual conversion to Catholicism and embrace of an 'ascetic ideal' (307).

The ascetic model of masculinity they adopt opens up queer forms of relationality in *Hungerheart*. When John-Baptist states that they envy men 'their prerogative as lovers' (245), the text strongly suggests that it is the prerogative to love women that is at stake here. Yet, ascetic masculinity also serves other purposes that are not exhausted by the articulation of lesbian desire. In England, Catholic asceticism was strongly associated with queer male–male attachments.[59] John-Baptist's masculinity is recognised and desired by male friends and structures their intimate relationships with men.[60] In childhood, their friend Ernest says he wants to marry John-Baptist, because he recognises and is attracted to their masculinity: 'You are – you are – well, you are just what I want. . . . I want a man!' (54). When John-Baptist is twenty-two, they form another intimate friendship with a married man called Jerome, who is forty-seven years old. Jerome is attracted to John-Baptist's 'strength and activity' and references 'Oscar Wilde's favourite description of hair as "honey-coloured"' to express his admiration for their beauty (194).

The homoerotic coding of John-Baptist's and Jerome's relationship is based on pederastic models of male–male friendship and comradeship derived from Ancient Greek culture, which were central to late nineteenth- and early twentieth-century constructions of male–male intimacy in Britain.[61] When John-Baptist learns about 'the friends of antiquity' in their studies, they are 'not shocked by the revelation that in these noble friendships there had been an element of sensuality' (186). What is enlightening for John-Baptist about these friendships is not the fact of their sensuality, but the idea that passionate male–male intimacy can also have a spiritual element: 'if they were noble they passed on and transformed their passions into something very spiritual, very noble' (187). John-Baptist understands retrospectively that this model of friendship would have allowed their relationship with Jerome to thrive, since their bond was based not on his 'passionate love' but on his comradeship and guidance: 'It was as comrades we had been most happy. All the virility in me responded to him. All the docile child in me felt the benefit of his guidance' (193).

The relationship with Jerome and the homoerotic male–male friendship traditions it evokes present a crucial moment in John-Baptist's development. It is through this encounter that John-Baptist learns how relationships can be transformed and elevated into spiritual bonds that are not limited by social conventions or individual physical needs. For John-Baptist, who recognises that love has to be 'learned like a language' (192), it is the model of ascetic masculinity that enables the shift from an individualistic search for pleasure towards a transcendent and spiritual relationality based on 'complete self-abnegation' (294). This ascetic ideal finds full expression in their conversion to Catholicism and spiritual friendship with a nun at the end of the book: 'I who had been very arrogant, very proud of my individuality [. . .] was now anxious to renounce my own will and yield it in complete submission' (298). For John-Baptist, ascetic masculinity holds out the promise of transformation and impersonality.

As mentioned above, critics have read St. John's decision to end the book on a note of ascetic renunciation as indicative of lesbian failure, humiliation and shame. David Trotter adds that, if read as a lesbian Bildungsroman, *Hungerheart* fails to be developmental due to the serial and repetitive nature of John-Baptist's seemingly transient and purposeless erotic attachments.[62] The allegedly unhappy conclusion of *Hungerheart*, with its emphasis on martyrdom and renunciation, has also been compared to the ending of *The Well of*

Loneliness, constituting a tradition of writing in which lesbian desire can only be expressed via its own negation.[63] In real life, St. John returned to Craig after the latter had briefly considered a marriage proposal from the musician Martin Shaw. In *Hungerheart*, Sally disappears from the narrative, creating room for John-Baptist's spiritual friendship with a nun. Ellen Terry's biographer, Nina Auerbach, argues that *Hungerheart*

> ends on an unresolved note of sexual torment and denial. John, the protagonist, has as little sexuality at the culmination of her spiritual odyssey as she does in adolescence. [. . .] John divides her soul from her body with a rigidity only the most moralistic of Victorians would have endorsed.[64]

Similarly, Cockin notes in her biography of Craig that St. John 'can only represent same-sex desire obliquely through the discourse of martyrdom, in terms of pain and suffering.'[65] These critical judgements are premised on reading *Hungerheart* as a lesbian novel of development that must culminate either in a declaration of lesbian identity or in the physical affirmation of lesbian sexuality. These readings are also exemplary of a wider tendency within queer studies to interpret the absence of (physical and genital) sexuality as indicative of failed or repressed homosexuality, which can obscure other ways of interpreting and valorising intimacy and relationality.[66]

John-Baptist, as the narrator of *Hungerheart*, anticipates these critical responses and knows that readers are likely to misunderstand the ending of the book: 'Abnormal, useless, starved, pale – these are the adjectives that the world keeps in stock for the lives of those who seek to subdue their earthly nature for the sake of liberating their spiritual nature' (310). To counter these readings, the narrative emphasises that John-Baptist's urgent hunger is finally satisfied through their spiritual conversion and friendship with the nun: 'One supreme Fact I was conscious of – that there behind the gold veil over the tabernacle was my God, and the Love for which I had been hungering all my life' (287). Thus, John-Baptist's alleged failure to embrace a lesbian identity and embodied experience of lesbian sexuality can also be read as their successful approximation of the ideal of ascetic masculinity. Far from signalling defeat or loneliness, the way in which John-Baptist transes gender allows them to interrogate and expand gendered possibilities and create relational bonds in which individuals are not defined by conventional gendered or sexual scripts. Understood within the framework of ascetic masculinity and celibacy, the emphasis on restraint and renunciation within the narrative does not need to be read as a form of lesbian failure; it can also be understood as a mechanism of joyful and pleasurable transformation that opens up different models of intimacy and kinship.[67] As explained in the final section of this chapter, ascetic masculinity in *Hungerheart* allows John-Baptist to experience a radical and capacious form of celibate friendship.

'THE STRONGEST EMOTION OF MY LIFE': CELIBATE FRIENDSHIP

On the final pages of the book, John-Baptist realises that '[t]he emotion of friendship has been the strongest emotion of my life' (313). In contrast to a sexual instinct that is directed towards people of the opposite sex, physical reproduction and/or genital sexual expression, John-Baptist's hunger is revealed to be a longing for spiritual love that extends to 'every one [*sic*] in the world' (288). The ability to experience this capacious love, which is not limited to a single or clearly defined romantic object of desire, is shared by 'the monk and the nun [who] are called into the cloister because of their capacity for a love, of which human love is a mere shadow' (308). The understanding of celibate friendship articulated here draws on the model of ascetic masculinity discussed above while also appropriating Catholic traditions of celibacy via the figure of the nun, which feminist and queer writers frequently associated with female independence from heterosexual marriage and motherhood.[68]

While John-Baptist's spiritual love is at least partially directed towards their 'Divine Friend' (313), the nun, the narrative makes it clear that they are not a couple: 'And often now with a *Sponza Christi* [spouse of Christ] for my friend, I feel like Endymion who had the moon for his bride' (314; italics in the original). Like Endymion, the shepherd in Greek mythology who was loved by the moon and put into an eternal sleep to preserve his youthful beauty, John-Baptist receives love at a distance without laying exclusive claim to the nun, who is already married to Christ. In addition to moving beyond the romantic convention of the couple form, John-Baptist's hunger for intimacy is not limited to alloerotic attachments to other people. They learn to embrace their capacity to experience a love that can also be directed at inanimate objects and the natural world: 'I poured it [the love in me] out on the wind when it touched my face, on the earth when I lay on it, on every human being who brought me joy for a moment' (154).

Although lesbian scholarship has understandably been keen to push beyond the models of romantic friendship and celibate attachment that have often served to desexualise relationships between women, *Hungerheart* demonstrates the importance of reclaiming friendship as a valuable and radical site of kinship formation, gender and sexual exploration, and creative expression.[69] John-Baptist's friendship with the nun may not be depicted as sexual in a physical and specifically genital sense, but it has significant intimate resonances that need to be acknowledged as part of lesbian and feminist traditions. In addition, their friendship leaves room for and affirms John-Baptist's ascetic masculinity, thus allowing them to trans gender and push beyond restrictive gendered conventions. Finally, it is through their ascetic masculinity that John-Baptist can access a deeply relational sense of self that inspires creative innovation and connects them with others. Indeed, *Hungerheart* presents this model of relationality as central to what Pamela Caughie has described as the modernist project of 'offering new narratives of embodiment that enable new configurations of gender and sexual identity.'[70]

Indeed, John-Baptist, as the narrator of *Hungerheart*, repeatedly comments on the ways in which the text deviates from conventional forms of narrative address and structure. As Elizabeth Hanna Hanson has argued, representations of asexuality tend to disturb conventional narrative plots, because asexuality, 'as the non-experience of sexual attraction, has no object, no aim, no tendency toward movement in any direction.'[71] Although the plot of *Hungerheart* is not driven by a gendered sexual instinct that finds expression in marriage, biological reproduction and/or genital sex, John-Baptist's hunger for spiritual enlightenment and intimacy does provide a certain teleological thrust, and the narrative culminates in their religious conversion and celibate encounter with the nun. Yet, as already noted above, the highly self-reflexive narrator of *Hungerheart* knows that the plot of the novel deviates from conventional scripts of gender and sexuality, such as the marriage plot, and therefore risks frustrating readerly expectations. John-Baptist, as narrator, repeatedly expresses their 'fear of being called "inartistic," or [. . .] of losing readers' (290). They hope that the book, which they describe as 'a history of my soul,' will find readers who can relate to their experiences: 'I call unto souls like me, and beg them to listen. It is for the "brotherly mind" I write, not for that of the foreigner' (89). At the end of the novel, the narrative shifts, as John-Baptist begins to address the nun in the second person, suggesting that the book is written for and addressed to their friend: 'How can I write *about* you? It comes more naturally to write *to* you' (311; emphasis in the original). Through this intimate form of address, the narrator expresses their hope of being understood by their friend, although the narrative does not confirm whether this understanding is granted. By drawing attention to the multiple implied readers of the text, *Hungerheart* puts emphasis on the relational dynamics involved in producing an idiosyncratic narrative that breaks with generic conventions and potentially frustrates readerly expectations. The text makes explicit the narrator's vulnerability to unsympathetic or fallacious readings while also foregrounding the pleasures involved in submitting oneself to the process of being read and, potentially, understood by others.

Conclusion

John-Baptist's direct address of their 'brotherly' readers invites us to partake in and reflect on this process of understanding. Given the autobiographical dimensions of *Hungerheart*, it is tempting to read the book as a text that gives access to St. John's inner sense of self. Moreover, the model of kinship outlined in the novel seems to anticipate the triadic relationship St. John built with Craig and Atwood in 1916, three years after the book was written and shortly after it was published. Similar to the model of friendship articulated in the book, the form of relationality lived by St. John, Craig and Atwood expands conventional understandings of the individual and the couple, and challenges how some readers may expect gender-sexuality to be navigated within relationships. According to Ricketts, 'the terms around which their relationship was structured were both communal and individual; the individual is posted as relation to a community, which itself is resistant to dominant cultural values.'[72] While *Hungerheart* suggests the radical lesbian, feminist and trans possibilities this kind of relationship may have opened up for St. John, Craig and Atwood over the course of the many decades they spent together, the novel also resists such autobiographical readings. The intimate address of the nun at the end of the novel in the second person reminds other readers that we do not have easy access to the relational dynamics through which John-Baptist comes to understand and experience themself.

With regard to St. John, Craig and Atwood, the fact that the details of the life and intimacy they shared may ultimately escape us is beautifully expressed by Vita Sackville-West in her contribution to the volume *Edy: Recollections of Edith Craig* (1949), a collection of essays about Craig published shortly after her death:

> Yet they are all one. Edy, and Tony, and Christopher, and the hedgehog, and Shakespeare – they are all one. They are all poetry, in this dark panelled room with the flower-piece glowing against the wall. They are so rare and unusual an experience that we can well believe that next time we come to Smallhythe we may find that Edy, Christopher and Tony have departed on a voyage where we cannot follow them.[73]

Sackville-West remembers Craig not as an individual but as part of a constellation made up of St. John and Atwood as well as the natural and creative world they inhabited together at Smallhythe.[74] Thinking about the intersections between lesbian, feminist and trans modernism, which this chapter has begun to explore, Sackville-West's observation reminds us that lives and intimacies often resist, blur and exceed the categories, explanatory models and narrative scripts available to us even as they invite us to relate to them. Occasionally, we have to acknowledge that 'we cannot follow' the authors and texts towards which we have turned our critical and emotional attention. One way in which we can try to engage with and honour these stories and lives nevertheless is by developing approaches that unsettle and expand the assumed boundaries of the scholarly fields we inhabit. As Stryker and Aizura remind us, our scholarly methods can 'actively participate in the proliferation and articulation of new modes of embodied subjectivity, new cultural practices, and new ways of understanding the world.'[75] Embracing and building on existing entanglements between trans, lesbian and feminist studies is one way of working towards this goal.

Notes

1. On the production and reception of *A Pageant of Great Women*, see Katharine Cockin, *Edith Craig (1869–1947): Dramatic Lives* (London: Cassell, 1998), 94–107; and Katherine Cockin, *Edith Craig and the Theatres of Art* (London: Methuen Drama, 2017), 64–6, 86–7.
2. Susan Stryker, *Transgender History* (Berkeley: Seal Press, 2008), 1. In addition to Snell/Gray, the pageant also featured Christian Davies, a white person who was assigned female at birth and joined the British Army as a male soldier in 1693. William Brown, a Black person assigned female at birth who fought in the British navy as a male soldier between 1804 and 1815, was among a group of historical figures that were researched for the play but not included. See Cockin, *Dramatic Lives*, 99.
3. Cicely Hamilton, *A Pageant of Great Women* (London: Suffrage Shop, 1910), n.p.
4. Cockin, *Dramatic Lives*, 105. Cockin's scholarship has been vital in recognising the important role St. John and Tony Atwood played in Craig's life.
5. Jen Manion, *Female Husbands: A Trans History* (Cambridge: Cambridge University Press, 2020), 68–81.
6. Ibid., 69, 74.
7. Like St. John, Atwood rejected her birth name and adopted a gender-ambivalent first name. Friends described Atwood and St. John as the 'Boys.' Cockin, *Dramatic Lives*, 22. There is very little scholarship on Atwood and, as Cockin notes, the 'Edith Craig Archive is almost silent about Tony Atwood' (ibid., 125). This makes it difficult to write about Atwood's gender or sexual identity in more detail.
8. St. John's first novel, *The Crimson Weed*, was published in 1900, identifying her as the author by name. *Hungerheart* was published without any authorial attribution, possibly to avoid censorship and to make it harder for readers to decode references to living people, including Ellen Terry, who was internationally famous.
9. I am referring to the fictional protagonist and narrator of *Hungerheart* as John-Baptist, using they/them pronouns. I am referring to the author of the book as St. John, using she/her pronouns. I have made this decision to try to respect what I believe to be the pronouns St. John and those closest to her used. This does not mean that St. John cannot or should not be read as trans masculine or non-binary. To be sure, the use of other pronouns can equally be justified, and my goal in this chapter is to open up trans and non-binary readings of St. John's life and work.
10. See, for instance, Nina Auerbach, *Ellen Terry: Player in Her Time* (New York: W. W. Norton, 1987), 405–7; Cockin, *Dramatic Lives*, 65–9; and Clare L. Taylor, *Women, Writing, and Fetishism, 1890–1950: Female Cross-Gendering* (Oxford: Oxford University Press, 2003), 57–61.
11. Prosser has influentially called on scholars to differentiate between texts that depict trans subjectivity (such as *The Well of Loneliness*) and those that deploy figures of gender-crossing for other, metaphorical purposes. See Jay Prosser, *Second Skins:*

The Body Narratives of Transsexuality (New York: Columbia University Press, 1998), 21–60.

12. My reading here is deeply informed by Benjamin Kahan's work on celibacy. Benjamin Kahan, *Celibacies: American Modernism & Sexual Life* (Durham, NC: Duke University Press, 2013), 3–6.
13. I am responding to the title of Diana Souhami's *No Modernism Without Lesbians* (London: Head of Zeus, 2020).
14. The importance of trans femininity within lesbian modernism remains under-researched, but see Emma Heaney, *The New Woman: Literary Modernism, Queer Theory, and the Trans Feminine Allegory* (Evanston, IL: Northwestern University Press, 2017). For more on early twentieth-century trans and cis lesbian communities, see Emma Heaney, '"I Am Not a Friend to Men": Embodiment and Desire in Magnus Hirschfeld's *Transvestites* Case Studies,' *Journal of Lesbian Studies* 22, no. 2 (2018): 136–52.
15. Jana Funke, 'Intersexions: Dandyism, Cross-Dressing, Transgender,' in *Late Victorian into Modern*, ed. Laura Marcus, Michèle Mendelssohn and Kirsten E. Shepherd-Barr (Oxford: Oxford University Press, 2016), 414–28; K. Allison Hammer, 'Epic Stone Butch: Transmasculinity in the Work of Willa Cather,' *TSQ: Transgender Studies Quarterly* 7, no. 1 (2020): 77–98; Prosser, *Second Skins*, 135–70; Chris Coffman, *Gertrude Stein's Transmasculinity* (Edinburgh: Edinburgh University Press, 2018).
16. There are important exceptions. In particular, my interest in the multiple meanings of masculinity and their unstable relationship to lesbian desire and identity is profoundly shaped by Laura Doan's field-defining work, including Laura Doan, 'Passing Fashions: Reading Female Masculinities in the 1920s,' *Feminist Studies* 24, no. 3 (1998): 663–700; Laura Doan, *Fashioning Sapphism: The Origins of a Modern English Lesbian Culture* (New York: Columbia University Press, 2001); and Laura Doan, *Disturbing Practices: History, Sexuality, and Women's Experience of Modern War* (Chicago: University of Chicago Press, 2013).
17. See, for instance, Cockin, *Dramatic Lives*, 21. Cockin, *Theatres of Art*, 113, argues that St. John's masculine name served to signal 'both her sexuality and her Catholicism.'
18. Jack Halberstam, *Female Masculinity* (Durham, NC: Duke University Press, 1998); Prosser, *Second Skins*.
19. Jack Halberstam, 'Butch/FTM Border Wars and the Masculine Continuum,' *GLQ: A Journal of Lesbian and Gay Studies* 4, no. 2 (1998): 287–310, 293. See also Manion, *Female Husbands*, 9.
20. See, for instance, Kevin Henderson, 'Becoming Lesbian: Monique Wittig's Queer-Trans-Feminism,' *Journal of Lesbian Studies* 22, no. 2 (3 April 2018): 185–203.
21. Susan Stryker and Paisley Currah, 'Introduction,' *TSQ: Transgender Studies Quarterly* 1, no. 1–2 (2014): 1–18, 6.
22. Manion, *Female Husbands*, 11. See also Clare Sears, *Arresting Dress: Cross-Dressing, Law, and Fascination in Nineteenth-Century San Francisco* (Durham, NC: Duke University Press, 2015).
23. In addition to Halberstam, *Female Masculinity*, and Prosser, *Second Skins*, see also Claudia Breger, 'Feminine Masculinities: Scientific and Literary Representations of "Female Inversion" at the Turn of the Twentieth Century,' *Journal of the History of Sexuality* 14, no. 1/2 (2005): 76–106.

24. Kadji Amin, 'We Are All Nonbinary: A Brief History of Accidents,' *Representations* 158, no. 1 (2022): 106–19, 107, explains that the term 'gender-sexuality' is preferable to 'gender and sexuality,' since 'the two are, in reality, indissociable.'
25. Cockin, *Dramatic Lives*, 155.
26. Vita Sackville-West to Virginia Woolf, quoted in Victoria Glendinning, *Vita: The Life of Vita Sackville-West* (London: Penguin, 1984), 250. See also Cockin, *Dramatic Lives*, 166.
27. Glendinning, *Vita*, 253.
28. Susan Stryker and Aren Z. Aizura, 'Introduction: Transgender Studies 2.0,' in *The Transgender Studies Reader 2*, ed. Susan Stryker and Aren Z. Aizura (New York: Routledge, 2013), 1–12, 6.
29. Amin, 'We Are All,' 115.
30. For more on trans masculinity in Hall's work, see Jaime E. Hovey, 'Gallantry and Its Discontents: Joan of Arc and Virtuous Transmasculinity in Radclyffe Hall and Vita Sackville-West,' *Feminist Modernist Studies* 1, no. 1–2 (2018): 113–37; and Prosser, *Second Skins*, 135–70.
31. Christopher St. John to Vita Sackville-West, quoted in Glendinning, *Vita*, 253.
32. Una Troubridge, quoted in Michael Baker, *Our Three Selves: A Life of Radclyffe Hall* (London: Hamish Hamilton, 1985), 271. See also Cockin, *Dramatic Lives*, 22.
33. Cockin, *Dramatic Lives*, 23.
34. One exception is *The Golden Book*, an intimate journal about St. John's relationship with Craig, which she wrote in the early 1910s. See Auerbach, *Ellen Terry*, 404–5; and Cockin, *Dramatic Lives*, 24.
35. Ellen Ricketts, 'The Fractured Pageant: Queering Lesbian Lives in the Early Twentieth Century,' *Peer English* 10 (2015): 82–94, 86.
36. Cockin, *Dramatic Lives*, 23; Ricketts, 'Fractured Pageant,' 87. *The Autobiography of Christopher Kirkland* (1885) by Eliza Lynn Linton anticipates *Hungerheart* in blurring the line between autobiography and fiction and crossing conventional boundaries of gender and sexuality. See Deborah T. Meem, 'Eliza Lynn Linton and the Rise of Lesbian Consciousness,' *Journal of the History of Sexuality* 7, no. 4 (1997): 537–60.
37. Cockin, *Dramatic Lives*, 23. David Trotter suggests that St. John rejects the concept of sexual instincts, because it was too 'impersonal.' David Trotter, 'Lesbians before Lesbianism: Sexual Identity in Early Twentieth-Century British Fiction,' in *Borderlines: Genders and Identities in War and Peace, 1870–1930*, ed. Billie Melman (New York: Routledge, 1998), 193–211, 207. While I agree with Trotter that St. John is interested in articulating a personal and idiosyncratic understanding of gender and sexuality, impersonality – understood as the transcendence of the self – is a central theme in *Hungerheart*. Auerbach, *Ellen Terry*, 404, recognises this about St. John, whom she describes as 'devoutly impersonal.'
38. Havelock Ellis and John Addington Symonds, *Sexual Inversion: A Critical Edition* (Basingstoke: Palgrave Macmillan, 2008), 96.
39. See Karli June Cerankowski and Megan Milks, eds, *Asexualities: Feminist and Queer Perspectives* (New York: Routledge, 2014).
40. Karli June Cerankowski and Megan Milks, 'Introduction: Why Asexuality? Why Now?,' in Cerankowski and Milks, *Asexualities*, 1–14, 2.

41. Kahan, *Celibacies*, 2. On the relationship between asexuality and celibacy, see Eunjung Kim, 'Asexualities and Disabilities in Constructing Sexual Normalcy,' in Cerankowski and Milks, *Asexualities*, 249–82. Kim stresses that the very distinction between celibacy (as a choice or practice) and asexuality (as an orientation or identity) is problematic in that it assumes 'that all celibate people are sexual' (269).
42. Kahan, *Celibacies*, 4. My goal here is not to draw a firm line between asexuality and celibacy, or to suggest that *Hungerheart* cannot be read as a text about asexuality. As Kahan also acknowledges, celibacy and asexuality are closely entangled historically and conceptually, and articulations of romantic asexuality, in particular, complicate attempts at differentiating between the two.
43. Kathleen Frederickson, *The Ploy of Instinct: Victorian Sciences of Nature and Sexuality in Liberal Governance* (New York: Fordham University Press, 2014), 121.
44. Ellis and Symonds, *Sexual Inversion*, 90.
45. Nancy F. Cott, 'Passionlessness: An Interpretation of Victorian Sexual Ideology, 1790–1850,' *Signs* 4, no. 2 (1978): 219–36.
46. Frederickson, *Ploy of Instinct*, 133.
47. Ibid., 129–30.
48. Ibid., 123.
49. Kahan, *Celibacies*, 13, 17.
50. Frederickson, *Ploy of Instinct*, 122.
51. Christopher St. John, *Hungerheart: The Story of a Soul* (London: Methuen, 1915), 60.
52. Kahan, *Celibacies*, 12.
53. Other scholars have recognised the ascetic qualities of St. John's work, most notably Ellen Ricketts, 'The Queer Movements of Ecstasy and Asceticism in *Hungerheart: The Story of a Soul* and *Madeleine: One of Love's Jansenists*,' in *Modernist Women Writers and Spirituality: A Piercing Darkness*, ed. Elizabeth Anderson, Andrew Radford and Heather Walton (London: Palgrave, 2016), 169–84. In contrast to Ricketts, I argue that St. John uses ascetic masculinity in ways that are not exhausted by a lesbian reading of the text.
54. For more on St. John's interest in St John the Baptist and *Salome*, see Cockin, *Dramatic Lives*, 126. For more on the fin-de-siècle fascination with Salome, see, for instance, Johannes Hendrikus Burgers, 'The Spectral Salome: Salomania and Fin-de-Siècle Sexology and Racial Theory,' in *Decadence, Degeneration, and the End*, ed. Marja Härmänmaa and Christopher Nissen (Basingstoke: Palgrave, 2014), 165–82; and Gülru Çakmak, '"For the Strong-Minded Alone": Evolution, Female Atavism, and Degeneration in Aubrey Beardsley's Salomé,' in Härmänmaa and Nissen, *Decadence*, 183–200.
55. Joseph Donohue, 'Distance, Death and Desire in Salome,' in *The Cambridge Companion to Oscar Wilde*, ed. Peter Raby (Cambridge: Cambridge University Press, 1997), 118–42, 128.
56. Wilde is also a key inspiration in St. John's first novel, *The Crimson Weed*. See Cockin, *Dramatic Lives*, 69–70.
57. Frederick S. Roden acknowledges that 'tensions between Hellenic sensual pleasure and Christian asceticism' reoccur across Wilde's work. Frederick S. Roden, *Same-Sex Desire in Victorian Religious Culture* (Basingstoke: Palgrave, 2002), 140.

58. Oscar Wilde, *De Profundis and Other Writings* (London: Penguin, 1986), 164.
59. On asceticism and queer male desire, see Dominic Janes, 'The Oxford Movement, Asceticism, and Sexual Desire,' in *The Oxford Handbook of Victorian Medievalism*, ed. Joanne Parker and Corinna Wagner (Oxford: Oxford University Press, 2020), 352–69; and Julia F. Saville, *A Queer Chivalry: The Homoerotic Asceticism of Gerard Manley Hopkins* (Charlottesville: University of Virginia Press, 2000).
60. As Coffman, *Stein's Transmasculinity*, 6, has shown in relation to Gertrude Stein, trans masculinity is frequently inscribed in homosocial male–male bonds.
61. See Linda Dowling, *Hellenism and Homosexuality in Victorian Oxford* (Ithaca, NY: Cornell University Press, 1997). For more on St. John and platonic love, see Jane Mackelworth, '"The Nature of My Love Had Never Been in Doubt . . ." Christopher St John (1871–960): Platonic Love and Sapphic Desire,' *Cultural and Social History* 17, no. 3 (2020): 375–89.
62. Trotter, 'Lesbians before Lesbianism,' 208.
63. See Joanne Glasgow, 'What's a Nice Lesbian Like You Doing in the Church of Torquemada? Radclyffe Hall and Other Catholic Converts,' in *Lesbian Texts and Contexts: Radical Revisions*, ed. Karla Jay and Joanne Glasgow (New York: New York University Press, 1990), 217–40.
64. Auerbach, *Ellen Terry*, 405.
65. Cockin, *Dramatic Lives*, 63.
66. Kahan, *Celibacies*, 3.
67. For more on the ways in which queer kinship could be articulated through engagements with Wilde and late-Victorian Decadence, see Kristin Mahoney, *Queer Kinship after Wilde: Transnational Decadence and the Family* (Cambridge: Cambridge University Press, 2022).
68. Kahan, *Celibacies*, 18–19. Marie Anne Pagliarini, '"The Pure American Woman and the Wicked Catholic Priest": An Analysis of Anti-Catholic Literature in Antebellum America,' *Religion and American Culture* 9, no. 1 (1999): 97–128, argues that Anglo-American anti-Catholic literature often responded to the perceived threat of nuns and convent life, which made it possible for women to live independently of marriage and motherhood. Nuns also play an important role within lesbian modernist literature. To name but a few examples, Radclyffe Hall's short story 'The Legend of Saint Ethelflaeda' describes the life of a medieval abbess. See Jana Funke, 'Introduction,' in *'The World' and Other Unpublished Works of Radclyffe Hall*, ed. Jana Funke (Manchester: Manchester University Press), 1–44, 16–19. Vita Sackville-West was inspired to write about Carmelite nuns St Teresa of Ávila and St Thérèse of Lisieux after visiting the latter's home and shrine in France with her sister-in-law and lover Gwen St. Aubyn, who converted to Catholicism. She eventually did so in her double biography of both saints, *The Eagle and the Dove* (1943). See Glendinning, *Vita*, 289. Sylvia Townsend Warner's novel *The Corners That Held Them* (1948) is centred around convent life. See Diana Wallace, 'The Convent Novel and the Uses of History,' in *Metafiction and Metahistory in Contemporary Women's Writing*, ed. Ann Heilmann and Mark Llewellyn (Basingstoke: Palgrave Macmillan, 2007), 158–71, 163–5.

69. Foucault's influential work on the radical potential of friendship focuses on male–male friendships, which, he argues, were more proscribed than female friendships. Michel Foucault, 'Friendship as a Way of Life,' in *Ethics: Subjectivity and Truth*, ed. Paul Rabinow, *The Essential Works of Michel Foucault, 1954–1984* (New York: The New Press, 1997), 135–40, 139. Subsequent scholarship has often continued to overlook the radical potential inherent in female and lesbian friendships.
70. Pamela L. Caughie, 'The Temporality of Modernist Life Writing in the Era of Transsexualism: Virginia Woolf's *Orlando* and Einar Wegener's *Man into Woman*,' *Modern Fiction Studies* 59, no. 3 (2013): 501–25, 520. See also Coffman, *Stein's Transmasculinity*, 17.
71. Elizabeth Hanna Hanson, 'Toward an Asexual Narrative Structure,' in Cerankowski and Milks, *Asexualities*, 344–74, 349.
72. Ricketts, 'Fractured Pageant,' 85.
73. Vita Sackville-West, 'Triptych,' in *Edy: Recollections of Edith Craig*, ed. Eleanor Adlard (London: Frederick Muller, 1949), 118–25, 124.
74. The reference to Shakespeare also honours the enduring presence of Ellen Terry, who was famous for her Shakespearean performances and who lived at Smallhythe with Craig, St. John and Atwood until her death in 1928.
75. Stryker and Aizura, 'Introduction,' 7.

3

THE ONTOLOGY OF THE PLURI-SINGULAR BODY IN NATALIE CLIFFORD BARNEY'S *THE ONE WHO IS LEGION* OR *A.D.'S AFTER-LIFE*

Katharina Boeckenhoff

Haunting the margins of the modernist canon, the 1930 novel *The One Who Is Legion or A.D.'s After-Life*, written by Natalie Clifford Barney, sporadically appears in publications on lesbian modernism as an example of lesbian representation in early twentieth-century fiction.[1] In comparison to works by other lesbian authors of the period, however, this novel is rarely discussed, its afterlife possibly compromised by a hardly legible, ambiguous prose of which its very title is an example: the singular 'one' is simultaneously a plural 'legion,' a possible name remains shrouded in the mysterious initials of 'A.D.' and the finality of the title is suspended by the conjunction 'or.'[2] Uncertainty over the possibility of a stable and distinctive identity across time and space not only animates the text's plot but also pervades its bewildering form. While the body of the protagonist morphs into different shapes throughout the story, the pages of the book change through typographical alterations. Similarly, the readerly conundrum of who and how many constitute the protagonist is further complicated by a narrative voice alternating between a plural 'we' and a singular 'I.' As the novel recounts the phantasmagorical story of the recreation of a woman's body and life in ways that radically depart from her previous mode of being in the world, content and form coalesce: the attempt to reimagine a new being outside of familiar identity categories of gender and sexual orientation is constantly re-enacted by the text's attempt to forgo narrative conventions of depicting a protagonist and relating a plot.

The One Who Is Legion presents text and world as mutually constitutive sites across which normative relational and sexual practices are constructed.

Canonical texts of religion, science, philosophy and literature, the novel suggests, produce and reproduce the dimorphic human body and its heterosexual couplings. Predicated on the assumption that the human body is never just matter, but always already an embodiment of established ideas delineated in authoritative discourses, the text's as well as the protagonist's mission is to fashion a paradoxically non-human and disembodied human body liberated from pre-determined paths through life. To interrogate the ontological distinction between representations and beings to be represented, the novel has a genderless protagonist, whose existence is based on an aggregate of material fragments held together by a corporeal frame, relive the life of a woman dead by suicide. In this way, matter itself becomes a character in a story which casts doubt on the knowledge contained in and continued by representational forms. Constituted of a multitude of discrete entities yet in a state of becoming, the main character struggles against the limitations of available representations. That a person comes to matter, physically and linguistically, as either a woman or a man and is embedded in a patriarchal structure sustained by procreative heterosexuality animates this undoing and redoing of the body effected in *The One Who Is Legion*.

Against this background, the possibility of lesbian identification serves as starting point for an imagined dismantling of the gendered body and a decoupling from heterosexual attachments. Outside the machinery of heterosexual procreation, the lesbian body defies the reproduction of sameness in biological terms.[3] Yet, Barney's novel ventures beyond textual inscriptions of lesbian desire and instead probes the lesbian's very conditions of existence. At a time when physicians and psychiatrists organised the messy field of sexuality into a sexological framework of sexual identities, *The One Who Is Legion* scrutinises identity's relation to sexual desire and the gendered body by exploring the ontology of the body and the metaphysics of matter. How material forces and discursive practices, biological and historical processes, entwine to have the human male or female body materialise is a question the protagonist pursues. *The One Who Is Legion* is a key example of a lesbian modernist text in which the lesbian figures not as an identity cast in literary form but as a site through which the text engages with those religious, philosophical and sexological discourses that have brought identities into being.

Couching a philosophical quest about the ontology of human matter across the mutually constitutive sites of representation and reality in literary form, Barney's novel negotiates central concerns of lesbian modernism as a genre and as a subject of study: how do sexuality and gender feature in the construction of a person as an individual and protagonist in this world? How do materiality and language figure in the (dis)assemblage of the lesbian? If lesbian modernism is associated with a reductive paradigm of identity, *The One Who Is Legion* illustrates how recourse to the lesbian may serve to take the notion of identity itself to task.[4] Likewise, if the lesbian – as a figure, a sign, an identity, a desire – always raises the problem of definition, then the unresolvable ambiguity around the definite (sexual) identity of the manifold characters in *The One Who Is Legion* makes this a very lesbian text.[5] Although it is possible to read the novel as an invocation of the lesbian (couple) by way of a supernatural, spiritual or sexological language, its concern with the very modalities of existence, the ontological conditions of being, also demands further scrutiny. The text juxtaposes mutable and multipliable 'beings,' variously termed spirits, shadows, fragments or selves, with a distinct identity embodied and rendered intelligible by an established system of representation. How matter comes to matter depends on its intelligibility within representational frameworks of language and authoritative discourses such as natural science. In its reconfiguration of a human organism, the novel outlines a materialist conception of the world in which the distinction between materiality and signification, reality and representation, collapses.

To tease out how the text itself, as a body verging on the edge of legibility, plays with readerly habits and narrative conventions, this chapter will first consider its metanarrative engagement with the production and reception of literary works. In experimenting with the human body and the written word, *The One Who Is Legion* suspends certainty and causality in its plot. Much like the protagonist who encounters an autobiographical book entitled 'The Love-Lives of A.D.' in A.D.'s house and deems it 'hardly a satisfactory documentation, no names, no dates, anecdotes,' the reader of Barney's novel, too, will have difficulties in following the course of events.[6] Shortly after, and more benevolently, the protagonist remarks that 'any other tale of events might have served as well' and '[i]n search of oppositions and differences between A.D. and ourselves' turns to the book's binding, its materiality, which 'had once been a human breast' (29). Alluding to the historic practice of anthropodermic bibliopegy, the text blurs the distinction between the material signifier and signified of autobiographical writing. The significance of matter is also evident in the text's blasphemous materialist refashioning of biblical scenes, which will be subject of the second part of this chapter. The recurrent differentiation between an a priori existence of material particles on the one hand and a composite organising fragments into one entity, on the other hand, draws from Aristotle's hylomorphic division between matter and form.[7] Following an examination of the text's engagement with sexological categories and religious narratives, the final part of this chapter shifts attention to larger questions posed by Barney's novel in relation to physical-philosophical contemplations on the ontology of matter.

Reading Barney's Recalcitrant Text

One of the challenges the prose of *The One Who Is Legion* poses to the reader is its disorientating traversal across narrative and meta-narrative dimensions, actual and possible worlds as well as decadent and avant-gardist styles. The text's refusal to adhere to narrative conventions is reflected in a potpourri of styles ranging from novelistic and poetic to philosophical and biblical and exploding the genre of the novel. Shari Benstock notes the near impossibility to situate the novel in any literary genre, and Elizabeth English describes it as a 'strange mesh of generic influences.'[8] Many passages use the biblical vocabulary and imploring rhetoric of religious speech, while others take the form of philosophical dialogues between interlocutors. Some sections brim with grand epigrammatic observations about life; others offer plain descriptions of food set off in verses. In a scene in which the protagonist flips through 'a bunch of press clippings criticising A.D.'s last book of poems,' the poet is 'taxed with obscurity' (103, 105) – a charge also levied on Barney's book.

The One Who Is Legion's evasive prose not only complicated Barney's search for publishers, who considered the novel 'incomprehensible,' but also elicited verdicts such as 'strange,' 'odd,' 'weird' and 'frustratingly abstract' among its readers.[9] Barney, the authorial persona, anticipated this reception as a comment in the 'Author's Note' reveals: 'For those who would have our obscurities brought into the opera-glass focus shall we as in the theatre, condense our argument?' (160). A playful provocation rather than a well-meaning concern, the note appears in the book's back matter, coming to the reader's attention only after they have wrestled through the story. Nevertheless, the publishers, more concerned about sales figures than the affluent Barney, 'suggest' on the very first page of the book 'that the *Author's Note* be read first' (emphasis in the original). Squeezed into a single long-winded sentence, Barney's summary of the phantasmagorical story remains rather vague:

> A.D., a being having committed suicide, is replaced by a sponsor, who carries on the broken life, with all the human feelings assumed with the flesh, until, having endured to the end in A.D.'s stead, the composite or legion is disbanded by the One, who remains supreme. (160)

Plot and protagonist have been variously interpreted. To some, A.D., the sponsor, the Glow-Woman and Stella are separate beings with their own subjectivity, to others these characters are one and the same. Both English and Suzanne Hobson, for example, identify a character named 'Stella' as a woman with whom A.D. is in love and the 'Glow-Woman' as a woman whom A.D. rejects, while for Karla Jay 'Stella' is simply the Glow-Woman's name.[10] The identity of the resurrected A.D. is also conceptualised differently: Benstock speaks of 'a sexually ambiguous hermaphrodite' but consistently uses female pronouns, Jay cites a 'gynandrous' being and uses 'she/he' as pronoun, Ana Livia sees 'a character who is plural in nature and both male and female,' and English refers to 'a gothic, inhuman and pluralised figure.'[11] On some accounts, A.D. assumes a new corporeal form, but retains their subjectivity, on other accounts a new being with its own subjectivity arises. Faithful to the novel's story of origin which Barney recounts in the 'Author's Note,' a few scholars have interpreted the myriad of characters mutating, merging and competing as the different and differing aspects constituting woman. For Benstock the multiplication of characters in *The One Who Is Legion* mirrors the effects of 'woman's self-division in patriarchal definitions of her.'[12] Hobson draws a similar parallel between 'norms relating to sex and gender' and 'A.D.'s divided consciousness.'[13] English, on the other hand, views the different voices entering A.D. as a form of 'occult transmission' which allows for a 'utopic transcendental union' between A.D. and the ghostly Stella.[14]

The question of the protagonist's numerical and corporeal properties, as this brief glance at some existing analyses indicates, yields multiple, even contradictory, answers. My aim here is not to endorse one reading over another but to highlight the surprisingly different ways in which we can make sense of the protagonists in a book devoid of 'coherence and explanation.'[15] Precisely this impossibility to distinguish ultimately between characters bespeaks the novel's preoccupation with the very boundaries of being and not-being: what does it take for a human being to come into existence and to acquire an identity which situates the self in the world are questions *The One Who Is Legion* explores. In its ontological inquiry into the genesis of living things and their modalities of existence, the novel is less interested in the psychological condition of the self than in its material composition. It explores the necessity of distinguishable bodily and textual matter as interceding substance – the material forms of representation – necessary to create and convey meaning to the reader or onlooker. From this angle, the novel's often noted strangeness is the inevitable outcome of a project aimed at pushing the boundaries of definite, readable forms and testifies to its persistent performative dimension: the text embodies the plot.

Scholars have analysed *The One Who Is Legion* from the vantage points of the supernatural, the spiritual, the religious and the decadent to pinpoint its vision of and concern with lesbian sexuality and subjectivity. This chapter shifts focus away from the differently conveyed representations of the lesbian to the lesbian as site through which authors challenge representational paradigms. Barney's novel manifests an acute interest in the power of matter and casts doubt on the assumed passivity of materiality as mere substance underlying words and other systems of representation. References to double-beings, hermaphrodites and angels alongside decadent motifs of death and decomposition have, as in the case of Bridget Elliott and Jo-Ann Wallace, underpinned an analysis of the novel as invested in the formulation of a distinctive lesbian identity. Elliott and Wallace view Barney's modification of fin-de-siècle decadence, associated with 'a marginal, deviant, and illegal sexuality,' as well as her nod to Baudelaire's poetry as literary strategies specific to the formulation of a 'specifically lesbian cultural identity.'[16] Despite the novel's allusions to sexological concepts and mythological notions of homosexual identities, however, it ultimately puts pressure on gender as a referential framework to differentiate between sexual identities.

RECONFIGURING THE BOUNDARIES OF BEING

In its undoing of the division of human matter into 'woman' and 'man' and its conception of a universe of corporeal spirits, *The One Who Is Legion* draws on the Bible, but undermines the very basis of the hierarchical distinction between the fallible mortal body and the infallible immortal God-sent or God-like spirit. The narrator compares spirits to 'separated atoms in a ray of light,' seeking to coalesce into one body (12). Other texts have similarly adopted and adapted motifs and elements from the Bible to conceive of a world filled with spirits. In Honoré de Balzac's *Séraphîta* (1834) and John Milton's *Paradise Lost* (1667) the term 'legion,' a central element in the title and story of Barney's novel, appears, too. *Séraphîta* uses 'deathless' and 'eternal' legions interchangeably with 'spirits' and 'myriads of angels,' all of which accompany the transfiguration of the 'seraph.'[17] In *Paradise Lost*, the legion appears as '[m]yriads of immortal Spirits' exiled from heaven but seeking 'to re-ascend.'[18] The legion of spirits in Barney's novel also participates in a process of transformation, but, importantly, not in a religious, otherworldly sense. In *The One Who Is Legion*, legions of spirits assemble around the corpse of A.D. to pass into the human body. From the beginning through to the end of the story, the human body plays a central role in the successful resurrection and redemption of the deceased A.D. In the first chapters the body is identified as the 'medium by which to realise and partake of this singular life,' and in the last chapter, entitled 'The One Takes Leave of the Legion,' the narrator begs the personified 'Flesh,' 'go your way, leaving us to our transparency. The body, our hero, has yet a part to play' (17, 158).

What prevents the reader from viewing A.D.'s suicide as an act of capitulation is Barney's fantastic reconceptualisation of death as an opportunity for metamorphosis. As the novel's subtitle, *A.D.'s After-Life*, implies, A.D.'s suicide does not relinquish her existence. Instead, her life is retraced and lived by someone else: 'a sponsor, who carries on the broken life' (160). The character who comes to live in A.D.'s stead is a multitude of fragments held together by an indeterminate corporeal form. To conceptualise the redemption of A.D., the novel mimics the biblical account of Jesus's resurrection. However, while in the scripture Jesus undergoes the stages of crucifixion, burial, death, the discovery of the tomb and resurrection, the text focuses on those three days of interim existence between death and resurrection which the Bible omits. These days constitute the temporal backdrop of Barney's novel and chronicle the attempt to assemble the multitude of spirits in a corporeal form. In thus turning to the

Bible as a template to modify, Barney targets one of the oldest and most influential accounts of rebirth, displaying an interest in origin stories, which also surfaces in Djuna Barnes's *Ladies Almanack* (1928). Barnes plays with readerly curiosity about lesbian love lives – Brian Glavey calls *Ladies Almanack* '[a] portrait of the lesbian coterie loosely organized around Natalie Barney' – by hinting at and yet withholding intimate knowledge about lesbian gatherings, resulting in an 'epistemological uncertainty,' which Glavey views as paradigmatic of the text's modernity.[19] In contrast to Barnes, who parodies narratives of creation, Barney embraces the idea of fashioning her very own account of a fantastic genesis. Although Barney's 'Author's Note' and metanarrative comments convey a humorous and parodic tone, *The One Who Is Legion* is a rather solemn interrogation of the material-discursive production of a definite being. If *Ladies Almanack* stages epistemological uncertainty, Barney's novel enacts 'ontological indeterminacy,' to borrow a term from Karen Barad.[20] Rewriting the scene of resurrection, Barney imagines a fantastic morphogenesis feeding on the numerous unintelligible particles the disintegrated body has left behind. At the end of the story, the precise nature of this new being, its bodily contours and its identity, remains unclear.

A cemetery in the Bois de Boulogne, a large public park in Paris featured in canonical works of French literature such as Gustav Flaubert's *Sentimental Education* (1869) and Marcel Proust's *In Search of Lost Time* (1913), provides the setting for the first two chapters of Barney's novel, titled 'An Adventure in Integration' and 'Brought to Life' respectively.[21] A symbolic and actual place of endings, at least for mortal life, the cemetery functions as a site for both the beginning of the book and the beginning of life for a protagonist whose journey the reader accompanies in the story to follow. The vitality of organic and inorganic matter freely 'intermingling' and 'entwining' as 'earth, wood, leaf, flesh, bone and stone' merge is a prerequisite for the utopian vision of the composition of a new human form (11). Among the many organisms alive at the cemetery is the first-person narrator who enters the scene as 'a living shadow' still lingering near the body of their deceased 'master-mistress' until, suddenly, a death occurs nearby, offering a new body to seize (11):

> Many of Death's cast-offs approach the radiation to be incorporated, like separated atoms in a ray of light. [. . .]
>
> All those out of a body must find again a body. Not to belong to a human make-up, not to become incorporated, not to lead or be led by a shape, is the worst thing that can befall even a shadow. (12–13)

In the quotation above, spirits do not denote an immaterial substance but are reconfigured as 'disembodied fragments' comparable to 'separated atoms' (12, 13). The result of breakage and separation, they no longer belong to a 'concrete entity' whose fixed solidity would render them identifiable and nameable but are nevertheless made of matter (12). This introductory scene in *The One Who Is Legion* is a modified version of a story in the Bible, titled 'Jesus Restores a Demon-Possessed Man' and narrated in the Gospels of Mark 5, Matthew 8 and Luke 8. In Mark 5: 1–20 Jesus encounters 'a man with an impure spirit' and asks for the impure spirit's name.[22] 'My name is Legion, [. . .] for we are many,' replies the chorus of impure spirits whereupon Jesus has them 'come out' of the man and enter 'into the pigs' grazing nearby.[23] The man, freed from the impure spirits, is again 'in his right mind.'[24] If we consider impurity as a marker for sexual transgression in the Bible, as some theologians have done, Barney reverses the biblical narrative in an embrace of sexual difference.[25] Whereas in the Gospel Jesus brings back to health a demon-possessed man through exorcism, in the novel the resurrection of an already dead woman is attempted precisely through the incorporation of various spirits. In Barney's adaptation of the scene, the reintegration of spirits into a 'human make-up' – becoming corporeal – is vital for the continuance of a life worth living. In *The Well of Loneliness* (1928), Radclyffe Hall also takes recourse to the biblical story when a crowd of people, 'the quick, the dead, and the unborn,' warn the lesbian protagonist, '"We are coming, Stephen – we are still coming on, and our name is legion – you dare not disown us!"'[26] In contrast to Stephen, however, the protagonist in *The One Who Is Legion* does not become an archetype for the previously unrepresented and invisible but rejects representation altogether.

A philosophical inquiry simulated by fantastic characters in a phantasmagorical plot, Barney's novel also reminds readers of Balzac's *Séraphîta*. Like *Séraphîta*, Barney's novel endows unidentified beings, forms and substances with life, but rather than exploring the spiritual world, *The One Who Is Legion* is concerned with the ways in which the human body matters on earth. The narrator's contemplation of angels takes up Balzac's idea that the full scope of angels remains yet unintelligible to ordinary human beings on earth:

> Wilfrid and Minna now understood some of the mysterious words of the being who on earth had appeared to them under the form which was intelligible to each—Seraphitus to one, Seraphita to the other—seeing that here all was homogeneous. [. . .] so that, everything existing in everything else, extension knew no limits, and the angels could traverse it everywhere to the utmost depths of the infinite.[27]

Barney does not simply adopt but extends Balzac's suggestion that the recognition of beings on earth depends on their embodiment of a specific gender. By alluding to a nascent system of classification through which human beings gain intelligibility on earth, namely the sexological nomenclature for individuals whose sexuality lies outside of opposite-sex attraction, Barney hints at yet another limitation placed on the full scope and potential of beings. During a horseback ride, which triggers a series of thoughts, the narrator also elaborates on angels: 'On earth they often appear with a woman's body and a man's desire, or vice versa. Two needed – No one entirely a woman or a man? Infinite variety of couples and couplings' (38). Desire for women, the narrator laments, is the stipulated property of the male subject, 'a man's desire,' and cannot be conceptualised beyond male sexuality. Among the ample taxonomies for sexual identities invented by early sexologists, the concept of the 'sexual invert' resembles the narrator's description of the angel as 'a woman's body and a man's desire' most closely. On this view, a woman would be a sexual invert if her behaviour, including her desire, corresponds to traits equated with masculinity.[28] The narrator's reference to an '[i]nfinite variety of couples and couplings' exploits the polysemy of the term 'couplings,' which can refer both to the pairing up of people into an amorous unit of two, the 'couple,' as well as to sexual intimacy. An infinite variety can hence suggest either erotic creativity or different pairings where, numerically, an infinity seems to indicate couplings beyond two genders. To forge a sexual identity by taking recourse to the gender binary is here contrasted with endless possibilities of different constellations. Similarly, the novel's title, *The One Who Is Legion*, achieves the disintegration of identity through the pluralisation of the grammatically singular.

The text reinforces the multiplication of a dualist conception at a later point in the story when the protagonist, having assumed the life of A.D., tries to familiarise themselves with their new strangely multiple singular self. To acquire self-knowledge, they need to choose a representational framework through which to organise yet unidentified parts constitutive of their identity: 'We must choose a system of classification – make our inventory, determine our composite. Establish an order where each might exist and serve' (97). This insight is followed by a contemplation of possible forms of representations such as musical notation to 'orchestrate' the various voices or orthographical manipulations – fonts, punctuation and shadings – to represent visually individual components. Ultimately, those systems are found to be wanting:

> Identified rather by the silhouette given by the letters than by the nomenclature. But in seeking to put each down as in a directory:
>
> Who's who
> and
> Whose whose
>
> we again realised that such inventions are irksome, and diminished by application. We dropped into a meditation on the origin of composite beings in general; on the duality of mind characterising several persons

in one; on an entity at variance with one of its selves, hoping in this way to throw a better light on our difficult case. (99–100)

To have the self expressed in the familiar shapes of writing, the narrator concludes, implicates the loss of sovereignty and agency. The act of identification, as undertaken in a directory, attributes to the individual a word by which they are known, establishing '[w]ho's who' and allowing for relations of ownership – '[w]hose whose' – to be determined. What is noticeable in this excerpt and throughout Barney's novel is its focus on shapes and materiality rather than on meaning and interiority in its exploration of personal identity. The 'silhouette given by the letters' rather than the semantic dimension of language is a candidate for the truthful depiction of the self: words are disconnected from a signified and reduced to their materiality. In the same chapter, the narrator terms writing 'printed matter,' again highlighting its materiality instead of the meaning it may convey (95).

Once disillusioned by the limits of orthography whose 'inventions are irksome,' the narrator shifts attention to the morphologies of life forms. From the 'single being' and the 'dual being' – the 'centaur,' 'the siren,' 'the sphinx,' 'the two-sexed hermaphrodite' and the 'angel' – to 'a trinity' and 'the three-in-one leading to four,' the narrator eventually is left with 'mystery' (100). Figures like the angel and hermaphrodites in *The One Who Is Legion* serve as a beginning for the further dismantling of familiar categories by which we gather knowledge about the world. The indication is that the human mind is not yet able to fathom an entirely new creation, which remains ineffable in language: 'To stretch the mind beyond its present possibilities may be to indicate a place towards which it will ultimately travel to the further discovery of itself,' muses the narrator, illustrating both the visionary tone of the novel and the utopian mission of the protagonist (100–1). The attention *The One Who Is Legion* pays to the interdependence between shapes, meaning and agency is also conveyed by its epigraph, a quote from Milton's *Paradise Lost*, which reads as follows:

> For Spirits, when they please,
> Can either sex assume, or both [. . .]
> Not tied nor manacled with joint or limb,
> Nor founded on the brittle strength of bones,
> Like cumberous flesh; but in what shape they choose.[29]

Milton's reference to the liberty of spirits to choose either or both sexes, the burden of flesh as matter fixed in form, and the malleability of shapes set the tenor for the story recounted in Barney's novel. The attraction of death and decay, the narrator later insinuates, is the liberating process associated with the 'decomposition of flesh, [. . .] to the architectural sexless skeleton'

(36). *The One Who Is Legion* also mimics *Paradise Lost* in basing its plot on unorthodox materialist interpretations of biblical scenes, although it misappropriates the biblical template to a greater extent.[30] Moreover, descriptions of living fragments of matter in *The One Who Is Legion* resemble Milton's conception of the material and animate essence of all things and thoughts existing in the world.[31] In *Paradise Lost* life springs from a 'formless Mass, / This worlds material mould' by assuming 'various forms,' which, as Beverley Sherry explains, 'are less bodily or corporeal the closer they are placed or move towards God [. . .] though, all remain material, the human mind and its products as well as rocks.'[32] Such a belief in material monism also underlies the cosmos of Barney's novel, in which the genesis of 'the One' commences with the coming together of various fragments that the narrator attempts to organise in vain. In *The One Who Is Legion*, however, writing as sequences of words on a surface plays a crucial role in determining which forms gain significance and prominence in the human world and which do not.

Writing, as a form of representation that endows a material entity with a specific kind of meaning, simultaneously embeds materiality in a larger story in which it plays a designated part. In attempting the redemption of A.D., the protagonist's challenge is first to identify and then to alter the well-trodden story of A.D., which has culminated in her suicide. 'Not to meet the story' may entail '[t]o be alive, and refuse a single track of life' (33). If we consider the Glow-Woman A.D.'s alter-ego when still alive – after all, the Glow-Woman, the narrator implies, has also died by suicide – we can surmise that A.D. has fallen victim to a heterosexual storyline, in which woman's freedom, including her romantic relations, depends on men.[33] The Glow-Woman represents the ideal woman in a patriarchal state, 'existing mostly as men appraised her' (120). Her extra-marital amorous affairs remain entrenched in reproductive functionality due to her 'limited vibrations of flesh,' which makes her a 'a slave to sexual habits, functioning absent-mindedly' for the purpose of 'full-sailed belly making' (80, 81). Both the Glow-Woman and A.D. or, indeed, the Glow-Woman as A.D., have suffered from an existence in the flesh as becomes clear when the narrator discovers A.D.'s memoir, which carries a 'hint at a tragedy of individual flesh' (29).

Repeatedly, the narrator implies a relation between available stories, books and representations, on the one hand, and possible bodily forms, identities and life paths, on the other. Barney's novel is not a fully-fledged philosophical study of the interaction between materiality and discursivity in the genesis of human corporeality and individuality, but it is clearly invested in disassembling and inspecting this connection. In a library 'from which there was no exit,' the narrator asks, '[w]hat books produced you?' (92). Touching 'the shelves and our ribs' simultaneously, they wonder '[w]hat books had passed from them into us? become part of our make-up' (96), and are 'we' not therefore 'each a circulating library spreading ideas, dreams, precepts, social and scientific prejudices' (95)? These quotations indicate a link between thoughts preserved and passed on in books and possible dimensions of one's identity. Parallel to this suggestion, the narrator infuses the narrative with indeterminacy by leaving open the question of whether 'we' includes the reader or merely registers the multiplicity of the protagonist (95, 96). Uncertainty over the precise referee of a word, constative utterances ending with a question mark, and statements followed by an equally possible alternative statement introduced with the conjunction 'or' abound in *The One Who Is Legion* from beginning to end. One of many examples occurs at a riding stable near A.D.'s house:

> The whinny of a horse in the uncertain light. A nightmare, or the stable-call of a horse? A staggering towards or away from reality?
> In the hall the empty standing boots; or was the invisible owner there? A dawn-shape rising from them? (31)

Both the ontological indeterminacy thematised in the novel as well as the text's inherent semantic indeterminacy, which the quoted passage illustrates, reverberate with new directions taken in the scientific discipline of physics in the early twentieth century.

ONTOLOGICAL AND SEMANTIC INDETERMINACY

We can read *The One Who Is Legion* as a story about how matter strives to matter in both senses of the word: to be of substance and significance. The novel's concern with material formations, provisionally fixed in place and rendered intelligible by familiar concepts, but otherwise entangled in an ongoing, open-ended process of potential becomings, echoes findings by the pioneers of quantum mechanics in the 1920s and beyond. Quantum mechanics revolutionised classical physics by proposing an entirely different depiction of the physical world. Physicists like Niels Bohr (1885–1962) have demonstrated, for example, that the observed phenomenon, 'the macroscopic manifestation of a measurement on an object,' is inseparable from the apparatus of observation.[34] An integral part of scientific experiments, the apparatus uncontrollably interacts with the object it measures, so that the object observed never exists independently from the observer: 'the state of the measuring device and the state of the object cannot be separated from each other during a measurement but they form a dynamical whole.'[35]

One ontological consequence is the so-called uncertainty principle, which underlies Bohr's notion of wave-particle duality. In the mid-1920s Bohr intervened in a discussion about the puzzling observation that, in the context of the so-called double-slit experiment, light and matter could, at different times, display the characteristics of a wave or the behaviour of a particle, both of which are mutually exclusive.[36] The unpredictable manifestation of either a wave or a particle picture of light on a photographic plate, Bohr suggested, did not correspond to actual physical reality but resulted from the uncontrollable interaction between a physical object and the measuring apparatus in a specific experimental set-up. Whether light has the qualities of a particle or the shape of a wave remains impossible to exhaustively determine. Despite this gap between actual physical reality and phenomena registered by way of a measuring apparatus, the result of a physical experiment is truthful under the conditions of the measurement context. Bohr believed, furthermore, that concepts of classical physics constitute the common language necessary to describe and communicate a physical experience otherwise incomprehensible. Since the interaction between physical object and apparatus is indeterminate, and thus 'unanalyzable,' the description of the phenomenon in terms of classical physics registers only characteristics of the object, falling short of providing an entire picture.[37] Even the attempt to analyse the interaction would simply yield the same issue of an indeterminate interaction between observer and observed object.

In probing the role of matter, language and boundaries in the emergence of a distinguishable, identifiable human body – what physicists might term a phenomenon – *The One Who Is Legion* contemplates ontological dilemmas comparable to those Bohr had raised. Barney's novel traverses the boundary between linguistic representation and material reality, determinate identity and indeterminate being, and, in the process, exposes the volatile nature of lines drawn between different entities. Occasionally, the narrator addresses the 'hardly discernible' or 'hardly distinguishable' line between an object and its doppelgänger in form of a projection onto a reflective surface or a shadow cast on a wall (79, 157). One passage explicitly highlights the difficulty of distinguishing between two phenomena:

> Which of these trees is real? Both are real differently: that willow moved by the breeze, and that same willow which the water sways. Everything takes on a value and loses a value as seen from my houseboat's window at the level of the rivers that pass me as I pass. (147)

In the fantastical world imagined in *The One Who Is Legion*, boundaries are malleable in ways that unsettle conventional notions of the identity of an object or a person. Its suggestion that physical objects can have two mutually exclusive and yet truthful states of beings – 'both are differently real' – resonates with Bohr's hypothesis. Barney's novel does not re-enact a physical experiment, but the narrator's reference to the observer's position, 'as seen from the houseboat,' acknowledges the effect of the apparatus of observation on the observed. Instead of a single true reality of the composite of an object, the viewer faces a '[n]ever-to-be conciliated choice of opposites' (13). Indeterminacy also surfaces in relation to the narrator who is in a 'state in which we were neither ourselves nor anyone else, – neither there nor here' (86).

Karen Barad's posthumanist account of material-discursive practices, which builds on Bohr's insights, offers a helpful perspective on *The One Who Is Legion*'s reworkings of the boundaries of the self as 'a something sitting in space' (141).[38] Albeit in differing ways – Barad in a comprehensive philosophical elaboration and Barney in an incoherent literary work – both authors connect a materialist understanding of the world with discursive practices and the constitution of the human body. Barad reworks Bohr's notion of a phenomenon as 'intra-activity in the ongoing reconfiguration of locally determinate causal structures with determinate boundaries, properties, meanings, and patterns of marks on bodies.'[39] In other words, the physical reality of, for example, the human body is the result of material-discursive processes, which have stabilised over time, feigning firm boundaries. Materiality, in Barad's account, is inherently indeterminate but can appear in 'local causal structures' within which it has definite boundaries and properties – much like the particles in a specified experimental setting. Correspondingly, Barad comprehends 'meaning' as inherently indeterminate unless inserted in 'particular discursive practices,' which 'define what counts as meaningful statements.'[40]

Against the background of such a framework, the opposing forces in *The One Who Is Legion*, free-floating indeterminate particles against identifiable petrified flesh, stage the revolt of matter against its discursive immobilisation with the aim to widen possibilities of mattering and acting in the world. A scene in the penultimate chapter, entitled 'The One Who Takes Leave of the Legion,' underpins such a reading by having the 'body confron[t] the spirit with all those who had composed it,' that is, with all of its 'false representations' (151). Adopting an increasingly utopian tone towards the end, the novel depicts the narrator as 'relieved from form and motion' and 'hardly distinguishable from the crystal objects' around them (157). Who, what and how many the protagonist is remains unanswered in a book that leaves the reader with a final conundrum: 'Is not our dead heart already with the dead – with those living otherwise?' (158).

Conclusion

The lack of consideration of the significance of *The One Who Is Legion* and Barney's oeuvre more generally to a comprehensive understanding of not only lesbian modernism but modernism at large bespeaks the selective criteria for inclusion still at work in (lesbian) modernist scholarship. A difficult prose, an anachronistic style, and a hard to place genre, as many have noted, have certainly complicated the incorporation, to invoke the novel's terminology, into the corpus of modernist literature. The prominence of Barney as the polyamorous lesbian, the heiress to a fortune, and host of parties, has also overshadowed an examination of Barney as the modernist writer. Given that most of her writing is in French we can also view the absence of her work in discussions of modernist aesthetics as reminder of a still existing bias towards English-language texts. The frequent omission of *The One Who Is Legion* even in publications focused on the entanglements of gender, sexuality and modernist literature is particularly unfortunate. Celebrating women's sexuality beyond heterosexual norms, *The One Who Is Legion* outlines a posthuman materialist account of the world, in which both materiality and signification remain entrenched in a state of becoming. Gendered bodies, in the novel's universe, are only a temporary materialisation in an ongoing process in which material forces and discursive practices dynamically interact to produce beings. Barney's novel is hence an important example of a lesbian-authored text in which the reader does not encounter a rendering of the lesbian persona, but in which the possibility of the lesbian only prepares a more encompassing exploration of the potential of matter to change shape and meaning.

Notes

1. Elizabeth English offers a rare in-depth study of *The One Who Is Legion* in *Lesbian Modernism: Censorship, Sexuality and Genre Fiction* (Edinburgh: Edinburgh University Press, 2015). Suzanne Hobson situates Barney's novel alongside H.D.'s writings in a discussion of 'the third sex angel' in modernist fiction. See Suzanne Hobson, *Angels of Modernism: Religion, Culture, Aesthetics 1910–1960* (Basingstoke: Palgrave, 2011), 125–31. Seminal studies on women writers in the early twentieth century also include discussions of *The One Who Is Legion*. See Bridget Elliott and Jo-Ann Wallace, *Women Artists and Writers: Modernist (Im)positionings* (London and New York: Routledge, 1994), 39–41; Shari Benstock, *Women of the Left Bank: Paris, 1900–1940*, 9th ed. (Austin: University of Texas Press, [1986] 2008), 298–301; and Sandra M. Gilbert and Susan Gubar, *No Man's Land: The Place of the Woman Writer in the Twentieth Century, Volume 2: Sexchanges* (New Haven and London: Yale University Press, 1989). Other publications on Barney primarily focus on her life as a polyamorous woman-loving woman and host of a legendary literary salon in Paris. See, for example, Joanne Winning, '"Ezra through the open door": The Parties of Natalie Barney, Adrienne Monnier and Sylvia Beach as Lesbian Modernist Cultural Production,' in *The Modernist Party*, ed. Kate McLoughlin (Edinburgh: Edinburgh University Press, 2015), 127–46.
2. Copies of Barney's novel can nowadays only be found in archives and libraries such as the John Rylands Library in Manchester, England, to which quotations in this chapter refer. Published by the Scholartis Press, which had issued 560 copies, 525 of which were up for sale, the book has since been out of print. A facsimile reprint issued by the National Poetry Foundation in 1987 is no longer obtainable.
3. To Valerie Rohy, homosexual reproduction is 'the ability to multiply non-biologically in an unsentimental process of replication, repetition, and representation.' Valerie Rohy, *Lost Causes: Narrative, Etiology, and Queer Theory* (New York: Oxford University Press, 2015), 24. Rohy contrasts the gay and lesbian reproduction of sameness

with the queer proliferation of difference (8). Benjamin Kahan identifies the potential and yet impossible reproductivity of the lesbian as a model of art for art's sake preoccupying decadent literature in France. 'Reproduction,' Kahan states, 'is the binary opposite of sodomy.' Benjamin Kahan, 'Queer Modernism,' in *A Handbook of Modernism Studies*, ed. Jean-Michel Rabaté (Chicester: Wiley-Blackwell, 2013), 347–61, 350–1.

4. With reference to gender as a selective category in the feminist recuperation of neglected early twentieth-century women writers, Jaime Hovey writes, 'work on the sexuality of modernism followed this identity model.' Jaime Hovey, *A Thousand Words: Portraiture, Style, and Queer Modernism* (Columbus: Ohio State University Press, 2006), 2. Writing more broadly on the lesbian in feminist and queer scholarship, Annamarie Jagose laments a chronological narrative in which the lesbian is equated with 'derivation, imitation, and secondariness.' Annamarie Jagose, 'Debating Definitions: The Lesbian in Feminist Studies and Queer Studies,' in *The Cambridge Companion to Lesbian Literature*, ed. Jodie Medd (New York: Cambridge University Press, 2015), 32–44, 32.

5. On the term 'lesbian' and definitional indeterminacy, see Jodie Medd, 'Lesbian Literature?: An Introduction,' in Medd, *Cambridge Companion to Lesbian Literature*, 1–16.

6. Natalie Clifford Barney, *The One Who Is Legion or A.D.'s After-Life* (London: Eric Partridge, 1930), 28. Subsequent references will cite page numbers in-text. Ironically, *The One Who Is Legion* has itself been read as a highly autobiographical account of Barney's turbulent love life during her residency at 20 rue Jacob in Paris. Elliott and Wallace describe *The One Who Is Legion* as 'teasingly autobiographical.' See Elliott and Wallace, *Women Artists and Writers*, 40.

7. 'Form is what unifies matter into a single object' is one of Aristotle's arguments in *Metaphysics*. See Thomas Ainsworth, 'Form vs. Matter,' in *The Stanford Encyclopedia of Philosophy* (Summer 2020 Edition), ed. Edward N. Zalta, accessed 13 February 2022, https://plato.stanford.edu/archives/sum2020/entries/form-matter/.

8. Benstock, *Women of the Left Bank*, 298; English, *Lesbian Modernism*, 68.

9. Scholars suggest that different friends, namely Djuna Barnes and Dolly Wilde, tried and failed to find publishers because they found it 'incomprehensible.' See Diana Souhami, *Paris, Sappho and Art: The Love Life of Natalie Barney and Romaine Brooks* (London: Quercus Publishing, [2004] 2013), 176. For references to the novel as 'strange,' 'odd,' 'weird,' and 'frustratingly abstract,' see, in order of appearance, Benstock, *Women of the Left Bank*, 298; George Wickes, *The Amazon of Letters* (New York: Putnam Publishing Group, 1976), 150; Suzanne Rodriguez, *Wild Heart: A Life* (New York: HarperCollins, 2003), 303; and Elliott and Wallace, *Women Artists and Writers*, 39.

10. In Jay's reading 'Stella, the Glow-Woman, reanimates the pair' composed of 'the genderless narrator' and 'the One.' Karla Jay, *The Amazon and the Page: Natalie Clifford Barney and Renée Vivien* (Bloomington and Indianapolis: Indiana University Press, 1988), 102.

11. Benstock, *Women of the Left Bank*, 298; Jay, *The Amazon and the Page*, 102; Anna Livia, *Pronoun Envy: Literary Uses of Linguistic Gender* (Oxford: Oxford University Press, 2001), 74; English, *Lesbian Modernism*, 67.

12. Benstock, *Women of the Left Bank*, 300.
13. Hobson, *Angels of Modernism*, 128.
14. English, *Lesbian Modernism*, 69.
15. Benstock, *Women of the Left Bank*, 301.
16. Elliott and Wallace, *Women Artists and Writers*, 51. Although she does not discuss *The One Who Is Legion*, Deborah Longworth makes a similar point in her study of the lesbian figure in decadent writing. To Longworth, Charles Baudelaire 'proclaimed Sappho's sapphism in *The Flowers of Evil*' and made her 'a mythic heroine of decadence.' Deborah Longworth, 'The Gender of Decadence: Paris-Lesbos from the Fin de Siècle to the Interwar Era,' in *Decadence and Literature*, ed. Jane Desmarais and David Weir (Cambridge: Cambridge University Press, 2019), 365. For a comprehensive study of representations of the 'lesbian mystique' in decadent art and writing, see Nicole G. Albert, *Lesbian Decadence: Representations in Art and Literature of Fin-de-Siècle France*, trans. Nancy Erber and William A. Peniston (New York: Harrington Park Press, 2016).
17. Honoré Balzac, *Séraphîta (and Louis Lambert & The Exiles)*, trans. Clara Bell (Sawtry: Dedalus, [1989] 2012), n.p.
18. See Book I, lines 622–34, in John Milton, *Paradise Lost*, ed. Stephen Orgel and Jonathan Goldberg (Oxford and New York: Oxford University Press, [1667] 2008), 24.
19. Brian Glavey, 'Modernity and Other Nocturnal Distempers,' *Modernism/modernity Print Plus* 1, no. 3 (2016), accessed 18 June 2022, https://doi.org/10.26597/mod.0020. Along similar lines, Daniela Caselli notes that *Ladies Almanack* 'promises access to the closed circle of the cult of Sappho while deferring right of entry and mocking the club.' Daniela Caselli, 'Novitiates, Saints and Priestesses: The Unreadable Pleasures of *Ladies Almanack*,' *Textual Practice* 20, no. 3 (2006): 463–89, 466.
20. Karen Barad, 'Posthumanist Performativity: Toward an Understanding of How Matter Comes to Matter,' *Signs: Journal of Women in Culture and Society* 28, no. 3 (2003): 801–31, 815.
21. On the significance of the Bois de Boulogne in Barney's social life, see Benstock, *Women of the Left Bank*, 82–3.
22. 'Jesus Restores a Demon-Possessed Man,' in *New International Version* (Biblica, 2011), Mark 5: 1–20, accessed 30 July 2022, https://www.biblica.com/bible/niv/mark/5/.
23. Ibid. The King James Bible speaks of an 'unclean' rather than an impure spirit. See *King James Online Study Bible* (MasonSoft Technology, 2022), accessed 30 July 2022, https://thekingsbible.com/Bible/41/5.
24. 'Jesus Restores a Demon-Possessed Man,' Mark 5: 15.
25. See Martti Nissinen, *Homoeroticism in the Biblical World: A Historical Perspective*, trans. Kirsi Stjerna (Minneapolis: Fortress Press, 1998); and Dale B. Martin, 'Heterosexism and the Interpretation of Romans:1:18–32,' *Biblical Interpretation: A Journal of Contemporary Approaches* 3, no. 3 (1995): 332–55.
26. Radclyffe Hall, *The Well of Loneliness* (London: Virago, [1928] 1982), 447. On reincarnation as a way to reimagine sexual identity in Hall's 'Miss Ogilvy Finds Herself,' see English, *Lesbian Modernism*, 58.

27. Balzac, *Séraphîta*, n.p.
28. German-born psychiatrist Richard von Krafft-Ebing spoke of 'the inversion of the sexual instinct' and of 'psychical hermaphroditism' as a mild and possibly curable version of sexual inversion in *Psychopathia Sexualis* (1886). See Richard von Krafft-Ebing, *Psychopathia Sexualis, With Special Reference to Contrary Sexual Instinct: A Medico-Legal Study* (Philadelphia: F. A. Davis, 1894), 230–2. Edward Carpenter's notion of the 'intermediate sex' also borrows from the idea that 'elements' or 'ingredients' of an individual 'represent the two sexes.' See Edward Carpenter, *The Intermediate Sex: A Study of Some Transitional Types of Men and Women* (London: George Allen & Unwin, [1908] 1921), 17. German physician Magnus Hirschfeld, on the other hand, sought to replace binary categories with a spectrum of 'sexual intermediaries.' See J. Edgar Bauer, 'On the Nameless Love and Infinite Sexualities: John Henry Mackay, Magnus Hirschfeld and the Origins of the Sexual Emancipation Movement,' *Journal of Homosexuality* 50, no. 1 (2005): 1–26, 1. In his early work on sexuality, Sigmund Freud referred to 'psychical hermaphroditism' as a phenomenon only detectable in 'inverted women.' Sigmund Freud, 'Three Essays on the Theory of Sexuality (1905),' in *The Standard Edition of the Complete Psychological Works of Sigmund Freud*, ed. James Strachey, vol. 7 (London: Vintage Books, 2001), 141–2.
29. Book I, lines 423–31, in Milton, *Paradise Lost*, 17.
30. For a demonstration of Milton's heretic rewriting of the biblical creation narrative in *Paradise Lost*, see Nigel Smith, 'Paradise Lost and Heresy,' in *The Oxford Handbook of Milton*, ed. Nicholas McDowell and Nigel Smith (Oxford: Oxford University Press, 2009), 510–24.
31. Following Stephen Fallon's discussion of 'animate materialism' in Milton's work, other scholars have likewise demonstrated his indebtedness to material monism, that is, the philosophical conception of the world as entirely composed of matter. See Stephen Hequembourg, 'The Poetics of Materialism in Cavendish and Milton,' *Studies in English Literature, 1500–1900* 54, no. 1 (2014): 173–92; Phillip J. Donnelly, '"Matter" versus Body: The Character of Milton's Monism,' *Milton Quarterly* 33, no. 3 (1999): 79–85; and D. Bentley Hart, 'Matter, Monism, and Narrative: An Essay on the Metaphysics of Paradise Lost,' *Milton Quarterly* 30, no. 1 (1996): 16–27.
32. Book III, lines 708–9, in Milton, *Paradise Lost*, 82; Beverley Sherry, 'Milton, Materialism, and the Sound of Paradise Lost,' *Essays in Criticism* 60, no. 3 (2010): 220–41, 220.
33. That the Glow-Woman and A.D. might be one and the same individual is suggested during the cemetery scene in the second chapter. After she has breathed life into the dead A.D., on whose forehead gapes the wound of a shot, the Glow-Woman arrives at her estate where her male companion apologises for the 'unwelcome restitution' and declares 'I return to you your papers, your revolver, your key, your solitude, your home' (19, 20). Whether she has returned from the dead or has been involved in the death of another remains unclear.
34. Jan Faye, 'Copenhagen Interpretation of Quantum Mechanics,' in *The Stanford Encyclopedia of Philosophy* (Winter 2019 Edition), ed. Edward N. Zalta, accessed 16 April 2022, https://plato.stanford.edu/archives/win2019/entries/qm-copenhagen/.

35. Ibid.
36. Jan Hilgevoord and Jos Uffink, 'The Uncertainty Principle,' in *The Stanford Encyclopedia of Philosophy* (Winter 2016 Edition), ed. Edward N. Zalta, accessed 16 April 2022, https://plato.stanford.edu/archives/win2016/entries/qt-uncertainty/. The double-slit experiment is a case in point.
37. Ibid. Hilgevoord and Uffink write that '[i]n every phenomenon the interaction between the object and the apparatus comprises at least one quantum. But the description of the phenomenon must use classical notions in which the quantum of action does not occur.'
38. Barad's interpretation and interdisciplinary use of Bohr's theory is not uncontroversial. See Jan Raye and Rasmus Jaksland, 'Barad, Bohr, and Quantum Mechanics,' *Synthese* 199 (2021): 8231–55.
39. Barad, 'Posthumanist Performativity,' 817. Bohr defined the phenomenon as 'the comprehension of the effects observed under given experimental conditions.' Niels Bohr, 'The Causality Problem in Atomic Physics,' in *New Theories in Physics* (Paris: International, 1939), quoted in Hilgevoord and Uffink, 'The Uncertainty Principle.'
40. Barad, 'Posthumanist Performativity,' 818–19.

PART II
GENRES AND FORMS

4

IMAGINATIVE BIOGRAPHY: MARGARET GOLDSMITH, VITA SACKVILLE-WEST AND LESBIAN HISTORICAL LIFE WRITING

Elizabeth English

INTRODUCTION

On 20 November 1928, the American Margaret Goldsmith (1894–1971) wrote to her lover, Vita Sackville-West (1892–1962), absolving her of any remaining sense of duty.[1] 'You owe me nothing,' Goldsmith wrote, 'except that which gives itself.'[2] Their affair, albeit short-lived, began in March 1928 in Berlin. Sackville-West arrived in the city in February to visit her husband, Harold Nicolson, who was already acquainted with Goldsmith and her British journalist husband, Frederick Voigt (whom she divorced in 1935). Writing to Virginia Woolf, Sackville-West claimed that Goldsmith, whose 'morals I strongly suspect,' was her 'one amusement.'[3] By early March their friendship had evolved: as Sackville-West suggestively wrote on 10 March, 'Margaret Voyt [sic] came in the morning with results I had foreseen.'[4] Although Sackville-West and Goldsmith shared what Victoria Glendinning calls an erotic 'fantasy loveworld at Long Barn' in the early summer of 1928, in which 'Margaret played the "peasant" to Vita's aristocrat, and Vita was "David" to Margaret,' by July the affair had dwindled with Sackville-West telling Nicolson in September that there were 'no misunderstandings or false positions between them.'[5] Whether Goldsmith was quite this stoic remains to be seen. Unlike Sackville-West, Goldsmith left no records, diaries or letters (other than those in Sackville-West's possession) that I am able to locate, so we can only presume her feelings on this topic. Hilda Matheson, the BBC producer and Goldsmith's romantic successor, did write to Sackville-West of the 'legend that you are so detached about people,' something which 'Margaret Goldsmith elaborated,' which perhaps suggests a less than clean emotional break.[6]

The above is the extent of Goldsmith's recorded significance in our literary history of the period.[7] If recalled as a writer, it is for her novel *Belated Adventure* (1929), said to include a character based on Sackville-West. Goldsmith is a bit part player in another woman's biography. Yet, if we probe further, we find a literary contribution that is significant in its own right and a woman who was well connected to leading cultural and political female figures. Goldsmith's career and interests were diverse and prolific: she had a significant economic advisory career with the US government, including a role as the first woman Assistant Trade Commissioner at the US Embassy in Berlin, but she also worked as a journalist, translator, literary agent and writer. She was politically active, sharing platforms with such women as the suffragette politician and activist Lady Rhondda, whom she spoke alongside at the 1924 International Federation of University Women's 3rd Biennial Conference.[8] In 1935, she was part of a deputation of ten women, including Monica Whately (Secretary of the Six Point Group), Naomi Mitchison and Storm Jameson, who approached the German Embassy to advocate for the rights of German women.[9] The National Portrait Gallery holds four photographic portraits of Goldsmith, with her striking shock of hair, taken in 1935 by Bauhaus photographer Lucia Moholy.[10] In a piece of literary criticism from the 1930s, *The School of Femininity*, Margaret Lawrence examines Goldsmith's work alongside that of Woolf, Katherine Mansfield and Willa Cather. Lawrence considers Goldsmith a 'rebel,' on a par with such writers as May Sinclair, for her representation of sexuality, female desire and modern marriage.[11] The above builds a picture of Goldsmith's significance, networks and activities in the period, entirely independent of her romantic affiliation with Sackville-West. Goldsmith has arguably received wider recognition in Germany, where she lived for periods throughout her life. Most likely this is because of Goldsmith's role as a translator of significant German writers but also because she published two novels, *Ein Fremder in Paris: Roman* (1930) and *Patience Geht Vorüber: Ein Roman* (1931), in German.[12] The second novel, translated as *Patience Passes By: A Novel*, was reissued in German in 2020 and is described by the publisher as a daring challenge to the sexual status quo, representing both love between women and polyamory.[13] Reviewing the novel on its reissue, Edelgard Abenstein argues that *Patience Passes By* 'puts the author in a series of big names of the 1920s.'[14]

While my emphasis here is on recovering Goldsmith's work and its significance for modernist biography and lesbian modernism, this chapter also explores the affinities and contrasts between Goldsmith's and Sackville-West's historical life writing. In the process I argue that Goldsmith is the more sexually bold, if perhaps not as nuanced or sophisticated, writer in the way that she deploys the biographical genre. The neglect of Goldsmith's contribution and her exclusion from the 'names' of the time is particularly unjust when one considers the fact that she spent her professional life documenting women's lives and achievements. In addition to her five novels, Goldsmith published thirteen biographical studies in English between 1929 and 1948, spotlighting such historical women as Florence Nightingale, Christina of Sweden, Marie Antoinette, Madame de Staël, Sappho of Lesbos and Maria Theresa of Austria. In tandem with this, her non-fiction publications, *Women and the Future* (1946) and *Women at War* (1943), aimed to document women's experiences – and expanded freedoms – of wartime, as well as to encourage women to build on these gains by demanding equal rights. While not quite as prolific in the biographical genre, Sackville-West also published a handful of studies of historical women during her writing career: Joan of Arc, Aphra Behn, Teresa of Ávila and Thérèse of Lisieux.

Much has been written about Sackville-West and Woolf's relationship and its influence on their literary output. More specifically, Karyn Sproles has examined how this applied to the writers' experimentation with biography, arguing that '[b]oth women were grappling with the problems of biographical representations of identity and sexuality in ways that still have revolutionary potential.'[15] While I do not suggest that Goldsmith and Sackville-West's creative, emotional or romantic relationship is comparable to that between Sackville-West and Woolf, it is notable that Goldsmith began her career as a biographer in 1929, shortly after meeting Sackville-West, with a biography of *Frederick the Great* (whose sexuality is often a contested topic) introduced by Sackville-West's husband, Harold Nicholson. Sackville-West had already begun writing women's histories with her biography of Aphra Behn in 1927, and her edition of *The Diary of Lady Anne Clifford* in 1923 suggests an earlier propensity for recording women's voices. Reading a wide range of Goldsmith's works, including *Christina of Sweden: A Psychological Biography* (1933), *Sappho: A Psychological Reconstruction of Her Life* (1936), *Venus in Scorpio: A Romance of Versailles, 1770–1793* (1940, co-authored with Katharine Burdekin) and *Women at War* (1943) alongside Sackville-West's *Aphra Behn: The Incomparable Astrea* (1927), *Saint Joan of Arc* (1936), *Pepita* (1937) and *The Women's Land Army* (1944), this chapter positions Goldsmith and Sackville-West as writers of lesbian modernist biography. Life writing allowed them to reclaim historical figures whose sexual and gender identities had been obscured, ignored or muted. In the process, their work queers the genre and its conventions, which are inherently heteronormative, patriarchal, and dependent on masculine definitions of truth and accuracy.

Queering Biography

Goldsmith and Sackville-West are, then, arguably part of the modernist 'new biography' movement, an attempt to revolutionise the genre and break away from what were perceived as the staid Victorian conventions of recording lives.[16] Studies of 'new biography' have in the past tended to focus on male writers, most notably Lytton Strachey whose *Eminent Victorians* (1918) serves as something of a manifesto for this revolutionary mode of life writing. Woolf is the only woman who regularly features in studies of modernist biography and indeed her contribution to this genre is significant. Most obviously, *Orlando: A Biography* (1928) and *Flush* (1933) satirise the inherited traditions of life writing, but more widely, Woolf's work consistently endeavoured to write women's lives into existence and into the record. The somewhat hardened evolutionary narrative, which tells us that modernist experimentation shook off the juvenile limitations and artificiality of Victorian biography and that Woolf began the recovery of women's historical lives, has been challenged by recent scholarship.[17] Juliette Atkinson and Alison Booth both contest the supposed dearth of women in history's annals by highlighting the proliferation of women's biographies in the nineteenth century.[18] In particular, they question the legitimacy of Woolf's supposed struggle to find maternal predecessors. Booth, for instance, states that 'Woolf inadvertently encouraged later feminist scholars in the view that a female tradition had been lost.'[19] This has, perhaps, not simply obscured earlier examples of women's biographical writing but also overshadowed the work undertaken by contemporaries such as Goldsmith. Claire Battershill argues that 'biographies and autobiographies still seem to play a relatively small role in current critical discussions about the period' and that this is in part because 'the canons of modernist biography include at present a relatively small number of books,' which, we might add, are mostly male authored.[20] Melanie Micir's excellent 2019 study of modernist women's biographical writing addresses this oversight by 'highlight[ing] the urgency of a critical return to biography studies, especially in the context of modernist, feminist, and queer studies, and [. . .] suggests that we should understand the archive as a site of bio-critical action for the writers and subjects long marginalized by dominant disciplinary narratives.'[21] For Micir, modernist biography is an 'activist genre' which resists the marginalisation and exclusion of its subjects from history.[22] Micir is interested specifically in 'passion projects,' the documentation of the lives of women lovers, partners, friends and peers. The biographies examined in this chapter are less intimate (though this does not preclude them from being personal) and, in the main, document historical rather than contemporary lives, but I argue that Goldsmith's and Sackville-West's biographical writing also belongs under Micir's heading of 'activist genre,' that is, the revolutionary, and modernist, recording of lesbian women's lives and desires.[23] 'Lesbian' in this context allows for an inclusive range of applications and meanings beyond the fact that these are biographies written by women who loved other women. In some texts examined here, historical figures are explicitly claimed and celebrated as lesbian – that is, women who loved, desired and had sex with women.

In others, a current of lesbian passion – unrequited, unsatisfied and almost unconscious – runs quietly through the pages, while a few of these texts might be claimed as lesbian for their challenge to heteronormative frameworks of sexuality and gender or for their representation of female masculinity.[24]

We might even read the way in which these narratives resist the traditional definition of the biography – with its linear chronology structured by standardised and heteronormative goals or life events (birth, education, marriage, career, etc.) – as part of what makes these texts 'lesbian.'[25] New Biographers turned away from the Victorian idealisation of their subjects – and often linear chronologies – to embrace their flaws and failings.[26] Although Goldsmith and Sackville-West published biographies to recover and record women's lives, neither writer romanticised her subjects. In fact, they consistently represent figures who fail, who struggle to 'mature' or achieve greatness, whose endings are disappointing and often flat. Sackville-West's biography of Aphra Behn repeatedly criticises the quality of Behn's work, bemoaning the task of trawling through her corpus, and going so far as to say that 'given her natural talent, [she] prodigally wasted her opportunities.'[27] Behn's significance is attributed solely to the fact that '[s]he was the first woman in England to earn her living by her pen' (12). Even Sackville-West's narrative of the French soldier and later saint Joan of Arc downplays Joan's heroism and military skill. Her success in leading the French in battle against the English is 'psychological rather than military'; she serves as 'inspiration' and 'symbol' rather than offering any tactical strength.[28] This is not, then, an unequivocal portrait of a hero; nor is it the story of a mystic. Although Sackville-West repeatedly addresses the question of the saint's supposed divine connection, she struggles to definitively credit Joan with any gift. The evidence appears, at times, to support Sackville-West's 'belief that certain persons are in touch with, or, shall we say, receptive to the influences of a unity for which we have no adequate name,' but at other times she is unconvinced, wondering whether, for instance, these voices are but 'dreams' (327, 284n1).

By Goldsmith's reckoning, Christina's and Sappho's lives are also somewhat disappointing. While Sappho is professionally and creatively successful, her personal life is 'empty,' primarily because she struggles to make meaningful emotional connections to her lovers.[29] Although a poet of love, she is a 'failure as far as love was concerned' (12). For Goldsmith, Sappho's decision to take her own life is not a dramatic gesture of love for Phaon, but rather is more mundanely motivated by an overwhelming sense of depression. Christina also experiences mental ill-health, described as a kind of modern 'nervous illness' or breakdown, often triggered by an abusive relationship with her mother.[30] And, although a monarch, she does not have a politically distinguished or historically significant career. Goldsmith opens her biography by minimising her importance, stating that 'she accomplished nothing at all' and 'left no impression on her own or any later age' (1–2). Neither Goldsmith nor Sackville-West celebrates her subjects' successes or achievements and in doing so they reject the inherited patriarchal and heteronormative models of history and life writing to redefine the value of a notable life and reconsider the traditionally hagiographic relationship between author and subject.

For Goldsmith this means redefining the nature of historical life writing. In *Christina of Sweden*, Goldsmith refers derisively to 'the writers of history, many of whom think in terms of power and conquests' (2), while in *Sappho* she lays the blame for misrepresentation of Sappho's death squarely at the feet of 'male biographers':

> These historians were all men, and they naturally preferred to believe that, at the close of her life, at least, this great woman found a man necessary to her happiness. [. . .] These historians [. . .] none of whom were apparently experts in the psychology of extra-ordinary women, judged her quite arbitrarily, adjusting their opinions to their prejudices. They never took into account her own point of view, so clearly expressed in every one of her poems. (271–2)

Taking advantage of the fact that there is little concretely known about Sappho, Goldsmith writes what she terms an 'imaginative' biography, using the fragments of Sappho's work to recreate her life and personality (v).[31] Notably, both this biography and that of Christina are positioned as 'psychological biography,' and although Goldsmith does not define this term explicitly, she does claim that 'I have tried to describe Sappho's life as it appears to me, as I myself am convinced that she must have lived it' (v). Rather than claim any sense of authority or objectivity, she acknowledges the subjective nature of her own, and any biographer's, interpretation of other people's lives.

Sackville-West's work also reflects on the inadequacy of facts as the definition of a life. *Aphra Behn* embraces this uncertainty, favouring the imaginative 'broader picture' (11), while *Saint Joan* begins with the admission that '[t]here are many deliberate omissions in this book' (Foreword). In place of an aggressive search for 'truth,' Sackville-West briefly allows herself to speculate. 'I have myself devised at least three theories,' she states in *Aphra Behn*, 'to explain Astrea's [Behn's] morals. All are equally satisfactory, all equally untrustworthy, and the truth probably lies, as usual, in a judicious mix of the lot' (48). But, unlike Goldsmith, Sackville-West refrains from indulging fully in imaginative biography because 'how dangerous [. . .] are these literary exercises! how fatally easy to construct a case, almost any case, by a little adjustment of the data!' (47). It is clear in *Pepita*, Sackville-West's biography of her Spanish grandmother, that she longs to abandon formalised history, to represent the personal, 'a family obscure and even disreputable, in no way connected with historical events or eminent figures.'³² However, she fears the power of invention, the 'comments as I myself could supply only from the depths of my own imagination' (32, 91). In *Pepita* she reports a conversation with her mother in which she explains the absence of a love interest in *Saint Joan*: she reflects that 'my book on St Joan isn't a novel; it is meant to be history. I can't introduce imaginary episodes' (279–80). Despite Sackville-West's experimentation with the genre, she clearly felt some duty to uphold the line between 'history' and 'fiction.'

Although Sackville-West seems hesitant to succumb to the temptations of imagining a life, Goldsmith gives in to them with pleasure. While Goldsmith includes a bibliography of sources in her study of Sappho, the referencing of this material, as in her other work, leaves much to be desired. It is rather telling, then, that Goldsmith includes Pierre Louÿs's *Les Chansons de Bilitis* in her bibliography. Louÿs's 1894 text purported to be the first publication of newly discovered erotic poems by Sappho's contemporary, Bilitis. The publication was ultimately revealed to be a hoax – Bilitis and her poetry were Louÿs's fabrication (though some of the poems attributed to Bilitis were in fact Sappho's), created to titillate a male audience.[33] By 1938, Goldsmith would likely have known this to be fraudulent and yet it still earns a place in her rather limited reference list. This is indicative of the tenor of her biographical writing in general, her willingness to invent scenes and events and to play with the 'truth.' In one instance, Goldsmith describes a conversation between Sappho and her lover Atthis, whose affair with Andromeda has been discovered. She refers to a fragment which Goldsmith claims, but obviously cannot have known, to have been written after that meeting. Sappho derides Andromeda as a woman 'which many may have for the asking' (251). Goldsmith states that all quotations from Sappho's work are taken from J. M. Edmonds's 1922 *Lyra Graeca*. In this instance, Edmonds notes that this line was probably a reference to Charaxus, Sappho's brother, and the courtesan Doricha.[34] Not only does Goldsmith ignore Edmonds's reading but she amends the quotation from 'which any man may have' to 'which many may have' to accommodate women's passionate relationships.[35] This is not to highlight the inaccuracies of Goldsmith's work but to indicate the way that she misrepresents and repurposes Sappho's fragments to suit her own needs. Rather than regurgitate the inherited 'facts,' she instead uses invention to craft her own personal understanding of Sappho. Absolutely central to this act is the rejection of inherited heteronormative narratives and the writing of her subjects' lives as lesbian: she reinscribes lesbian desire and writes her subjects as women who loved, physically and emotionally, other women.

Intimate Lives

While not all of the historical women examined by Goldsmith and Sackville-West are explicitly lesbian, they both chose subjects whose lives were sexually unconventional or non-heteronormative – women who refused marriage entirely, were non-monogamous, who had sex outside of marriage for pleasure, or who refused to adhere to the gender and sexual status quo. However, many of their subjects – Sappho, Christina of Sweden, Marie Antoinette, Joan of Arc – were rumoured to enjoy the love of other women and were already on their way to becoming queer cult figures. Goldsmith was not, then, the first to present these women as lesbian but she does so in a non-sensational way and, as she saw it, without judgement or 'moral prejudice' (*Sappho*, v). She also places their sexual identities as central to the narrative and to our understanding of who they are. 'None of her biographers,' Goldsmith states of Christina, 'venture to discuss the delicate reasons prompting her to remain unmarried' (67). But Goldsmith is unequivocal: 'many contemporary documents, and Christina's own letters, make it quite clear that she was attracted by her own sex' (67). Goldsmith shuts down every attempt to associate Christina with male lovers. In their place emerge a cast of female partners and romantic adventures. There is, amongst others, Ebba Sparre, with whom she has an 'unconventional but thoroughly fine attachment' (71); the Countess de Suze, who behaves like a '*schwärmerisch[es]* schoolgirl' (220); Ninon the Courtesan, with whom she is 'alone [. . .] for many hours' (221); and a young Roman singer who is her 'constant companion' in later life (310). Unlike Christina, who takes time to understand her own identity, Sappho is conscious of, and comfortable with, her desire from an early age. Although Sappho struggles to find fully satisfying love, Goldsmith is at pains to detail the many love affairs that Sappho enjoys, from her first experience as a young adolescent with Chloe the dancing-girl (43) to the 'cool and soothing, and yet stimulating' (219) affairs she embarks on later in her life with women in her Academy.

In contrast, the relationship depicted in *Venus in Scorpio: A Romance of Versailles, 1770–1793*, is not explicitly sexual. This historical romance, co-authored with Goldsmith's friend Katharine Burdekin, charts the relationship between Marie Antoinette and her lady-in-waiting Marie de Lamballe. The novel shares many of the characteristics of Goldsmith's other work. The foreword, for instance, praises psychological rather than moral readings of the Queen and states that, rather than being a 'historical treatise,' this is simply the authors' 'own personal interpretation of her human relationships.'[36] But unlike Goldsmith's other historical work, this text focuses primarily on the emotional and romantic quality of the women's relationship: Marie de Lamballe, put simply, is in love with Marie Antoinette. She spends much of the text playing the part of forlorn lover, fantasising about the Queen and their encounters. Before they even meet, she is drawn to her erotically. As she tells her father-in-law, '"Marie Antoinette is just—Marie Antoinette." She said the name the first time gaily, and the second time in a lower, slower, more caressing voice, as if she liked the sound of it and was loth to let it go' (34). She dreams of Marie Antoinette, of kissing her and being loved by her: 'the dream figure of the young girl ran down the steps of the throne and took Marie's hand and kissed her cheek. It was delicious, that light touch, like a cool leaf, and it filled Marie with extraordinary happiness. "She loves me!"' (40). This is undoubtedly a romance novel, employing the tropes and language of a love story – longing, desire, jealousy, rejection, sorrow, separation, reunion and self-sacrifice. More than this, it is a fantasy of desire (felt if not actualised) between two historical women and, in particular, of the erotic appeal of Marie Antoinette. Terry Castle's fascinating article on the 'Marie Antoinette Obsession' examines the Queen's position as 'a kind of cult figure – the object of a widespread and often curiously eroticized group fixation' as evidenced by nineteenth-century biographical representations.[37] Twentieth-century writers continued to use Marie Antoinette to evoke love between women but they 'affirm rather than obfuscate the sexual nature of her intimacies with women.'[38]

Although Goldsmith and Burdekin acknowledge the scandalous rumours of Marie's relationships with women, her connection with Lamballe is never physical. Given Goldsmith's frankness elsewhere in declaring her subjects' sexualities, I suspect that this can be accounted for by Burdekin's influence.[39] While she frequently wrote about same-sex love in her own novels, she privileged spiritual and emotional connections. Although Lamballe does not fully understand her feelings for the Queen, she is quite clear that she wants nothing to do with heterosexuality: 'I don't want to be in love with a man, I don't want to be touched, I don't want to bear children – I don't want any *of that*. But I do want something. Friendship – love – love of some kind, something to use up the whole of me' (39; emphasis in the original). The 'something' which she cannot quite articulate is, of course, a passionate relationship with another woman. She is treated by a doctor who is, in essence, a modern-day psychoanalyst: they talk of her repression and neurotic fears of stags and imaginary men with forked tongues like snakes, which are crudely symbolic of her fear of male penetration. Although this pathologises Lamballe's longing for women to some extent, one might argue that the pathology here is her repression of this desire rather than the desire itself. The book ends with the Queen's realisation that Lamballe, whom she has treated disgracefully, is in fact her one true love. Of course, by this point it is too late: Lamballe essentially sacrifices herself for Marie Antoinette and is brutally killed by French revolutionaries, as she was in real life. Again, these tropes of self-sacrifice and epiphany are reminiscent of many romance narratives. Even though much of this remains implicit, Marie Antoinette or rather Lamballe's love for her certainly signifies lesbian desire, and while Lamballe's passion for the Queen is never satisfied, her longing for her is nevertheless an erotic fantasy made for their readers – and perhaps their authors – to indulge in.

Sackville-West does not approach the topic of her subjects' sexuality or their desire for other women with as much frankness as Goldsmith, no doubt in part due to Sackville-West's significantly more public social and marital position. *Saint Joan* makes fleeting references to her relationships with women – 'the list of women whose admiration she had gained,' the hostess with whom she shared a bed 'as her hostess later implied, on terms of considerable intimacy' – but these do not evolve into a direct staking out of sexual identity (7, 94). *Saint Joan* is a complicated and perhaps ambivalent portrait of sexuality which does not focus on desire or sex acts but on gendered appearance and masculinity. This is arguably where Goldsmith's and Sackville-West's work aligns most distinctly. Christina, Sappho and Joan are, we are repeatedly told, unattractive, even ugly, women (though they have a hidden beauty or charm apparent on closer acquaintance). What this 'ugliness' entails is unclear (the definition of what is 'attractive' is, of course, subjective), but for Christina and Joan this is inextricably connected to markers of masculinity. The question of Joan's appearance – in terms of both her physicality and dress – preoccupies Sackville-West throughout her biography: what did she really look like; was she attractive; what did she wear; why did she choose to wear men's clothes and so on. She repeatedly emphasises that Joan was not 'pretty' or in possession of 'feminine attractions' (3). She is not, Sackville-West insists at length, attractive to men:

> one of the principal accusations against her was that she adopted men's clothes and fashions; naturally, her apologists and rehabilitators, awkwardly embarrassed by her masculine career, aspired to present her under as feminine an aspect as possible. [. . .] I think it is not unfair to qualify her as unattractive. Men attempted no rape, nor were women jealous. (6)

This biographer is in no way embarrassed by Joan's masculinity: she embraces 'those thick short thighs, those truncated arms' (6). And although this female masculinity becomes equated with unattractiveness, Sackville-West is using this to position her outside of heteronormative standards rather than to deride Joan. Sproles argues that, although Joan is 'a woman dressed as a man, [. . .] her clothing, though necessary to the pursuit of her task, did not alter her identity,' and that the biography 'fails to do more than imagine active femininity as drag – not a third option but simply the masculinization of women.'[40] But I argue that her masculine clothes are not presented as a disguise of her 'real' identity, not simply a necessity, but as a representation of Joan's innate self. The fact that men do not find Joan physically attractive, we are repeatedly told, protects her from sexual violence (although this logic is obviously faulty). If adoption of male dress is unnecessary as a strategy for survival, it emerges as a choice motivated by other needs and desires.[41] Elsewhere, Sackville-West claims that Joan's masculine dress is evidence of 'the practical inconvenience of belonging to the wrong sex' (8).

Giving birth to Joan, her mother had 'hatched an eagle' 'instead of a chicken,' we are told (28). We might read these statements as an acknowledgement of the limitations imposed on a fifteenth-century woman's life – Joan wants more than her gender and social station can provide – but we cannot ignore the familiarity of this phrasing. Given the popularity of sexology in the early twentieth century, with its central tenet of gender and sexual inversion, and Sackville-West's interest in this discourse, we might confidently read Joan's masculinity as a rendition of sexual inversion, a masculine soul within a feminine body. Joan, we are told, possesses a 'queer [. . .] mixture of feminine and masculine attributes,' again indicative of the invert's commingling of the sexes (11). Indeed, this statement seems to echo Sackville-West's understanding of her own sexuality as an example of 'dual personality [. . .] in which the feminine and the masculine elements alternately preponderate.'[42]

Jaime Hovey suggests an alternative interpretation of Joan's masculinity. Hovey rightly argues that Sackville-West is 'both drawn to and perplexed by Joan's dually gendered history': although Sackville-West does, at times, attempt to feminise Joan, Hovey points out that she vacillates between alternately gendered readings, resisting any definition of identity.[43] In Hovey's excellent article, they situate Sackville-West's reading of Joan as part of a larger cultural trend interested in Joan's 'virtuous transmasculinity': 'The production of Joan during The Great War and its aftermath as a figure of what I am calling virtuous transmasculinity offered her gender comportment – gallant chivalry, courage, fortitude, and self-sacrifice – as a noble way of being queer.'[44] In light of this, we might think about Sackville-West's representation of female masculinity, then, as not simply a means of articulating lesbian desire or as indicative of sexual inversion, but rather as an identity position explored in its own right – a form of transmasculinity or identification with masculine gender characteristics.[45] Joan may have loved women, Sackville-West gently implies, but her masculine gender identity exists independently of that. What this indicates is that there are multiple ways to interpret Joan's masculinity and that Sackville-West's slippery and non-committal text allows for plural readings.

Like Sackville-West, Goldsmith repeatedly addresses Christina's appearance and need to present as a man, and like the heroic Joan she is known for her gallantry and masculine charm. When appealing to the Assembly regarding her abdication, she wins their support not on the basis of feminine vulnerability but because of her gallant and proud masculinity:

> And they recognised in her that rare gallantry, which now, despite her illness, caused her to conceal from them that she was feeling ill and miserable, and prevented her from stooping to appeal to them on the grounds that she was not well, and a woman. (123)

Immediately after her abdication, Christina is free to embrace her masculinity, cutting her hair, adopting male clothes and assuming a male pseudonym. The source of this masculinity can be traced not to Christina's inner self but to her upbringing. Christina's parents long for a boy and at her birth she is mistaken for male because her body is covered by a caul. Not to be deterred in his wish, the King reflects that 'he had welcomed this child into the world as a son, and a son she would remain to him' (8). He provides Christina with the life and privileges of a prince (most importantly, a masculine education), and eventually she is crowned King. But, growing up, Christina is made to feel shame (mostly by her mother) both for having been born female and, confusingly, for her inability to perform femininity appropriately. As Christina ages, she feels 'a profound contempt for her own sex,' and increasingly identifies with men while finding the prospect of sexual contact with them repulsive (50). We are told that Christina, '[n]ever forgetful of her father's wishes [. . .] watched and imitated men before she was ten years old' (34). The echoes of Radclyffe Hall's character Stephen Gordon (*The Well of Loneliness*, 1928) resound clearly here and elsewhere in the biography. As Sarah Waters also points out, Goldsmith replicates fundamental aspects of Hall's story: '[o]ver-influential father, distant mother, inappropriate education, boyishness, self-discovery and exile.'[46] 'Christina as Stephen,' Waters continues, is 'an attempt to reopen a space for the articulation of lesbian desire and an implicit protest against its closure.'[47] However, unlike Joan and Stephen, whose masculinity is innate, there is the implication that Christina's gender identity (and, it seems to follow, her lesbianism) is a product of her psychological environment and conditioning (her father's expectations and mother's mistreatment of her, for instance). Goldsmith tells us that 'the words [had not] been invented in which she could have described her inferiority complex at being born a woman, who yet did not feel towards other women as a woman should' (133). Unlike Joan, Christina's masculine gender identity and sexual identity seem to be interdependent and productive of one another. Given that Christina is treated by 'a seventeenth-century psychoanalysis doctor without the Freudian jargon' (133), it is obvious that Goldsmith is presenting Christina through the lens of psychoanalysis. Waters acknowledges that this is problematic because it frames her lesbianism as pathological and 'curable.'[48] However, Waters argues that 'we must acknowledge that it is precisely Goldsmith's construction of her text as a "Psychological Biography" that allows her to extend the implications of her project,' that is, to create a space for lesbian desire.[49] And while this masculinity is not innate, there is no suggestion that Christina should deny that identity. In fact, when she attempts to conform to the expectations of femininity, the result is decidedly strange: 'her rare attempts to dress conventionally were pathetically unsuccessful. The queer mixture of men's and women's clothes, which she wore on such occasions, was commented on, and often cruelly ridiculed' (170). While her masculinity is not necessarily accepted by society, her attempt to feminise that masculine identity is the oddity here.

We can trace this interest in masculinity and gallantry in both Sackville-West's and Goldsmith's non-fiction work on women's experiences of the Second World War. Sackville-West was involved in the administration of the Women's Land Army (WLA) and wrote *The Women's Land Army*, which Glendinning describes as a 'propaganda book' (published for the Ministry of Agriculture and Fisheries) that Sackville-West did not take particularly seriously, in 1944.[50] Nevertheless, this text is intriguing as a continuation of Sackville-West's interest in female gallantry. Notably, while working for her local WLA in 1943, she also began writing *The Eagle and the Dove*, a biography of two saints, Teresa of Ávila and Thérèse of Lisieux. As Glendinning states of this time, '[h]er regular companions, she said, were "saints and landgirls."'[51] And, indeed, *The Women's Land Army* is partly concerned with detailing the courageous and heroic – and perhaps saintly – deeds of the women soldiers. The charm of these women soldiers is not lost on the author, who paints a remarkably romanticised picture:

> One of the prettiest sights I ever saw was four Land-girls sitting on upturned packing-cases under an oast house in the warm September sun. They sat round a huge sea of Orange Pippins, and I don't know which were the rosier – the apples or their cheeks. [. . .] The browns came pale in the wood of the boxes, the wicker of the bushel-baskets, the corduroy breeches, darker in the sunburnt hands moving amongst the fruit, and in the immense Mexican straw hats which for some odd reason two of the girls were wearing, giving them a startlingly foreign appearance in that very English farmyard.[52]

It is worth noting that when she visited the headquarters of the WLA, she observed 'innumerable women all rather reminiscent of Hilda Matheson,' who was, of course, one of Sackville-West's lovers in the 1930s.[53] These masculine and heroic women, in their breeches and 'familiar jerseys, so close-fitting to the young figures' (84), undoubtedly hold an erotic appeal for Sackville-West. Yet, even though this is supposedly propaganda, it is not an entirely glowing assessment of the WLA. In particular, Sackville-West is highly critical of their dishevelled appearance and, intriguingly, their combination of masculine uniform and feminine fashions:

> I have sometimes thought also that if this minority [. . .] could hear the remarks passed upon them behind their backs [. . .] they might pause to consider that uniform properly worn is smart, whereas uniform adapted to the personal whimsy of the wearer looks like nothing but a confused

and unsuccessful fancy-dress. [. . .] Yet they themselves will cheerfully go about in a flowery frock showing under their khaki overcoat, or a magenta jumper combined with dungarees. (42–3)

This criticism is odd given Sackville-West's own 'eccentric' style of dress.[54] Glendinning reports Peter Quennell's assessment of Sackville-West's appearance in 1936 as a strange mix of the feminine and masculine: 'Though she wore long earrings and a small pearl necklace, the end tucked inside a lacy shirt, they were accompanied by a heavy corduroy jacket; while her legs [. . .] were encased in a gamekeeper's breeches and top-boots laced up to the knee.'[55] We might remember here the 'pathetically unsuccessful' combination of men's and women's clothes for which Goldsmith's Christina is mocked (170). Perhaps Sackville-West was in part inspiration for Goldsmith's depiction of the Swedish monarch. Indeed, Goldsmith describes Christina as walking 'in great jerky strides' much as Sackville-West (and her fictional representative, Orlando) was known to do.[56] It is surprising, then, that Sackville-West's assessment of the Land Girls' appearance is not more forgiving. If only the Land Girl would wear her regulation hat appropriately, Sackville-West imagines, then 'she could look as romantic as a cowboy' or 'the once popular [Western film star] Tom Mix' (43). Of course, Sackville-West also enjoyed the erotic frisson of adopting the persona of the male hero – and at times, injured soldier – when she dressed as 'Julian' during her relationship with Violet Trefusis.[57] Sackville-West's criticism of the Land Girl is, essentially, a dislike of the intrusion of femininity onto female masculinity as well as a potentially erotic fantasy of the masculine woman as Western hero.

Sackville-West's book also offers guidance to Land Girls on their future: what are their options when men return and reclaim their jobs? With free passage to the dominions, one possibility is to go abroad:

> I can visualise a new 'Mayflower,' blossoming on every deck with the waving hands of a new sort of pioneer, a sort which would have astonished our Mayflower forefathers whose women were encumbered even more by the convenient prejudices established by man for the control of his subservient woman. My new Mayflower carries a different muster. It carries gay young creatures, untrammelled by bulky clothes; legs are allowed to appear as legs, breeched and gaitered; the soft loose jersey replaces the whale-boned bodice, the elastic belt replaces the rigidity of the unnatural corset. And above all the liberty of the spirit replaces the rigidity of the conventional mind. (162)

As in *Saint Joan*, the Land Girl does not sacrifice her masculine clothes even when she no longer needs to wear them. In contrast, Sackville-West did not have the liberty to wear trousers when she pleased: as late as the mid-1950s Nicolson 'would not allow her to wear her breeches on holiday.'[58] Sackville-West takes pleasure in imagining the masculine woman's appearance, her free legs 'breeched and gaitered,' her 'loose jersey.' This is a fantasy of the masculine woman as free, as a pioneer, sailing off to heroically create a 'new world.' These women, we might surmise, in their rejection of conventionality and embrace of heroic and gallant masculinity, are the future.

Goldsmith's *Women at War* is the more incisive and politically committed exploration of the impact of war on women's lives. While Sackville-West sees no problem, for instance, in women being paid less for the same work as men – 'a man is fully justified in receiving the high wage: he gives better value for his time and money' (166), she claims – Goldsmith's piece unequivocally advocates for equal pay and equal compensation to those women injured in the war effort. More than this, Goldsmith's text is a call to reinvent women's roles in a post-war world, capitalising on gains made and revolutionising their relationship to work and the home. She explores childcare, birth control, and domestic labour-saving devices as ways to free women from the burden of domestic responsibility. And yet this is not simply a vehicle for Goldsmith's political opinions. *Women at War* is also a collection of stories, voices and experiences from a range of women across the social strata.[59] As with Sackville-West's work, Goldsmith focuses on specific tales of women's heroism, which she believes to be under-reported and crucial to a successful outcome in the war. Goldsmith sees these women heroes as encroaching on the territory of men, even replacing them:

> Englishmen are proud of the women, there is no doubt of that, but I sometimes wonder whether, mixed with this pride, there is not in some of the men a feeling of sad regret, for many of them must wonder whether their chivalrousness has not perhaps become a little obsolete.[60]

She would not be the first to recognise that women's gender identity had morphed over the course of the war, although unlike others she celebrates rather than fears this change. Goldsmith understands the revolutionary effect of the war on women's identities and lives, and this text is a call for these heroic and masculine women to force the next stage of their political and social emancipation, to 'have exactly the same opportunities, exactly the same working conditions, exactly the same salaries or wages as their male colleagues' (210).

It is possible that these biographical works also allow Goldsmith and Sackville-West the chance to articulate their own female masculinity. As Janet Beizer has argued with respect to more recent biographical work by women, 'the quest for foremothers [. . .] is personally motivated, [and] becomes a search for the self and its biological maternal origins.'[61] Might Goldsmith and Sackville-West be using historical women to articulate their own identities? Several critics have commented on Sackville-West's use of biographical writing to make sense of her own bisexuality and gender identity.[62] Sproles sees Joan as an object of transference, a fantasy through which Sackville-West tries to reconcile her competing sense of masculinity and femininity.[63] But Sproles believes that Sackville-West fails in this endeavour, that she cannot resolve the ambivalences of Joan's, or her own, identity.[64] Perhaps her treatment of the Land Girls and her disdain for their confused dress, despite the affinities between them, is part of this struggle to understand the self. Sackville-West's research for *Saint Joan* takes her to France, where she quite literally follows in Joan's footsteps, visiting key sites from Joan's story, imagining her thoughts and feelings were she to see the modern French landscape, the very same landscape which Sackville-West faces in the twentieth century. When considering the possibility that Joan may have told the local curé of her visions, she is highly amused by the coincidence of her own contact with the curé of Domremy:

> How queerly life turns out! How impossible that Jeanne [Joan], in spite of all her prescience, could have foreseen that I, trying in 1935 to interpret all the facts of her existence from 1412 to 1428, should receive a visiting-card from the *Curé-Doyen de Domremy-la-Purcelle*. (77)

What we see here is the coming together of Joan and Sackville-West, the mapping of the modern woman onto the historical: they walk the same paths, take in the same views, and have contact with the same religious representatives. Perhaps they are even mystically connected across time; perhaps Joan foresaw Sackville-West's enterprise? This sense of being haunted by the historical woman, and the embrace of this spectral connection across time, is repeated in *Pepita*. Sackville-West calls on Pepita's spirit, almost as if this were a séance: 'Pepita, can I re-create you? Come to me. Make yourself alive again' (32). She often addresses Pepita as if her spirit were in collaboration: 'There was an evening once in Seville, years ago, when your ghost seemed to stand very close behind me, so close almost as to lay a soft hand upon my shoulder' (33). As with Joan, there seems to be an affinity here between Sackville-West and Pepita, though it is not one rooted in female masculinity. Although Pepita is not positioned as a lesbian woman, she is undoubtedly socially and sexually unconventional, an outsider in many ways. And, like her granddaughter, Pepita was 'married' to a diplomat but non-monogamous. Central to this sense of affinity is Pepita's duality as 'half gypsy and half aristocrat' (23). For Sackville-West, this explains her mother's complicated character:

> Although on one side of her lineage she had the opulent Sackvilles aligned behind her, on the other she had all that rapscallion Spanish background,

that chaos of the underworld, tohu-bohu, struggling and scheming and bargaining and even thieving for a living. It was the descendant of all those people [. . .] that her critics expected to behave as an ordinary English lady. (232)

By implication, Sackville-West is also a descendent of both aristocratic and Romani blood, a person pulled in two directions but expected to conform. But, of course, this is a fantastical and romanticised vision. Pepita, dead many years, can easily fulfil this dream, but when Sackville-West is faced with her real Spanish relations at the 1910 trial to determine the inheritance of the familial estate, she is disappointed by the fact that they look 'so like plumbers' (226). Kirstie Blair's article on the significance of the 'gypsy' figure in this period and the way in which they are used to signify desire between women examines Sackville-West's fantasy of her origins. As Blair states in relation to Sackville-West and Trefusis's relationship, 'it is clear that their private elaboration of the gypsy myth provided both lovers with an intense fantasy of escape and a way of referring to an illicit but natural sexuality.'[65] There is no explicit connection in this particular text between the Romani and desire for women but Pepita, and the Spanish Romani heritage she represents, is undoubtedly used by Sackville-West to try to gain an understanding of her difference as well as her mother's uncompromising character.

We lack detailed knowledge of Goldsmith's life or insight into her understanding of her own gender and sexual identity, so we cannot make the same kind of biographical connections. However, Goldsmith does position her historical subjects as inherently modern, sisters to women such as herself. Christina is compared to a suffragette (Goldsmith equates Christina's wearing of men's shoes with the suffragettes' cutting of their hair), modern professional women 'who refuse to forget their work after they have left the office,' a maladjusted 'expatriate' like those found on the Parisian Left Bank, and an English spinster (53, 76, 289). Had she been given the chance, and of course lived in the twentieth century, she might have been a 'brilliant international journalist' or 'become a passionate visitor of peace conferences' (303, 255). Goldsmith is in essence describing herself here: highly educated, expatriate, feminist, professional woman, international journalist and political activist. Goldsmith uses contemporary discourses and models of sexuality to represent historical figures in new and sympathetic ways and position them as recognisable and inherently modern. In mapping herself and other women onto figures such as Christina, Goldsmith also collapses the space between a seventeenth-century queen and the modern woman.

Sackville-West similarly recognises an affinity with her subjects when she acknowledges the difficulty of truly understanding another person and, by implication, herself: 'Pepita is an unfathomable character. But then so are most of us unfathomable characters, even to ourselves' (144). What she admits here is the impossibility of representing the biographical subject as cohesive and stable, and by implication the impossibility of truly defining the self. In this, she is perhaps the writer more obviously affiliated with the modernist New Biographers. Goldsmith, in contrast, relishes her subjects as solid entities. The very fact that these are 'psychological' biographies necessitates Goldsmith's habitation of her subjects' minds, imagining their thoughts, feelings and desires. She claims to know them, presenting their identities, and more specifically their sexualities, with a definitiveness which is absent from Sackville-West's work. But Goldsmith's eagerness to rework inherited narratives and facts liberally is also in line with the methods of modernist biographers such as Strachey. Both Goldsmith and Sackville-West use historical biography to understand the self – and by this I mean the individual self as well as the collective. These historical women are part of a lineage, the matriarchal ancestors of the modern lesbian woman. While Sackville-West struggles to find certainty in this endeavour, Goldsmith does not. Both investigate the lines between truth and imagination, fact and fiction. Goldsmith embraces imaginative life writing and the possibilities this provides for reversing the erasure of women's lives, identities and desires for one another, while Sackville-West explores the nuances of this binary and the representation of women's sexuality with greater trepidation and complexity.

Notes

1. Dates sourced from the National Portrait Gallery. 'Margaret Goldsmith (Margaret Leland) (1894–1971), Writer,' National Portrait Gallery, accessed 21 June 2021, https://www.npg.org.uk/collections/search/person/mp101062/margaret-goldsmith-margaret-leland
2. Quoted in Victoria Glendinning, *Vita: The Life of Vita Sackville-West* (London: Weidenfeld & Nicolson, 1998), 208.
3. Sackville-West, letter dated 29 February 1928, in *The Letters of Vita Sackville-West and Virginia Woolf*, ed. Louise DeSalvo and Mitchell Leaska (San Francisco: Cleis Press, 1985), 258.
4. Quoted in Glendinning, *Vita*, 191.
5. Ibid., 196.
6. Ibid., 213.
7. I am aware of one piece of scholarly work examining Goldsmith's writing, which is Sarah Waters's article, '"A Girton Girl on a Throne": Queen Christina and Versions of Lesbianism, 1906–1933,' *Feminist Review* 46 (Spring 1994): 41–60. See also Elizabeth English, *Lesbian Modernism: Censorship, Sexuality and Genre Fiction* (Edinburgh: Edinburgh University Press, 2015).
8. See 'House and Home,' *The Daily Mail*, 7 August 1924, 6.
9. The deputation was turned away because details of the meeting were reported in the press. See 'British Women Banned: Embassy Refuse Meeting,' *Daily Herald*, 19 July 1935, 9.
10. 'Margaret Goldsmith (Margaret Leland) (1894–1971), Writer,' National Portrait Gallery.

11. Margaret Lawrence, *The School of Femininity: A Book for and about Women as They Are Interpreted Through Feminine Writers of Yesterday and Today* (New York: Frederick A. Stokes, 1936), 274.
12. Margaret Goldsmith published three novels in English: *Karin's Mother* (1928), *Belated Adventure* (1929) and *Venus in Scorpio: A Romance of Versailles, 1770–1793* (1940).
13. See https://www.aviva-verlag.de, accessed 21 June 2021.
14. Edelgard Abenstein, 'Margaret Goldsmith: Patience geht vorüber. Eine Frau zwischen den Stühlen,' Deutschlandfunk Kultur, accessed 21 June 2021, https://www.deutschlandfunkkultur.de/margaret-goldsmith-patience-geht-vorueber-eine-frau.950.de.html?dram:article_id=489973.
15. Karyn Sproles, 'Virginia Woolf Writes to Vita Sackville-West (and Receives a Reply): *Aphra Behn, Orlando, Saint Joan of Arc* and Revolutionary Biography,' in *Virginia Woolf: Texts and Contexts Selected Papers from the Fifth Annual Conference on Virginia Woolf*, ed. Beth Rigel Daugherty and Eileen Barrett (New York: Pace University Press, 1996), 189–93, 190. See also Karyn Sproles, *Desiring Women: The Partnership of Virginia Woolf and Vita Sackville-West* (Toronto: University of Toronto Press, 2006).
16. On the importance of biography in the period and 'new biography,' see, for instance, Ruth Hoberman, *Modernizing Lives: Experiments in English Biography, 1918–1939* (Carbondale and Edwardsville: Southern Illinois University Press, 1987); and Claire Battershill, *Modernist Lives: Biography and Autobiography at Leonard and Virginia Woolf's Hogarth Press* (London: Bloomsbury Press, 2018).
17. Battershill sees a shift not in the biographies themselves but the discussion about the nature of biography. See Battershill, *Modernist Lives*, 67.
18. Juliette Atkinson, *Victorian Biography Reconsidered: A Study of Nineteenth-Century 'Hidden' Lives* (Oxford: Oxford University Press, 2010); Alison Booth, *How to Make a Woman: Collective Biographical History from Victoria to the Present* (Chicago: University of Chicago Press, 2004). Mary Jean Corbett's recent work, *Behind the Times: Virginia Woolf in Late-Victorian Contexts* (Ithaca, NY: Cornell University Press, 2020), also re-examines Woolf's debt to the Victorian period.
19. Booth, *How to Make a Woman*, 229.
20. Battershill, *Modernist Lives*, 87.
21. Melanie Micir, *The Passion Projects: Modernist Women, Intimate Archives, Unfinished Lives* (Princeton, NJ: Princeton University Press, 2019), 8–9.
22. Ibid., 3.
23. Other than that on Woolf and Sackville-West, there seems to be little work on lesbian modernist biography. Georgia Johnston's 2007 study examines queer modernist autobiography, and Micir obviously turns her attention to queer biographical 'passion projects.' However, I am not aware of any critical work on what we could call lesbian modernist historical biography. See Micir, *Passion Projects*; and Georgia Johnston, *The Formation of 20th Century Queer Autobiography: Reading Vita Sackville-West, Virginia Woolf, Hilda Doolittle, and Gertrude Stein* (New York: Palgrave Macmillan, 2016).
24. On female masculinity, see Jack Halberstam, *Female Masculinity* (Durham, NC: Duke University Press, 1998).

25. Johnston and Micir both comment on the heteronormative pattern of biography. See Johnston, *Formation*, 10–11; Micir, *Passion Projects*, 114.
26. Hoberman comments on the ways New Biographers embraced their subjects as failures. See Hoberman, *Modernizing Lives*, xii–xiii.
27. Vita Sackville-West, *Aphra Behn: The Incomparable Astrea* (London: Gerald Howe, 1927), 72. Subsequent references will cite page numbers in-text.
28. Vita Sackville-West, *Saint Joan of Arc* (London: Sphere Books, [1936] 1990), 143. Subsequent references will cite page numbers in-text.
29. Margaret Goldsmith, *Sappho of Lesbos: A Psychological Reconstruction of Her Life* (London: Rich & Cowan, 1938), 124. Subsequent references will cite page numbers in-text.
30. Margaret Goldsmith, *Christina of Sweden: A Psychological Biography* (London: Arthur Barker, 1933), 57. Subsequent references will cite page numbers in-text.
31. On the lesbian modernist fascination with Sappho, see, for instance, Diana Collecott, *H.D. and Sapphic Modernism 1910–1950* (Cambridge: Cambridge University Press, 1999).
32. Vita Sackville-West, *Pepita* (London: Virago, [1937] 1991), 14. Subsequent references will cite page numbers in-text.
33. On Louÿs's hoax, see Tama Lea Engelking, 'Translating the Lesbian Writing: Pierre Louÿs, Natalie Barney, and "Girls of the Future Society,"' *South Central Review* 22, no. 3 (Fall 2005): 62–77.
34. J. M. Edmonds, *Lyra Graeca: Being the Remains of All the Greek Lyric Poets from Eumelus to Timotheus Exception Pinda: Vol. I* (Cambridge, MA: Harvard University Press, [1922] 1952), 251.
35. Ibid.
36. Margaret Goldsmith and Murray Constantine [Katharine Burdekin], *Venus in Scorpio: A Romance of Versailles, 1770–1793* (London: John Lane The Bodley Head, 1940), 10. Subsequent references will cite page numbers in-text.
37. Terry Castle, 'Marie Antoinette Obsession,' *Representations* 38 (Spring 1992): 1–38, 14.
38. Ibid., 25.
39. It is hard to judge the distribution of labour on this project. Daphne Patai notes that Goldsmith gave Burdekin 'the extensive research notes she had been accumulating on Marie Antoinette' when Burdekin was experiencing a period of depression, and Burdekin 'wrote up the material.' Daphne Patai, 'Afterword,' in Katharine Burdekin, *The End of This Day's Business* (New York: The Feminist Press, 1989), 166.
40. Karyn Z. Sproles, 'Cross-Dressing for (Imaginary) Battle: Vita Sackville-West's Biography of Joan of Arc,' *Biography* 19, no. 2 (Spring 1996): 158–77, 159, 174.
41. Admittedly, the text contradicts itself. In another instance, while trying to grapple with Joan's rationale for continuing to wear men's clothes after her imprisonment, Sackville-West acknowledges that '[o]ne can understand her adoption of men's clothes as a reasonable and indeed necessary precaution for the preservation of her virginity' (303).
42. Quoted in Nigel Nicolson, *Portrait of a Marriage: Vita Sackville-West and Harold Nicolson* (New York: Atheneum, 1973), 106.

43. Jaime E. Hovey, 'Gallantry and Its Discontents: Joan of Arc and Virtuous Transmasculinity in Radclyffe Hall and Vita Sackville-West,' *Feminist Modernist Studies* 1, no. 1–2 (2018): 113–37, 132.
44. Ibid., 114. On the way that Joan served as an example of female masculinity in this period, see also Steven Macnamara, 'Joan of Arc and Radclyffe Hall: Martyrdom and Masculinity,' in *Reimagining Masculinities: Beyond Masculinist Epistemology*, ed. Frank K. Karioisis and Cassandra Loeser (Oxford: Inter-Disciplinary Press, 2014).
45. Chris Coffman offers a useful definition of transmasculinity: 'By "transmasculinity," I refer to a broad range of masculine traits in persons assigned female at birth. My choice of terminology encompasses not only those who embody what Halberstam calls "female masculinity" but also those who consider themselves transgender or transsexual. Moreover, it includes those who understood their masculinity in relation to earlier constructs of gender variance (such as late nineteenth- and early twentieth-century "inverts") or who fashioned their own style of masculinity outside of any official discourses.' Chris Coffman, *Gertrude Stein's Transmasculinity* (Edinburgh: Edinburgh University Press, 2018), 2.
46. Waters, 'Girton Girl,' 57.
47. Ibid.
48. Ibid.
49. Ibid.
50. Glendinning, *Vita*, 302, 325.
51. Ibid., 322.
52. Vita Sackville-West, *The Women's Land Army* (London: Unicorn Publishing Group, [1944] 2016), 84. Subsequent references will cite page numbers in-text.
53. Quoted in Glendinning, *Vita*, 325.
54. Ibid., 273.
55. Quoted in ibid., 286.
56. Ibid., 143.
57. Hovey, 'Gallantry,' 130. Glendinning also mentions that Sackville-West took on the male persona of 'David' with her lovers. Glendinning, *Vita*, 196.
58. Glendinning, *Vita*, 381.
59. This is not to idealise Goldsmith's politics. She does not go so far as to say that women might forgo marriage and children altogether and agrees that women should be encouraged to improve the birth rate. Her wish is to address the conditions under which women are expected to fulfil this role.
60. Margaret Goldsmith, *Women at War* (London: Lindsay Drummond, 1943), 127. Subsequent references will cite page numbers in-text.
61. Janet Beizer, *Thinking Through the Mothers: Reimagining Women's Biographies* (Ithaca, NY: Cornell University Press, 2008), 2–3.
62. See, for instance, Sproles, 'Cross-Dressing,' and Hovey, 'Gallantry.'
63. Sproles, 'Cross-Dressing,' 159.
64. Ibid., 161.
65. Kirstie Blair, 'Gypsies and Lesbian Desire: Vita Sackville-West, Violet Trefussis, and Virginia Woolf,' *Twentieth Century Literature* 50, no. 2 (2004): 141–66, 150.

5

MODERNISM AT THE MARGINS: MARIETTE LYDIS'S PRINT PORTFOLIO *LESBIENNES*

Abbey Rees-Hales

On ne peut oublier Mariette Lydis une fois qu'on l'a vue, et bien moins, quand on s'est mis à aimer cet art amer et voluptueux, tendre et cruel, viril et féminin.

[You cannot forget Mariette Lydis once you have seen her, and much less, when you have come to love this bitter and voluptuous, tender and cruel, virile and feminine art.]

– Lucienne Florentin, 1930[1]

Heavily vignetted to the point of obscurity, the image of a woman's torso, as viewed from behind, emerges out of a shadowy background (Figure 5.1). Reminiscent of a fragment of antique statuary, this truncated form is in fact the subject of a black and white photographic reproduction of an original hand-coloured etching (Figure 5.2) by the Austrian painter and illustrator Mariette Lydis (1887–1970). Fêted in her lifetime as a 'great artist, with the fatal lyricism of Sappho,' the now largely forgotten Lydis unequivocally and unapologetically articulated lesbian intimacy and desire in a large body of paintings, drawings and prints that she produced in Paris between 1926 and 1939, the year that she, a bisexual woman of Jewish heritage, fled mainland Europe.[2] Far from reticent when it came to visualising female same-sex intimacy, Lydis defiantly depicted women as desirable and desiring Sapphic subjects. Yet one gets little sense of Lydis's artistic audacity from this strangely censorial reproduction of her original lesboerotic etching.[3]

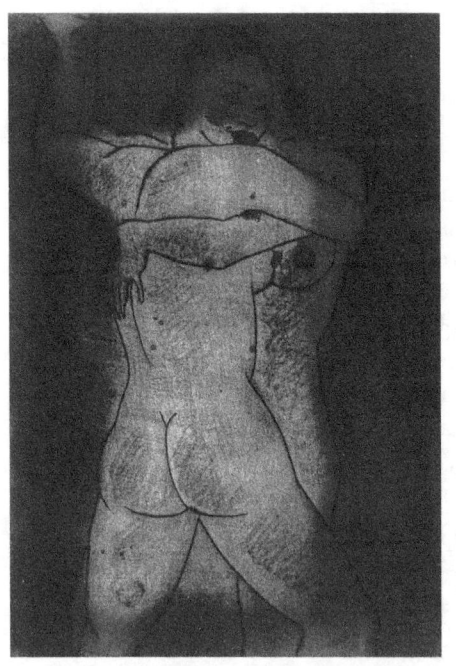

Figure 5.1 Marc Vaux, Black and white photographic reproduction of hand-coloured etching from Mariette Lydis's *Lesbiennes* portfolio (1926), date of photograph unknown. Scan of original glass plate negative: © Centre Pompidou – MNAM/CCI – Bibliothèque Kandinsky – Fonds Marc Vaux

Figure 5.2 Mariette Lydis, Untitled print from *Lesbiennes* [Lesbians], 1926. Hand-coloured etching, print size: 15 × 11 cm. Private collection; image courtesy of honesterotica.com

One of a series of 375 photographs of Lydis's work captured by the Parisian photographer Marc Vaux (1895–1971) during the 1920s and 1930s, the darkness and indistinctness of this particular image is entirely at odds with Vaux's customary technique for faithfully translating graphic images into photographic ones.[4] Lydis's original hand-coloured print, one of the twenty-five signed and unbound etchings comprising her deluxe print portfolio *Lesbiennes* [Lesbians] (1926) (Figures 5.2–5.4), had focused upon a dancing female couple, their naked bodies locked in a close embrace. The viewer of Vaux's black and white photographic reproduction could be forgiven for missing such lesboerotic content. Rather than focusing the viewer's attention upon the actual subject of Lydis's intaglio print – the lesbian couple – the extreme vignetting serves to transform the subject of the image altogether.

Entirely effacing the secondary female from the image, as well as the background dancing couples, the lesbian is, to quote Terry Castle on the subject of the apparitional lesbian, relegated to a 'recessive, indeterminate, misted-over space,' simultaneously there but not there.[5] This apparitional lesbian instead resides, as Castle muses, 'somewhere else: in the shadows, in the margins, hidden from history, out of sight, out of mind, a wanderer in the dusk.'[6] If, as Teresa de Lauretis asserts, 'it takes two women, not one, to make a lesbian,'

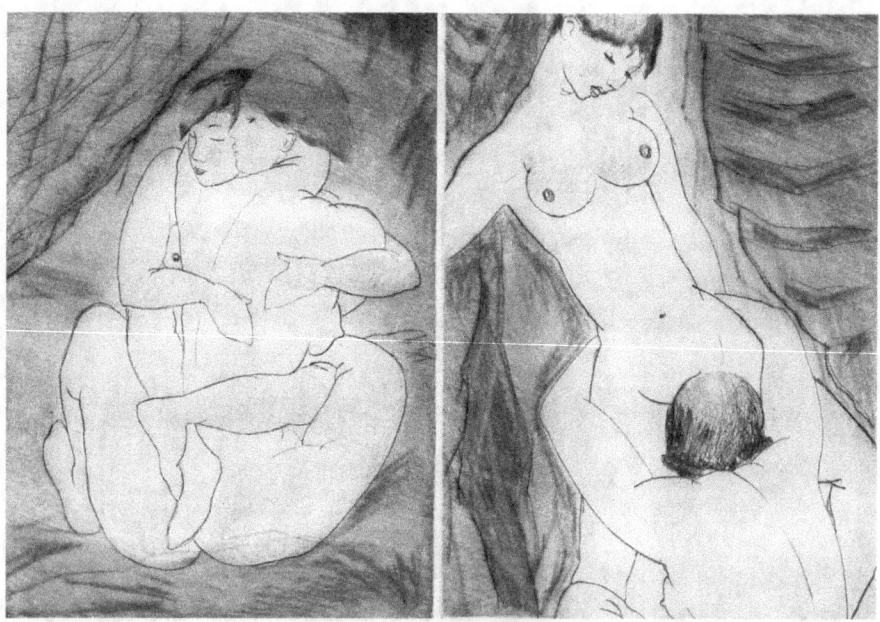

Figure 5.3 Mariette Lydis, Two untitled prints from *Lesbiennes* [Lesbians], 1926. Hand-coloured etchings on paper, each print measures: 15 x 11 cm. Private collection; image courtesy of honesterotica.com

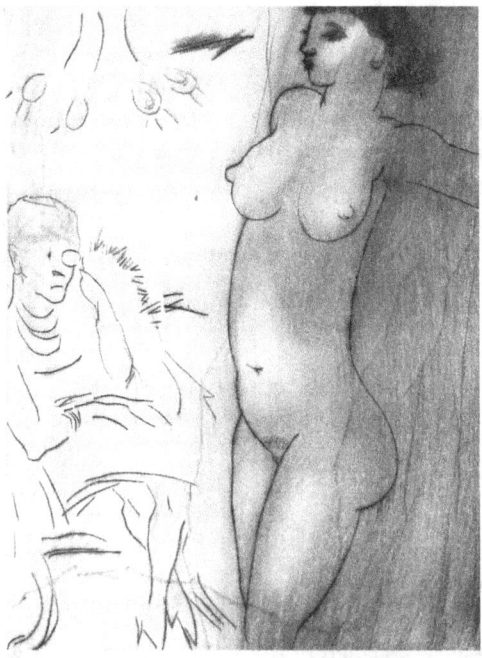

Figure 5.4 Mariette Lydis, Untitled print from *Lesbiennes* [Lesbians], 1926. Hand-coloured etching, print size: 15 × 11 cm. Private collection; image courtesy of honesterotica.com

then Vaux's obfuscatory technique serves to remove the lesbian from the photographic picture, just as Lydis and her Sapphic subjects have been removed from the art historical one.[7] Shrouded in obscurity and presenting a misleading impression of Lydis's work, Vaux's shadowy image serves as a symbol for Lydis's reputation today, a reputation entirely at odds with the fame and critical acclaim that she once enjoyed.

Reflecting in 1931 upon Lydis's meteoric rise to fame in the French capital, the Danish novelist and journalist Karin Michaëlis remarked that the artist's star had 'soared with a force that we normally only experience when it comes to singers, film heroes or actors.'[8] This was an artist who was photographed by Germaine Krull (c. 1926), Man Ray (1929) and Laure Albin-Guillot (c. 1930). She was also painted by the British artist Gluck (Hannah Gluckstein), commemorated in a poem by the Belgian-American lesbian poet May Sarton, and celebrated in a laudatory essay by Colette.[9] Images by and images of Lydis graced avant-garde periodicals, mass-market magazines, feminist weeklies, soft-pornographic pamphlets and connoisseurial journals in France, Austria, Germany and the United Kingdom alike. Her art was purchased by the Italian and French states, and displayed in such hallowed institutions as the Uffizi, the Salon d'Automne, the

Galerie Bernheim-Jeune and that transatlantic temple of modernism, the Museum of Modern Art (MoMA).[10] Her works were even included in the first international exhibition dedicated to the work of women artists, *Les femmes artistes d'Europe* at the Jeu de Paume (1937), where they were displayed alongside paintings by Tamara de Lempicka, Marie Laurencin, Vanessa Bell and Romaine Brooks, amongst others.[11]

Lydis won extensive praise from those notoriously sceptical about the abilities and alleged sensibilities of the female artist. The influential French art critic Louis Vauxcelles – best remembered for naming those quintessential modernist *isms*, Cubism and Fauvism – praised her as 'one of the authentic artists of today.'[12] Her art, he wrote in 1926, bore 'no trace of female assimilation.'[13] Writing in the British journal *Artwork* two years later, Thyra Clark echoed such comments whilst ramping up the gendered rhetoric:

> More than one lyrical critic [...] hailed Mariette Lydis as an angel, whilst others would burn her as a witch. Whichever she be, she is certainly a rare thing in art; a woman painter who follows no one, with much to say that is really worth saying.[14]

If Vauxcelles and Clark lavished praise upon Lydis, then it was couched in disparagingly gendered terms, casting doubt upon women's capacity for original thought and technical mastery. Setting her apart from her female peers, critics would routinely other Lydis as the exceptional woman. Michaëlis might have been inflating Lydis's fame when she asserted that her name was known to 'every artist, every art historian, every journalist' in her adopted country of France.[15] Nevertheless, Michaëlis's comments hint at the extent of Lydis's former renown. Today, however, Lydis's sonorous name has been almost entirely erased from the art historical record. Her works now gather dust in museum storage racks and rare book departments, largely passed over by curators and art historians.[16]

In feminist art historical scholarship, it has become something of a truism to observe how influential accounts of modernism as promoted from the late 1930s onwards by the likes of the Museum of Modern Art's founding director, Alfred Barr, and the American art critic Clement Greenberg have largely left women outside of their decidedly formalist frame.[17] Feminist art historians have long since sought to redress this masculinist conceptualisation of modernism. Yet with avant-garde art having 'become the official art of our time,' it is little wonder that a privileging of the more formally experimental, abstract end of the modernist spectrum is apparent in much of this recuperative work. This tendency has made its presence felt in which female artists have been salvaged from obscurity and selected as the subject of major exhibitions and monographs (Hannah Höch, Anni Albers and Sonia

Delaunay, amongst others), and which ones continue to be relegated to it.[18] However, one only needs to peruse the art historical studies of Paula Birnbaum, Bridget Elliot and Gill Perry and, if we extend our geographical focus slightly eastwards, Marsha Meskimmon and Sabine Plakolm-Forsthuber, to grasp just how many female artists during the 'heyday of modernism' missed 'the avant-garde boat,' or point-blank refused to embark the vessel.[19] Such women as Lydis, Lene Schneider-Kainer and Gertrude Sandmann, amongst countless others who worked in the figurative tradition, may have embraced modernity in terms of the subjects that they depicted, subjects that included the modern lesbian nude.[20] Yet in rejecting the more explicitly experimental tendencies now synonymous with art of the modernist period (pure abstraction, the flattening of three-dimensional space, the use of geometric forms, collage, photomontage), they have proved to be simply 'not modern enough' for art historical posterity.[21]

Whilst Greenberg's modernist artist (characteristically gendered male) turned 'his attention away from subject matter of common experience' and towards 'the medium of his own craft,' Lydis failed to satisfy such disciplinary purity in actively turning her attention towards the 'subject matter of common experience.'[22] Or more specifically, towards common lesbian experience, as my examination of her *Lesbiennes* folio will demonstrate. Moreover, as Greenberg was defining avant-garde art in opposition to the kitsch, Lydis was veering all too closely towards the latter for modernist approbation.[23] If Lydis's sex, coupled with her émigré status, was not enough to see her written out of history even within her own lifetime, then the kitschy 'excesses' of her work from the late 1930s onwards, which include a wealth of strangely sinister and saccharine portraits of doe-eyed children and a highly camp reworking (Figure 5.5) of the Fontainebleau school painting *Gabrielle d'Estrées et une de ses sœurs* (c. 1595; Louvre), have guaranteed that she continues to reside in the art historical wilderness. Presenting a veritable affront to modernist purity and restraint, Lydis's work of the late 1930s onwards has lamentably overshadowed the strident lesbian modernity of her early Parisian artworks.

In recent decades, scholars in the field of lesbian modernist studies have sought to expand our understanding of modernism to include works that do not conform to the formal experimentation synonymous with modernism, an objective shared by many of the contributors to this present volume. Despite the stylistically plural vision of lesbian modernism that has emerged, lesbian modernist scholarship (like modernist studies more generally) has remained focused upon literature and moreover, anglophone literature. Regrettably, the visual arts have received limited attention from a self-avowedly lesbian modernist perspective, the work of Bridget Elliott, Whitney Chadwick and Tirza True Latimer providing notable exceptions. Perhaps the greatest beneficiary of the all too infrequent intersection of feminist art history and lesbian modernist

Figure 5.5 Mariette Lydis, Untitled, 1937. Oil on canvas, size and current whereabouts of the original painting unknown. Scan of original glass plate negative: © Centre Pompidou – MNAM/CCI – Bibliothèque Kandinsky – Fonds Marc Vaux, photograph: Marc Vaux

studies has been the American-born painter Romaine Brooks.[24] Creating 'the all-time ultimate gallery of all the famous dykes from 1889 to 1935,' as Truman Capote reportedly quipped, it is perhaps not surprising then that Natalie Clifford Barney's long-term partner has undoubtedly been admitted to the pantheon of lesbian modernism.[25] Yet as Jo Winning cautions, lesbian modernism should strive to avoid instilling 'its own reductions and exclusions.'[26] It is, Winning contends, 'simply not possible to incorporate women into a kind of lesbian 'inner circle' on the grounds of their avowed sexual identities, or to exclude them from it.'[27] Such a lesbian modernist 'inner circle' does exist in literary and art historical scholarship, and despite the absolute centrality of female same-sex desire to Lydis's art of the interwar period, there has been no place in this privileged coterie for the artist once branded 'the Archangel of Perversity.'[28] If we accept Shari Benstock's assertion that lesbian modernism 'wore many necessary and elaborate disguises,' be it the neo-Decadence of Brooks or the Sapphic Surrealism of Claude Cahun, then, I believe, there should be room at the *invert* inn for Lydis.[29]

Bringing Lydis out of the shadows, this chapter seeks to redress the erasure of Lydis and her lesbian modernist legacy. Given her obscurity in the anglophone world, this chapter proceeds with a biographical overview before turning to an examination of *Lesbiennes*, Lydis's suite of etchings depicting naked women engaging in an array of lesbian sexual acts. With only two copies of *Lesbiennes* known to survive to this day, both of which are incomplete and secreted away in private collections, it is perhaps not surprising that this elusive portfolio has, until now, been entirely overlooked by academics.[30] As with Vaux's obfuscatory reproduction, we can only glimpse a partial image of Lydis's earliest-known suite of lesbian images. Influenced by lesbian modernism's pluralising turn, this chapter seeks to re-establish Lydis as a notable contributor to an interwar lesbian aesthetic that was resolutely modern, if not categorically modernist in the formalist sense.

In Transit and Transition

Whilst notoriously reluctant to reveal biographical information, Lydis was born as Marietta Ronsperger in the Austrian spa town of Baden bei Wien in 1887 into an affluent and highly cultured Jewish family.[31] Little is known of her until 1910 when she formally converted to Catholicism; her faith provided inspiration for the many religious works that she would produce from the mid-1920s onwards, whereby depictions of the Virgin Mary (Figure 5.6) sit alongside sexualised renderings of lesbian women. That same year she married the first of three husbands: the Viennese manufacturer Julius Koloman Pachhofer-Karny.[32] It was during the First World War that she first displayed her work in public in an exhibition at Emmy Zweybrück-Prochaska's applied art school in Vienna in 1915, though it seems surprising that the adult artist, who would later boast of being self-taught, should have enrolled at Zweybrück-Prochaska's school for teenage girls.[33] Amongst Lydis's surviving artworks from the war years are a series of whimsical oval-shaped watercolours. The series, which includes *La Pudeur* [Modesty] (Figure 5.7), a cartoonish depiction of three naked bathers aghast at the discovery of a camera hidden in the nearby bushes, hints at the preoccupation with the naked female form that would come to define her works of the 1920s and 1930s.

Lydis largely disappears from view until January 1921 when she re-emerges in an elegant studio photograph by the fashionable Viennese photographer Madame D'Ora (Dora Kallmus) (Figure 5.8). Mistakenly identified as Frau Bachhofen – seemingly a corruption of the name Pachhofer – the true identity of the elusive figure peeking out from beneath a brimmed hat is concealed, just as her lesbian legacy has likewise been concealed. Lydis's self-fashioning harnesses the tensions involved in the performance of female masculinity during the interwar period. Her modish attire in masculine equestrian garb can variously be interpreted as a Sapphic sartorial code, an expression of her class and

Figure 5.6 Mariette Lydis, Untitled (Virgin Mary holding the Holy Shroud), 1926. Gouache and graphite, size and whereabouts of the original artwork unknown. Scan of original glass plate negative: © Centre Pompidou – MNAM/ CCI – Bibliothèque Kandinsky – Fonds Marc Vaux, photograph: Marc Vaux

Figure 5.7 Mariette Lydis, *La Pudeur* [Modesty], c. 1915. Watercolour and ink on paper. Private collection

Figure 5.8 Madame D'Ora, *Frau Bachhofen mit Reitkleid* [Mrs Bachhofen in riding dress] (Portrait of Mariette Lydis), 1921. Scan of original glass-plate negative, 18 x 24 cm. Vienna, Österreichische Nationalbibliothek

social status, or a declaration of her position as the adventurous, self-assured New Woman.[34]

Demonstrating Chadwick and Latimer's assertion that the New Woman was 'a figure in transit and transition' who 'travelled unescorted, distancing herself from her national and/or familial points of origin' to relocate to places anew, Lydis left Pachhofer-Karny and relocated to the outskirts of Athens in the early 1920s.[35] In 1922, she married the Greek millionaire Jean Lydis, and although she would wed for a third and final time, marrying the aristocratic Italian art publisher and Gabriele D'Annunzio acolyte Count Giuseppe Govone (1885–1948), she retained the name Lydis for professional purposes.[36] Lydis may have married three times but it was women who would inspire and inflame her imagination, for as she once remarked, 'every woman is interesting.'[37]

Looking back upon Lydis's time in Greece, Michaëlis sardonically cast Lydis as the bored bourgeois wife who began 'fiddling with chalk and paint, probably more like women play with handicrafts to find an easy pastime.'[38] A sarcastic riposte to the misogynistic cliché of the bourgeois female amateur artist – a cliché which found visual form in Kees van Dongen's oil on canvas painting

Passe-temps honnête [An Honest Pastime] (c. 1920) – Michaëlis's tongue-in-cheek portrait of Lydis is entirely at odds with the image of the masculine emancipated woman constructed by D'Ora. Moreover, it is entirely at odds with the alleged portrait of Lydis that the Austrian bisexual author Grete von Urbanitzky crafts in her New Woman novel *Die goldene Peitsche* [The Golden Whip] (1922), where she appears in the guise of the painter Karla Jarl.[39] Described in the novel as a 'sinner' who worships 'at the altar of the mighty Eros,' Urbanitzky's transgressive modern artist struggles to reconcile a heterosexual relationship with her blossoming artistic career.[40] Heterosexual relationships do not concern Alexandra Pseleuditi, the emancipated female artist in Urbanitzky's *Der wilde Garten* [The Wild Garden] (1927), the first-known Austrian novel to address lesbian desire.[41] Described as 'famous, independent, excessively proud and of a wild, peculiar beauty,' Pseleuditi – a seductive lesbian sculptor who hails from Greece and who eventually escapes to the equally Sapphically coded environs of Paris – bears more than a passing resemblance to Lydis, the one-time Athenian denizen.[42] Lydis's rumoured friendship with Urbanitzky, and the influence that she appears to have exerted upon the latter's artist characters, might suggest Lydis's involvement in Sapphic circles in her home city. Unlike the hard evidence that survives documenting Lydis's three marriages and heterosexual liaisons, evidence pertaining to her intimate relationships with women, including Gluck and the British poet and publisher Erica Marx, is regrettably, and perhaps all too inevitably, elusive and anecdotal.[43] Accepting such absence, ambiguity and uncertainty is necessary when researching lesser-known figures on the 'lesbian continuum,' women whose personal correspondence is less likely to have survived and been afforded the honour of an archival afterlife.[44]

Echoing the plot of *Die goldene Peitsche*, within a year of its publication Lydis's second marriage had broken down. She relocated to a palatial villa on the outskirts of Florence and spent the next few years residing in Italy or travelling in Europe, Turkey and Morocco, as documented in her sketches of the period.[45] It was then that she began pursuing seriously an artistic career, producing orientalist illustrations for a number of limited-edition books, including a sacrilegious translation of the Qur'an.[46] Having garnered 'polite words of praise' for these early illustrative undertakings, Lydis, as Michaëlis noted, 'tasted blood' and like so many artists before her set her stall upon moving to Paris to become 'a "real" painter.'[47]

Paris-Lesbienne

Seeking Sappho in Lesbos was a futile task, the journalist Maryse Choisy cautioned in the French satirical magazine *Le Rire* [Laughter] in 1932. Sappho, she proclaimed, 'is an artist. So, she moved to Paris.'[48] Fusing ancient and modern, Choisy positioned the original lesbian poet as having found – like so many female artists, poets and novelists – her spiritual home in the French capital with its renowned transnational artistic and literary communities, fabled nocturnal indulgences, and its celebrated lesbian circles. Like Choisy's modern Sappho and Urbanitzky's Sapphic sculptor, Lydis was drawn to the artistic opportunities and, one might speculate, to the putative sexual freedoms that the city promised. 'I knew I had to live in Paris,' Lydis later reflected; 'I had to experience the atmosphere of this unique city.'[49]

Relocating to the French capital in 1926, Lydis set about relaunching herself and her artistic career for the competitive Parisian modern art market. Her decision to inhabit, however briefly, the city's fabled Left Bank, and exhibit in the cosmopolitan artists' colony of Montparnasse, suggests a desire to keep abreast of the latest developments in the city's vibrant art scene.[50] Turning her back on the richly hued orientalist illustrations that had defined her works of the early 1920s, Lydis now replaced her early interest in exoticism with a fixation upon what the French author Henry de Montherlant branded 'rare vices,' taking as her subjects '[p]rostitutes, lesbians, criminals, young girls who have just discovered their bodies, and abuse their discovery.'[51] Lydis announced this change of direction by not only producing but also self-publishing her first of many lesbian-themed works: the print portfolio *Lesbiennes* (Figures 5.2–5.4).

Published in an edition of just seventy-seven signed and numbered copies, *Lesbiennes* presents Lydis's emphatically modern response to the professional and personal opportunities presented by the French capital. By the time that Lydis unveiled her portfolio of twenty-five erotic etchings in 1926, modernism had long since rendered academic history paintings, that veritable excuse for the depiction of copious amounts of bare female flesh, as distinctly *arrière-garde*. Yet the time-(dis)honoured belief that 'the wellsprings of authentic art are fed by the streams of male libidinous energy' ensured that the central place occupied by the female nude in Western art remained largely uncontested during the era of modernism.[52] Regardless of their aesthetic or their avowed justification, the genre of the female nude continued to present the primary vehicle in which artists, whether of the *avant-garde*, *juste milieu* or *arrière-garde*, could assert their 'mastery' over women's bodies and likewise their professional standing. For proof of this, one need only look to the nudes produced by Lydis's Parisian contemporaries Van Dongen, Jules Pascin, Moïse Kisling and Foujita, or the veritable subgenre of portraits and self-portraits depicting male artists clutching the phallic tools of their craft whilst their nameless female models hover behind.[53] For women artists, such as Lydis, wanting to compete on the same playing field as their male peers – even if that field was anything but a level one – they needed to *master* the female nude.[54] With the genre built upon heterosexual power play and the commodification and subjugation of women's bodies, for the female artist and particularly for the doubly deviant female artist who possessed talent and desire deemed unnatural for her sex, the female nude represented something distinctly different.

Rather than chronicling the multi-faceted realities of lesbian life, *Lesbiennes* offers a series of autonomous 'snapshots' of female same-sex sexual practices. The etchings range from tender depictions of women dancing (Figure 5.2) and embracing (Figure 5.3, left), to explicit renderings of mutual masturbation, cunnilingus (Figure 5.3, right), group sex and lesbian prostitution (Figure 5.4). Eliminating an obvious narrative and rejecting sexological taxonomies, as will be discussed further, *Lesbiennes* implies that the lesbian needs no justification or explanation for her existence. In portraying sexually explicit subjects and not shying away from showing female genitalia, Lydis's suite of etchings highlights just how porous the boundaries can be between art, erotica and pornography, evidencing Lynda Nead's belief that the female nude is an artistic genre central to Western art but also one which 'risks losing its respectability and spilling out and over into the pornographic.'[55] Flirting with the obscene and the pornographic can also be seen as something of a modernist hallmark, as Allison Pease, Rachel Potter and Chris Forster have all shown, albeit with reference to text rather than image.[56] If, as Forster contends, 'nothing better captures modernism's power to upset convention and tradition than obscenity,' then should we interpret Lydis's engagement with explicit Sapphic subject matter as not simply a modernist act but a defiantly lesbian modernist one?[57] Moreover, in producing and self-publishing sexually explicit lesbian material, Lydis can be seen to have challenged assumptions regarding the abilities and sensibilities of the so-called fairer sex, sequestering privileges that had formerly been the preserve of the male artist and publisher. In depicting the female nude in such an unapologetically sexual manner, Lydis *inverted* that pugnacious association of artistic creativity with untrammelled male (hetero)sexual libido, as embodied in Renoir's apocryphal assertion, 'I paint with my prick.'[58] Lydis, as Joseph Delteil proclaimed in 1927, 'paints with her breasts. Mariette Lydis is painting made sex.'[59]

Characterised by a sober, matter-of-fact quality, redolent of German *Neue Sachlichkeit* [New Objectivity] art, Lydis's technical approach rebuts pervasive early twentieth-century assumptions of a distinctly feminine style that was whimsical, graceful, decorative and derivative.[60] For the Austrian art historian Hans Ankwicz-Kleehoven, Lydis's apparent masculinity – a quality which he, drawing upon the work of his compatriot Otto Weininger, deemed a prerequisite for women's creativity – was not borne out in her 'fine, ethereal face' but in 'the masculine attitude with which she confronts things.'[61] This allegedly masculine attitude manifested itself in her choice of subject matter, as well as in her technique, as Montherlant would likewise note.[62] Rendered without idealisation, the female body is pared by Lydis to its essential outlines, crisply delineated with a velvety-black etched line. Translucent washes of intense magenta ink are sparingly applied to suggest the fullness of breasts and abdomens, as well as to draw attention to erogenous zones. Lydis left a hazy veil of black ink on selected areas of the plate surface, so that the naked female form looms out from the shadowy, nebulous backgrounds. There is only one instance where she locates the figures in any kind of discernible setting, the etching which depicts a claustrophobic curtained interior, a space that I contend represents a Parisian *maison close* [state-regulated brothel] (Figure 5.4).

The aforementioned print sees a young woman, coded as a prostitute, presenting her voluptuous nude body for the scrutiny of an older bourgeois woman. Older women had for centuries figured in prostitution scenes as brothel madams, yet to assume that Lydis's etching could only depict a scene between a madam and one of her workers would be to close one's eyes to the image's queer potential and to impose a heteronormative reading of an image which is anything but. Breaking with artistic convention, Lydis depicts the older woman as purchaser of sex, scrutinising the 'goods' on offer – surely a more fitting subject for a portfolio entitled *Lesbiennes*. In doing so, Lydis alludes to Paris's reputation for what the German lesbian writer Ruth Margarete Roellig (best remembered for authoring the first-known lesbian travel guide) described in 1930 as a centre for 'tribadic Prostitution.'[63] Lydis's inclusion of the bourgeois female not only corresponds with contemporaneous sexological understandings of the class of women patronising Parisian brothels but also suggests that same-sex relationships can be as exploitative and unequal as heterosexual ones.[64]

In depicting a brothel catering to lesbian clients, Lydis records a lesbian establishment of sorts, albeit not the kind of affirmative lesbian locale that we might ordinarily associate with the same-sex subcultures of interwar Paris. Whilst the number of self-avowedly lesbian establishments in Paris paled in comparison with those in Berlin, by 1926 the French capital counted amongst its many nocturnal attractions La Fétiche.[65] This lesbian cabaret-bar in Montmartre, the district which had been the nucleus of Parisian lesbian life since the nineteenth century, was described by one voyeuristic male travel writer as a venue where one could ogle 'dashing dames of magnetic masculinity.'[66] Carefully constructed images of interwar lesbian bars, including La Fétiche, routinely record same-sex couples dancing the tango.[67] Typically, a tuxedo-clad woman with close-cropped hair is shown assuming the traditionally masculine role, leading her feminine partner around the dance floor.[68] Lydis likewise depicts a female couple performing this popular dance in the etching alluded to at the beginning of this chapter (Figure 5.2). Without recourse to sartorial signifiers or a discernible setting, Lydis suggests the importance of dance venues as sites of same-sex sociability.[69] Far from mirroring the traditional gendered division of dance roles, Lydis's monumental nudes perform an *inverted* tango, whereby both women assume the dominant male position. The couple are presented as equal in role, and equal in stature, as they dance the dance that it was feared simulated and stimulated sex.[70] Whilst Lydis's dancers queer the dance floor, Vaux obscured this very aspect of lesbian sociability in his shadowy photographic reproduction.

Whilst the lesbians who populate sexological texts wore their 'inversion' conspicuously on their crisply tailored shirt sleeves, the lesbians who populate *Lesbiennes* are distinguished from the 'normal' woman by their sexual acts and not by dress, appearance or physique. Whilst popularised at the turn of the century in the writings of Karl Heinrich Ulrichs, Richard von Krafft-Ebing and Havelock Ellis, the influential model of the female sexual invert, a woman who possessed a 'masculine soul, heaving in the female bosom' (Krafft-Ebing), continued to hold considerable sway in the interwar period.[71] It was, after all, the sexological model that members of interwar Paris's elite lesbian community, including Djuna Barnes, Sylvia Beach, Adrienne Monnier and Claude Cahun, were not only conversant with but one which they both critiqued and imbibed in both art and life, as Latimer has shown.[72] Yet it was a model of lesbianism in which Lydis appears to have had little interest. Indeed, Lydis's depiction of the feminine lesbian counters the idea that same-sex desire stemmed from an inversion of gender traits and could almost be seen to illustrate Magnus Hirschfeld's conviction that alongside the masculine lesbian woman there existed an equal number of lesbian women 'so thoroughly feminine in their expression of feeling, taste, and thought, that no one would consider them homosexual.'[73]

The inconspicuousness of the feminine 'shadow-lesbian' could, in certain contexts, make her a more disturbing spectre for the heteronormative imagination than the masculine lesbian, as Sherrie Inness has argued in her discussion of the ill-fated Broadway staging of Édouard Bourdet's *La Prisonnière* [The Captive], a play which premiered in Paris the year that Lydis published *Lesbiennes*.[74] Yet a commodified and confined version of the feminine lesbian served as the submissive object of what Jack Halberstam branded the 'heteropornographic imagination.'[75] Prurient depictions of lesbians – lesbians whose alleged deviance did not mar heterosexual man's scopophilic pleasure – populate French interwar erotica. They can be found in the graphic works of George Barbier, Edouard Chimot and Sylvain Sauvage, amongst others, and bear out Adrienne Rich's assertion that 'lesbian pornography, created for the male voyeuristic eye,' is bereft of 'emotional context' and 'individual personality,' and exists to deny lesbian women sexual autonomy.[76] Female artists were by no means immune from producing this type of lesbian imagery, as evidenced by Gerda Wegener's illustrations for Louis Perceau's pseudonymously published *Les délassements d'Éros: douze sonnets lascifs* [The Amusements of Eros: Twelve Lustful Sonnets].[77] Lydis offered an altogether different interpretation of female same-sex desire, one that emphasises neither hyper-sexualised performativity nor what Camilla Smith terms 'grotesque alterity.'[78] *Lesbiennes* is devoid of the coquettish expressions, submissive poses, phallic props, and the customary fetishistic uniform of stockings, heeled footwear and dishevelled undergarments that populate interwar erotic imagery. Lydis's statuesque nudes emanate a physical power that counters the symbolic violence enacted upon the lesbian body in male-orientated erotica. Her refusal to gratify the frequently cited heterosexual male preference for the partly clad female body might be symptomatic of the fact that she did not conceive of *Lesbiennes* solely with male desires in mind, as I will return to shortly.[79]

Lydis may not have been the first European female artist to transgress gender norms by producing erotic or lesboerotic graphic art; Wegener, Schneider-Kainer and Charlotte Berend-Corinth all slightly precede her in that respect.[80] However, Lydis's decision to self-publish *Lesbiennes* and assume the associated risks sets her apart. Erotic graphic folios and illustrated books were seldom conceived of, or published by, the artists who illustrated them. The financial risk and reward were usually subsumed by a private press, invariably male-owned. Lydis's privileged economic position undoubtedly afforded her certain freedoms, including the ability to fund self-publication. Nevertheless, it was a daring move to issue such an explicit work just as she was beginning to receive official recognition, with the publication of *Lesbiennes* taking place the same year that the French state made the first of several purchases of her work.[81] It also took place the year that the editor and publisher of *Inversions*, France's second-ever gay journal, were imprisoned for an affront to public decency.[82] Yet the small edition size of *Lesbiennes*, its high ticket price, and its apparent lack of marketing enabled Lydis to circumvent the watchful eye of public prosecutors, who were more concerned with mass cultural forms than elite ones.[83] That is not to say French police completely turned a blind eye to the fine arts but rather, in the rare instances when fine art depictions of the nude were subjected to levels of censorship, they had been prominently exhibited in public locations.[84] It was, after all, 'the places where the images could be seen and distributed, that was the chief source of their obscenity,' as Forster and others have shown.[85] The public visibility of a journal such as *Inversions*, which was briefly available at newsstands, certainly did not apply to a costly print folio like *Lesbiennes*. Nevertheless, Lydis's willingness to risk censure, if not necessarily censorship, may have stemmed from the fact that her investment in same-sex desire ran deeper than shock tactics or careerist opportunism.[86]

Despite (or perhaps because of) how radical Lydis's rendering of female same-sex desire was, *Lesbiennes* was neither publicly promoted nor reviewed at the time of its publication. Whilst ten copies of the folio had been marked as *hors commerce* [non-trade], if these had been intended as promotional copies (a common strategy with fine art print publications), then given the wall of silence that met its publication, this strategy does not appear to have paid off. Far from its lesbian content creating a *succès de scandale* – as had been the case with Victor Margueritte's best-selling novel *La Garçonne* (1922) – such a frank image of lesbian desire that was produced by a bisexual female artist was, it would seem, too audacious for the patriarchal Parisian artworld.[87] A copy of the folio was, however, included in an exhibition of Lydis's work the following year at the Galerie d'art contemporain, one of a number of small commercial galleries lining Montparnasse's Boulevard Raspail.[88]

It is not known for how much copies of *Lesbiennes* retailed, nor the channels through which they were marketed and sold. A limited-edition, signed and numbered art folio, printed on fine paper as *Lesbiennes* was, would have undoubtedly been a decidedly costly offering, accessible only to the select few with the appropriate means and contacts. The fact that Lydis self-published and the lack of promotional material opens up the possibility that interested parties would have purchased *Lesbiennes* directly from her, testifying to the level of control that Lydis appears to have exerted over each stage of its production and dissemination. If copies did change hands in such a manner, might this have increased the likelihood of a female audience? With no known sales ledger listing the original purchasers, and little in the way of provenance information relating to the few surviving copies, it is doubtful we will ever know the identities of the folio's original buyers. We should not, however, rule out the possibility of an audience on the lesbian continuum, particularly as *Lesbiennes* offered something distinctly different from the heterosexist male fantasy of lesbian sex.

Since the publication of Laura Mulvey's frequently cited essay 'Visual Pleasure and Narrative Cinema' (1975), much ink has been spilt debating the gendered gaze. Whilst I do not have space in this chapter to address this theoretical debate in detail, it is worth reflecting that whilst the 'determining gaze' of Western art and visual culture has overwhelmingly been that of the male, too often feminist art historical scholarship has refused to entertain even the possibility of a disobedient female gaze. From the statuesque nudes of Michelangelo to the classicising, androgynous ephebes of Anne-Louis Girodet, the male nude is frequently subsumed under the category of the homoerotic but as Tamsin Wilton observes, to consider the female nude in a comparable light 'never seems to occur to anyone.'[89] Moreover, the possibility of queer female spectatorship is all too infrequently addressed in art historical studies pertaining to the female nude.[90] Centring the possibility of alternative spectatorial subjectivities enables an exploration of what Wilton terms the 'disobedient lesbian consumption of supposedly heterosexual marks.'[91] Foregrounding the question of queer female spectatorship is, perhaps, all the more relevant when the artist under study was, as is true of Lydis, a bisexual woman who doggedly explored lesbian eroticism in her work. There was nothing 'supposedly heterosexual' about the marks made by this etcher's needle.[92] Inevitably, heterosexual men would have constituted part of the original market for *Lesbiennes*, just as they constitute a sizable part of the market for Lydis's work today. Nevertheless, we should resist what Wilton describes as the 'absolute presumption of heterobinary dynamics.'[93]

Whilst undoubtedly cognisant of the potential male market for lesbian erotica, that does not mean that Lydis necessarily produced *Lesbiennes* with male appetites exclusively in mind.

Lydis's *Lesbiennes* presented and still presents an astonishing declaration of the artistic, social and sexual autonomy of the modern female artist. Yet the folio's marginal positioning at the junction of art and pornography has arguably contributed to the fact that it is a declaration of lesbian modernity that has remained little known, or rather known to few aside from male erotica collectors. Whilst flirting with obscenity may be deemed something of a modernist standpoint, a sure-fire way to *épater les bourgeois* [shock the bourgeois], did Lydis venture too far into the obscene for art historical posterity? Moreover, Lydis's decision to privately publish *Lesbiennes* in a highly limited print run may have been in part an attempt to evade being hauled over the pornographic coals, however unlikely such a fate would have been. Far from simply safeguarding *Lesbiennes* from the attentions of police chiefs and public prosecutors, such protective strategies have proved so effective that Lydis's declaration of lesbian modernity has inadvertently remained, at least until now, 'in the shadows, in the margins, hidden from history, out of sight, out of mind.'[94]

Notes

1. Lucienne Florentin, *La Suisse* (Geneva), October 1930, quoted in *Dessins et Peintures de Mariette Lydis* (New York: Marie Sterner Galleries, 1936), n.p.
2. 'Une grande artiste, avec la lyrisme fatal de Sapho,' Marius-Ary Leblond [George Athénas and Aimé Merlo], 'Mariette Lydis,' *L'Ère nouvelle*, 7 October 1928, 2–4. All translations are my own.
3. I favour the Sapphic specificity of 'lesboerotic' over the ostensibly more generic but in reality, decidedly androcentric 'homoerotic.'
4. From the 1920s until his death in 1971, Vaux created an archive (now housed in the Bibliothèque Kandinsky at the Centre Pompidou) of over 250,000 glass plate negatives documenting the work and Parisian studios of 6,000 artists. 'Fonds Marc Vaux,' Bibliothèque Kandinsky – Archives et documentation, accessed 28 May 2021, https://archivesetdocumentation.centrepompidou.fr/ead.html?id=FRM5050-X0031_0000173#!{%22content%22:[%22FRM5050-X0031_0000173_FRM5050-X003195403%22,true,%22%22]}.
5. Terry Castle, *The Apparitional Lesbian: Female Homosexuality and Modern Culture* (New York: Columbia University Press, 1993), 30.
6. Ibid., 2.
7. Teresa de Lauretis, *The Practice of Love: Lesbian Sexuality and Perverse Desire* (Bloomington and Indianapolis: University of Indiana Press, 1994), 92.
8. 'Ihr Ruhm ist in die Höhe geschnellt mit einer Wucht, die wir sonst nur erleben, wenn es sich um Sänger Filmhelden oder Schauspieler handelt.' Karin Michaëlis, 'Das unbewußte Talent,' in *Die Kultur der Frau: Eine Lebenssymphonie der Frau des XX. Jahrhunderts*, ed. Ada Schmidt-Beil (Berlin: Verlag für Kultur und Wissenschaft, 1931), 246–53, 247.

9. According to Diana Souhami, Gluck met Lydis 'frequently, if fleetingly, in a Paris hotel.' Diana Souhami, *Gluck, 1895–1978: Her Biography*, 2nd paperback ed. (London: Phoenix Press, 2001), 95. Gluck's portrait of Lydis was reproduced in 'Gluck on Talented People' in the *Daily Sketch* on 3 November 1937, and included in an exhibition at the Fine Art Society (London) that month. May Sarton, 'For Mariette Lydis,' in *Encounter in April* (Boston: Houghton Mifflin, 1937). Lydis refers to her friendships with Colette and the psychoanalyst Marie Bonaparte in E.M.S., 'Die Wienerin, die den Koran illustrierte: Seltsame Karriere einer Österreicherin. — Gespräch mit Mariette Lydis,' *Neues Wiener Journal*, 4 August 1936, 7. Colette, *Bal des petits lits blancs* (Paris: Société nouvelle Publicitas, 1934).
10. An oil on panel self-portrait (1931) resides at the Uffizi. In 1926, the graphite and gouache study *Aveugles* (1925), now in the collections of the Centre Pompidou, became the first work by Lydis to be purchased by the French state. See Pierre Sanchez, *Dictionnaire du Salon d'Automne: répertoire des exposants et liste des œuvres présentées, 1903–1945* (Dijon: Echelle de Jacob, 2006), 894; and Robert Rey, 'Les arts expositions,' *L'Europe nouvelle* 9, no. 418 (20 February 1926): 249.
11. Paula Birnbaum, 'The Exhibitions of the Femmes Artistes Modernes (FAM), Paris, 1931–38,' *Artl@s Bulletin* 8, no. 1 (2019): 152–65, 153; *Les femmes artistes d'Europe exposent au Musée du Jeu de Paume: catalogue d'exposition* (Paris: Jeu de Paume des Tuileries, 1937), exhibition catalogue.
12. 'Mariette Lydis est une des artistes authentiques d'aujourd'hui.' Louis Vauxcelles, 'Mariette Lydis,' *Excelsior* (Paris), 23 February 1926, 2.
13. 'D'abord, son art est à elle. Aucune trace d'assimilation féminine.' Ibid.
14. Thyra Clark, 'Mariette Lydis,' *Artwork* 4, no. 16 (Winter 1928): 236–8, 236.
15. 'In Frankreich wird jeder Künstler, jeder Kunsthistoriker, jeder Journalist den Namen Mariette Lydis kennen.' Michaëlis, 'Das unbewußte Talent,' 247.
16. Notable exceptions are Christian Maryška's biographical essay, as well as brief but insightful critical engagements with Lydis's varied oeuvre by Sabine Plakolm-Forsthuber and Paula Birnbaum. See Christian Maryška, '"Mon travail est mon refuge": The Painter and Book Illustrator Mariette Lydis – An Unknown Woman,' in *Die bessere Hälfte: Jüdische Künstlerinnen bis 1938 / The Better Half: Jewish Women Artists before 1938*, ed. Andrea Winklbauer and Sabine Fellner (Vienna: Jüdisches Museum Wien and Metroverlag, 2016), exhibition catalogue, 183–9; Sabine Plakolm-Forsthuber, *Künstlerinnen in Österreich 1897–1938: Malerei, Plastik, Architektur* (Vienna: Picus, 1994), 178–9; and Paula Birnbaum, *Women Artists in Interwar France: Framing Femininities* (London and New York: Routledge, 2011), 208–12.
17. On the exclusion of female artists from mainstream modernist histories, see Camilla Smith, 'Women's Contributions to Modernism: Discover, Recover, or Revise?,' *Oxford Art Journal* 32, no. 3 (2009): 453–8.
18. Carol Duncan, 'Virility and Domination in Early Twentieth-Century Vanguard Painting' (1973), in *Feminism and Art History: Questioning the Litany*, ed. Norma Broude and Mary D. Garrard (New York: Harper and Row, 1982), 293–313, 293.
19. Birnbaum, *Women Artists*; Bridget Elliott, 'Deconsecrating Modernism: Allegories of Regeneration in Brooks and Picasso,' in *The Modern Woman Revisited: Paris*

between the Wars, ed. Whitney Chadwick and Tirza True Latimer (New Brunswick, NJ and London: Rutgers University Press, 2003), 35–51, 35; Gill Perry, *Women Artists and the Parisian Avant-Garde: Modernism and Feminine Art* (Manchester and New York: Manchester University Press, 1995); Marsha Meskimmon, *We Weren't Modern Enough: Women Artists and the Limits of German Modernism* (London and New York: I.B. Tauris Publishers, 1999); Plakolm-Forsthuber, *Künstlerinnen in Österreich*.

20. Schneider-Kainer is the subject of my chapter '"The Woman Thoroughly Dominates": Lene Schneider-Kainer (1885–1971) and Weimar Lesbian Erotica,' in *Women in Print: Volume 1, Design and Identities*, ed. Artemis Alexiou, Rose Roberto and John Hinks (Oxford: Peter Lang, 2022), 245–71. The German-Jewish lesbian artist Gertrude Sandmann is the focus of Anna Havemann's short catalogue essay, 'Gertrude Sandmann – Skizze zu Leben und Werk einer wiederentdecken Künstlerin / Gertrude Sandmann: The Life and Work of a Rediscovered Artist,' in *Strassen und Gesichter / Streets and Faces: Berlin 1918–1933*, ed. Annelie Lütgens (Berlin: Kerber Verlag, 2013), 111–17. Despite this, Sandmann remains little known and woefully under-researched, particularly outside Germany.

21. Here I am drawing upon the title of Meskimmon's aforementioned book.

22. Greenberg's essay 'Avant-Garde and Kitsch' was originally published in the *Partisan Review* 6 (Autumn, 1939): 34–49. Citation details in this study refer to the revised edition published in Clement Greenberg, *Art and Culture: Critical Essays* (Boston: Beacon Press, 1961), 3–21. Citation taken from 6.

23. Greenberg, 'Avant-Garde and Kitsch.'

24. Whitney Chadwick, ed., *Amazons in the Drawing Room: The Art of Romaine Brooks* (Berkeley and Los Angeles: University of California Press, 2000), exhibition catalogue; Tirza True Latimer, *Women Together/Women Apart: Portraits of Lesbian Paris* (New Brunswick, NJ: Rutgers University Press, 2005), 43–67; Elliott, 'Deconsecrating Modernism.'

25. Truman Capote, quoted in George Plimpton, *Truman Capote, in which Various Friends, Enemies, Acquaintances, and Detractors Recall His Turbulent Career* (New York: Doubleday, 1997), 86.

26. Joanne Winning, *The Pilgrimage of Dorothy Richardson* (Madison and London: University of Wisconsin Press, 2000), 9.

27. Ibid.

28. 'l'Archange de la Perversité.' Francis de Miomandre, 'Artistes contemporains: Mariette Lydis,' *Le Cousin Pons: revue des collectionneurs*, 7 June 1927, 31.

29. Shari Benstock, 'Expatriate Sapphic Modernism: Entering Literary History,' in *Lesbian Texts and Contexts: Radical Revisions*, ed. Karla Jay and Joanne Glasgow (New York: New York University Press, 1990), 183–203, 185.

30. The copy of *Lesbiennes* from which the images accompanying this chapter are taken belongs to a collector who wishes to remain anonymous. A second copy of *Lesbiennes* went to auction in 2019 at the Swann Auction Galleries, New York, as part of their Pride Sale but appears to have gone unsold. Unfortunately, the Swann Auction Galleries did not respond to my repeated enquiries about the folio. See https://catalogue.swanngalleries.com/Lots/auction-lot/MARIETTE-

LYDIS-(1887-1970)--Lesbiennes?saleno=2514&lotNo=46&refNo=756711, accessed 20 September 2022.
31. Jorge Luis Correa, 'Mariette Lydis' (unpublished Winchcombe Museum manuscript, undated), typescript.
32. 'Mariette,' in *MALYDIS* (blog), 6 July 2010, accessed 20 September 2022, https://www.malydis.eu/article-mariette-53514447.html.
33. On the exhibition, see Anton Jaumann, 'Die Kunstschüle von Emmy Zweybrück—Wien,' *Deutsche Kunst und Dekoration* (July 1915): 279–85. Hans Ankwicz-Kleehoven, 'Mariette Lydis,' *Die Graphischen Künste* 55, no. 2/3 (1932): 65–8, 67.
34. On the multiplicity of meanings connoted by the performance of female masculinity during the 1920s, see Laura Doan, 'Passing Fashions: Reading Female Masculinities in the 1920s,' *Feminist Studies* 24, no. 3 (1998): 663–700.
35. Whitney Chadwick and Tirza True Latimer, 'Becoming Modern: Gender and Sexual Identity after World War I,' in Chadwick and Latimer, *Modern Woman Revisited*, 3–19, 3.
36. Maryška claims she married Jean Lydis in 1917 but a photograph of 'Frau Marietta Pachhofer-Karny, Athen' appears in the Viennese magazine *Moderne Welt* 3 (Salzburger Festspiele issue), no. 3 (1921): 12. The earliest print reference to 'Mariette Lydis' that I have found dates from 28 April 1922 and appears in the Viennese Hungarian newspaper, the *Becsi Magyar Ujsag*. Given Lydis's Catholic faith, it seems more likely that she remarried after the death of her first husband in 1922. Maryška, 'Mon travail est mon refuge,' 183. Govone served as one of D'Annunzio's so-called legionaries in Fiume and would later publish a number of his works. Lydis and Govone are known to have visited D'Annunzio's Lake Garda estate and, in 1947, Lydis illustrated the cover of a French translation of D'Annunzio's novel *Il piacere* (first published 1899) for the French publisher Calmann-Lévy. It is feasible that like other elite lesbian and bisexual women in interwar Paris, including Natalie Barney, Romaine Brooks and Gertrude Stein, Lydis may have been drawn to elements of fascist ideology. On the appeal of fascism to elite Paris lesbians more generally, see Shari Benstock, 'Paris Lesbianism and the Politics of Reaction, 1900–1940,' in *Hidden from History: Reclaiming the Gay and Lesbian Past*, ed. Martin Duberman, Martha Vicinus and George Chauncey, Jr. (New York: Meridian Book, 1989), 332–46.
37. 'Glauben Sie mir: jede Frau ist interessant.' C. Benedek, 'Marietta Lydis und ihre Modelle,' *Neues Wiener Journal*, 25 August 1934, 8.
38. 'Sie lebt nun in Griechenland, und hier fängt sie an, mit Kreide und Farben herumzuhantieren, wohl mehr, wie Frauen mit Handarbeiten spielen, um einen leichten Zeitvertreib zu finden.' Michaëlis, 'Das unbewußte Talent,' 247.
39. Grete von Urbanitzky, *Die goldene Peitsche* (Leipzig: H. Hassel Verlag, 1922). On Lydis as the inspiration for Grete von Urbanitzky's Karla Jarl, see Christa Bittermann-Wille, '*Erotik*-theoretischer Diskurs und literarische Chiffren in der Frauenliteratur des Fin-de-siècle,' in *Der verbotene Blick. Erotisches aus zwei Jahrtausenden*, ed. Michaele Brodl (Klagenfurt and Vienna: Österreichische Nationalbibliothek, with Verlag Ritter, 2002), exhibition catalogue, 156, 179.
40. 'Sünderin,' 'am Altare des mächtigen Eros.' Urbanitzky, *Die goldene Peitsche*, 69, 209.

41. Viktoria Pötzl, 'Lesbische Literatur und Zwischenkriegszeit: Mythos und Entmystifizierung am Beispiel Der wilde Garten von Grete von Urbanitzky,' *Journal of Austrian Studies* 51, no. 4 (2018): 63–82.
42. 'berühmt, unabhängig, maßlos stolz und von einer wilden, seltsamen Schönheit.' Grete von Urbanitzky, *Der wilde Garten* (Leipzig: Hesse & Becker, 1927), 24. The parallel between Lydis and Pseleuditi was previously noted in Hanna Hacker, *Frauen und Freundinnen: Studien zur 'weiblichen Homosexualität' am Beispiel Österreich 1870–1938* (Weinheim and Basel: Beltz Verlag, 1987), 263.
43. The Getty Research Institute holds approximately 240 love letters that Lydis sent to the Italian poet and novelist Massimo Bontempelli during the 1920s. 'Massimo Bontempelli papers, 1865–1991,' Getty Research Institute accessed 20 September 2022, http://archives2.getty.edu:8082/xtf/view?docId=ead/910147/910147.xml;chunk.id=ref18;brand=default.
44. Adrienne Rich, 'Compulsory Heterosexuality and Lesbian Existence,' *Signs: Journal of Women in Culture and Society* 5, no. 4 (1980): 631–60, 648.
45. Elisabeth Janstein, 'Mariette Lydis,' *Das Leben*, November 1927, 22; Vicomte de Lascano Tegui [Emilio Lascanotegui], 'Mariette Lydis,' *Paris Montparnasse*, 15 June 1929, 6, 8. See, for instance, Lydis's *Ftoma II, Maroc* (1925).
46. *42 Miniaturen zum Koran* (Berlin: Brandus Verlagsbuchhandlung, 1924); *Le Coran, quarante-deux miniatures* (Paris: Société du livre d'art ancien et modern, 1927).
47. 'Sie illustriert ein Buch und erntet höfliche Lobesworte. Was sie damals zeigte, ist sehr unvollkommene Nachahmung persischer Kleinkunst. Aber jetzt hat sie Blut geleckt, sie führt nach Paris und will "richtige" Malerin warden.' Michaëlis, 'Das unbewußte Talent,' 247.
48. 'Non. Il ne faut point chercher *Sappho ni* à Mytilène, *ni* à Leucade, *ni* à Alexandrie, ni même dans les couvents ... C'est une artiste. Donc *elle a* déménagé à Paris.' Maryse Choisy, 'Dames seules,' *Le Rire*, numéro spécial, 21 May 1932, 3.
49. 'Je savais qu'il fallait que je vive à Paris, que je connaisse l'atmosphère de cette ville unique.' Mariette Lydis, Souvenirs de Mariette Lydis (handwritten manuscript), quoted in Gérard Barbier, 'Actualité? Frantz-Jourdain,' in *MALYDIS* (blog), 15 July 2011, accessed 20 September 2022, https://www.malydis.eu/article-actualite-frantz-jourdain-79514770.html.
50. Lydis's address is listed in the Salon d'Automne catalogue of 1926 as 284, rue de Vaugirard (Left Bank). The following year, she is listed as living at 18, rue Troyon, close to the Arc de Triomphe; she would remain a resident of the Right Bank for the rest of her time in Paris. Sanchez, *Dictionnaire du Salon d'Automne*, 894. I am grateful to C. Reed for sharing this source with me.
51. 'Vices rares [. . .] Prostituées, lesbiennes, criminelles, gamines qui viennent de découvrir leur corps, et abusent de leur découverte.' Henry de Montherlant, 'Mariette Lydis,' *Arts et métiers graphiques* 20 (15 November 1930): 82.
52. Duncan, 'Virility and Domination,' 306.
53. See, for instance, paintings each entitled *Self Portrait with a Model* by Lovis Corinth (1903); Ernst Ludwig Kirchner (1910); and George Grosz (1928).
54. See Birnbaum, *Women Artists*, 161–4.

55. Lynda Nead, *The Female Nude: Art, Obscenity and Sexuality* (London and New York: Routledge, 1992), 103.
56. Allison Pease, *Modernism, Mass Culture and the Aesthetics of Obscenity* (Cambridge: Cambridge University Press, 2000); Rachel Potter, *Obscene Modernism: Literary Censorship and Experiment, 1900–1940* (Oxford: Oxford University Press, 2013); Chris Forster, *Filthy Material: Modernism and the Media History of Obscenity* (Oxford: Oxford University Press, 2019).
57. Forster, *Filthy Material*, 2.
58. Pierre-Auguste Renoir, quoted in Susan Ratcliffe, ed., *Oxford Treasury of Sayings and Quotations*, 4th ed. (Oxford and New York: Oxford University Press, 2011), 323.
59. 'elle peint avec ses seins. Mariette Lydis est la peinture faite sexe.' Joseph Delteil, 1927. Delteil's quip was widely quoted at the time, including in Marcel Coulaud, 'Une méprise,' *Paris-midi*, 17 March 1927, 1. The reference to 'seins' [breasts] was changed to 'cœur' [heart] when Delteil's essay was reproduced in a Dutch exhibition catalogue. See Joseph Delteil, 'Les illustrations de Mariette Lydis,' in *Exposition de Peintures et d'aquarelles par Mariette Lydis Paris* (Amsterdam: Firma J.S. Fetter, 1927), exhibition catalogue.
60. Taking its name from an exhibition organised by Gustav Hartlaub in 1925, the term *Neue Sachlichkeit* [New Objectivity] is widely used to refer to the work of a diverse array of German artists active during the Weimar Republic, including Otto Dix, George Grosz, Christian Schad and Grethe Jürgens.
61. 'deren feines, durchgeistigtes Frauenantlitz nichts von der ganz männlichen Einstellung verrät, mit der sie den Dingen gegenübertritt.' Ankwicz-Kleehoven, 'Mariette Lydis,' 66.
62. Montherlant, 'Mariette Lydis,' 84.
63. Ruth Margarete Roellig, 'Lesbierinnen und Transvestiten,' in *Das lasterhafte Weib: Schriften zur weiblichen Sexualität*, ed. Agnes Gräfin Eszterházy (Vienna: Verlag für Kulturförschung, 1930; repr., Frankfurt am Main and Berlin: Ullstein Buch, 1989), 67–81, 72.
64. The sexologist Iwan Bloch commented that the women frequenting brothels were of a higher social position. Iwan Bloch, *Beiträge zur Aetiologie der Psychopathia Sexualis*, vol. 1 (Dresden: H. R. Dohrn, 1902), 246. Leslie Choquette refers to the interwar 'vogue of high-class brothels among society ladies.' Leslie Choquette, 'Paris-Lesbos: Lesbian Social Space in the Modern City, 1870–1940,' in *Proceedings of the Western Society for French History: Selected Papers of the 1998 Annual Meeting*, ed. Barry Rothaus (Denver: University of Colorado Press, 1998), 122–32, 127.
65. La Fétiche was allegedly operational from 1923 to 1944. See Mel Gordon, *Horizontal Collaboration: The Erotic World of Paris, 1920–1946* (Port Townsend, WA: Feral House, 2015), 219.
66. Bruce Reynolds, *Paris with the Lid Lifted: A New Sort of a 'Travel Cocktail'* (New York: G. Sully, c. 1927), 198–9.
67. Such a photograph of La Fétiche was reproduced in the male-orientated soft pornographic weekly *Paris-Plaisirs* on 1 January 1927.

68. The Berlin artist Jeanne Mammen featured such a scene in her ill-fated suite of lithographs illustrating Pierre Louÿs's Sapphic pseudograph *Les chansons des Bilitis* (1894; c. 1931).
69. On the importance of dance to interwar lesbian subcultures, see Lowry Martin, 'Desire, Fantasy, and the Writing of Lesbos-sur-Seine, 1880–1939' (PhD diss., University of California, Berkeley, 2010), ProQuest (3555804), 77–83.
70. Jeffrey H. Jackson, *Making Jazz French: Music and Modern Life in Interwar Paris* (Durham, NC: Duke University Press, 2003), 28.
71. Richard von Krafft-Ebing, *Psychopathia Sexualis: A Medico-forensic Study*, trans. F. J. Rebman (London: Heinemann, 1927), 399.
72. Choquette, 'Paris-Lesbos,' 127. The late Mel Gordon claimed that one such interwar brothel was the Temple de Sappho in the 2nd Arrondissement but as he was wont to do, Gordon does not reference such assertions, whilst Luc Sante alludes to the existence of a number of 'Women-only bordellos' in Paris by the 1930s but provides no further details. Gordon, *Horizontal Collaboration*, 102; Luc Sante, *The Other Paris: An Illustrated Journey Through a City's Poor and Bohemian Past* (London: Faber and Faber, 2015), 134; Latimer, *Women Together/Women Apart*, 15–19.
73. 'in ihren Gefühls-, Geschmacks- und Gedankenäußerungen so durchaus weiblich, daß sie niemand für homosexuell halten würde.' Magnus Hirschfeld, *Die Homosexualität des Mannes und des Weibes* (Berlin: Louis Marcus, 1914), 272, quoted in Cyd Sturgess,'"Die zarte Haut einer schönen Frau": Fashioning Femininities in Weimar Germany's Lesbian Periodicals,' in *Edinburgh German Yearbook 10: Queering German Culture*, ed. Leanne Dawson (Rochester, NY: Camden House, 2018), 59–62.
74. Sherrie A. Inness, 'Who's Afraid of Stephen Gordon?: The Lesbian in the United States Popular Imagination of the 1920s,' *NWSA Journal* 4, no. 3 (Autumn 1992): 303–20, 315.
75. Jack Halberstam, *Female Masculinity* (Durham, NC: Duke University Press, 1998), 61.
76. Louÿs's *Les chansons de Bilitis* was the preferred interwar vehicle for lesbian subject matter, illustrated by artists including Georges Barbier (1922), Edouard Chimot (Paris: Devambez, 1925) and Sylvain Sauvage (Paris: Chez Sylvain Sauvage, 1927). Rich, 'Compulsory Heterosexuality,' 638, 641.
77. Alexandre de Vérineau [Louis Perceau], *Les délassements d'Éros: douze sonnets lascifs* (Paris: Érotopolis, 1925).
78. Camilla Smith, 'Sex Sells! Wolfgang Gurlitt, Erotic Print Culture and Women Artists in the Weimar Republic,' *Art History* 42, no. 4 (2019): 780–807, 782.
79. On the preference for partial nudity, see Magnus Hirschfeld, *Sexual Anomalies and Perversions: Physical and Psychological Development and Treatment* [. . .] [anonymous translation] (New York: Emerson Books, 1948), 482.
80. On Berend, see Abbey Rees-Hales,'"Mit einer ziemlich weitgehenden weiblichen Indiskretion": Charlotte Berends Anita Berber: Acht Originallithographieen (1919),' in *Wolfgang Gurlitt Zauberprinz: Kunsthändler – Sammler*, ed. Hemma Schmutz and Elisabeth Nowak-Thaller, LENTOS Kunstmuseum Linz (Munich: Hirmer, 2019), exhibition catalogue, 169–76.

81. The year 1926 also witnessed the unprecedented number of Lydis's works exhibited at the Salon d'Automne, her appointment as a member of the Salon d'Automne and considerable critical praise.
82. Carolyn J. Dean, *The Frail Social Body: Pornography, Homosexuality, and Other Fantasies in Interwar France* (Berkeley: University of California Press, 2000), 54–63. I am very grateful to Dean for sharing further insights with me pertaining to patterns of censorship in interwar France.
83. French censorship legislation of the interwar period was still governed by the *Loi sur la liberté de la presse* [Law on the Freedom of the Press] of July 1881.
84. For instance, female nudes by Kees van Dongen and Amedeo Modigliani were the subject of censorship scandals during the 1910s.
85. Forster, *Filthy Material*, 44.
86. There is no evidence to suggest that *Lesbiennes* was the subject of censorship.
87. On *Margueritte*'s novel and the controversy it caused, see Mary Louise Roberts, *Civilization Without Sexes* (Chicago: University of Chicago Press, 1994), 53.
88. André Warnod, 'Beaux Arts: les expositions de la semaine,' *Comoedia*, 10 March 1927, 3.
89. Tamsin Wilton, *Lesbian Studies: Setting an Agenda* (London and New York: Routledge, 1995), 141.
90. See, for instance, James Smalls, 'Making Trouble for Art History: The Queer Case of Girodet,' *Art Journal* 55, no. 4 (1996): 20–7.
91. Wilton, *Lesbian Studies*, 141.
92. Ibid.
93. Ibid., 140.
94. Castle, *Apparitional Lesbian*, 2.

6

INVERTING THE GAZE: RADCLYFFE HALL AND MALE SEXUAL IDENTITIES

Steven Macnamara

INTRODUCTION

'Inverting the Gaze' is a homage to Radclyffe Hall's self-identification as an invert, but it also signals that the central aim of this chapter is to explore how Hall used sight and vision to indicate difference in relation to male sexual identities.[1] This is a shift in critical perspective concerning Hall as their work is more commonly associated with female identities and sexuality, because of their own sexual relationships with women and the representation of Stephen Gordon in *The Well of Loneliness* (1928).[2] However, the term 'sexual inversion' did encompass the sexuality/gendered identity of both women and men, and Hall's oeuvre, including the lesbian novel *The Well of Loneliness*, reveals that they were psychologically interested in all human sexuality and gender.[3] Acknowledging that lesbian modernism can (and does) explore masculinity and male sexuality, this chapter focuses on Hall's representation of heterosexual male characters who share a common literary motif that is connected to their vision. The chapter argues that Hall developed and used this motif throughout their career to indicate non-conforming cis masculinity and male sexuality during the interwar years.

Written during the modernist period, *The Well of Loneliness* has a traditional chronological narrative style and is melodramatic, sentimental and overtly religious in its tone. Judged through a modernist lens and based mainly on the critical reaction to *The Well of Loneliness*, the assumption is that all of Hall's work is non-experimental and middlebrow. However, Elizabeth English contends that modernism and middlebrow do seem to be intimately connected. What we witness then, is not a clear separation but a mutual reciprocity between the high and low, the serious and the fun, and an indication that the boundaries between these forms (and across the divide) are permeable.[4]

As such, framing Hall's work as middlebrow overlooks their ability to be subversive within a conventional space and dismisses their contribution to the concerns that were being discussed by modernist writers – for example, the impact of the war on men and its relationship to their identities. Hannah Roche also argues that *The Well of Loneliness* may appear traditional, but its subject matter is progressively modern and that Hall uses the romantic genre to explore a space 'previously reserved for heterosexuals.'[5] Roche's challenge to how Hall and *The Well of Loneliness* have previously been read and interpreted opens up the possibilities of using lesbian modernism to revisit and review texts from alternative perspectives.

This chapter follows Roche's example by considering Hall's representation of the following heterosexual cis male characters: Hilary Brent in *The Forge* (1924), Gian-Luca Boselli in *Adam's Breed* (1926), Martin Hallam in *The Well of Loneliness* and Christophe Bénédit in *The Master of the House* (1932). The characters are presented as heterosexual men, but they all have some physical or psychological divergence connected to their vision, which indicates their sexual difference. The chapter argues that Hall developed and evolved this motif following the success of their poem 'The Blind Ploughman' (1913), in which masculine difference is associated with blindness. In their post-war writing, the concept of how one *sees* and is *seen* is played out in multifarious ways as Hall connects blindness, sight/insight and physical disability to a sense of queer masculine identity. This chapter helps to reveal how Hall appropriated this motif – often in problematic ways – to suggest an ambiguity about the authenticity of the characters' heterosexuality. It also demonstrates how Hall was able to represent different male sexualities at a time when male homosexuality was illegal in the UK and many other countries.

Sowing Blindness

Published the year after Hall had converted to Catholicism, 'The Blind Ploughman' describes how the Ploughman works with no sight and implies that, in doing so, his soul is truly able to see and appreciate the natural world around him. The short poem ends with the Ploughman declaring, 'God, who took away my eyes, / That my *soul* might see!'[6] 'The Blind Ploughman' is typical of the majority of Hall's poetry, in that it is unashamedly and unapologetically sentimental. There is no hint of realism as Hall romanticises not only the hardship of rural manual working life but also blindness. Written during the modernist period, the poem lacks any obvious experimental use of language or form, and thematically is the antithesis of agnostic or atheistic branches of modernism as it is overtly religious. The poem also draws on problematic classist and ableist tropes: it treats physical labour and blindness as an allegory to imply that the Ploughman not only is in harmony with nature but also has a powerful understanding and awareness of the omnipresence of God because of his working-class status and disability. The allegorical depiction of the Ploughman appears to explore the Biblical concept of blind faith, in which 'The Blind See, but the Seeing are Blind.'[7] In the poem, Hall depicts the Ploughman blindly working in the same world as those who can see, but his experience and understanding of that world are different because of his blind faith. The Ploughman is an early example of Hall's fascination with the outsider, the 'misfits' and the lonely – those individuals who occupy the margins of society, but who are different and rarely seen.[8]

In his introduction to Hall's *Songs of Three Counties and Other Poems* (1913), Robert Bontine Cunninghame Graham singled out 'The Blind Ploughman' poem by stating, 'This shows the poet in an unusual light, for most poets write on far different subjects; but here is one which is eternal, and has been since the time of Œdipus.'[9] Oedipus is a famous literary example of blindness, which is connected to the neglect of the truth, but Graham's reference comes three years after Sigmund Freud had coined the term 'Oedipus complex' to describe a key stage in the development of human sexuality.[10] Graham, a politician, writer and literary patron, was an astute reader, and his mention of Oedipus may indeed be referring to Freud's developing psychological theories, but he is also linking the Ploughman's blindness to one of classical Greek mythology's most notorious examples of a sexual misdemeanour. It is an indication that Graham was acutely aware that something deeper was happening within Hall's work beyond its romantic and spiritual sentimentalisation. Graham does not explicitly state that Hall's work contains radical sexual and social ideas, but he is hinting at this possibility by mentioning Oedipus as an example of an individual whose lack of insight leads to his downfall as he kills his father and marries his mother. Hall's poetry may appear to reflect a more traditionalist Victorian quality, which is counter to the experimental modernist period that Hall was writing in, but Graham is suggesting (long before *The Well of Loneliness*) that there is another way to view their work as sexually subversive.

Hall's poetry offers many examples of queer and alternative readings beyond the assumed heteronormative interpretation, but only if the reader recognises Hall's coded use of language and motifs. The metaphorical connection between the plough(man) and homosexuality is explicitly present in Hall's post-war speech 'Ghosts' (undated), in which there is an ardent plea for the surviving inverts of the war to recognise that their battle for acceptance is far from over:

> For we have a harder furrow to hoe – a hard, long, gruelling furrow to hoe. And we dare not take our hands from the plough – [nor look back,

for so much as a moment] till this furrow is driven home straight and true, we dare not to relax our grip for a moment.[11]

The blindness of the Ploughman therefore could be a commentary on homosexuality, particularly at a time when male homosexuality was illegal. In the Bible, angels blind the men who threaten to rape Lot, which suggests that God will punish men who engage in or threaten to commit acts of homosexuality – in the poem, the Ploughman states God has taken his eyes.[12] However, throughout the poem, the blindness the Ploughman experiences is not a penalty for sin, even if the world may view it differently. Instead, the poem aims to convince the reader that the Ploughman's blindness is a gift, which enables him to feel and experience God's love and to appreciate and understand the world differently. The Ploughman's blindness signifies both insight and the celebration of positive difference.

Hall could not have anticipated how 'The Blind Ploughman,' written before the outbreak of the First World War, would gain traction and become imbued with alternative meaning as it was adapted into a song by the composer Robert Coningsby Clarke. Adopted as an anthem for men who were blinded and/or physically harmed in other ways in the war, 'The Blind Ploughman' became an international success and was regularly performed at concerts to raise funds for the injured men.[13] At a time of international crisis, the song offered a sense of hope and purpose to men wounded in the war. The song's phenomenal success and the social and cultural association with war-injured men were tangible catalysts in Hall's writing career, changing their artistic perspective of themselves from an amateur to a professional writer. The creative significance and importance of 'The Blind Ploughman' can be traced through each of Hall's novels as an emblematic commentary on the damaged and fractured sense of both physical and psychological masculinity in the interwar years. Hall explores the impact of the war on their male characters by evolving the concept of vision and difference, which was present in 'The Blind Ploughman,' by reimagining this in their post-war writing.

Forging a Vision of Ambiguous Male Sexuality

In Hall's first published novel, *The Forge*, the opening chapter describes how the male protagonist, Hilary Brent, an upper-class English author, wears an eye-patch, due to an injury he sustained in the First World War:

> At the moment only one of these queer eyes showed, the other being covered by a black patch. This patch was the only trophy that its wearer had brought back from the war, and curiously enough, it was not unbecoming or so his friends thought.[14]

The Forge is a light comedy novel, but Hilary reflects how the war has physically marked him, just as it had millions of other men. Later in the same chapter, it is revealed that Hilary's injury occurred because of a bizarre accident, and before any fighting, which undermines and lampoons the gravity of his war effort. The scenario is humorous, and Hall is playing with the reader's expectations (particularly at the time of the novel's publication shortly after the war), because Hilary's wartime injuries do not reflect the expected narrative of military masculinity that might be associated with the loss of sight during the war. Hall is setting the comedic tone at the start of the novel, as Hilary's character is a figure whose masculinity can easily be mocked. As the story continues, there is a repetition of his wartime fate, because his best intentions are generally foiled and ridiculed. Much of the comedy in *The Forge* comes from how Hilary envisages both himself and situations which rarely reflect reality. Hilary is pedantic and petty, but his perception of himself is that of a noble English gentleman. He also tends to romanticise the past and his expectations for the future. Consequently, Hilary is often disappointed by the reality of the present. Hall is using humour to show that how the individual views the world may not always reflect reality, but this in turn also includes how the reader sees and interprets Hilary's character.

As Graham suggested in his introduction to *Songs of Three Counties and Other Poems*, Hall is a subversive writer who works within the boundaries of convention and Hilary is a character who can be viewed through a simple or more complex lens. Hilary is a stock comedy character – a bumbling, misguided, upper-class, pompous, but harmless, fool – who ultimately returns to the comfort and familiarity of his wife, Susan, following their separation. *The Forge* pre-empts Noël Coward's play *Private Lives* (1930) by six years, but it reflects a similar comedy of manners which satires class, marriage and the tragicomic fate of characters who repeat the same mistakes. There is a campness to *The Forge* and *Private Lives*, which lends itself to interpreting both works as frivolous and nonsensical, but Terry Castle argues that Coward was celebrating 'a creative marriage of male and female homosexual sensibilities.'[15] Similarly, in *The Forge*, Hall, a lesbian writer, explores a heterosexual relationship, with binary male and female characters that blur the expected gendered roles within marriage because they are a reflection of each other rather than being polar opposites. Hilary and Susan are both artistic, dramatic and impractical in dealing with everyday life, but their eccentricities and behaviours are comically believable because of the social stereotypes associated with their class and wealth. It is possible that Hall was portraying a sophisticated post-war heterosexual relationship, in which Hilary and Susan are indifferent to socially expected gender roles and sexual identities. Jana Funke points out that Hall's work is concerned with both heterosexual and homosexual relationships and 'questions of national identity and national belonging in conjunction with questions of gender, sexuality and class.'[16] How Hilary is viewed within this context depends on the reader, but even contemporary readers recognised that the relationship in the novel was an affectionate depiction of Hall and their partner, Una Troubridge. Richard Dellamora states that '[i]n presenting a partnership between two women under the fictional guise of marriage between a man and a woman [. . .] Hall signalled, as she does more directly in *The Unlit Lamp* [1924], her interest in a crossgendered protagonist.'[17] Rather than dismissing *The Forge* as a light comedy and Hilary as a stock comedy character, the novel presents a fascinating fictionalised and parodied version of Hall and their relationship with Troubridge.

Hilary, more so than Stephen Gordon in *The Well of Loneliness*, is a character that Hall aligned themself to and/or identified with, and significantly, as well as being male, part of that association includes physical injury and visual disability. It suggests that, for Hall, there was a developing relationship between queerness, physical injury and vision, which was present or evolved from the success of 'The Blind Ploughman.' The reflective character types of Hilary and Susan include a mirrored ambiguity concerning their sexuality. The couple's wealth and class allow the marriage to be bohemian and unconventional and, as a result, the fluidity attached to their attraction and awareness of queer culture around them is part of their avant-garde lifestyle. This is slightly more evident in the novel with Susan and her fascination with Venetia Ford (a version of the lesbian artist Romaine Brooks), but Hilary's visual disability is a symbolic indication that he is different at a time when male homosexuality was illegal. Hall signals Hilary's difference not only in the way that he looks but in their frequent use of the word 'queer' to describe him or his associated mannerisms or actions (as in the quote above that describes his eyes). The *Oxford English Dictionary* records that the first use of the word 'queer' in relation to homosexuality was in 1914, but it would have been used in conversation and discourse before being officially recorded.[18] Hall often uses the word 'queer' to describe something as strange or peculiar in their oeuvre, but there are times when its meaning is open to interpretation, especially when it is used to describe individual characters. In *The Well of Loneliness*, even as a child, Stephen is described as queer: 'she could not but feel a new interest in the child whom she and the cook had now labelled as "queer", and Stephen basked in much surreptitious petting, and her love for Collins grew daily.'[19] Hall is playing with the ambiguity of the word; in *The Forge*, after a group of children in Italy mock and attack Hilary, Susan attempts to justify the assault as being occasioned by his eye patch:

> 'But, my dear, if they haven't seen such a thing before, it would look queer.'
> 'What, never seen a black patch, with all the wounded during the war?'
> 'But perhaps none of the wounded they've seen happened to have an injured eye. You must be just.'

'Just! Perhaps you think I'm a kind of Guy Fawkes! Perhaps you think I *look* queer!'

'Don't be ridiculous! I merely said that to them you probably *did* look queer.'

'Oh, all right, I'm a freak! Where's the Pond's Extract?'[20]

This humorous exchange between Hilary and Susan reveals the contemporary sensitivity around the word 'queer' – as no one wants to be queer, even (or especially) if its meaning is related to difference or indeed homosexuality. In these few lines of dialogue, the reader is reminded that Hilary is visibly different from other men, and whilst many men were injured in the war, Hall swiftly, but with humour, undermines his association with military masculinity with the request for the Pond's Extract Company's most popular beauty product, a vanishing cream. Hall is playing with language and with the concept of masculine identities, but thematically they are linking sight (not only how Hilary looks but also how he is seen) to difference and the notion of queerness, whether the meaning is peculiar or homosexual. Hilary's sexuality is questionable throughout the novel, and by associating the word 'queer' with him in addition to his visual disability, Hall is reinforcing an uncertainty regarding the character's heterosexuality.

The Forge also explores the folly of Hilary's attempt to achieve personal happiness, but it is an ideal that he is perpetually chasing and never finding. The comic pathos is introduced as the couple venture on a tour of Europe, which presents Hilary with an opportunity to revisit the places he had been to as a single man. The impact of the war has altered Hilary's happy memories of the places he visits, and the fact that his wife is with him is spoiling his enjoyment and independence. Whilst in Santa Chiara he witnesses a bird singing in a small cage. The image of captivity disturbs him, because it reminds Hilary of his own feeling in his marriage to Susan. At this moment Hilary achieves some clarity when he realises that his vision is not restricted by his eye-patch but by his own symbolic cage.[21] Hilary's revelation occurs in Santa Chiara, the Italian name for Saint Clare. Saint Clare was a follower of Saint Francis of Assisi and is the patron saint for eye diseases. The connection between Saint Clare and eyes is inventive and not immediately obvious, but the location is symbolic, as it is becoming increasingly clear to both Hilary and Susan that their marriage and relationship is floundering.

As Hilary reflects on his relationship with Susan, he considers them to be '[p]oor, striving, struggling, blind men and women, how little they ever really knew of each other, how little they really penetrated beyond the surface of each other's lives; pathetic creatures!'[22] Although Hilary is aware that they do not truly see or understand each other, they inevitably return to the comfort of their domestic arrangements. In the book's final scene, Hilary admits, '"After all, [. . .] I'm free – But it didn't work, darling, I couldn't make love, not with the proper conviction. They all saw through me, the women, I mean: I expected they saw you in my eyes."'[23] The confession is surprising, as Hilary talks of his sexual relationships with other women, but unlike the colluded intimacy with Susan, which sustains the charade of their marriage, the other women see the real Hilary and recognise his queerness. The working title for the novel was *Chains*, with the implication that – like *The Unlit Lamp* – it explored the ties that bind people together, the metaphor being that Hilary and Susan are fatefully bound together.[24] However, 'forge' also has another meaning, which relates to a fake or imitation. Hall presents Hilary and Susan as heterosexual, but there is a sexual queerness that is also part of their identity, and, as such, *The Forge* could also be read as a novel that documents and comments on marriages of convenience. Hilary may have had a moment where he knew his marriage to Susan was a sham, but rather than explore his authentic self, he continues to make the same mistakes. In the end, both Hilary and Susan are fooling themselves and the reader who wants to believe their heterosexual façade, but for the reader who sees behind their constructed identities, the ending reveals one of the ways in which lesbian/bisexual women and gay/bisexual men had to hide in public in the early twentieth century.

Visualising Injured Masculinity in *The Well*

The Well of Loneliness enables Hall to explore the contribution and sacrifice that both lesbian women and gay men made to the war effort through Stephen's and Jonathan Brockett's war experience.[25] In the novel, war physically and visibly changes the inverts Stephen and Jonathan. Before the war, Stephen, a masculine woman, has a deep-rooted sense that their inverted difference is aligned with concepts surrounding personal nobility, martyrdom and suffering. In part, this comes from Stephen's name and the association with the eponymous Saint, but it is also emphasised when they discover a book by sexologist Richard von Krafft-Ebing, presumably *Psychopathia Sexualis* (1886), and they realise that their father knew they were a sexual invert – a term that many sexologists associated with deviance and as such the notion of suffering. As they search for comfort in the Bible, Stephen reads, 'And the Lord set a mark upon Cain.'[26] At a critical moment of self-discovery and naming, Hall creates a connection between inverted identity and physical injury through the mark of Cain. War liberates Stephen and allows them to valorise their own sense of inverted difference, first, by serving their country and, second, by establishing a mutually beneficial relationship with Mary where they are the protector. When Stephen suffers a facial injury during the war, the scar is both a mark of honour and a symbolic reminder of their difference. Stephen reiterates the connection between physical injury and inverted identity by telling their lover, Mary, 'Like Cain. I am marked and blemished.'[27] Through one of Hall's most important and significant literary characters, they create an association between psychological and physical difference, as well as linking the shame of sexuality to a Biblical story of a God vengefully marking a human as different, so that others can recognise them and their sin. Jonathan also returns from the war physically changed and aged by the discipline of military life and the hardship of fighting in the Mesopotamian campaign. Stephen notes 'that his face had certainly aged; little bags were showing under his eyes, and rather deep lines at the sides of his mouth – war had left its mark upon Brockett.'[28] Compared with Stephen's noble mark of war, Jonathan's would appear superficial, but the war has marked him as he has sacrificed his youth and looks.

In contrast to the inverted characters Stephen and Jonathan, Martin Hallam's war injury and its connection with his vision are perhaps the most interesting in *The Well of Loneliness*. Martin, like Hilary in *The Forge*, is presented as a heterosexual man. During the war, Martin is hit in the face by a bullet, and when they meet again, Stephen observes how '[j]ust beside the right temple was a deep little scar – it must have been a near thing, that bullet.'[29] Not only is Martin's face scarred, but the bullet has also damaged his optic nerve, and he is at risk of losing his sight in one eye – eyes that Stephen notes 'looked so normal.'[30] Martin has a minor and a slightly noticeable injury, but in addition, he has problems with vision that could lead to the possibility of blindness in one eye. At this stage in Hall's writing career, it is not a coincidence or accident that they are returning to a motif they had used in the past, which connects masculine sexual ambiguity to physical difference and vision. Martin, like Hilary, is written as a bisexual character, but the fact that the scar is hardly noticeable is an indication that he is a depiction of a man who passes as heterosexual and even heteronormative. He is the type of man that Edward Carpenter would describe as 'the more normal type of the Uranian man.'[31] Whilst Martin is not marked in the same obvious way as Hilary, Stephen or Jonathan, he is still presented as different. Beneath his relatively minor surface injury, there is a risk that Martin may lose his sight, which suggests there are other layers to Martin's character which are not visible.

The view that Martin can be read as bisexual or gay has been acknowledged by other scholars. Laura Doan argues that both Martin and Mary 'conform to Carpenter's typology of the intermediate sex.'[32] For Carpenter, an individual may present as male or female physically but have a differently gendered soul and experience same-sex attraction. Clare Hemmings also refers to Martin's sexuality when discussing Havelock Ellis's theory that a heterosexual man may be able to 'cure' a feminine female invert:

> If we think for a moment of Martin Hallam, the man to whom Mary runs at the end of the novel, we can see this ambivalence in action [according to Ellis's theory]. Martin's status as ideal heterosexual male

is cast in doubt in a number of ways throughout *The Well*. First, there is perhaps too gentle a love of trees, and his curious isolation. In terms of desire, Martin has already proved his judgement to be flawed, through his declaration of love for Stephen earlier in the novel. Additionally, when Martin reappears in the novel he suffers from a very particular war wound – a bullet to the head that 'affected the optic nerve rather badly'. The very gaze required to structurally seduce a feminine invert away from the masculine woman is damaged.[33]

Hemmings argues that Mary, based on Ellis's hypothesis, is not the type of woman a heterosexual man would be interested in, and, therefore, for Martin to fall in love with her suggests there is something suspicious about his proclaimed heterosexuality. By identifying factors that undermine the legitimacy of Martin's heterosexual masculinity, his fondness for nature and his initial attraction to the masculine Stephen, Hemmings suggests that the character is homosexual or bisexual. This is a brief aside in a paper that otherwise focuses on Mary, but Hemmings's suggestion regarding Martin's sexuality is further discussed by Laura Erickson-Smith and Jennifer Mitchell in their essay 'Queering Queer Theory, or Why Bisexuality Matters':

> Hemmings is right to question the unquestioning ascription of heterosexuality to Martin Hallam. Martin is attracted to the masculinity that Stephen embodies and the femininity that is easily located in Mary; because the gender identities of the two objects of his desire are not the same Martin is, in one way or another, not monosexual. His bisexual tendencies – perhaps less obvious and more complicated than other instances of literary bisexuality – are nonetheless a reality.[34]

Doan, Hemmings, Erickson-Smith and Mitchell all recognise that something is misleading in the concept of Martin's heterosexuality. This is questionable in the marriage proposal to Stephen and then his attraction to Mary, but also the fact that Martin is thirty-nine, unmarried and living with his aunt when he re-enters Stephen's life in Paris. In conversations with Mary, Martin reveals that he is familiar with the alternative Paris scene: 'Mary would talk to him freely as she did very often of such people as Wanda, of the nightlife of the cafés and bars of Paris – most of which it transpired he himself had been to.'[35] It is a minor, but important insight into how Martin occupied his two months in Paris, before re-establishing contact with Stephen. Martin's admission raises an obvious question of doubt in the text as to why a heterosexual man (even in 1920s bohemian Paris) would know and frequent these bars and cafés – what is Martin looking for in these queer spaces? The novel never fully answers this question, but his lonely exploration of queer Paris prompts Martin to contact

Stephen again, and, in doing so, he finds Mary, a lesbian/bisexual woman with whom he can envisage having a relationship, suggesting that he may have been seeking a woman in the bars and cafés to hide his same-sex attraction.[36] Doan states that the union of Martin and Mary demonstrates the 'potential in pairing normal female and male intermediate types.'[37] Couples like Martin and Mary, and Hilary and Susan, can pass and be seen as heterosexual, but Hall is signalling Martin's and Hilary's difference with the motif that is connected to their vision.

Spiritual Intersubjective Vision: *Adam's Breed* and *The Master of the House*

As shown so far, there is a correlation between masculine facial injury, visual disability or blindness, and male sexual ambiguity in Hall's work. However, in *Adam's Breed* and *The Master of the House*, the two male protagonists, Gian-Luca and Christophe, are not injured or physically disabled. In fact, both are conventionally handsome working-class men, who are presented as heterosexual. Nevertheless, they are viewed as singularly different from their communities. *Adam's Breed* tells the story of Gian-Luca, whose mother dies in childbirth without revealing the identity of his father. Gian-Luca's status as an illegitimate British-Italian person adds to his innate sense of un-belonging and difference. He works as a waiter as an adult and spends the war in the catering corps, but is frustrated at not being able to fight. Post-war, he spirals into a deep depression and starves to death as a hermit in the woods. Whereas Gian-Luca always felt like an outsider, Christophe in *The Master of the House* is very much a part of his community, as Hall reimagines a Christ story in contemporary France. Christophe grows up experiencing sensations of déjà vu that appear to align with the story of Christ. When war breaks out, he enlists with his cousin Jan, but the novel ends with his being crucified by his enemies. Gian-Luca's and Christophe's distinct difference stems from how they see the world around them and how others (including the reader) observe their spiritual and intersubjective vision – the ability to view and sense the world as other people might. Hall is building on the dichotomy between sight and insight, which was already present in 'The Blind Ploughman,' but in *Adam's Breed* and *The Master of the House*, they explore a more complex and sustained hypothesis around vision and insight and its relationship to ambiguous masculine identities.[38]

In her discussion of Gian-Luca, Roche argues that 'it would be difficult to make a convincing case for Gian-Luca as a gay man,' but Hall's depiction of male sexuality is not always as clearly delineated as either 'straight' or 'gay.'[39] Hilary and Martin both demonstrate how Hall can hide bisexuality within heteronormative narratives focused on men who are married or who appear to be interested in sexual or romantic relationships with women while still making these characters' queerness visible and recognisable to those who understand the clues. In *Adam's Breed* and *The Master of the* House, Hall is exploring a more complex depiction of male sexuality with Gian-Luca and Christophe inasmuch as both characters struggle to understand the possibilities of other sexual options for them beyond that of heterosexuality. As early as 1936, Margaret Lawrence (a Canadian academic and feminist) claimed that '*The Master of the House*, like *The Well of Loneliness*, deals with inversion.'[40] One of the frustrations with Christophe's character is that despite his compassion and spiritual insight, he fails to realise that his male cousin Jan is in love with him. As a result, he cannot see the opportunities that homosexuality might offer him as an expression of his sexuality. During their military training, Christophe and Jan suddenly realise that they might die fighting in the war. It is a moment of revelation, shock and clarity for the pair, and Hall describes how '[t]heir eyes met, Christophe's pale and bright and tormented, Jan's dark and disturbed by the rising anger. Then a fearful thought struck like a lash on Jan's mind – ah, but no, not Christophe, the man he loved.'[41] This open discussion of love between men is socially acceptable, because Christophe and Jan are cousins who have grown up together. In this context, the love Jan has for Christophe is valid and appropriate, but it also has a homosexual/bisexual subtext.

In contrast, homosexuality is alluded to as an option for good-looking working-class men in *Adam's Breed*, when a poet offers to introduce Gian-Luca to an artist who will paint him:

> 'You're a handsome boy, why don't you go as a model? I can get you taken on by Munster, if you like; he's looking for a sort of John the Baptist.'
> 'What would he pay me?' inquired Gian-Luca promptly.
> 'That depends on his circumstances. When he's flush he pays well; otherwise, my true Italian, he might pay you nothing at all.'
> 'Then I think I am better where I am,' smiled Gian-Luca, 'for some day I shall be a head-waiter.'[42]

There is an undertone of something sexual in the offer, an economic trade-off for his good looks. Alan Sinfield describes how culture and the arts were a way of signalling homosexuality and that 'cross-class liaison, between the effete gent and the "manly" lower-class boy, was the most significant consequence of the queer stereotype.'[43] Gian-Luca rejects the proposition, mainly because there is no financial guarantee for his services. Even though Gian-Luca marries a woman, there remains a degree of uncertainty about the authenticity of his heterosexuality, which is compounded by the lack of children in the marriage:

> Finally he would feel aggrieved and unhappy; angry, too, as the blind may feel angry, who stumble and hurt themselves in their blindness. He

would go back to work with the uncomfortable conviction that he did not understand his wife, that he did not quite understand himself either.[44]

Hall links Gian-Luca's frustration with his wife for wanting children and his inability to father them with blindness. The text hints at his sexual ambiguity, because Gian-Luca has been married for a year and his wife has not had a baby and is not pregnant, which would be an expected outcome for a marriage at the time. The situation reveals that Gian-Luca has no insight into understanding either his wife's sexuality or his authentic self. At the time of publication, Hall could not depict explicit male homosexuality with either Gian-Luca or Christophe without risking censorship. At the same time, ambiguous sexuality does not automatically relate to suppressed homosexuality. Fundamentally, Gian-Luca and Christophe are not representative of hyper-masculine or archetypal heterosexual male characters. They may be gay, but there is also the possibility that they could be bisexual, pansexual or asexual, which opens up a much broader and interesting range of sexual identities in Hall's work.

The intersubjective visions of Gian-Luca and Christophe, where they feel or sense another being or moment in time, point to their difference. This engagement with temporality also shows that Hall was more experimental in their writing than critics have often assumed. Hall, like Virginia Woolf, is exploring the continuum of time as the past, present and future merge into each character's 'separate moments of being [that] were however embedded in many more moments of non-being.'[45] Particularly, in *The Master of the House*, Christophe's déjà vu reflects the tiny fragments of sensations and feelings that would have formed part of Christ's everyday life:

> It was almost as though it had happened before, even to the minutest personal details – a new pair of sandals given to a boy of eight years by his parents' neighbour, and that boy sitting down to examine the gift in a room which was bare but flooded with sun, and the boy very conscious of idling his time when instead he should have been diligently working.[46]

This is not Christ the child in the temple conversing with his elders, but Christophe reliving a simple moment of trying on new sandals, which is too unremarkable and quotidian to be included in the Bible. Hall is exploring the humanity of Christ by suggesting that there are parallels in Christophe's contemporary life as well as in the lives of the readers. Gian-Luca's intersubjective vision occurs later in *Adam's Breed* when he encounters a beggar and her blind son. He is initially horrified to see that the child's eyes have been removed, but as Gian-Luca continues to stare at the child he feels as though 'he were suddenly suffering with him, as though in some curious way he belonged to those woe-begone, sightless eyes.'[47] The child's empty eye sockets metaphorically reflect the emptiness that

Gian-Luca has felt all of his life. Unaware of his father's identity and made to feel responsible for the death of his mother, Gian-Luca's unknown dual heritage alienates him from his family and displaces him within both the Italian and British communities. As with 'The Blind Ploughman,' there is a troubling rhetoric around blindness in which a higher sensibility or morality is associated with physical disability, because the child acts as a catalyst to change Gian-Luca's vision. Following the encounter, the child haunts Gian-Luca's dreams and awakens his spiritual intersubjective vision with an intense empathy for all the suffering in the world, which includes both people and animals.

Christophe's intersubjective vision is associated with the figure of Christ, whilst Gian-Luca's is comparable to Saint Francis of Assisi – a saint who is associated with the patronage of animals and the natural environment. The intersubjective vision suggests their difference, but the overtly religious overtone also contributes to Christophe's and Gian-Luca's ambiguous masculine sexuality. Callum G. Brown describes how at the turn of the twentieth century, Christianity was perceived as gendered:

> Christian culture of the early twentieth century inherited from the Victorians a highly gendered notion of religion and piety. Men and women were conceived in cultural terms as having different religious attributes. This cultural division affected how religion was discussed, portrayed and experienced by individuals.[48]

In essence, Brown suggests that women had become associated with religious piety that was unattainable to men, because it involved suppressing their natural masculinity. Christianity was encouraging men to be 'meek and mild, and had thereby alienated great swathes of manhood and boyhood.'[49] The spiritual masculinity of Christophe and Gian-Luca, therefore, at the time of publication, had a societal perception that associated religion with femininity, which further contributes to their ambiguous heterosexual masculinity.

The religious nature of Hall's work has fundamentally led to their disassociation from modernism, because, as Roger Luckhurst states, the '[o]ne central way of defining modernity is to emphasize its rejection of religion.'[50] Yet, to reject religion one must be aware of its existence, which leads to an interesting tension between modernism and religion. Erik Tonning argues that there is a 'continuing influence of Christianity as cultural and political force throughout the Modernist period.'[51] Whilst *Adam's Breed* and *The Master of the House* (and *The Well of Loneliness*) are thematically religious, they are not celebrating the power of the Church. Instead, Hall is reimagining the lives of saints and martyrs in contemporary settings. As with Stephen (who is named after a saint), the sense of queer difference is aligned with the concept of martyrdom. In his discussion of Hall's and Oscar Wilde's fascination with the passion of

Christ, Dellamora argues that '[t]he suffering of Christ provides a context for experiencing, troping, and narrativizing the negativities, psychic and social, that accompanied nonconformity of these individuals.'[52] Hall is transposing the narratives of Christ, saints and martyrs who were persecuted, suffered and, in many cases, killed onto the lives and experiences of those within the LGBTQIA+ community. It is another example, alongside physical injury and vision, where Hall uses the motif of saints and martyrs in their writing to signal queer difference, which supports the questioning of Gian-Luca's and Christophe's heterosexual masculinity.

Conclusion

The Well of Loneliness will always be core to critical studies on Hall, and it will continue to provoke dialogue around its feminist and lesbian/trans themes. However, this chapter has aimed to demonstrate that Hall was also interested in cis masculine identities and sexualities by exploring the development and evolution of the blindness and physical injury motifs, following the success of their early poem 'The Blind Ploughman.' The connection between queerness, physical injury and vision enabled Hall to present seemingly heterosexual male characters with a degree of sexual ambiguity. Recognising these motifs and their meaning, which are also part of the depiction of their most famous character, Stephen Gordon, illustrates Hall's sustained interest in representations of male queer experiences in the interwar years. In their characterisation of Hilary, Martin, Gian-Luca and Christophe, Hall explored more ambiguous queer male lives in their novels than has previously been acknowledged. Through these characters, Hall, like other contemporary modernist writers, was interrogating the impact of war on men and their relationship to their masculinity and sexuality. The perception of Hall's work as middlebrow and predominantly focused on depictions of queer female desire conceals their innovative engagement with male characters whose sexuality is ambiguous. Expanding lesbian modernism to consider the ambiguities around cis male sexuality demonstrates the inventive, experimental and often encoded ways in which Hall's work represented queer male lives.

Notes

1. In a letter to Evguenia Souline, dated 24 October 1934, Radclyffe Hall states, 'I am a born invert,' in *Your John: The Love Letters of Radclyffe Hall*, ed. Joanne Glasgow (New York: New York University Press, 1997), 78.
2. Stephen Gordon's characterisation can also be interpreted as an example of literature that explores an emerging trans experience. See Jay Prosser, '"Some Primitive Thing Conceived in a Turbulent Age of Transition": The Transsexual Emerging from *The Well*,' in *Palatable Poison: Critical Perspectives on The Well of Loneliness*, ed. Laura Doan and Jay Prosser (New York: Columbia University Press, 2002), 135–70.

3. See Radclyffe Hall, 'Paris; and on Sexual Inversion' [Notebook] (Undated), Harry Ransom Center (hereafter HRC), The Radclyffe Hall and Una Troubridge Papers, Container 12. Folder 5. The notebook documents Hall's research into the gay bars of Paris for *The Well of Loneliness* and not only contains a draft of the ending of the novel but also includes evidence of their equal fascination with the wide variety of men and women who occupied these queer spaces.
4. Elizabeth English, *Lesbian Modernism: Censorship, Sexuality and Genre Fiction* (Edinburgh: Edinburgh University Press, 2015), 17.
5. Hannah Roche, *The Outside Thing: Modernist Lesbian Romance* (New York: Columbia University Press, 2019), 89.
6. Marguerite Radclyffe-Hall, 'The Blind Ploughman,' in *Songs of Three Counties and Other Poems* (London: Chapman & Hall, 1913), 32 (emphasis in the original).
7. John 9: 35–41.
8. Glasgow, *Love Letters*, 78.
9. R. B. Cunninghame Graham, 'Introduction,' in Radclyffe-Hall, *Songs of Three Counties*, xii.
10. The term 'Oedipus complex' was first used in Sigmund Freud's essay 'A Special Type of Choice of Object Made by Men' (1910). See *The Standard Edition of the Complete Psychological Works of Sigmund Freud*, ed. James Strachey, vol. 11 (London: Vintage, 2001), 171.
11. Radclyffe Hall, 'Ghosts' (c. 1930s), HRC, The Radclyffe Hall and Una Troubridge Papers, Container 18. Folder 8.
12. Genesis 19: 11: 'And they smote the men that were at the door of the house with blindness, both small and great: so that they wearied themselves to find the door.'
13. The estimated number of English soldiers who lost their sight in service was approximately 3,000, and most of these converged on London for treatment and recovery. See Gabriel Farrell, *The Story of Blindness* (London: Oxford University Press, 1956).
14. Radclyffe Hall, *The Forge* (London: Falcon Press, [1924] 1952), 10–11.
15. Terry Castle, *Noël Coward & Radclyffe Hall: Kindred Spirits* (New York: Columbia University Press, 1996), 30.
16. Jana Funke, 'Introduction,' in *'The World' and Other Unpublished Works of Radclyffe Hall*, ed. Jana Funke (Manchester: Manchester University Press, 2016), 1–44, 20.
17. Richard Dellamora, *Radclyffe Hall: A Life in the Writing* (Philadelphia: University of Pennsylvania Press, 2011), 116.
18. See 'queer, n.2.,' in *OED Online*, Oxford University Press, December 2021, accessed 31 December 2021, https://www.oed.com/view/Entry/156235.
19. Radclyffe Hall, *The Well of Loneliness* (London: Virago, [1928] 1982), 20.
20. Hall, *The Forge*, 141 (emphasis in the original).
21. As the couple prepare to separate, Susan tells Hilary, '"Yes, I want you to go," she replied quietly. "I've opened your cage door wide."' Ibid., 206.
22. Ibid., 203.
23. Ibid., 242.
24. See Michael Baker, *Our Three Selves: A Life of Radclyffe Hall* (London: Hamish Hamilton, 1985), 106: 'Despite its comic approach, *The Forge* deals with a theme

which also preoccupied John in *The Unlit Lamp*, namely the ties which bind people to each other.'
25. See Hall, 'Ghosts.' Hall politicises the contribution of lesbians and gay men in the war in the unpublished talk 'Ghosts.' The lecture draft reveals a concern for the war wounded, who are rarely seen on the streets and in society after the war. Hall notes how the disappearance of the injured war veterans is similar to the fate of lesbians and gay men who served in the war without their contributions being recognised.
26. Hall, *Well of Loneliness*, 207.
27. Ibid., 303.
28. Ibid., 333.
29. Ibid., 420.
30. Ibid.
31. Edward Carpenter, *The Intermediate Sex: A Study of Some Transitional Types of Men and Women* (London: George Allen & Unwin, [1908] 1921), 14.
32. Laura Doan, '"The Outcast of One Age Is the Hero of Another": Radclyffe Hall, Edward Carpenter and the Intermediate Sex,' in Doan and Prosser, *Palatable Poison*, 166.
33. Clare Hemmings, '"All My Life I've Been Waiting for Something . . .": Theorizing Femme Narrative in *The Well of Loneliness*,' in Doan and Prosser, *Palatable Poison*, 183–4.
34. Laura Erickson-Smith and Jennifer Mitchell, 'Queering Queer Theory, or Why Bisexuality Matters,' in *Bisexuality and Queer Theory: Intersections, Connections and Challenges*, ed. Jonathan Alexander and Serena Anderlini-D'Onofrio (Abingdon: Routledge, 2012), 105–24, 120.
35. Hall, *Well of Loneliness*, 424.
36. In Martin's letter to Stephen, he writes that he has 'been in Paris for two months,' and that he is 'a lonely sort of fellow.' Hall, *Well of Loneliness*, 416.
37. Doan, 'Outcast of One Age,' 172.
38. In *The Well of Loneliness*, this type of spiritual and intersubjective connection with other humans only occurs at the end of the novel when all the inverts of the world appear before Stephen and they famously ask, 'Acknowledge us oh God, before the whole world. Give us also the right to our existence.' Hall, *Well of Loneliness*, 447. Prior to this, Stephen is able to view the world through the eyes of animals: Peter, the Swan; Raftery, the horse; and David, the dog.
39. Roche, *Outside Thing*, 101.
40. Margaret Lawrence, *The School of Femininity: A Book for and about Women as They Are Interpreted Through Feminine Writers of Yesterday and Today* (Toronto: Musson Book Company, [1936] 1972), 329. Dellamora also reads Christophe as a gay man: 'Christophe is another of Hall's inverted protagonists, but libido in this novel is thoroughly sublimated into a sacrificial humanism. A virginal, feminine male, the great love of Christophe's life is his cousin Jan (in terms of Christian allegory, read John the Baptist).' Dellamora, *Radclyffe Hall*, 204.
41. Radclyffe Hall, *The Master of the House* (London: Jonathan Cape, 1932), 441.
42. Radclyffe Hall, *Adam's Breed* (London: Virago, [1926] 1985), 120.

43. Alan Sinfield, *The Wilde Century: Effeminacy, Oscar Wilde and the Queer Movement* (London: Cassell, 1994), 149.
44. Hall, *Adam's Breed*, 282.
45. Virginia Woolf, 'Sketch of the Past,' in *Moments of Being: Autobiographical Writings*, ed. Jeanne Schulkind (London: Pimlico, [1939] 2002), 83.
46. Hall, *Master of the House*, 135.
47. Hall, *Adam's Breed*, 282.
48. Callum G. Brown, *Religion and Society in Twentieth-Century Britain* (Harlow: Pearson, 2006), 69.
49. Ibid., 73.
50. Roger Luckhurst, 'Religion, Psychical Research, Spiritualism, and the Occult,' in *The Oxford Handbook of Modernisms*, ed. Peter Brooker, Andrzej Gąsiorek, Deborah Longworth and Andrew Thacker (Oxford: Oxford University Press, 2010), 429–44, 429.
51. Erik Tonning, *Modernism and Christianity* (Basingstoke: Palgrave Macmillian, 2014), 4.
52. Dellamora, *Radclyffe Hall*, 166.

PART III
RELATIONALITY, NETWORKS AND KINSHIP

7

WRITING WIDOWS OF LESBIAN MODERNISM

Hannah Roche

In the opening chapter of her autobiography *What Is Remembered* (1963), Alice B. Toklas recalls the unwelcome arrival of her baby brother, born when she was ten years old. 'I wanted to kiss my mother and confide my horror to her,' writes Toklas. 'He is red like a lobster, I said, are you going to love him? Taking me in her arms she said, Not like you, darling, you will always come first. And I was satisfied.'[1]

For a woman who has been remembered not as a writer but as a writer's wife, whose fame has rested on her willingness to come second to 'genius' Gertrude Stein, Toklas's decision to foreground her own primacy is both compelling and telling. Where photographic portraits of the couple show Toklas positioned firmly behind Stein, with Cecil Beaton's 1937 portrait placing Stein's 'wife' so far in the background that she appears to be in miniature, *What Is Remembered* brings Toklas into focus. At the time of Stein's death in July 1946, Stein's typist, editor, general secretary and devoted supporter had long been seen to live in her partner's shadow – a position and perspective that Toklas may publicly have welcomed. While biographer Linda Simon observes that 'at the side of the gregarious Gertrude, Alice believed there was little in her own personality that acquaintances would find interesting,' the couple's friend Donald Sutherland points out that the 'self-effacement which Alice seems to have cultivated [. . .] became a form of publicity in itself.'[2] For Sylvia Beach, Toklas was the more sophisticated of the two: 'Obviously they saw things from the same angle, [but] Alice had a great deal more finesse than Gertrude.'[3] Stein's tricksy *The Autobiography of Alice B. Toklas* (1933) might present Toklas as its subject, but the narrator ensures that 'Gertrude Stein,' a name repeated so often that it gains the hypnotic power and seductive pull of a marketing slogan or trademark, is the text's main attraction.

Two years before the publication of *What Is Remembered*, another lesbian 'widow' had at last published her biography of her writer-partner. In *The Life and Death of Radclyffe Hall* (1961), Una, Lady Troubridge, narrates the life of her beloved John 'both before and since I shared it,' claiming to provide 'the truth, the whole truth, and nothing but the truth' about the author of *The Well of Loneliness* (1928).[4] A sculptor, translator and daily diarist, Troubridge was eager to imply that her own skills lay in faithful reproduction and record-keeping rather than creation, imagination or composition: 'I am no scribe,' she writes in the foreword, 'except that I am much addicted to letter-writing.'[5] But when she claims to be 'unskilled in writing,' Troubridge is not to be taken at her word.[6] Sally Cline is right to approach Troubridge's 'hagiographic' biography with caution, describing the 'colorful drama drawn and redrawn by Lady Troubridge' in the diaries and day books kept during Hall's lifetime and pointing out that facts 'were often for bending.'[7] Where Troubridge prefaces her biography with the claim that she and Hall 'dwelt of choice in the palace of truth,' Cline draws attention to Troubridge's autocracy and artfulness as well as her 'alert artistic sense,' suggesting that Hall 'began to believe in and act out' the character that her partner created for her.[8] 'From 1915 onwards,' Cline writes, 'biographers have been hard put *not* to see the domestic and literary world of Radclyffe Hall according to Una's version.'[9] The monocle and arch eyebrow in Romaine Brooks's portrait of Troubridge (1924) serve as fitting reminders of the subject's wry lens, while the firm grip on the dachshund's collar points to authority and control.

The relationship between truth and fiction in lesbian auto/biography is far from straightforward. Diana Souhami is right that there would be no modernism without lesbians, but it is also true that there would be no lesbian modernism without imaginative life writing.[10] In 1928, the year that saw the publication and ban of *The Well of Loneliness*, two books charted new spatial and temporal territory for both lesbian writing and life writing: Djuna Barnes's satirical *Ladies Almanack* cast a fanciful eye at Natalie Clifford Barney's Sapphic salon, while Virginia Woolf's fantastical tribute to Vita Sackville-West, *Orlando*, pushed the limits of what biography might be. Woolf's vision of 'The New Biography' (1927) extended to her suitably playful *Flush: A Biography* (1933), a life of Elizabeth Barrett Browning's cocker spaniel that presented readers with a curious crossbreed of biography and fiction. Stein, whose indirect and altogether inventive take on autobiography was published in the same year as *Flush*, observed in 1934 that 'it is of course perfectly natural that autobiographies are being well written and well read.'[11] Three very different queer autobiographies had emerged in 1930: the new decade began with Ruth Fuller Field's frank and accessible *The Stone Wall*, published under the pseudonym Mary Casal; *The Little Review* founder Margaret Anderson's witty and absorbing *My Thirty Years' War*, with a chapter devoted to partner, co-editor and 'the world's best talker' Jane Heap; and surrealist photographer and writer Claude Cahun's 'literary mosaic' *Aveux non avenus* (*Disavowals, or Cancelled Confessions*), which had been rejected by Adrienne Monnier in 1928.[12] Cahun has a cameo of sorts in *The Autobiography of Alice B. Toklas*: Stein refers to her fellow guest at Sylvia Beach's apartment simply, and dismissively, as 'the niece of Marcel Schwob.'[13] But where Stein, Barnes and Woolf were bending genres and blending fact and fiction, less celebrated lesbian writers were laying claim to the truth. The mysterious Diana Frederics's *Diana: A Strange Autobiography* (1939), which shares significant aspects of plot and structure with *The Well of Loneliness*, repeatedly insists upon the authenticity of its 'characters' and events.[14] Like *The Well*, which was prefaced with a commentary by sexologist Havelock Ellis, *Diana* benefited from an introductory statement by a medical professional who could substantiate its narrative of inborn sexual difference.[15] Literary flair and avant-garde experimentation were important to some, but Hall paved the way for lesser-known lesbians who were determined to show simply that we exist.

My recent book, *The Outside Thing* (2019), explores the connection between literary production and reproduction for Stein and Hall, observing that both writers conceived of their creations as jointly produced offspring, or the happy results of a happy relationship. Though markedly different in their aesthetics, Stein and Hall engaged in imaginative role play in strikingly similar ways: Stein, who was both 'Baby boy' and 'little hubby' to 'wifey' Toklas, produced 'babies' using Toklas's 'little pen,' while Hall fostered the idea of her affair partner, Evguenia Souline, as both child and mother of the child – the text – that Hall herself would produce.[16] An encouraging letter from Souline, with whom Hall conducted an affair from 1934 until her death in 1943, 'would hit the right spot, thus enabling Hall to (pro)create.'[17] Troubridge, who had given birth to daughter Andrea in 1910, did not inseminate Hall's works but instead claimed to have 'christened' them, stating in her biography that she came up with the titles of four of Hall's novels (81). The idea of Toklas impregnating Stein while Troubridge named and nurtured Hall's children clearly has far-reaching implications for discussions of gender identity, butch/femme role play and queer family. But while it is tempting to linger on partnership and collaboration, celebrating the input and influence of modernist lesbian wives, the writing produced in sadness and in solitude by modernist lesbian widows also demands attention.

This chapter reads Toklas and Troubridge as strategic modernist memoirists, proposing an alternative to the accepted narrative of the lesbian writer's wife as subordinate amanuensis, secretary and muse. In *The Passion Projects* (2019), Melanie Micir casts light on the 'intertwined' archives of an extensive range of queer couples and collaborators, showing how surviving partners and friends sought to shape and sustain writers' literary legacies.[18] Taking a closer look at memoirs by Toklas and Troubridge, this chapter makes a case for two lesbian widows not only as caretakers of their partners' pasts and futures but also as creative practitioners of lesbian modernism. What happens when the seemingly self-effacing supporter is left alone in the spotlight, and the continuous present of life together has become the past? What becomes of the lesbian writer's wife once literary labour is no longer a shared reproductive endeavour? How, when memories have faded and 'making it new' has long grown old, might the lesbian modernist widow both remember and be remembered? Leigh Gilmore has argued that the form of the autobiography allows a writer to 'emerge through writing as an agent of self-representation, a figure, textual to be sure but seemingly substantial, who can claim "I was there" or "I am here."'[19] How might the recently reinvigorated field of late modernism be expanded and enhanced by the inclusion of these belated or delayed memoirs, both of which recapture or resurrect a late writer-partner and reinforce readers' sense that the author 'was there' and 'is here'?[20]

What Is Remembered

It is somehow symbolic that a telegram composed on the day of Stein's death simply reads 'Gertrude died this afternoon. I am writing. Dearest love / Alice.'[21] In the years between Stein's death and the composition of *What Is Remembered*, Toklas authored *The Alice B. Toklas Cook Book* (1954) along with articles in the *New York Times Book Review*, the *New Republic* and the *Atlantic Monthly*.[22] With the publication of the *Cook Book*, a 'mingling of recipe and reminiscence' that bears little resemblance to a conventional cookbook, Toklas proved herself a creative writer despite the text's concluding claim to the contrary: 'As if a cook-book had anything to do with writing.'[23] In her autobiography, Toklas draws attention to her own talents not as a writer but as a classical pianist, suggesting that her musical training allowed her to attain 'a professional accuracy and speed' as Stein's typist: 'I got a Gertrude Stein technique, like playing Bach' (59). While Toklas is clear that her work was secondary – reminding us that it was she who typed, edited, printed and published Stein's writing, under the couple's own Plain Edition imprint – she also emphasises the vital significance of, and her own unique suitability for, the role of Stein's primary supporter. There are telling moments in *The Autobiography*, as Charles Caramello points out, where the narrator describes Stein's texts as 'my books.'[24]

It would be wrong to suggest that Toklas's centrality to Stein's life and writing has not been remembered. In 1984, Catharine Stimpson acknowledged the inseparability of Stein and Toklas while expressing concerns about scholarly prurience and misinterpretation: 'Perhaps the danger now is not that we will avoid their wedding and their bedding, but that we will linger there too long.'[25] In 1991, a second essay with 'Gertrice/Altrude' in its title, by Leigh Gilmore, cautioned against narrow biographical readings that threaten to 'miniaturize [Stein] as a member of a spatting couple.'[26] Karin Cope has since suggested that Toklas may be seen as 'architect' rather than 'satellite' of Stein, and Janine Utell has similarly argued that all of the 'arrangements' in Stein's world and work 'depend on their arranger – Alice B. Toklas.'[27] In 2006, Anna Linzie placed Toklas centre stage with a monograph that would tell *The True Story of Alice B. Toklas*, reading Toklas's own autobiographical writing in relation to Stein's *The Autobiography*. While Linzie's work provides a detailed and persuasive analysis of Toklas's oeuvre, its series of 'intertextual close readings' that point out places where Toklas's autobiography 'mimics or echoes *The Autobiography*' can only go so far in convincing readers of the value of *What Is Remembered* as a text in its own right.[28]

It is significant that *The Autobiography* receives only brief mention in *What Is Remembered*. On 24 October 1934, having at last achieved fame in her homeland with the publication of *The Autobiography*, which the *Atlantic Monthly* had published in an abridged form in four monthly instalments from May 1933, Stein embarked on a triumphant lecture tour of America. Toklas, who accompanied her partner for the duration of the six-month trip, does not explain that *The Autobiography* had made Stein's name in America but instead presents the tour in passive and prosaic terms: 'In 1934 it was suggested by a lecture bureau that Gertrude should go to New York' (149). In *Everybody's Autobiography* (1937), a text that aimed to build on (but ultimately failed to replicate) the success of her first autobiography, Stein reveals that advances on *The Autobiography* paid for a new Ford car, a bespoke Hermès coat, two studded collars for Basket the poodle, and the installation of a telephone at each of the couple's two homes.[29] 'Being a celebrity,' Stein recalls of the voyage to New York, beginning in the singular before turning tellingly to the plural, 'we paid less than the full price of a small room and we had a very luxurious one' (173). But where Stein expresses excitement about having earned both celebrity status and her 'first dollar' (42), Toklas remembers that 'Bernard Faÿ got us passage on the S.S. *Champlain* at a reduced rate' (149) and goes on to downplay an invitation to dine at the captain's table: 'They seemed to think that Gertrude deserved that distinction' (152). When purchasing fruit on arrival in New York, Toklas is surprised to be recognised by an attendant: 'How did he know who I was?' (154). Five paragraphs later, after Toklas has seen a revolving electric light in Times Square announcing 'Gertrude Stein has arrived in New York, Gertrude Stein has arrived in New York' (154), the bestselling book that led to the lecture tour is finally introduced: 'Mr Harcourt, who had published

The Autobiography of Alice B. Toklas by Gertrude Stein [. . .]' (155). Whether Toklas's curious decision to decentre *The Autobiography* from the story of Stein's success can be explained by coyness about a text bearing her own name or by a desire for readers to accept her work on its own terms, this episode serves as one illustration of the narrative play and temporal trickery that characterise *What Is Remembered*.

As an autobiography is written in the present about the past, by a writer who has the benefit of future knowledge about the events they describe, the relationship between autobiographical narrative and time is naturally unstable. The chronology of Toklas's ostensibly accessible autobiography is further disrupted, repeatedly and often confusingly, by the past perfect tense and the introduction (to the text) of friends whom the couple have long known. After the discussion of the lecture tour, for instance, Stein and Toklas visit their good friends the Abdys, whom readers have not yet encountered. 'It was Bertie, Sir Robert Abdy,' Toklas recalls, 'who had said to Gertrude, You should write the history of your friends and time. Which she did, *The Autobiography of Alice B. Toklas*' (172). Many of Toklas's paragraphs begin with markers of time – 'One day,' 'One afternoon,' 'That night,' 'When,' 'Later' – but events do not always unfold in logical or linear fashion. 'In the summer of 1931,' begins one paragraph in chapter 8, 'Aaron Copland and Paul Bowles came to visit us at Bilignin' (147). Toklas then provides, in four paragraphs, anecdotes about Copland and Bowles, ending with the recollection that she met Bowles's wife 'later in Paris after Gertrude died' (148). The following two paragraphs open thus: 'One day Madame de Clermont-Tonnerre came to see Gertrude and took off her hat and said, What do you think of it? She had had her beautiful hair cut'; 'That night Gertrude said to me, Cut off my braids. Which I agreed to do.' Stein's famous haircut was carried out by Toklas in 1926. After a one-sentence paragraph on forgetting – 'Later Gertrude forgot that she had ever had two long braids' (149) – Toklas turns to 1934 and the lecture tour. Moving from 1931 to 1934 via the unwritten dates of 1946 (Stein's death) and 1926, the narrative distorts and manipulates time, forcing readers to attempt to piece together individual stories ('One day') into a coherent narrative. While Stein observes in *Everybody's Autobiography* that '[a]n autobiography is not a novel no indeed it is not a novel' (200), the nonlinear storytelling, temporal distortion and narrative fragmentation of *What Is Remembered* require serious interpretative work.

Describing their good friend the Baroness Pierlot, Toklas writes that 'Gertrude used to say she had a memory that rivalled mine' (131). It goes without saying, however, that the elderly Toklas – who was eighty-one when she began work on *What Is Remembered* in 1958 – may have struggled to arrange events into the 'correct' order. In an interview six years earlier, Toklas had been quick to correct the impression that her 'recollection of times and places and dates [was] quite astounding':

I don't think so. Oh, you should have known what it was. I could have begun with the beginning and given you *everything* connected with *every* day along the line, until Gertrude died. I lost my memory then, because I think I was upset and my head, when it came back, just wasn't clear about things.[30]

Both Simon and Linzie document Toklas's aborted collaboration with Max White, a writer-friend who was enlisted to work with Toklas on her memoirs but who eventually gave up and threw away his notes, citing his subject's tendency to 'lie and deny it and contradict herself' as reason for the failure of the project.[31] Linzie is right that White's search for a 'preexisting, factual, pure, complete, and verifiable' autobiographical 'truth' could only ever have been futile, but we might also understand Toklas's creative approach to autobiography as a narrative strategy rather than a simple failure to remember.[32] Where Stein uses informative chapter headings to enforce a semblance of order and chronology on *The Autobiography*, Toklas's memoir appears purposely disordered and often impishly deceiving. Revealingly, the Toklas that we hear in the 1952 interview takes pleasure in teasing and misleading interested interlocutors. Having rejected interviewer Roland Duncan's suggestion that she may have 'contributed' to *The Autobiography*, Toklas recalls a conversation with a friend: '"I suppose you are helping Miss Stein write her books, aren't you, Alice?" "Oh, surely. Most of them are mine," I said.'[33] Similarly, in *What Is Remembered*, Toklas draws attention to her own unreliable narration: when meeting Charlie Chaplin, 'I said to him, The only films we have seen are yours, which flattered him but which was not exactly exact' (163–4). Discussing 'the kind and degree of "truth" that can be expected from autobiographical writing,' Laura Marcus recognises that 'the "intention" to tell the truth, as far as possible, is a sufficient guarantee of autobiographical veracity and sincerity.'[34] Toklas, however, is quite clear in her intention to secure her reader's (and Chaplin's) trust and affection through charm and beguilement rather than factual accuracy.

Elsewhere in her memoir, Toklas alerts readers to instances of interplay between reality and fiction. Remembering a little girl who asked her for money outside the Gothic cathedral in Burgos, Spain, Toklas writes that her 'green eyes and her ways suggested Becky Sharp [from Thackeray's *Vanity Fair*]' (74). So many of Toklas's memories are bound up in reading, from her paternal grandfather's 'read[ing] aloud to me Grimm's fairy tales' (8) and school days spent with Louisa May Alcott and Dickens (11) to her first walk with Stein, where Stein asked 'what books I had read on the steamer and were the Flaubert letters translated into English' (28). Where the appreciation and purchase of art are central to Stein's autobiography, Toklas spends her time in Paris 'looking at and buying books' (51). The impact of this literary preoccupation is twofold: Toklas reminds her readers that her bookish sensibilities are as fine-tuned as

Stein's, and she draws attention to the novelistic qualities of her own writing. Weaving references to fiction into her narrative, Toklas establishes interconnections among her own 'store of well-wrought anecdotes,' to quote Simon paraphrasing White (302), and the expansive 'store' of stories that she has read. As she recalls that her daily typing of *The Making of Americans* (1925) was 'like living history,' with 'characters or incidents of the previous day' making their way into Stein's monumental family saga (60), Toklas again shows that the line between real life and fiction is not always easy to discern.

Reviewing *What Is Remembered* for the *New Republic*, Joseph Barry (mis)identifies the couple as a 'Platonic pair' while commenting upon 'the fullness of a relationship that makes wife a feeble household word.'[35] Although she is careful to conceal specific details, Toklas provides key insights into her intimate relationship with Stein. Stein appears as 'Gertrude Stein' throughout *The Autobiography* – and Toklas is 'Alice Toklas' in *Everybody's Autobiography* – but Toklas pinpoints the moment at which she 'was to call her Gertrude' (39) and continues to do so for the remaining nine chapters. Toklas chooses not to give away any secrets about the beginnings of the relationship, but her explicit refusal to tell makes it clear that there is something worth telling. Toklas recalls having arrived half an hour late to their second meeting:

> I did not know what had happened or what was going to happen.
> Nor is it possible for me to tell about it now. After she had paced for some time about the long Florentine table made longer by being flanked on either side by two smaller ones, she stood in front of me and said, Now you understand. It is over. It is not too late to go for a walk. You can look at the pictures while I change my clothes. (27)

Moving swiftly from ignorance to secrecy to closure ('It is over') to possibility ('It is not too late'), Toklas not only shows readers that it was Stein who drove the relationship forward but also uses Stein's voice to ask for acceptance: 'Now you understand.' After providing some detail about the walk, Toklas tells travelling companion Harriet Levy 'only of the walk and nothing of what had occurred before' (28) before symbolically tearing into shreds a letter that she had received from a commodore with whom she may have 'lacked discretion' (23) on the voyage to Paris. As Linzie argues, this incident represents a 'slight but significant subplot of heterosexual (im)possibility.'[36] 'Well, that episode was closed' (29), Toklas declares emphatically, at once consigning heterosexuality to the past and echoing Stein's 'It is over,' demonstrating the similarity and inseparability of Stein's voice and her own.

While temporal shifts, silences and deferrals allow Toklas to sidestep the subject of sexuality, there are moments where she favours an 'exactly exact' approach to time, punctuality and the details of domestic life. Picasso is introduced as being always 'on time' (30); Stein 'had her breakfast coffee at the lunch table at one o'clock' (60); and, narrating a bizarre episode where Levy claims to have seen God, Toklas remembers that 'I looked at my watch. It was half-past eight' (42). Such claims for temporal 'truth' serve as carefully placed reminders that Toklas *can* remember, but as writer and narrator she is in a position to decide what to share and what to obscure. Readers are not initially privy to Toklas's plans to move in with Stein at the rue de Fleurus, hearing the news belatedly via a conversation between Toklas and a friend: 'it is already arranged that I should go to stay with Gertrude and Leo' (67). But while Toklas appears a passive spectator in certain private affairs – 'it is already arranged' – she does not shy away from seizing narratives of public, professional and philanthropic life. 'We decided that we would at once have to busy ourselves with some war work,' Toklas begins chapter 6 (100), before switching from 'we' to 'I' in the next sentence. 'I suddenly saw a Ford car' is followed by 'I said to Gertrude, wait a minute, I am going in to enquire about this.' Toklas is insistent that it was she who secured the couple's war work for the American Fund for French Wounded, and she who arranged for the printing of postcards to produce additional funds (104). With the amusing recollection that 'I gave Gertrude a half cold chicken to eat in one hand while she was driving' (104), readers are playfully reminded that while Stein was in the driver's seat in a literal sense, Toklas fuelled their endeavours in more ways than one.

Though Toklas's character is in no way subsumed by Stein, their togetherness is emphasised by unexpected slips in subject/object positions and by the merging of autobiography and biography. On a trip to Seville, 'I ate innumerable ices during the day, which disturbed Gertrude's stomach' (81). *What Is Remembered* poses as straightforward autobiography, beginning 'I was born and raised in California' (5), but it ends with Stein's death. While Toklas introduces her text as autobiography, the idea that the text offers a performance of the autobiographical mode is subtly suggested by the first chapter's preoccupation with theatre and spectacle. In the opening five pages, we encounter opera, the circus, and a young Toklas waltzing and dancing the cachucha, and in chapter 3, the theatre is host to both modernism and modernity. After having seen and been shocked by 'the most questionable of the comedies,' Toklas attends a Henri Bernstein play where she sees 'one of the first portable telephones' (50) on the stage. The audience 'buzzed with excitement as the curtain went up and revealed it' (50). Toklas's interest in technology and machinery extends from her delight in her 'formidable' new Smith Premier typewriter (59) to a charming anecdote about Stein's wartime attempt to repair their truck's fan belt using a hairpin (110). Aspects of artistic and literary modernism are introduced with more scepticism. Toklas overhears 'not entirely friendly' discussions at the vernissage of the Salon d'Automne, and she appears to observe rather than participate in applause for a 'very small Russian girl' who claims that her art strives for '[t]he modern, the new' (33). Joyce and Stein have little to say to one another (141), and 'Mrs. [Vanessa] Bell' and the 'very beautiful' Woolf – 'daughters of Sir Leslie Stephen' (88) – are noted not for their work but for their part in the Dreadnought Hoax, 'a very English prank' (89). Continuing the work of *The Autobiography*, where the narrator insists that it was Stein's 'Melanctha' (in *Three Lives*, 1909) that made 'the first definite step away from the nineteenth century and into the twentieth century in literature' (61), *What Is Remembered* upholds the idea of Stein as the most prominent and pioneering of literary modernists.

It is easy to see why Linzie would argue that *What Is Remembered* 'repeats and mimics Stein's text in such a way as to unsettle the fantasy of originality.'[37] Along with the 'double takes' that Linzie identifies, there are clear nods to the earlier text in Toklas's narrative: the bells that ring in San Francisco in the second paragraph, for instance, echo the first chapter of *The Autobiography*, where a bell rings within Toklas each time she encounters a 'genius' (9). Similarities in style and structure place the two texts in a 'classical chicken/egg situation,' familiar to readers of collaborative queer writing: did Toklas write her autobiography in the voice that Stein had assigned her, or was the narration of *The Autobiography* an attempt by Stein to capture Toklas's authentic voice?[38] As Toklas ends her own autobiography with Stein's death, we might conclude that the literary construct of Toklas, first introduced in *The Autobiography*, dies with Stein. Toklas herself may well have supported this idea, as is evident in a particularly poignant letter written to curator Donald Gallup on 11 March 1947: 'You realize surely that Gertrude's memory is all my life.'[39] But as this chapter has shown, Toklas's writing life extended beyond Stein, and her modernist legacy amounts to much more than the texts that she typed and printed for her partner. Where Stein claims in *Everybody's Autobiography* that 'autobiography is easy like it or not autobiography is easy for any one' (4), *What Is Remembered* is a deceptively complex and challenging amalgam of auto/biography and invention by a writer with an unexpectedly unique literary imagination.

The Life and Death of Radclyffe Hall

While the title of *What Is Remembered* does not claim Stein as the book's subject – Toklas's suggested title, *Things I Have Seen*, an echo of Stein's 1945 memoir *Wars I Have Seen*, was ignored by the publisher – *The Life and Death of Radclyffe Hall* makes its status as biography clear. In her foreword, Troubridge introduces her text as 'a perfectly truthful biography [. . .] in the form of a long letter addressed to those who will read it.'[40] Gilmore's claim that biography 'begins in mourning' and 'give[s] voice to the dead, [who] seem to be withholding something that the living want' is apposite here: as Micir has observed, Troubridge's decision to document Hall's past was driven in part by a desire to secure her partner's 'posthumous reputation' and to 'provide necessary information about Hall to generations of future readers.'[41] But, unsurprisingly, Troubridge's insistence upon the veracity of her narrative has been met with scorn. Souhami observes that 'Una had a psychopath's skill to convince herself of the truth of her lies,' while an otherwise forgiving Richard Ormrod admits that 'in a court of law some of her statements and omissions would amount to perjury!'[42] Reflecting on her own experience of writing Hall's life, Cline outlines the 'fraudulent' actions taken by a woman who was 'utterly determined that only her version of Hall as a stern lesbian icon should be in the public domain.'[43] Troubridge's letter-biography was written at great speed from 19 February to 18 March 1945, but it remained unpublished until 1961, three years after the death of Hall's affair partner Souline – who, as Troubridge was well aware, could have sued for libel.

The inclusion of 'Lady' on the book's cover may raise eyebrows. Troubridge had taken the title in June 1919, despite having been legally separated from her newly knighted husband Admiral Sir Ernest Charles Thomas Troubridge for four months. While the 'form of a long letter' may seem like a reasonable choice for a woman who had continued to write to Hall every day since her death on 7 October 1943, aspects of the text's structure and style might also arouse suspicion. Troubridge kept meticulous records of Hall's professional life, but the absence of chapter breaks and scarcity of specific dates here do not point to a partner bent on precise documentation. For Ormrod, the form of Troubridge's biography goes some way in letting its author off the hook: 'It meanders confusingly, showing little concern for accurate dating, but in fairness some license must be granted in a "letter."'[44] Troubridge quite clearly uses any 'license' granted by a letter to her advantage, presenting her biography not as a carefully edited record but rather as a spontaneously produced 'story' (44) or string of recollections that may at any point pull her off track: 'as I write this, a memory crops up' (20); 'once again I have wandered up by-ways' (93, 134). At the same time, Troubridge does pay attention to certain conventions of biography: the narrative starts reluctantly with a discussion of Hall's ancestry and family crest ('I suppose I ought to begin [. . .],' 7), and there is an attempt to impose chronology despite the many distractions and digressions. Acknowledging the tension between the present narrating self and the past subject who could not foresee future events, Troubridge looks back 'with the eye of one who knows the sequel' (42), often providing flashes of what 'was hidden in the impenetrable future' (47). 'Being now nearly sixty,' she writes, 'most of my vision works backwards and I can visualize what seemed at the time a mere vortex of impulses and coincidence and tragedy as a pattern' (47). Though Hall's death does not occur until we reach the last page, we are made privy to a discussion that took place 'shortly before her death and when we both knew that bodily separation was imminent' (60) in the first third of the narrative. Where temporal disorder in Toklas's narrative has been interpreted as confusion or a failure to remember, Troubridge's apparently effortless leaps across time create a confident impression of comprehensive knowledge and god-like omniscience.

Cline may be right to describe Troubridge's biography as hagiographic, but the Hall who emerges from the first part of the text does not inspire veneration. 'Throughout her adolescence and her maturity until the age of thirty-four,' claims Troubridge, 'she was idle, bone idle' (18). When Troubridge first encounters Hall on 1 August 1915, she finds her 'not only devout but, to my mind, bigoted in the extreme' (48). Most repellent to readers is a second-hand account of a year spent in America as a reckless twenty-something, where Hall 'drove her cousin Jane Randolph (later Caruth) all over the States in a primitive car with one spark-plug at the back and a revolver handy for obstreperous negroes [sic]' (19). The couple's later politics are troubling to say the least: forerunner to Italian fascism Gabriele D'Annunzio is given more space in the narrative than any other acquaintance (118–25), and both partners prize their 'Fascist medal' (68) and a dedicated photograph of 'the Duce' (151) – though Hitler, whom they see in person during his visit to Florence in 1938, is 'a criminal lunatic' (150). While Troubridge does not explicitly marry up the age of thirty-four and the date when she and Hall met, the not-so-subtle implication is that Hall was not only 'a mass of sharp corners, prejudices and preconceptions that she was sure nothing was ever going to modify' (48) but also 'resolutely and remorselessly idle' (28) until she had the fortune of falling for Troubridge. Thus, although Troubridge claims that she will 'try to omit, so far as possible, my personal concerns and history' (44) from her narrative, to the point that she does not once mention her own daughter, she nonetheless presents herself as the sole saviour and architect of Hall's life and career. Her supposed self-effacement is nothing but performance.

Like Toklas, whose 'fingers were adapted only to Gertrude's work' (*What Is Remembered*, 59), Troubridge felt herself uniquely suited to the role of 'watching, serving and subordinating everything in existence to the requirements of an overwhelming literary inspiration and industry' (39). 'Serving' Hall involved deciphering handwriting, reading aloud, correcting spellings, incorporating revisions, exercising tact, and 'repeatedly read[ing] the riot act' (77) when it came to the destruction of early drafts. Describing the 'one respect in which I trained John,' as though she were one of the couple's pet dogs, Troubridge explains that she 'exacted a solemn promise that never, never again would she destroy anything until we had finally examined it together and she had confirmed her verdict' (77–8). Though Troubridge credits Hall's first long-term partner, her own cousin 'Ladye' Mabel Batten, with recognising Hall's talent 'even in the egg' and taking steps that led to her career (39), she questions whether Batten would have been up to the task of sustaining Hall's writing life. Souline was certainly not fit for the role: 'She had less than no appreciation of the conditions essential to the production of creative work' (116). Only Troubridge, in whose hands the decision to write *The Well of Loneliness* was apparently placed (82), could achieve an intimate knowledge of Hall's working mind. 'I have reason to believe,' Troubridge asserts, 'that even after a number of years Evguenia hardly knew the names of the characters that John had created' (116).

In Troubridge's memoir, Hall's fictional characters are very much alive. Troubridge recalls how, 'collecting copy' for *Adam's Breed* (1926), the couple followed the novel's hero 'step by step to the New Forest [. . .] and found him at last' (80). Travelling through Fréjus, on the Côte d'Azur, Hall spies the place where Christophe Bénédit was 'born' (101) before writing his character in *The Master of the House* (1932). According to Troubridge, Hall 'wrote herself' (103) into the martyred Christophe, a carpenter's son with spiritual healing powers, only to develop 'an angry-looking red stain' (105) at the centre of each palm. Though she admits that Hall shared 'practically none of her circumstances or experiences' (103) with her earlier martyred messiah, Stephen Gordon, Troubridge also hints at connections between Hall and the protagonist of *The Well of Loneliness*. From childhood, Hall had 'protection mania' (16); later, '[a]thletic diversions' give way to 'intellectual, artistic and religious understanding' (42). The descriptions of Hall's working practices, where she writes and smokes through the night with Troubridge growing ever weary of her outbursts of temper and self-doubt, mirror scenes between Stephen and Puddle in the third book of *The Well*. Two aspects of Troubridge's own writing style are of particular note: like Hall, she has a tendency to begin sentences with 'And,' and she often describes how she and Hall were 'like' fictional characters. 'Like Hilary and Susan Brent in *The Forge*, [. . .] we decided that what we wanted was a small house in London' (65); 'like Stephen Gordon, we both loved [the Sacré Cœur]' (84). While Troubridge evidently imagines the recipient of her 'letter' to have a detailed knowledge of Hall's oeuvre, her phrasing also implies that fictional characters somehow prefigure reality.

Fiction shapes Troubridge's biography in other ways, too – and not just because Troubridge, like Toklas, was a voracious reader who 'seemed to breed' books (181). We are confronted with significant omissions and outright lies: Troubridge claims that Hall's affair with Phoebe Hoare in 1913–14 was a 'trivial, passing lapse' that Batten dismissed 'with a tolerant smile' (38), but Cline has pointed out that Batten meticulously 'measured and calculated' Hall's meetings with Hoare in her diaries and grew increasingly estranged from Hall.[45] Troubridge discusses the couple's sittings with trance medium Gladys Osborne Leonard and their 'war work' (59) for the Society for Psychical Research (SPR), but she does not make reference to Hall's 1920 slander trial against SPR member St George Lane Fox-Pitt, who had described her as a 'grossly immoral woman.'[46] Both Cline and Souhami have documented Troubridge's active role in shaping – or sculpting – lasting perceptions of Hall's mannish persona. When

Hall was ten or eleven years old, her stepfather Alberto Visetti made sexual advances towards her. Having initially described this abuse and its effects in forty pages of her biography, Troubridge then removed all trace of it 'lest we have psycho analytic know alls saying she would have been a wife and mother but for that experience.'[47] Ever insistent upon the innate masculinity of her 'John,' Troubridge arranged for a portrait of a five-year-old Hall with long curls, which would appear in the biography, to be doctored in order to depict a more boyish child. Hall was forty when she cropped her waist-length hair, on 17 December 1920: much like Stein before Toklas carried out the 'monk' haircut in 1926, the younger Hall usually wore her hair 'in tight plaits closely twisted round her small and admirably shaped head.'[48] Nonetheless, for her partner, Hall's face was always that of 'a very handsome young man' (46).

Throughout the biography, Troubridge works hard to convince her reader of the 'truth' of her account, drawing attention to both spontaneous memories and her sustained effort to remember. As we have seen, she also uses her 'backward' vision to allow her to identify 'patterns' in the past. Though she admits to knowing very little about Hall's childhood, Troubridge reports that she 'hated dolls, loved drums and noisy toys, but such tastes are common to many girl children and might seem to have had little if any significance had the future not confirmed the fact of her sexual inversion' (19). The discussion of a photograph of Hall as a 'sturdy-looking baby' with 'hard-clenched fists' appears to borrow directly from *The Well*, where Hall describes the infant Stephen's 'hard little arrogant fists.'[49] As Troubridge is writing about this photograph, which is not reproduced in the biography, 'a memory crops up that she was told at one time that throughout her infancy strangers always mistook her for a boy' (20). In this way, Troubridge nurtures a narrative of gender difference while also suggesting that her own role is merely that of messenger or medium. Though some recollections appear to reach Troubridge as if from nowhere, she also takes pains to record her attempts to remember on the page: 'And there the curtain – so far as my memory serves – comes down on the anecdotes [. . .]. No, there is one more glimpse' (12). Making repeated turns to metaphor, describing any forgotten moments as 'dropped stitches in the fabric of my knowledge' (25), Troubridge creatively diverts attention away from her many deliberate fabrications and omissions. The holes in the text are not 'dropped stitches' but rather purposely placed gaps – or, to mix Troubridge's metaphors, an obfuscating 'curtain' – between her subject and the reader-recipient. While her style is lively and her tone often intimate, Troubridge-as-biographer maintains a careful distance: she knew Hall 'better than anyone on this earth' (103) and will not readily share her knowledge.

Though she claims to be 'unskilled' as a writer (182), Troubridge is quite clearly in control of her story. At times, the perceived interests of the letter's recipient are taken into account – 'And, you may begin to ask, where in all this do we find any traces of Radclyffe Hall, the future writer?' (27) – but Troubridge will rarely be swayed from her narrative path. Having introduced an American cousin with whom Hall was romantically involved in her mid-twenties, Troubridge states that 'Dorothy Clarke [was Diehl] is dead now, and you might well say, "*de mortuis*", but this record is to be the truth, the whole truth, and nothing but the truth' (27) before giving a one-sided account of Clarke as ungrateful and disloyal. Troubridge's dismissal of her love rival, the 'violent and uncontrolled' (112) Souline, is to be expected, but her insistence on Hall's and her own mutual dependence and isolation from others is concerning. Recognising that she has included 'very little' about friends, Troubridge claims that 'the very fact of our perfect companionship precluded their assuming any great importance or entering very closely into our lives' (113). In a chapter on Hall in her 1963 work *Me – and the Swans*, the couple's friend Naomi 'Mickie' Jacob writes as though she were trespassing on another's property: Troubridge, who 'understood her as no one else could possibly do,' is 'the only person who could really write' an account of Hall's life.[50] Jacob reports her regret at having dared to ask to see Hall on her deathbed, a request that Troubridge firmly refused, and makes it clear that she will not attempt to cross boundaries again. In my work on Hall's obsessive relationship with Souline, I identify Hall's behaviour as coercive control.[51] Here, asserting absolute authority over her subject, Troubridge exercises a form of textual control, excluding family and friends (the word 'friends' is placed in inverted commas on page 128) and manipulating her reader – through wit, charm and a feigned intimacy with 'you' – into accepting her distorted version of events.

Noting that others remember Hall for her laughter (177), Troubridge steers her narrative between grief and humour, offering telling insights into the couple's domestic and intimate life together. The word 'orgy' describes the pleasures of homemaking (62, 108), reading (74) and sightseeing (143). We are invited to smile at the description of Hall and Troubridge filling the bottom of their car with ten kilograms of cherries on a journey from Châteauneuf-du-Pape to Avignon (98), and at the account of how Hall, Troubridge, Souline and a tan dwarf pinscher named Mary Rose travelled from Merano to Florence in a 'turquoise-blue charabanc of immense proportions' (127). In Florence, a domestic servant surprisingly refers to 'Donna Una and the Signorina' (133). Troubridge's steadfast dedication to Hall, particularly as she nears the end of her life, is presented in powerful, moving and increasingly distressing terms. Recalling how she prayed for a miracle as Hall's condition worsened, despairing at the thought of surviving her beloved, Troubridge observes that 'separation on earth was the universal lot unless people had the amazing luck to die or be killed together' (189). The couple's Catholic faith provided hope for reunion, and – though she carried out Hall's wish that she destroy the draft of her last novel – Troubridge evidently found comfort in the knowledge that Hall's texts would survive. The biography brims with pride in Hall's fiction: the obscenity trials of *The Well of Loneliness* are given little space, but chance encounters with admirers and supporters are interspersed throughout. Importantly, Troubridge highlights the positive after-effects of censorship, drawing attention to the notorious novel's extraordinary reach. Hall 'would have felt less tired' at the time of the trials, she observes wryly, 'had she known that fourteen years after publication *The Well of Loneliness* in America alone would have a steady annual sale of over one hundred thousand copies' (94). The last line of the biography is spoken by Hall herself, as Troubridge quotes from a letter by Hall discovered in her widowhood: 'God keep you until we meet again . . . and believe in my love, which is much, much stronger than mere death' (190). Where *The Well* ends with Stephen sacrificing her relationship with Mary Llewellyn, Troubridge's life of Hall concludes with an enduring and emphatic lesbian love.

Conclusion

Attending her first bullfight with Stein, Toklas wears 'what I called my Spanish disguise, so that I remained unnoticed' (78). Although they have not reserved tickets, Toklas requests and receives 'the very best [seats] in the first row in the shade under the President's box' (78). Showing a curious combination of invisibility and prime positioning, with more than a hint of privilege and entitlement, this short episode somehow captures the character and self-presentation of the lesbian modernist wife.

Despite differences in style and approach, there are remarkable similarities between the two memoirs discussed here. Ormrod briefly outlines 'surprising parallels' (292) between Toklas and Troubridge, and we might enhance his discussion by adding a number of shared passions: the association of past happiness with 'food and drink' (*Life and Death*, 90), for instance, or an insatiable appetite for reading. Both writers' accounts of domestic life with adored pet dogs have much to offer to scholarship on alternative families; both texts' temporal disruption could contribute to debates around queer time. Both memoirs – written by women who only took up their own 'little pens' after the death of the author-partner-parent – might enrich the fertile fields of late modernist and lesbian auto/biography studies. When it comes to sexual and textual relationships, the queer force of this work is clear: only through writing about their late partners do Toklas and Troubridge find their own voices as lesbian modernists.

Notes

1. Alice B. Toklas, *What Is Remembered: An Autobiography* (London: Cardinal, 1989), 7–8. Subsequent references will cite page numbers in-text.
2. Linda Simon, *The Biography of Alice B. Toklas* (Lincoln and London: University of Nebraska Press, 1991), 266; Donald Sutherland, 'Alice and Gertrude and Others,' *Prairie Schooner* 45, no. 4 (1971/2): 284–99, 288.
3. Sylvia Beach, *Shakespeare and Company* (Lincoln: University of Nebraska Press, [1959] 1991), 27.

4. Una, Lady Troubridge, 'Foreword,' in *The Life and Death of Radclyffe Hall* (London: Hammond, Hammond, 1961), n.p.
5. Ibid.
6. Ibid., 182.
7. Sally Cline, *Radclyffe Hall: A Woman Called John* (London: John Murray Publishers, 1997), 108.
8. Ibid., 110, 108.
9. Ibid., 108.
10. Diana Souhami, *No Modernism Without Lesbians* (London: Head of Zeus, 2020).
11. Gertrude Stein, 'Portraits and Repetition,' in *Lectures in America* (Boston: Beacon Press, 1957), 184.
12. Margaret Anderson, *My Thirty Years' War: An Autobiography* (New York: Covici-Friede, 1930), 103. Tirza True Latimer describes *Aveux non avenus* as a 'literary mosaic' in her chapter on '"Narcissus and Narcissus": Claude Cahun and Marcel Moore,' in *Women Together/Women Apart: Portraits of Lesbian Paris* (New Brunswick, NJ: Rutgers University Press, 2005), 68–104, 80.
13. Gertrude Stein, *The Autobiography of Alice B. Toklas* (London: Penguin Classics, 2001), 211. Subsequent references will cite page numbers in-text.
14. As Julie Abraham points out, 'On the cover, in the introduction, and in the text, *Diana* tells you that what it is telling you is true.' Julie Abraham, 'Introduction to the New Edition,' in Diana Frederics, *Diana: A Strange Autobiography* (New York and London: New York University Press, 1995), xxii. Frederics claims that the 'characters and events in this book are real' in her foreword (xxxix).
15. Physician and medical journalist Victor Robinson, MD, provides the introduction to Frederics's text.
16. See Hannah Roche, *The Outside Thing: Modernist Lesbian Romance* (New York: Columbia University Press, 2019), 61–6, 114–18.
17. Ibid., 115.
18. Melanie Micir, *The Passion Projects: Modernist Women, Intimate Archives, Unfinished Lives* (Princeton, NJ: Princeton University Press, 2019), 10.
19. Leigh Gilmore, *The Limits of Autobiography: Trauma and Testimony* (Ithaca, NY and London: Cornell University Press, 2001), 9.
20. See Julia Jordan, *Late Modernism and the Avant-Garde British Novel: Oblique Strategies* (Oxford: Oxford University Press, 2020). Jordan acknowledges scholars including Laura Marcus, David James, Rebecca Walkowitz and Urmila Seshagiri who have 'recently made the field of late modernism so capacious' (25n87).
21. Alice B. Toklas to W. G. Rogers, 27 July 1946, in *Staying on Alone: Letters of Alice B. Toklas*, ed. Edward Burns (London: Angus and Robinson, 1974), 3.
22. For a full list of Toklas's publications, see Simon, *Biography*, 374–5.
23. Alice B. Toklas, *The Alice B. Toklas Cook Book* (New York: Anchor, [1954] 1960), 298. Toklas describes the text as a 'mingling of recipe and reminiscence' in its preface, 'A Word with the Cook,' n.p.
24. Charles Caramello, *Henry James, Gertrude Stein, and the Biographical Act* (Chapel Hill: University of North Carolina Press, 1996), 160.
25. Catharine R. Stimpson, 'Gertrice/Altrude: Stein, Toklas, and the Paradox of the Happy Marriage,' in *Mothering the Mind: Twelve Studies of Women and Their*

Silent Partners, ed. Ruth Perry and Martine Watson Brownley (New York and London: Holmes and Meier, 1984), 122–39, 128.
26. Leigh Gilmore, 'A Signature of Lesbian Autobiography: "Gertrice/Altrude,"' *Prose Studies* 14, no. 2 (1991): 56–75, 56.
27. Karin Cope, *Passionate Collaborations: Learning to Live with Gertrude Stein* (Victoria, BC: ELS Editions, 2005), 166; Janine Utell, *Literary Couples and Twentieth-Century Life Writing* (London and New York: Bloomsbury, 2020), 59.
28. Anna Linzie, *The True Story of Alice B. Toklas: A Study of Three Autobiographies* (Iowa City: University of Iowa Press, 2006), 107, 103.
29. Gertrude Stein, *Everybody's Autobiography* (Cambridge, MA: Exact Change, [1937] 1993), 173. See 41, 44–5.
30. Alice B. Toklas, 'The Bancroft Library Interview,' conducted by Roland Duncan, November 1952 (Regional Oral History Office, University of California, Berkeley, 2012), 94.
31. Quoted in Simon, *Biography*, 303.
32. Linzie, *True Story*, 116.
33. Toklas, 'Bancroft Library Interview,' 93.
34. Laura Marcus, *Auto/biographical Discourses: Criticism, Theory, Practice* (Manchester and New York: Manchester University Press, 1994), 3.
35. Joseph Barry, 'Miss Toklas on Her Own,' *The New Republic*, 30 March 1963, 21.
36. Linzie, *True Story*, 130.
37. Ibid., 125.
38. Ibid., 133.
39. Toklas, *Staying on Alone*, 54.
40. Troubridge, 'Foreword,' n.p. Subsequent references will cite page numbers in-text.
41. Gilmore, *Limits of Autobiography*, 93; Micir, *Passion Projects*, 25.
42. Diana Souhami, *The Trials of Radclyffe Hall* (London: Weidenfeld and Nicolson, 1998), 360; Richard Ormrod, *Una Troubridge: The Friend of Radclyffe Hall* (London: Jonathan Cape, 1984), 290.
43. Sally Cline and Carole Angier, eds, *Life Writing: A Writers' and Artists' Companion* (London: Bloomsbury, 2013), 38–9.
44. Ormrod, *Una Troubridge*, 291.
45. Cline, *Radclyffe Hall*, 91.
46. See Jodie Medd, 'Séances and Slander: Radclyffe Hall in 1920,' in *Sapphic Modernities: Sexuality, Women and National Culture*, ed. Laura Doan and Jane Garrity (Basingstoke: Palgrave Macmillan, 2006), 201–16.
47. Quoted in Souhami, *Trials*, 17.
48. Toklas, *What Is Remembered*, 148, recalls how Sherwood Anderson told Stein that she looked 'like a monk'; Troubridge, *Life and Death*, 45.
49. Troubridge, *Life and Death*, 20; Radclyffe Hall, *The Well of Loneliness* (Paris: The Pegasus Press, 1928), 16.
50. Naomi Jacob, *Me – and the Swans* (London: William Kimber, 1963), 121.
51. See chapter 4 of Roche, *Outside Thing*.

8

LESBIANISM IN/AND THE FAMILY: EVA GORE-BOOTH AND THE MAKING OF FEMINIST MODERNISM

Kathryn Holland

Families occupy nuanced and sometimes vexed places in modernist literature, as its subjects and as historical structures shaping its creation. In work across the later nineteenth and early twentieth centuries, modernist authors frequently depict multigenerational family units as sites of recognition, tension, exchange and transformation. Relationality develops via birth, adoption, marriage, divorce and death, along with intimate bonds not codified by blood or law, all of which usher individuals in and out of the life of each group. While generations extend in multiple directions, their complex genealogies are inseparable from the larger culture they inhabit together and represented in the art of the time.

This chapter explores the influence of multigenerational family in the networks of feminist, lesbian modernism. It argues that historical families developed by marriage and birth also supported queer members and relationships, visibly and tenaciously, and such families were vital to the work of wider cultural collectives and institutions. Attending specifically to the feminist, lesbian writing and life of Eva Gore-Booth (1870–1926) within her immediate and more expansive creative network that includes two generations of her family and her partner Esther Roper, it aims to advance what we know of intertextual and social relations in modernism. With an examination of Gore-Booth's suffrage and labour activism, poems 'Women's Rights' and 'Women's Trades on the Embankment' (1907), along with her foundational contributions to the queer periodical *Urania* (1916–26), I argue that her life's work indicates how historical family units were not simply at odds with the social and intellectual experiments of the modernist project. Instead, some became flexible spaces for the development of feminist and lesbian lives and writing, and are crucial to our understanding of the social forces that animated modernism.

Gore-Booth lived and wrote among her contemporaries' diverse perspectives on and experiences with kinship structures that indicate how queer relationality can be, as Tyler Bradway argues about kinship in contemporary writing, 'not so much the family one chooses as a family that accumulates over time. Its diagram is dynamic, and the categories are neither exclusive or closed.'[1] Adjacent to modernist writing itself, productivity stirred within historical families. In the Stein and Sitwell families, for instance, members' queer sexualities and work were embraced without the dismantling of their attachments to earlier generations, the pooling of material and social capital, or the concept of biological kinship as they launched, respectively, the rue de Fleurus studio-salon in 1903 and *Wheels: An Anthology of Verse* in 1916.[2]

Queer modernist writing also is replete with scenes of shifting, complex kinships. Radclyffe Hall's *The Well of Loneliness* (1928) is a narrative of conflicted acknowledgement of notions of familial tradition, through Stephen Gordon's movements as a woman who identifies as an 'invert' in her family and culture. Her father's acquisition of books on sexology and his love for her indicate the potential security of her place in their lineage, but his death and her mother's fury at her romance with a woman prompt Stephen to seek community elsewhere. After her time with Valérie Seymour's Sapphic coterie in Paris and the ambulance unit in which she meets Mary Llewellyn, she offers her belief that love is most securely expressed within marriage. Stephen urges Mary to enjoy a 'more normal' life that would, she claims, offer her a 'complete existence,' and prepares her lover for a new family by pairing Mary with her friend Martin Hallam, though such relations are not for herself.[3] In Dorothy Bussy's Sapphic novella *Olivia* (1949), the titular protagonist discusses her departure from her biological family in pursuit of a fulfilling intellectual and erotic life modelled on that of her object of affection and school headmistress. Olivia positions her family's values and interests in contrast with the school's richly queer world that shapes her life and is the foundation of her writing, but reflects on her mother's long friendship with the headmistress and her female partner, which enabled Olivia's attendance at her school, and the lingering influence of her aunt, who did not attend the school but set the foundation for Olivia's aesthetic life.[4]

Suggesting the powerful hold of familial relationships on the imaginations and experiences of modernist writers, metaphors of sustained kinship are prominent even in writing that emphasises the value of turning from the past to effect experiment and change. The central text of feminist modernism, Virginia Woolf's *A Room of One's Own* (1929), harnesses the language of genealogy to depict affiliations formed by authors in extrafamilial systems that are vital to their creative output. Fascinated by the vitality of the past and formation of creative lineages, Woolf's narrator also deploys familial metaphors that mark exclusion and loss along with continuity in literary traditions, and that support her embrace of the world-making possibilities of writing by women in her present and future. 'For we think back through our mothers if we are women' is one of the book's best-known statements.[5] With it, Woolf highlights consequences of the under-representation of women writers in the canon of her time and foreshadows her narrator's peroration urging the women in her audience to forge literary traditions by taking up their own pens, 'hesitating at no subject however trivial or however vast,' with the recognition that each woman already prominent in literary history 'is an inheritor as well as an originator' whose body of writing is part of a capacious genealogy that includes the work of obscure authors lost to history as well as blazing forebears.[6]

Studies of modernism, particularly those dedicated to queer and feminist writing, frequently articulate the importance of departures from traditional kinship structures and the assembly of alternatives. Such research draws on ample representations of writers' resistance to their forebears and immersion in cultures forging innovative approaches to gender and sexuality, with alternative kinships founded on affinities that are artistic, intellectual and political.[7] Studies of queer intimacies within pairs, groups and more expansive communities in modernist writing and culture also frequently align with what Bradway, considering the interplay between contemporary queer literature and queer theory's emphasis on transgression and rupture as the most radical alternative to kinship codified by marriage and birth, calls 'one of the foundational plots of queer people': 'being expelled from heteronormative nuclear families' and turning to the cumulative process of 'making family under conditions of being kinless.'[8] Yet the kinship structures of the early twentieth century tell nuanced stories of 'contingent contiguities' rather than 'explosive discontinuities.'[9] In their sustained engagements with varied but not discrete familial models, texts and creative networks of the modernist period invite us to consider the tenacious value of families as generative sites in literary history, including those involved in feminist and queer writing.

Familial, Unfamiliar Collaborations

Eva Gore-Booth's feminist, lesbian life was frequently collaborative and animated consistently by familial connections. An Irish suffragist author and organiser who was born in 1870 at her family's estate, Lissadell House in County Sligo, and died in Fitzroy Square, London in 1926, where she lived with her partner Esther Roper, Gore-Booth undertook feminist collaborations developed in and beyond generations of her family. Interweaving suffrage and labour concerns, her activism also encompassed key relationships with members of other families at the core of the feminist movement, such as Emmeline and Christabel Pankhurst. Her works of the imagination were admired by her contemporaries, including Katharine Tynan and George William Russell (Æ).[10] W. B. Yeats was close to the Gore-Booth family for decades and encouraged her early writing, describing her first book to her as 'full of poetic feeling and [. . .] great promise,' as Roper notes in her edited collection of Gore-Booth's poetry.[11] He remained an attentive reader of her work. But his later poem 'In Memory of Eva Gore-Booth and Con Markievicz' (1927) is a bitter homage to the two sisters. Yeats's poem follows Gore-Booth's seizing and refashioning of his 'The Stolen Child' (1886) in her poem 'Women's Rights.'[12] Published in Gore-Booth's 1907 collection *The Egyptian Pillar*, the text is included among other feminist poems including 'Women's Trades on the Embankment,' which, like some of her sister's writing of the same time, experiments with language beyond the gender binary.[13] Gore-Booth's subsequent collaborative work with Roper and their peers, funded partly by her family, resulted in *Urania*, a newsletter of new and republished writing about aspects of queer culture falling under its motto, coined by Gore-Booth, 'Sex is an accident.'

Her creative life in and adjacent to her family demonstrates that members' relationships – collaborations – in such social structures of the time were not siloed. Advancing the period's feminist and queer innovations, they inspired thematic and formal intertexts between their work and those by their contemporaries. Introducing a *Literature & History* issue on modernist collaboration, Claire Battershill and Alexandra Peat observe:

> collaborative work can be hard to recognise, often occurring behind the scenes and in the margins . . . [C]ollaboration is complicated by political and social circumstances – from the power dynamics inevitably infusing transnational relationship in an imperial era to racial and gender inequalities – but can, at the same time, be a way for marginalised people or groups to create community and, moreover, strategies of resistance.[14]

Battershill and Peat address collaboration in communities and platforms that are primarily extrafamilial, such as P.E.N., the Book Society, and the *Workers' Dreadnought* newspaper. But their views about lesser-known collaborations and the nuanced objectives of people undertaking them align with the argument in this chapter about the roles of historical feminist families in modernist culture, supporting political and literary experimentation rather than inhibiting or rejecting it.

By examining the intertextuality and collaborations within Gore-Booth's work, this chapter sharpens the visibility of families as productive hubs in modernist culture, building on the prominence of the network as a paradigm for exploring multidirectional systems of association and influence in modernist literary history. From a perspective similar to that of Battershill and Peat in a study of the Hogarth Press, Helen Southworth identifies the value of network study for understandings of systems of exchange that became some of modernism's collaborative foundations along with the generative relationships among specific individuals and collectives regardless of their places in the modernist canon.[15] Families, clearly comprising powerful but not exclusive modes of belonging, contributed to wider networks of the time, where figures, groups and institutions that function as nodes are connected by relationships, texts and events that function as lines among them. Three generations of the Gore-Booth family itself are part of *Kindred Britain*, a digital resource that tracks the vitality of families for cultural production. It examines 'the centrality of family experience to the formation of British culture' via network graphs, maps and timelines representing genealogical ties among more than 30,000 individuals. Though it spans 1200–2012 CE, the influence of modernists on its structure and objectives is clear: the epigraph for *Howards End* – 'Only connect . . .' – is adopted by *Kindred Britain*, and its team's curiosity about glimpses of W. H. Auden's family history in his poetry was a catalyst for their collaboration.[16] Considerations of the scope and impact of historical families' collaborations, including those advanced by Eva Gore-Booth, indicate the complex relationality of modernist creativity and how lesbian, feminist work was fostered by it.

Feminist Families of Modernism

Gore-Booth's life in and extending from her family demonstrates how and to what ends kinship structures could incorporate varied instances and forms of queer intimacy and influence creative work beyond them. Emma Donoghue describes Gore-Booth's early years at Lissadell House in County Sligo as 'the base from which all her work sprang,' partly because of its matriarchal culture driven by her mother, Georgina Gore-Booth, her maternal grandmother (who lived with the Gore-Booths) and the fertile natural landscapes she constantly explored with her family.[17] The sibling to whom she was closest, her older sister Constance Markievicz, was an Irish nationalist leader who drew much media coverage for her work, particularly during the Easter Rising of 1916. After both of their deaths, W. B. Yeats, who was a long-time friend of the family, wrote of them in his 1927 poem 'In Memory of Eva Gore-Booth and Con Markievicz.' The text begins with a portrait of the sisters in their youth, at home in an idyllic summer glow: 'The light of evening, Lissadell, / Great windows open to the south, / Two girls in silk kimonos, both / Beautiful, one a gazelle.'[18] This vision then shifts, with the passage of time, to harsh portraits of the two in light of the activism they undertook well beyond their first home: to the poem's speaker, Gore-Booth 'seems / When withered old and skeleton-gaunt, / An image of such politics.'[19] In contrast with Yeats's vision of her life's work as enervating, Gore-Booth developed a rich body of feminist writing and activism drawn directly from her exchanges with her mother, sister Constance Markievicz, and partner Esther Roper.

In activism and writing that developed via multiple forms of collaboration, the women shared commitments to suffrage and labour politics, dissident spirituality and Celtic myth, while the Gore-Booth family expanded to include Esther Roper from the first years of her intimate relationship with Eva. Georgina Gore-Booth established a needlework school for women on the family estate, where they earned an independent and steady income through the sales of their completed work and honed skills that led to other employment opportunities. Her daughters modified this approach in their early suffrage activities, looking simultaneously to their mother's work and to the commitments of Esther Roper, who met Eva Gore-Booth in 1896 and became her partner soon after. Lauren Arrington launches a discussion of Roper's place in Gore-Booth's and Markievicz's political activism by aptly noting that the 'sisters were inspired by personal relationships and public reforms.'[20]

Gore-Booth's intimate life with Roper and her family of origin was inextricable from their feminism in Ireland and England. Their first focus with Markievicz, on a complete parliamentary franchise, led to their co-founding of a branch of the Irishwomen's Suffrage and Local Governance Association and expanded into a commitment to women's trade activism based in Manchester and London, where Gore-Booth and Roper lived together. Inspired by Roper's social reform efforts, Gore-Booth joined the executive of the National Union of Suffrage Societies (or the NUWSS) from 1899 onwards and used her voice and writing to highlight what she, her sister and Roper called 'the industrial concern' within suffrage for the group's leaders, who included Millicent Garrett Fawcett, her sister Elizabeth Garrett Anderson, and her niece Louisa Garrett Anderson, members of one of several multigenerational feminist families with whom they collaborated.[21]

The visible, extensive feminist activism carried out by Gore-Booth and Roper was imbricated with their personal, erotic intimacy and participation in the Gore-Booth family. The couple visited Lissadell each summer, Roper became the beneficiary of Gore-Booth's will, and in a letter to Roper marking Gore-Booth's death in 1926, Markievicz imagined the comparative intensity of Roper's grief over her own because Roper had been 'so much nearer her body than I.'[22] Roper became the steward of Gore-Booth's writing after her death, editing and introducing the *Poems of Eva Gore-Booth* (1929) with the inclusion of a previously unpublished essay on her early years, 'The Inner Life of a Child,' and commentary on Gore-Booth's correspondence with family and friends. Five years later, Roper published (and financed) *Prison Letters*, a volume of correspondence between Gore-Booth and Markievicz, supplemented by the former's poetry and prose about the Easter Rising.[23] Gore-Booth and Roper were buried together when the latter died in 1938, with a headstone whose inscriptions of lines from Gore-Booth's poem 'In Praise of Life' is an elegy to Sappho, simultaneously signalling their lesbian intimacy and their focus on

Gore-Booth's writing life.[24] Their partnership was recognised and incorporated by generations of Gore-Booth's family, and it accrued value that was personal, social and political.

The Gore-Booth women, working closely with Roper, were not unique in their shared focus on feminist issues of their time and they collaborated with other multigenerational families who led suffrage and labour activism, particularly the Pankhurst and Strachey families in addition to the Fawcetts.[25] Members of such families included generations of writers whose established forms of relationships facilitated their political activism, and whose inclusion of lesbian and other queer intimacies indicate the plasticity of their views and of forms of familial and broader social engagement that became, directly and indirectly, part of modernism's cultural production.

The impact of kinship structures on the acceleration of feminist writing and activism is suggested in accounts of the first large-scale suffrage demonstration in Britain, the 'United Procession of Women' or the 'Mud March.' Held in London on 7 February 1908, it brought together 3,000 participants. Gore-Booth and Roper were featured speakers, listed in the event's promotional flyer, and represented the Women's Trades Council and Women Textile Workers' Committee respectively.[26] Led by multiple families, the event played a central role in the expanding public life of feminism in the modernist period. The secretary of the NUWSS's London branch, Philippa Strachey, coordinated the march; her mother, Jane Strachey, and Millicent Garrett Fawcett, who were the group's Vice-President and President, headed the procession and spoke at its conclusion. Elinor Rendel, one of Jane Strachey's granddaughters, walked with Ray Costelloe (later Strachey), both of whom were students at Newnham College, Cambridge, which was founded in 1871 by people including Fawcett and later would have Pernel Strachey, another of Jane's daughters and Philippa's sister, as its Principal.[27] Members of divergent groups came together for the event, including the more militant Women's Social and Political Union (WSPU) led during this period by Emmeline Pankhurst and her daughters Christabel and Sylvia, with their peers.

This United Procession of Women initiated a new mode of engagement between feminist groups and the public, launching an era of large-scale suffrage marches and pageants. Four months later, another NUWSS march attracted more than 10,000 marchers while the WSPU led a march with more than 30,000 participants. The 'United Procession' became one event through which multigenerational contact and collaboration, in and near the Gore-Booth family, directly informed the acceleration of feminist activity and linked such activity to writing of the period.

Key participants in the march became the subjects of others' writing and created platforms for authors in and beyond the feminist movement. Emmeline Pankhurst was a founder of *Votes for Women*, a WSPU journal to which Dora Marsden contributed when she was employed by the group, before she left it to found *The Freewoman: A Weekly Feminist Review* in 1911, which published articles by such writers as Dorothy Richardson and Rebecca West.[28] West went on to write about the Pankhursts' feminism in several venues: she addressed their work in her journalism of the early 1910s, and her essay on Emmeline Pankhurst, 'A Reed of Steel,' is part of *The Post-Victorians* (1933) biographical collection.[29] When Woolf visited Newnham College to deliver one of the 1928 lectures fictionalised in *A Room of One's Own*, she stayed with its Principal, Pernel Strachey, later wrote letters to her about her mother's, Jane Strachey's, feminist life during her composition of the book, and transmuted their visit in the book's account of its narrator's time with Fernham's Principal. Sylvia Pankhurst's 1930s publications include a biography of her mother and a history of feminism that highlighted her opposition to the work of her mother and sister; she also launched an anti-fascist paper, collaborating on it with such writers as Nancy Cunard.[30]

Gore-Booth and Roper remained part of this network and feature directly in narrative histories of feminism written in the 1920s and 1930s by its members. As these texts highlight the intermingling of groups whose work is frequently depicted as oppositional, especially those running along suffragist/suffragette lines, they also demonstrate the centrality of multigenerational families in them. Ray Strachey notes the significance of Gore-Booth's labour feminism in *The Cause: A Short History of the Women's Movement in Britain* (1928), one of two books Strachey wrote after the death of Fawcett, perhaps her own closest mentor. There, Strachey argues that Gore-Booth's collaboration with Emmeline Pankhurst and other leading members of the Manchester Suffrage Society drove the agitation for suffrage among women in trade unions in about 1901–2, manifest in the delivery of a petition signed by 67,000 textile workers to Parliament, which in turn caught the attention of the nascent Labour Party.[31] In *The Suffragette Movement: An Intimate Account of Persons and Ideals* (1931), Sylvia Pankhurst articulates the importance of Gore-Booth and Roper in her sister Christabel's intellectual and political life, beginning via the Women's Trade Union in Manchester.[32] The two successfully urged her to study law, and when she and Annie Kenney were released from prison after unfurling a Votes for Women banner at a Liberal Party gathering in 1905, Gore-Booth and Roper made a prominent celebration of their release, along with roughly 200 other supporters, by greeting them at the prison gates with flowers.[33] These relationships, represented in the activist material and historical accounts of feminism, unfolded alongside Gore-Booth's own body of writing and periodical work spanning the early 1900s and mid-1920s.

WORKS OF THE FEMINIST-MODERNIST IMAGINATION: SUFFRAGE POETRY

Gore-Booth complemented her activism with suffrage poetry that enters modernism's broader networks via its handling of immediate political issues; its response to poetry by Yeats, within their long exchanges facilitated by familial contacts; and its links to the work of her contemporaries who explored feminism implicitly and explicitly in their own poetry. This is evident in her collection *The Egyptian Pillar*, published in 1907 and dedicated to her sister, Constance Markievicz. *The Egyptian Pillar*'s title points to Cleopatra's Needle on the Victoria Embankment in London and the centrality of feminist themes in the volume, serving as the setting of multiple poems including 'Women's Trades on the Embankment.' Building on Gore-Booth's years of labour feminism, undertaken at that time for more than a decade with her family, her lesbian partner, and their peers, this poem delves into and seeks to accelerate the long history of feminist activism by women workers, from its epigraph (an incisive quotation, 'Have patience!' by Prime Minister Henry Campbell-Bannerman, to a suffrage delegation at Parliament in 1906), through its conflation of the lives of enslaved people in Egypt with the circumscribed conditions of tradeswomen without the franchise.[34] Yet the poem's title and epigraph contain the text's only direct references to women workers seeking the vote. Throughout the rest of the poem, the language of its core subject is ungendered and addressed only as a 'human soul.' Arrington sees a shift in language used repeatedly in *The Egyptian Pillar*, moving away from a gender binary comprised of women and men, via the repeated use of such terms as 'comrade' in texts about the pursuit of fellowship, namely 'Comrades' and 'The Visionary,' which 'mark a transition from poetry that is clearly engaged with the fight for women's suffrage to an esoteric verse that challenges the very notions of gender.' Continuing on, she argues that these poems begin to demonstrate that 'sexual equality is the natural and spiritual state of humanity' for their author.[35] Arrington identifies this as a turn evident in both sisters' writing, marking the emergence of this language in Markievicz's Irish propaganda poem 'To the Citizen Army,' which she published in 1915 under the pseudonym 'Maca,' the name she also took for some of her pro-suffrage writing.[36] The sisters' intellectual and personal proximity with each other is manifest across genre and time.

'Women's Rights,' published in the same collection, encourages consideration of the more expansive complexity of Gore-Booth's feminist poetry. In 'A Love Song' and 'February at Adare,' from her first collection, *Poems* (1898), she personifies Spring in nature as a waking woman desired by her observer.[37] 'Women's Rights' shifts the balance of Gore-Booth's abiding interest in the alignment of women's intimacy and nature from the erotic to the political. It returns to these settings of her earlier poems and makes them sites of liberation and collectivity. This poem's title immediately turns readers' attention to women's political agency during a historical moment when the fight for suffrage was slow and victories remained uncertain. The poem's stanzas, however, unfold a feminist space that attends to possibilities for women's community. With such lines as 'Every little thrush that sings / Quells the wild air with brave wings' and 'Oh, whatever men may say, / Ours is the wide and the open way,' Gore-Booth represents an invigorating escape from patriarchal culture.[38]

'Women's Rights' forges an explicit intertext with Yeats's poetry. In modernist literary history, Gore-Booth is best known for appearing in poetry, not writing it: as we have seen, she and her sister are the objects of Yeats's memory and creative gaze in his poem 'In Memory of Eva Gore-Booth and Con Markievicz,' with Gore-Booth initially the 'gazelle' in the window of 'that old Georgian mansion' nestled in her family's bucolic haven at Lissadell, eventually wasted by a lifetime of striving for inscrutable and ultimately undesirable political change.[39] Her poem offers starkly different visions of her family's immediate surroundings and their political work, identifying the natural beauty of her first home with what she sees as the wonder and force of feminist community. Gore-Booth rewrites Yeats's ballad 'The Stolen Child' (1886), which brings together Yeats's own memories and experiences in County Sligo's landscapes with Irish folklore to retell the changeling myth of a boy enchanted by faeries away from society to a natural idyll.[40] Shifting the formal qualities of Yeats's original through its own stricter flow, the thirteen rhyming couplets of 'Women's Rights' comprise a schema that helps indicate the poem's proximity to Yeats's text, which includes alternative rhyme and rhyming couplets within the fifty-three lines of its four stanzas. Similarly, the content of Gore-Booth's poem gestures back to Yeats's work while moving in another direction. Rather than concentrating exclusively on natural spaces, the sustained comparison of natural and urban realms in 'Women's Rights' offers a remarkable separatist vision of the modern world, juxtaposing the arid towers, walls and offices occupied by impotent men locked into 'the dark and dreary town' with fecund spaces open to women.[41] While 'The Stolen Child' takes a small boy as its central figure and preserves his youthful innocence via his escape from worldly concerns, women's subjectivity dominates Gore-Booth's writing.

A deeper look into the poems' shared setting, made clear in their opening lines, cracks open a reading of their intertextuality. Gore-Booth's poem takes place 'Down by Glencar Waterfall,' set very close to Lissadell House, the Gore-Booth family home.[42] Gore-Booth uses this text to connect this imagined haven of and for women to her familial past and present, inspired strongly by her mother and sister, and to sharpen her feminist reworking of Yeats's 1886 poem. In the first and second lines of 'The Stolen Child,' which locate the spot 'Where dips the rocky highland / Of Sleuth Wood in the lake,' Yeats embeds a direct reference to County Sligo, then extends it at the opening of the third stanza, at the place 'Where the wandering water gushes / From the hills above Glen-Car.'[43] Throughout, the ballad imagines a solemn boy successfully lured by fairies into the woods, away from the cares of human existence. Here is its refrain: 'Come away, O human child! / To the waters and the wild / With a faery, hand in hand, / For the world's more full of weeping than you can understand.'[44]

Gore-Booth uses the changeling myth for feminist purposes instead, reimagining this natural space and the life in it by depicting collective movement by women and inviting readers to question the parameters of the world and the identity of those with whom it is most richly aligned. Whereas the forces in Yeats's poem have enchanted the boy successfully ('Away with us he's going'), Gore-Booth's speaker continues to seduce her internal audience away from human society: 'Rise with us and let us go / To where the living waters flow / [. . .] / All the green world is on our side.'[45] By playing on the structure and concerns of 'The Stolen Child,' 'Women's Rights' exemplifies intertextuality as rewriting, a response that sets a discussion on a new path, and is drawn from familial intimacy and cultural history while depicting alternative forms of belonging. Reimagining Yeats's vision from 'The Stolen Child' and countering the image of feminist women Yeats would create of Gore-Booth and Markievicz at Lissadell's window twenty years after the publication of *The Egyptian Pillar*, the poem generates a distinctive view of feminism's objectives beyond suffrage and offers us one instance of the familial, political and literary converging.

Representing the interplay between activism and works of the imagination, Gore-Booth's poetry also extends our awareness of the heterogeneous approaches to feminism in modernist networks that are apparent in the work of her better-known contemporaries Marianne Moore, Dora Marsden and Mina Loy. Points of contact among their texts emerge when we compare embedded references to sites of feminist protest in Gore-Booth's title for her volume *The Egyptian Pillar* and her poem 'Women's Trades on the Embankment' with Moore's integration of her activism with her mother and friends in the late 1900s and early 1910s in her writing, with an analogous approach to feminist intertextuality informed by familial and broader social relationships. Mary Chapman observes the value of Moore's use of direct quotes by suffrage leaders and texts about feminism, particularly J. M. Barrie's play *What Every Women Knows* (1908), in personal and public correspondence as she developed her own pro-suffrage views, and argues that Moore leverages her citations and politically charged imagery in such poems as 'Silence' (1924) to simultaneously 'assert a feminine voice within a male literary tradition' and critique aspects of anti-suffrage culture, particularly British Parliament's 'Cat and Mouse' Act of 1913 that had been attacked in speech and print by the WPSU, still led by the Pankhurst family.[46]

Whereas Gore-Booth and Moore experimented with multiple forms of intertextuality as feminist response, the former's writing links to work by Marsden and Loy via their similar curiosity about the limits of feminism. The natural world of 'Women's Rights,' which evokes a collective of women who are liberated beyond suffrage as a comparatively narrow form of political autonomy, invites comparison with texts published in *The Freewoman* in the same period. Marsden's collection of articles on 'A New Morality,' for example, addresses the complexity of women's sexual identities and desires beyond marriage and gendered roles within it, discussing free love, same-sex desire, and the necessity of women's financial agency, particularly if they are mothers. Marsden writes, for example:

> If the Freewoman is not going to be the protected woman, but is to carve out an independence for herself, she must produce within herself strength sufficient to provide for herself and for those of whom Nature has made her the natural guardian, her children. To this end she must open up resources of wealth for herself. She must work, earn money.[47]

In their study of Loy's career, Suzanne W. Churchill, Linda Kinnahan and Susan Rosenbaum note that in her 'Aphorisms on Futurism' (1914) and visual collages of the 1940s onwards, Loy 'understood that transforming values and conventions need not entail strident opposition, violent rupture, or breakage. It might, for example, accommodate strategies of renovation or rehabilitation.'[48] In her 1914 *Feminist Manifesto*, which identifies the organised movement as 'Inadequate' and in need of 'Absolute Demolition,' Loy's emphasis on the urgency of women's rejection of patriarchal approaches to gender and sexuality connects back to Gore-Booth's separatist world of 'Women's Rights' and the norms Marsden attacks in her essays.[49] Considered together, the work of these writers demonstrates the range of explorations of feminism from varied perspectives on the movement, some invested and others distant, along with the range of places that feminism occupied in modernist networks.

Queering Feminism: *Urania*

The later phase of Gore-Booth's work, from the mid-1910s to her death in 1926, also gestures to the outcomes of change in and across generations of feminist activism and perspectives on gender and sexuality that emerged in the later nineteenth and early twentieth centuries. It supported the growth of a privately published and circulated magazine called *Urania*, in which feminist and queer discourses are interleaved. By the early 1910s, Gore-Booth and Roper had formed views about women's labour and economic agency that combined with their dedication to Theosophy to inspire their rejection of sex difference.[50] They shared these views with Thomas Baty, a lawyer based in London and then Japan, who also lived and wrote as Irene Clyde. Together the group sought new methods for shaping mainstream feminist groups to which they belonged. In 1911, Baty wrote to Fawcett, asking the NUWSS to 'adopt the elimination of gender distinctions as one of its aims.'[51] When she declined, Baty founded a new political organisation, the Aëthnic Union, with Gore-Booth, Roper and others. Gore-Booth and Roper maintained some connections to established feminist groups but their concerns about the limits of such organisations are apparent in the Union's advertisements to attract new members, which links

Gore-Booth's work more closely to her better-known peers Marsden and Loy. For instance, one Union flyer announces:

> Modern suffragists, while anxious to remove the superficial disabilities which stand in the way of political influence and economic advantage, seem disposed to accept [. . .] the far deeper hindrances to self-development imposed by the clumsy differentiation which divides the race into 'men and women.'[52]

It welcomed new members, 'those who are anxious to maintain that the ideal is a single ideal.'[53]

The group also grew via its contacts in modernist periodical culture, with the Union's focus shifting to the work of publication. Its founders addressed *The Freewoman*'s audience by publishing articles in that journal, founded by Marsden when her dispute with Christabel and Emmeline Pankhurst, about their differences regarding the focus and structure of the Women's Social and Political Union, prompted her departure from it. The Union's links to emerging ideas about gender beyond feminism and the hubs of Gore-Booth's larger creative network were reinforced in a February 1912 *Freewoman* piece signed by Baty, about the Union as a collective dedicated to 'a real necessity of modern life,' the recognition 'that upon the fact of sex there has built up a giant superstructure of artificial convention which urgently needs to be swept away' but 'cannot be swept away unless sex is resolutely ignored.'[54] The argument continues in the same piece:

> the idea of sex inevitably carries with it a whole flood of associations which rivet on the soul the fetters of a warped ideal. It submerges the mind in waves of that autocratic sternness which one has been taught is the ideal of the masculine, or that of narrow triviality which one is (less successfully) taught to consider the mark of the feminine.[55]

The article's concepts and imagery are strikingly close to Woolf's reflections on the androgynous mind in *A Room of One's Own*, whose narrator observes a falling leaf 'pointing to a force which one had overlooked. It seemed to point to a river, which flowed past' and soon carried a young man and woman riding together in a taxi, 'swept on by the current elsewhere' and prompting her suggestion that understanding 'one sex as distinct from the other is an effort. It interferes with the unity of the mind.'[56] By addressing the impact of sex and gender binaries with language that anticipates one of the best-known assessments of gender of the time, the Union accelerated its participation in a network of feminist modernism where varied forms of queerness and intimacy effected cultural production.

The group built upon their claims, in *The Freewoman* and elsewhere, through the long life of *Urania*. During its run from 1916 to 1940, they produced between three and six issues per year and distributed them at no charge to subscribers, estimated at 200–250 readers. Identifying as a single unnamed 'editor,' the journal's editorial collective of five, including Gore-Booth and Roper, wrote its editorials collaboratively and ensured its stability by funding its publication and distribution. One of *Urania*'s mottos, 'Sex is an Accident,' is given as the epigraph of a 1921 issue and attributed to Gore-Booth, with the editors describing it as 'the nearest and clearest expression of our views.'[57] Gore-Booth's use of funds from her family to support the journal offers one instance of how kinship informed the material conditions of possibility for queer expression in this period.[58]

Each issue of *Urania* is a bricolage of original writing by its editorial team and reprinted articles about the politics of modern sex, gender and sexuality. Its editors held a nuanced dedication to multiple mainstream feminist goals. Many issues discuss the importance of women's enfranchisement and seats in Parliament, some cover debates around the legislation of pay standards for women, and the January 1921 issue marks the admission of women students at Oxford to full membership in the university. Karen Steele observes the proximity of *Urania* and *Freewoman* in her reading of their content and objectives, stating that the journals share 'a far broader set of objectives for feminism than the equality and social reform campaigns undertaken by feminist organisations in the period.'[59]

Telegraphed by its group's earlier writing in *The Freewoman*, *Urania*'s approach to gender and sexuality looked well beyond feminist issues of suffrage and access to education, critiquing heteronormativity and gender essentialism in its content and the larger creative network in which it developed, which includes relationships among its editors, other individuals, and the varied discourses to which they contributed. Steele argues that *Urania*'s significance in modernist culture lies in its role as 'a queer archive dedicated to dismantling gender norms and documenting examples of [trans] identity, intersexuality, cross-dressing, and lesbian lives.'[60] *Urania* turns away from what it sees as constraining discourses of the past and present. For example, the journal's editorial collective conveys its resistance to the sexological concept of inversion in a review of *The Well of Loneliness*, published on the front page of the journal's mid-1929 issue. Here, they praise the story as 'delicate and touching and full of beautiful and sympathetic observation,' yet claim that Hall's insistence on the characterisation of Stephen Gordon as an invert is 'a profound artistic and psychological mistake,' one rooted in the persistent standards of the time, when lovers were frequently drawn to each other by their discrete masculine and feminine qualities.[61] *Urania* is replete with accounts of the lives of people who did not fit into binary and heteronormative models of gender and sexuality, rejecting them through relationships, wardrobes and medical procedures to affirm their identities. The journal's strategies complicated sexological discourses about the complexities of bodies and lives while extending the concept of Uranism as an intermediate and unfixed position.[62]

Within this scope of subjects, *Urania* attends to historical and contemporaneous depictions of lesbian culture particularly, foregrounding representations of Sapphic desire and community. Reprinting and thereby extending the reach of writing published elsewhere, its issues chronicle varied models of love and desire between women. A special feature on 'A Girl's Question' begins with a short article reprinted from the *London Evening News*, 'Do Unmarried Women Miss the Half of Life?,' that includes the claim that for most women, 'life, so far as understanding is concerned, is finished when the marriage knot is tied.'[63] It is followed immediately by Katharine Tynan's 'An Irish School-Girl,' an excerpt from her *Twenty-Five Years: Reminiscences* (1913) where she reflects on an unexpected kiss from her 'passion,' an older classmate about to join a convent in Lisbon: 'Oh, rapture! Oh, delight! Oh, ecstasy! What there anything in more mature passions quite as good?'[64] A 1933 lead article titled 'Sappho Up-To-Date' critiques recent representations of Sappho and her writing as heteronormative. Though the reviewer acknowledges, 'We know next to nothing about Sappho, except that she wrote magnificently, and surrounded herself with ladies with whom she was accused of physical intimacy,' they ultimately celebrate her as a 'passionate and possessive adorer of beauty and charm in women,' ending with a cheeky riposte to those who remain welcome to imagine that she 'preferred in her last days to die for the embraces of a masterful man.'[65] A 1936 issue features a review of Suzanne Howe's 1935 biography of Geraldine Jewsbury that critiques Howe's apparent attempt to 'tone down' her subject's attraction to Jane Carlyle and fills the page with quotations from letters in which Jewsbury declares her love for Carlyle, then ends with the sentence 'We may leave it at that.'[66]

Apart from the texts by Tynan, Hall and Howe, the journal often limits its engagement with contemporaneous queer women's writing and lives, dedicating space to historical sources. With its reflections on the objects of Sappho's desire and subjects of her writing, however, the journal directly contributed to the development of erotic intimacy between women as a concept running through queer writing of the time. Such writing builds on what Elaine Marks identifies as the 'Sappho model' of queer women's lives, particularly in pedagogical settings, depicted in writing of the late nineteenth and early twentieth centuries.[67] Sources for this model include Charles Baudelaire's identification of Sappho the poet with women's homoeroticism, and it appears throughout writing by canonical modernists, such as Woolf's short story set at Newnham College, Cambridge, 'A Woman's College from Outside' (1926). Along with the story's depiction of a kiss between its protagonist and the student she admires, the college's erotic culture is suggested by lyrical night-time scenes:

> Elderly women slept, who would on waking immediately clasp the ivory rod of office. Now smooth and colourless, reposing deeply, they lay surrounded, lay supported, by the bodies of youth recumbent or grouped at the window; pouring forth into the garden this bubbling laughter, this irresponsible laughter ... immensely fertilising, yet formless, chaotic, trailing and straying and tufting the rose-bushes with shreds of vapour.[68]

Urania joins these texts to thicken the lesbian literary discourse of the time and illuminate more of its breadth beyond the texts and genres central to modernist studies. Though *Urania*'s circulation was limited, its run was long and its concerns were radical. It gestures to the multistrand, collaborative development of perspectives on creative and political agency across its time, along with the role of familial kinship in it, suggesting the influence of varied relationships in the making of feminist, queer modernism.

Conclusion

'Where we find feminism matters; from whom we find feminism matters. Feminism as a collective movement is made out of how we are moved to become feminists in dialogue with others.'[69] In this short passage from *Living a Feminist Life*, Sara Ahmed focuses on the orientations of everyday encounters, intellectual and social, in our historical moment. But her assertion also is relevant to how we study modernism. To better comprehend the significance of feminist, lesbian writing in modernist culture, we must explore the diverse structures through which it circulated along with the specific exchanges among authors and their fellow contributors to modernism, canonical and lesser-known together. This consideration of networked collaboration in and near Gore-Booth's multigenerational feminist family builds on recent and established studies of modernist relationality, aligning, for instance, with Urmila Seshagiri's identification of the necessity of taking feminism as 'a mode of critical discourse as well as an object' of investigation in modernist studies and her claim that '*any* account of modernism is also an account of women's art and women's lives.'[70] It seeks to advance ongoing conversations about the tenaciously formative power of families in modernist culture, with an emphasis on the dynamics that supported the rise of feminism by lesbian writers within the movement during the later nineteenth and early twentieth centuries.

Gore-Booth's creative intimacies invite exploration through the lenses of studies of women's specifically queer texts, lives and kinship beyond families of origin. In an examination of the 'passion projects' of such authors as Sylvia Townsend Warner and Hope Mirrlees, who developed accounts of their shared lives with their queer partners that foregrounded the deferred, the unspoken and the unfinished, Melanie Micir highlights the archive 'as a site of bio-critical action for the writers and subjects long marginalized by dominant disciplinary narratives.'[71] Taking an approach that aligns provocatively with Micir's in their shared focus on the futurity of modernist writing and cultural activities, Hannah Roche identifies experiments with parent–child dynamics within queer relationships comprising 'alternative families,' along with the 'radically queer repurposing' of reproduction, pregnancy, childbirth and family units in Hall's *The Well of Loneliness* (1928) and across the culture of lesbian modernism.[72] This discussion of Gore-Booth's experience of kinship also builds on studies of how other modernist women writers queered the family in ways that enriched their intellectual and creative activities, such as H.D. and Bryher's leveraging of marriage and shared parenting with Kenneth Macpherson, and Christopher St John's life with Edith Craig, which included other important intimate partners and their working connections to Craig's mother, Ellen Terry.[73]

Like writers working well beyond her communities, Gore-Booth wrote with her peers and forebears, creating sustained exchanges with her family, including her partner, and members of the larger networks to which they belonged. The interplay among Gore-Booth and members of multiple generations points to some of the ways familial dynamics fostered the production of feminist, lesbian writing in the early twentieth century, when writers were occupied with points of contact among manifold groups and questions of continuity and change between the later nineteenth century and their own time. Their work gestures to the significance of protean kinships formed simultaneously in domestic and public spaces, where multigenerational family dynamics of the period were not exclusively or inherently restrictive in their maintenance of heteronormativity. They could be capacious enough to foster political change and queer intimacies, shaped by 'contingent contiguities' instead of 'explosive discontinuities.'[74] They became integral to the development of modernist literature, visible in its intertexts. As a kinship structure that grew in unprecedented decades of debate about gender, power and creativity, especially the parameters of women's political agency, the multigenerational feminist family became a catalysing force in domestic spaces, in the street and on the page. Swathes of modernism are at once lesbian, feminist and familial.

Notes

1. Tyler Bradway, 'Queer Narrative Theory and the Relationality of Form,' *PMLA* 136, no. 5 (2021): 711–27, 723.
2. Deborah Longworth, 'The Sitwells and Sitwellism: An Ornamental Modernism,' in *The Many Faces of Edith Sitwell*, ed. Allan Pero and Gyllian Phillips (Gainesville: University Press of Florida, 2017), 21–40.
3. Radclyffe Hall, *The Well of Loneliness* (New York: Covici-Friede, 1932), 447.

4. Dorothy Strachey (Dorothy Bussy), *Olivia*, ed. André Anciman (London: Penguin Classics, 2020).
5. Virginia Woolf, *A Room of One's Own* (London: Hogarth Press, 1929), 44.
6. Woolf, *Room*, 78, 83.
7. Examples include Benjamin Bateman, *The Modernist Art of Queer Survival* (Oxford: Oxford University Press, 2018); Brenda Helt and Madelyn Detloff, eds. *Queer Bloomsbury* (Edinburgh: Edinburgh University Press, 2016); Diana Souhami, *No Modernism Without Lesbians* (London: Head of Zeus, 2020); and Francesca Wade, *Square Haunting: Five Writers in London between the Wars* (New York: Penguin Random House, 2020).
8. Lena Mattheis, '"Queer Kinship" with Tyler Bradway,' in *Queer Lit* (podcast), 14 March 2022, accessed 20 March 2022, spreaker.com/user/14328383/queer-lit-tyler-bradway.
9. Bradway, 'Queer Narrative Theory,' 721.
10. Susan Brown, Patricia Clements and Isobel Grundy, eds, 'Eva Gore-Booth,' in *Orlando: Women's Writing in the British Isles from the Beginnings to the Present* (Cambridge: Cambridge University Press, 2022), accessed 20 September 2022, https://orlando.cambridge.org/profiles/goreev.
11. Quoted in Esther Roper, 'Biographical Introduction,' in *Poems of Eva Gore-Booth*, ed. Esther Roper (London: Longmans, Green, 1929), 1–46, 9.
12. W. B. Yeats, 'The Stolen Child,' in *Selected Poems*, ed. Timothy Webb (London: Penguin, 1991), 18–21.
13. Eva Gore-Booth, *The Egyptian Pillar* (Dublin: Maunsell, 1907).
14. Claire Battershill and Alexandra Peat, 'Introduction: Modernism and Collaboration,' *Literature & History* 28, no. 1 (2019): 3–9, 7–8.
15. Helen Southworth, 'Introduction,' in *Leonard and Virginia Woolf, the Hogarth Press, and Networks of Modernism*, ed. Helen Southworth (Edinburgh: Edinburgh University Press, 2010), 1–25, 14, 16–17.
16. Nicholas Jenkins, 'Originating *Kindred Britain*,' *Kindred Britain*, ed. Nicholas Jenkins, Elijah Meeks and Scott Murray (2013), accessed 20 September 2022, https://kindred.stanford.edu/notes.html?section=originating.
17. Emma Donoghue, '"How could I fear and thee by the hand": The Poetry of Eva Gore-Booth,' in *Sex, Nation, and Dissent in Irish Writing*, ed. Éibhear Walshe (New York: St. Martin's Press, 1997), 16–42, 16.
18. W. B. Yeats, 'In Memory of Eva Gore-Booth and Con Markievicz,' in *The Winding Stair and Other Poems* (London: Macmillan, 1933), 1–2, 1.
19. Yeats, 'In Memory,' 1.
20. Lauren Arrington, 'Liberté, egalité, sororité: The Poetics of Suffrage in the Work of Eva Gore-Booth and Constance Markievicz,' in *Irish Women's Writing, 1878–1922: Advancing the Cause of Liberty*, ed. Anna Pilz and Whitney Standlee (Manchester: Manchester University Press, 2016), 209–26, 217.
21. Brown et al., 'Eva Gore-Booth.'
22. Arrington, 'Liberté, egalité, sororité,' 210.
23. Sonja Tiernan, *Eva Gore-Booth: An Image of Such Politics* (Manchester: Manchester University Press, 2012), 261–2.

24. Michael D. Higgins, 'The Poetic Life of Eva Gore-Booth,' in *Eva Gore-Booth: Collected Poems*, ed. Sonja Tiernan (Dublin: Arlen House, 2018), 13–59, 51; Tiernan, *Image of Such Politics*, 262.
25. For accounts of these families' roles in early feminism, see Barbara Caine, *Bombay to Bloomsbury: A Biography of the Strachey Family* (Oxford: Oxford University Press, 2003); Jane Marcus, *Suffrage and the Pankhursts* (London and New York: Routledge and Kegan Paul, 1987); and Ray Strachey, *Millicent Garrett Fawcett* (London: John Murray, 1931).
26. Kathryn Holland and Jana Smith Elford, 'Textbase as Machine: Reading Feminist Modernism with *OrlandoVision*,' in *Reading Modernism with Machines: Digital Humanities and Modernist Literature*, ed. Shawna Ross and James O'Sullivan (London: Palgrave Macmillan, 2016), 109–34, 110.
27. Ibid., 109–10.
28. Cary Franklin, 'Marketing Edwardian Feminism: Dora Marsden, *Votes for Women*, and the *Freewoman*,' *Women's History Review* 11, no. 4 (2002): 631–42, 633, 635–7.
29. Rebecca West, 'A Reed of Steel' (1933), in *Rebecca West: A Celebration*, ed. Samuel Hynes (Harmondsworth: Penguin, 1978), 665–80.
30. June Purvis and Maureen Wright, 'Writing Suffragette History: The Contending Autobiographical Narratives of the Pankhursts,' *Women's History Review* 14, no. 3/4 (2005): 405–33; Maureen Moynaugh, 'Introduction,' in Nancy Cunard, *Essays on Race and Empire*, ed. Maureen Moynagh (Peterborough: Broadview Press, 2002), 9–63, 14.
31. Ray Strachey, *The Cause: A Short History of the Women's Movement in Britain* (London: Virago, 1978), 289.
32. Sylvia Pankhurst, *The Suffragette Movement: An Intimate Account of Persons and Ideals* (London and New York: Longmans, Green, 1931), 5–6.
33. Brown et al., 'Eva Gore-Booth.'
34. Eva Gore-Booth, 'Women's Trades on the Embankment,' in *Egyptian Pillar*, 19–20.
35. Arrington, 'Liberté, egalité, sororité,' 216–17.
36. Ibid., 216–17.
37. Higgins, 'Poetic Life,' 23–4.
38. Eva Gore-Booth, 'Women's Rights,' in *Egyptian Pillar*, 29–30, 29, 30.
39. Yeats, 'In Memory,' 1.
40. Peter McDonald, 'Yeats's Early Lake Isles,' *The Review of English Studies* 70, no. 294 (April 2019): 312–31, 325–6.
41. Gore-Booth, 'Women's Rights,' 29.
42. Ibid.
43. Yeats, 'The Stolen Child,' 18.
44. Ibid., 19.
45. Gore-Booth, 'Women's Rights,' 29–30.
46. Mary Chapman, *Making Noise, Making News: Suffrage Print Culture and U.S. Modernism* (Oxford: Oxford University Press, 2014), 120–38.
47. Quoted in Barbara Green, 'Introduction to *The Freewoman*,' *Modernist Journals Project*, ed. Robert Scholes and Sean Latham (2012), accessed 20 September 2022, https://modjourn.org/introduction-to-the-freewoman/.

48. Suzanne W. Churchill, Linda A. Kinnahan and Susan Rosenbaum, 'Theories of the Avant-Garde and En Dehors Garde: Feminist Challenges,' in *Mina Loy: Navigating the Avant-Garde*, ed. Suzanne W. Churchill, Linda A. Kinnahan and Susan Rosenbaum, University of Georgia (2020), accessed 20 September 2022, https://minaloy.com/chapters/avant-garde-theory-2/feminist-challenges/; Suzanne W. Churchill, Linda A. Kinnahan and Susan Rosenbaum, 'Handiwork: Mina Loy, Collage, and the En Dehors Garde,' *Modernism/modernity Print Plus* 5, no. 2 (2020), accessed 20 September 2022, https://modernismmodernity.org/forums/posts/handiwork.
49. Mina Loy, 'Feminist Manifesto,' *Mina Loy Online*, ed. Andrew Pilsch, accessed 7 December 2021, https://oncomouse.github.io/loy/feminist.html.
50. Arrington, 'Liberté, egalité, sororité,' 220–1.
51. Thomas Baty, quoted in Tiernan, *Image of Such Politics*, 145.
52. Tiernan, *Image of Such Politics*, 145.
53. Ibid.
54. T. Baty, 'The Aëthnic Union,' *The Freewoman* 1, no. 14 (February 1912): 279.
55. Ibid.
56. Woolf, *Room*, 95.
57. 'Science Confirms Intuition,' *Urania* nos. 29–30 (September–December 1921): 1.
58. Karen Steele, 'Ireland and Sapphic Journalism between the Wars: A Case Study of *Urania* (1916–40),' in *Women's Periodicals and Print Culture in Britain, 1918–1939: The Interwar Period*, ed. Catherine Clay, Maria DiCenzo, Barbara Green and Fiona Hackney (Edinburgh: Edinburgh University Press, 2018), 329–39, 338–9.
59. Ibid., 336.
60. Ibid., 331.
61. '"The Well of Loneliness" or, "Cut by the Country,"' *Urania* nos. 75–6 (May–August 1929): 1–2.
62. Steele, 'Ireland and Sapphic Journalism,' 330–1.
63. 'Do Unmarried Women Miss the Half of Life?,' *Urania* no. 19 (March–April 1919): 6.
64. Katharine Tynan, 'An Irish School-Girl,' *Urania* no. 19 (March–April 1919): 6–7.
65. 'Sappho Up-To-Date,' *Urania* nos. 99–100 (May–August 1933): 1–2.
66. 'Geraldine Jewsbury,' *Urania* nos. 115–16 (January–April 1936): 8.
67. Elaine Marks, 'Lesbian Intertextuality,' in *Homosexualities and French Literature*, ed. George Stambolian and Elaine Marks (Ithaca, NY: Cornell University Press, 1979), 353–78, 356–7.
68. Virginia Woolf, 'A Woman's College from Outside,' in *A Haunted House: The Complete Shorter Fiction*, ed. Susan Dick (London: Vintage, 2003), 139–42, 141.
69. Sara Ahmed, *Living a Feminist Life* (Durham, NC: Duke University Press, 2017), 130.
70. Urmila Seshagiri, 'Mind the Gap! Modernism and Feminist Praxis,' *Modernism/modernity Print Plus* 2, no. 2 (2017), doi.org/10.26597/mod.0022 (emphasis in the original).
71. Melanie Micir, *The Passion Projects: Modernist Women, Intimate Archives, Unfinished Lives* (Princeton, NJ: Princeton University Press, 2019), 9.
72. Hannah Roche, 'The Reproductive Futures of Lesbian Modernism,' paper presented at English at Loughborough University, Cultural Currents Research Seminar Series, online, 12 May 2021.

73. See Susan Brown, Patricia Clements and Isobel Grundy, eds, 'Bryher' and 'Christopher St John,' in *Orlando: Women's Writing in the British Isles from the Beginnings to the Present* (Cambridge: Cambridge University Press, 2022), both accessed 20 September 2022, https://orlando.cambridge.org/profiles/bryh_ and https://orlando.cambridge.org/profiles/stjoch. In *Orlando*'s bespoke semantic XML tagset, discussions of both authors' queer families are encoded in multiple ways, using <Family> and <IntimateRelationships><EroticYes> tags to represent modes of kinship.
74. Bradway, 'Queer Narrative Theory,' 721.

9

LESBIAN JOYCE

Katherine Mullin

James Joyce was enabled by lesbians. In 1914, *A Portrait of the Artist as a Young Man* was initially serialised in *The Egoist*, a radical little magazine first founded as *The Freewoman* by Dora Marsden, then sustained as *The New Freewoman* by her intimate friend Harriet Shaw Weaver. Joyce acknowledged his debut and debt by reviving the former feminist title in *Finnegans Wake*: 'I'm so keen on that New Free Woman with novel inside.'[1] 'Dear Miss Weaver' was Joyce's champion and financier for the rest of his life, although censorship constraints meant that *Ulysses* was first issued by two other lesbian couples. In New York, Jane Heap and Margaret Anderson serialised two-thirds in their avant-garde *The Little Review*, until the New York Society for the Suppression of Vice suppressed it.[2] In Paris, Sylvia Beach and Adrienne Monnier ushered *Ulysses* through their new Shakespeare and Company publishing house, before passing the plates to Weaver for her own Egoist Press imprint. Joyce's indebtedness to these Sapphic midwives of modernism was anticipated and obliquely repaid through sympathetic interest. His sense of the possibilities of queer attractions eddies through and disturbs the ostensibly heterosexual dynamics of *Dubliners* and *Ulysses*.[3] Although his treatment of the women who facilitated his writing was not always gracious, Joyce's sensitivity to tenderness, intimacy and love between women nonetheless stands as tribute to lesbian comrades and friends.

On 15 February 1912, Kathlyn Oliver disrupted the letters column of *The Freewoman* by contending that 'the abstinence of many single women' was 'not injurious,' since they were 'sexually anaesthetic.'[4] Her disclosure was characteristic of *The Freewoman*'s boldly confessional mode. Launched in November 1911 by renegade suffragists Dora Marsden and Mary Gawthorpe, it debated 'free love,' birth control, sex work, and 'Uranianism,' by which it meant sex between men.[5] It prided itself, as contributor Rebecca West later put it, on 'its unblushingness—*The Freewoman* mentioned sex loudly and clearly and repeatedly and in the worst possible taste.'[6] The journal was committed to promoting possibilities for women beyond heterosexual reproductive marriage, most strenuously through the contributions of the socialist feminist Stella Browne. Under the pseudonym 'A New Subscriber,' Browne argued that heterosexual abstinence was unwholesome and unhealthy for women, provoking Oliver's eloquent defence of what she termed chastity:

> from my knowledge of many single women and girls I deny that I am not a normal woman. Of course, girls and women do not discuss the sex question as it affects themselves, but from my observation of unmarried girls and women whom I have known intimately, there is not the least ground to suppose that they are in any way troubled or affected diversely by complete chastity. I think I speak for most women when I say that until they love, the idea of the sex relationship seldom enters their thoughts, but if it does it appears repulsive rather than attractive.[7]

Oliver's claim about 'unmarried girls and women whom I have known intimately' dissolves into a telling tangle of negations: 'I deny that I am not a normal woman.' But Oliver was scarcely a 'normal woman.' As Laura Schwartz has shown, she was remarkable: whilst still in her twenties and working as a cook, she had founded the Domestic Workers' Union in 1909, recruiting and organising through *The Woman Worker*, where she also explored her sexual orientation. In 1909, she wrote, 'I have been more in love with women than I have with any of the opposite sex [. . .] I cannot explain this (perhaps) unnatural state of things, but I know it is so.'[8] Within three years of *The Freewoman* controversy, she was corresponding with Edward Carpenter and advertising in *The Daily Herald* for a 'woman who could fill the emptiness in her life': in 1917 she joined the British Society for the Study of Sex Psychology – proposed by Stella Browne, who was by now a close friend.[9] Nonetheless, Oliver's defensive presentation of her sexuality as 'chastity' stands as an apt illustration of the difficulties of naming lesbian selfhood in 1912 – even in *The Freewoman*. Her discussion of absences rather than presences indicates how love between women hovered in the shadows, obscure and inchoate.

Here is a familiar parable of lesbian invisibility: Oliver's sexuality haunts the margins of *The Freewoman* as inference or apparition. It kept company with other ghosts. Marsden and Gawthorpe began *The Freewoman* with the help of Marsden's domestic partner Grace Jardine. The three were members of the

Manchester network of suffragette trade unionists initiated by another lesbian couple, Eva Gore-Booth and Esther Roper. Weaver, independently wealthy, self-effacing, and committed to radical aesthetic and political activism, was an early *Freewoman* subscriber. In 1970, Weaver's biographers – her goddaughter Jane Lidderdale and Lidderdale's friend Mary Nicholson – explained her 'total lack of interest in the other sex' as being 'by no means uncommon among young women of her generation, class and interests,' adding that '[i]t was enough, for them, not to marry.'[10] They conceded that Weaver had 'strong personal reasons' for investment in *The Freewoman*, being 'well equipped to understand the emotional relief that free discussion can give, to people who have suffered in secret,' 'particularly evident in the contributions from homosexuals.'[11] Weaver was part of the Freewoman Discussion Circle, a fledgling queer social network which met monthly at Eustace Miles's vegetarian restaurant in Covent Garden. It hosted ardent debates about sexuality led by guest speakers including 'Mrs Havelock Ellis,' otherwise the well-known lesbian Edith Lees. For Rebecca West, Freewoman meetings were characterised by 'an epidemic of kissing,' symptomatic of lesbian exuberance.[12] When *The Freewoman* folded in October 1912 following a boycott by W H Smith's, Weaver hastened to answer Marsden's call for support, financing and otherwise practically enabling its relaunch as *The New Freewoman* nine months later. On first meeting in London in February 1913, the pair 'took an instant liking to each other,' Weaver finding Marsden 'a remarkable person, a genius, and also very beautiful to look upon,' petite and with the 'face of a Florentine angel.'[13] So began Weaver's lifelong emotional, practical and financial support of Marsden, sustained until Marsden's death in 1960. Love between women may not quite have made it into print, but it was essential to the network from which print flourished.

As owner-editor, Weaver helped Marsden broaden *The New Freewoman*'s focus from sexual politics to literary modernism. The two converged in the championing of Joyce, then languishing unpublished in Trieste. On 15 December 1913, Ezra Pound wrote to Joyce for the first time on the recommendation of W. B. Yeats. He explained he was 'informally connected with a couple of new and impecunious papers,' principally '*The Egoist* which has coursed under the unsuitable name of *The New Freewoman*.'[14] Pound had just petitioned Marsden and Weaver to change the title to one which might 'mark the character of your paper as an organ of individualists of both sexes.'[15] Within a month, he was introducing Joyce as a new 'author of known and notable talents' in the rechristened *Egoist*, and reprinting Joyce's open letter about his difficulties in publishing *Dubliners*.[16] Joyce had first circulated 'A Curious History' in the Irish press in summer 1911, detailing a decade of struggles over *Dubliners'* improprieties, first with London publisher Grant Richards and later with the Dublin firm Maunsel & Co. Readers were thus primed to understand him as a victim of prudery when *The Egoist* began to serialise *A Portrait of the*

Artist as a Young Man on 2 February 1914. Joyce's recruitment was part of Pound's broader strategy to 'fire the sex problem,' and *The New Freewoman*'s transformation is often read as a paradigmatic conflict between modernism and feminism.[17] But Joyce's introduction as sex-radical raises the question of how far he might be assimilated within Pound's ideological project.[18] Focusing on Stephen Dedalus, *A Portrait* does not address the most shadowy of *The Freewoman*'s concerns: lesbian identity. But its serialisation was the start of Joyce's *annus mirabilis*, since *The Egoist*'s championship ultimately prompted Grant Richards to publish *Dubliners* on 15 June 1914.[19] Its role as catalyst precipitating Joyce to international acclaim is strangely apt, for aspects of *Dubliners*' understanding of female sexuality anticipate the possibilities that *The Freewoman* barely named.

Specifically, there are continuities between Oliver's passionate account of 'sexual anaesthesia,' and *Dubliners*' sketch of the consequences of compulsory heterosexuality. As Maria Luddy has established, the number of women who would never marry doubled in Ireland between 1901 and 1911, indicating rising female precarity in an era of scant alternatives.[20] Accordingly, *Dubliners*' courtships are cursory, anxious and desperate. Eveline Hill contemplates elopement to Buenos Aires with a man she hardly knows because '[f]irst of all it had been an excitement for her to have a fellow' – and she longs for 'Escape!'[21] Polly Mooney's bleak seduction of Bob Doran is furtively choreographed by her mother, conscious of 'some mothers she knew who could not get their daughters off their hands' (48). Lily the caretaker's daughter in 'The Dead' speaks for a generation of disenchanted young women when she answers Gabriel's mild pleasantry about her future wedding with '[t]he men that is now is only all palaver and what they can get out of you' (140). Romance is illusionary, ardour transactional, and the resulting marriages sketched with deft economy: 'Miss Devlin had become Mrs Kearney out of spite' (106) begins 'A Mother.' Mr Kearney, 'much older than she,' is a pragmatic prospect – 'Mrs Kearney perceived that such a man would wear better than a romantic person' – but nonetheless she continues her maidenly habit of 'trying to console her romantic desires by eating a great deal of Turkish Delight in secret' (106). Mrs Kearney's appetite for Turkish Delight is the closest any married woman gets to pleasure in *Dubliners*. Certainly, she is better off than Mrs Kernan in 'Grace': 'After three weeks she had found a wife's life irksome and, later on, when she was beginning to find it unbearable, she had become a mother' (121). Motherhood is no escape: Polly's mother is separated from a husband who 'went for his wife with the cleaver' (46), whilst Eveline's late mother endured a 'life of commonplace sacrifices closing in final craziness' (28). In comparison, Gabriel Conroy in 'The Dead' seems uxorious. But Gretta's hidden longing for the lover of her youth, Michael Furey, is revealed after a delicately devastating glimpse of her evasion of her husband's 'keen pang of lust' (169) at the Gresham Hotel.

These vignettes together sketch an emotional landscape which is not far away from Oliver's declaration that she and her friends find heterosexuality 'repulsive rather than attractive.'[22] *Dubliners*' wives and would-be wives are united by a shared indifference, bordering on distaste.

Like Oliver, Joyce stops short of contemplating affective alternatives for any of his disappointed women. *Dubliners* describes no lesbians – but the collection is book-ended by two pairs of elderly sibling spinsters. Eliza and Nannie Flynn, and Kate and Julia Morkan feature in stories whose titles could be swapped – 'The Sisters' is about the dead, and 'The Dead,' about sisters – framing Joyce's careful attention to women's circumscribed emotional lives. Tellingly, these sibling pairs exhibit more sustaining domestic intimacies than any of *Dubliners*' marriages. Eliza's care for her deaf, downtrodden sister – '—There's poor Nannie, said Eliza, looking at her, she's wore out' (8) – is recapitulated in Kate's protective outrage over Julia's lifelong exploitation: 'She had worked herself into a passion and would have continued in defence of her sister for it was a sore subject with her' (153). Kate's anger over Pope Leo XIII's 1903 decree removing women from church choirs and so terminating Julia's brilliant singing career is one of several discords unsettling the seemingly harmonious hospitality of *Dubliners*' final story.[23] Other 'back answers' include Lily's sharp retort and Gretta's conjugal snub, but they are most overtly expressed by the nationalist feminist Molly Ivors, who tasks Gabriel with being a 'West Briton' (147) for writing for the jingoistic *Daily Express*. Whilst recognising Miss Ivors's 'warm grasp' and 'soft friendly tone' (148), Gabriel struggles to 'keep his good humour under the ordeal' (148). He improvises an attack on 'the new and very serious and hypereducated generation' for his speech as 'one for Miss Ivors' (151), only to be balked when he finds her 'buttoning her cloak' (153) and good-humouredly resisting the entreaties of Gretta and his cousin Mary Jane that she stay for supper. Joyce's narrative is filtered from Gabriel's perspective, and thus coloured by a sense of what he misses. He chances upon Gretta and Mary Jane's attempts to persuade Miss Ivors to stay for supper, just glimpsing the latter's dejection: '—I am afraid you didn't enjoy yourself at all, said Mary Jane hopelessly' (154). What may linger is the frisson of a possibility.

Miss Ivors's unsettling qualities might be understood through Bonnie Zimmerman's useful conception of the 'metaphorical lesbian' – a fictional character who is never explicitly outed, but who is nonetheless a 'disrupter of heterosexuality,' 'a hole in the fabric of gender dualism,' a 'radical absence.'[24] Certainly, the temptation to read Miss Ivors along these lines is evident from her introduction as:

> a frank-mannered talkative young lady, with a freckled face and prominent brown eyes. She did not wear a low-cut bodice and the large brooch which was fixed in the front of her collar bore on it an Irish device and motto. (147)

Miss Ivors's severe neckline – inappropriate for an evening party – is an early intimation of her evasion of contemporary codes of femininity. Her university education and teaching career, her political commitment, her willingness to confront Gabriel, and her enthusiasm for travel together create an aura that Gabriel finds altogether disconcerting. Their conversation during a Christmas-time quadrille arranged by couples makes her status as a 'disrupter of heterosexuality' the clearer. The occasion seems ripe for tipsy flirtation, but her 'warm grasp,' her lively teasing, and quizzical glance 'from under her brows' (148) are no more than friendly. Revealingly, Gabriel cannot place 'the girl or woman, or whatever she was,' resorting in his private thoughts to vengeful slights about her 'staring at him with her rabbit's eyes' (149). But Gabriel, as usual, misses the point: Miss Ivors's charm is not for him. Mary Jane, another spinster in her mid-thirties with a dual career as gifted musician and teacher, is the mainstay of her aunts' household, and, whilst she is keen that the festivities should please her paying pupils, she also seems particularly troubled that one guest is leaving early. Mary Jane and Miss Ivors share qualities of intelligence, competence and independence – Miss Ivors laughingly refuses Gabriel's escort home – and 'Mary Jane gazed after her, a moody puzzled expression on her face,' distressed by 'her abrupt departure' (154). The disappointment takes the shine off her evening, leaving Mary Jane to run errands, smooth disagreements and 'settle down quietly to her supper' (156).

Molly Ivors and Mary Jane Morkan are good friends, but is there anything more? We cannot know, and the narrative, focalised through Gabriel's blinkered perceptions, does not tell. But friendship, Hannah Roche reminds us, can conceal something else – especially in early modernism. Roche's reading of Djuna Barnes's 1915 short story 'Paprika Johnson' unveils 'the lesbian romance plot running parallel to the marriage plot' in the form of a queer intimacy between Paprika and her '"bosom friend", the "thin and pock-marked and colorless" Leah.'[25] For Roche, the story is an extension of Sharon Marcus's 'plot of female amity,' which hides lesbian attachments 'in plain sight': although the erotic connection between Paprika and Leah is 'the only authentic partnership in the story,' it is 'nonetheless easy to miss.'[26] In *Dubliners* too, we have 'plots of female amity' counterpointed with inauthentic heterosexual partnerships, characterised by estrangement, disaffection and even violence. If Molly Ivors – like Barnes's Leah, unattractive to men, or to Gabriel at least – is a lesbian, she is also easy to miss. Nonetheless, 'The Dead's' Sapphic *sillage* indicates how it came to pass that queer women became Joyce's earliest and most stalwart champions. Djuna Barnes did not meet Joyce until the autumn of 1921, although they had published alongside one other in *The Little Review* since 1918.[27] They quickly became friends: Joyce presented Barnes with a prized signed copy of the first edition of *Ulysses*, dated a mere fortnight after its launch.[28] Mutual affection shines from Barnes's April 1922 profile of Joyce for *Vanity Fair*, in which she explains, 'I had read *Dubliners* over my coffee during the war' and gives a flavour of their conversations 'in the café of the Deux Magots':

> It has been my pleasure to talk to him many times during my four months in Paris. We have talked of rivers and religion, of the instinctive genius of the church which chose, for the singing of its hymns, the voice without 'overtones' – the voice of the eunuch. We have talked of women, about women he seems a bit disinterested.[29]

The vignette suggests intimacy without attraction, consonant with their conversation's curious turn to castrati in church choirs – a subject intersecting with the contretemps over women's exclusion from church music in 'The Dead.' Barnes's use of the term 'disinterest' is odd: as the common solecism for 'uninterested,' it implies the absence of an ulterior motive – flirtation – which made Joyce particularly appealing to women like her. Her interview half-articulates a quality ripe to be inferred: Joyce liked queer women, and queer women liked him.

Joyce's subtle sympathy shines from Sylvia Beach's account of their first meeting at a Paris literary party 'in the summer of 1920, when my bookshop was in its first year.'[30] Beach attended as the initially bashful partner of her neighbour-bookseller Adrienne Monnier, and they were introduced together before Beach could settle into *tête-à-tête*:

> We talked on. Joyce's manner was so extremely simple that, overcome though I was in the presence of the greatest writer of my time, I somehow felt at ease with him. This first time and afterward, I was always conscious of his genius, yet I knew no one so easy to talk with.[31]

Beach's experience of rapport ultimately prompted her celebrated offer the following spring: 'Would you let Shakespeare and Company have the honor of bringing out your *Ulysses*?' (47). Her account of her proposal underscores her lover's role as its arbiter:

> We parted, both of us, I think, very much moved. He was to come back next day to hear what Adrienne Monnier, 'Shakespeare and Company's Adviser,' as Joyce called her, thought of my plan. I always consulted her before taking an important step. She was such a wise counselor, and she was, besides, a sort of partner in the firm. (47)

Monnier duly proved instrumental in the practicalities of publication, supplying the printer and guiding Beach through 'the mysteries of limited editions'

(49), the prospectus and the subscription list. Joyce's understanding of Monnier's significance to Beach compares to his punctilious enquiries after 'Miss Marsden' in his letters to Weaver.[32] As he would later acknowledge, '[t]hroughout my life women have been my most active helpers' – but crucially, they were women who loved women.[33]

It is tempting to speculate about the affective roots of Joyce's affinity. His own life partnership was a strange hybrid of the conventional and the irregular, anticipating *The Freewoman*'s spirited advocacy of 'free unions' as a reconfiguration of reproductive heterosexuality. He eloped with Nora Barnacle in 1904, yet the couple did not marry until 1931, long after the birth of two children and the establishment of a nomadic, chaotic mode of living. In May 1922, Joyce's ophthalmologist attended his patient in one of the succession of furnished apartments which served the Joyce family as temporary homes, and was astonished at the disarray. Amid half-unpacked trunks, scattered papers and 'toilet articles,' Joyce and Nora were squatting on the floor, wrapped in blankets, sharing a roast chicken and a bottle of wine.[34] The Joyces' union was the inverse of a lavender marriage, insofar as the social forms of legal contract, home-making and child-rearing were precarious at best, whilst the emotional essentials of erotic love and lifelong companionship were authentically present. These unconventionalities flavoured the writing and its reception. *Ulysses* had already captivated Beach well in advance of their fateful first meeting in the summer of 1920: 'I worshipped James Joyce,' she wrote in her memoir (35). Beach had read instalments first in *The Egoist*, where it was initially serialised until Weaver could no longer find a willing printer, then in its New York counterpart *The Little Review*. Editors Margaret Anderson and Jane Heap had fallen in love with Joyce's writing not long after they fell for one another. For Anderson, meeting Heap was a revelation – a gifted pianist, she found her 'a hand on the exact octave that is me' – and, for both, reading Joyce was almost as transformative.[35] They reviewed *A Portrait* side by side in the April 1917 issue of *The Little Review*. To Anderson, it was 'the most beautiful piece of writing and the most creative piece of prose anywhere to be seen on the horizon to-day': for Heap, Joyce's triumphant achievement was his flouting of a prudish 'geography of the body' which meant 'some parts' were meet subjects for art 'but others must be treated like the Bad Lands.'[36] Neither Anderson nor Heap met Joyce in person, but his fiction was enough. As they prepared to serialise *Ulysses*, their bold advertisement brooked no argument: 'We are about to publish a prose masterpiece.'[37]

Ulysses ran in *The Little Review* from March 1918 until the July–August number carrying the 'Nausicaa' episode was confiscated by the New York Society for the Suppression of Vice. The subsequent conviction of Anderson and Heap on obscenity charges in February 1921 banned *Ulysses* from publication in the United States and, in effect, the wider English-speaking world, forcing Joyce's New York publisher Ben Huebsch's regretful withdrawal, Beach's offer, and Joyce's grateful acceptance.[38] *Ulysses* was passed like a baton between lesbian couples – from Marsden and Weaver to Anderson and Heap, then to Beach and Monnier – before finally appearing in book form in time for Joyce's fortieth birthday on 2 February 1922. Speculation about affective investments should not undermine the courage and radicalism of these women's literary tastes – but we might also ask whether there was something about *Ulysses* that appealed at a more personal level. To be sure, queer female figures make fleeting appearances as cross-dressed minor characters disturbing gender binaries through costume and manner. In 'Nausicaa,' Gerty MacDowell remembers her friend 'Madcap' Cissy Caffrey, 'dressed up in her father's suit and hat and the burned cork moustache,' walking 'down Tritonville road, smoking a cigarette.'[39] In 'Circe,' 'massive whoremistress' (15: 2742) Bella Cohen transforms into 'Mr Bello,' a 'ma'amsir' (15: 2880) 'with bobbed hair,' 'green silverbuttoned coat, sport skirt and alpine hat with moorcock's feather' (15: 2857). Bello's sartorial codes are borrowed from contemporary butch stylings – indeed, s/he resembles 'Tilly Tweed-In-Blood,' Djuna Barnes's affectionate satire of Radclyffe Hall in *Ladies Almanack* (1928). But these apparitions are pranks or fantasies, passing incidents of fancy-dress or phantasmagoria, rather than serious or sustained portraits. Instead, I would propose that *Ulysses* elaborates *Dubliners'* interest in women's heterosexual indifference – a quality, as Oliver reminds us, important to many lesbian women's journey to self-knowledge. Heterosexuality is both abundantly and abrasively present in *Ulysses* – the reason for these publication difficulties – but also curiously absent, in the sense that it is attenuated and performative. It is Joyce's vision of female heterosexuality as mediated rather than authentically felt which may have proved imaginatively compelling to his first lesbian readers.

Mediation is essential to the mode in which female heterosexuality enters *Ulysses*. 'Calypso' introduces Leopold Bloom chatting to his cat whilst preparing breakfast at 7 Eccles Street when two letters arrive, the first from the Blooms' fifteen-year-old daughter, Milly, to her father, and the second from Molly Bloom's singing manager, Blazes Boylan. Both withhold erotic secrets. Milly writes, 'There is a young student comes here some evenings named Bannon his cousins or something are big swells and he sings Boylan's (I was on the pop of writing Blazes Boylan's) song about those seaside girls' (4: 406–9). Milly, her father rapidly intuits, hints at a budding flirtation – 'A wild piece of goods' (4: 429–30) – but this teenage romance is twice filtered, first through the popular song through which Bannon registers his interest in Milly, and second through the letter itself. The episode's second letter, from Boylan to Molly to arrange the afternoon appointment where they will become lovers, is still more retentive:

—Who was the letter from? he asked.
Bold hand. Marion.
—O, Boylan, she said. He's bringing the programme.
—What are you singing?
—*La ci darem* with J. C. Doyle, she said, and *Love's Old Sweet Song*. (4: 310–14)

Molly conceals her letter 'under the dimpled pillow,' but its contents are displaced into the two songs of seduction and fulfilment she plans to rehearse. Female heterosexuality is thus doubly mediated through song and letter, complementing other stylised representations, including Molly's erotic novella '*Ruby: the Pride of the Ring*' (4: 345), or the picture from the softcore magazine *Photo Bits* hanging over the marital bed. In the next episode, 'Lotus-Eaters,' Bloom furtively collects a third letter from the Westland Row Post Office. The subterfuge is necessary, since Bloom has been conducting a clandestine erotic correspondence under the name 'Henry Flower' after placing an advertisement in *The Irish Times*: 'Wanted, smart lady typist to aid gentleman in literary work' (8: 326–7). Receiving forty-four replies, Bloom has selected Martha Clifford because of her willingness to humour his masochism: 'I am awfully angry with you. I do wish I could punish you for that' (5: 243–4), she writes. Bloom is pleased by her complaisance, particularly since he feels he '[w]ent too far last time' (5: 59), but his pleasure is qualified by suspicions that her ardour is feigned. Bloom is paying her – in 'Sirens,' he replies, '[a]ccep my poor litt pres enclos' (11: 865–6), a postal order for two shillings and sixpence, before imploring her to tell him in return '[h]ow you will pun? You punish me?,' 'It will excite me. You know how' (11: 890–1, 888–9). Martha is an enigma, refracted through advertising column, typewriter and contact details; Bloom writes to her 'c/o P. O. Dolphin's Barn Lane' (11: 899–900) but cannot be sure that Martha Clifford is even her real name. Martha's identity and motivations remain uncertain, the mystery highlighted by her postscript: 'P. S. Do tell me what kind of perfume does your wife use. I want to know' (5: 258). This alarming turn to Molly's scent unsettles Bloom and mars the fantasy, suggesting that Martha may have opaque investments of her own. Martha's interest in Molly can hardly be read as queer – after all, the women have not met – but it nonetheless points up the essential performativity of her masquerade of longing. Joyce gives us a 1904 version of virtual sex, where the other's identity or motive cannot be ascertained.

These letters are three instances of mediated female heterosexuality in *Ulysses*, where women's desire for men repeatedly appears as culturally imposed rather than organically felt. Strategy, Joyce slyly suggests, underpins the compliance of other sexy women characters – most obviously, the gaudily performative sex workers Kitty, Zoe and Florry in the 'Circe' episode, or Miss

Douce and Miss Kennedy, the 'Sirens' barmaids who flirt obligingly, yet cower 'under their reef of counter' (11: 109) on their tea-break. Significantly, Bloom's consciousness of Martha's artifice inhibits him from masturbation: 'Damned glad I didn't do it in the bath this morning over her silly I will punish you letter' (13: 785–6). The context is his more successful later encounter with another mysterious young woman, Gerty MacDowell, who in 'Nausicaa' choreographs her desirability from romantic fiction, fashion plates, women's magazines, and the early striptease films which animated the turn-of-the-century craze for Mutoscopes. Watching Gerty's routine as she swings her leg back and forth, conscious of his voyeuristic arousal, Bloom is quick to make the connection between this high-kicking show and the erotica he relishes: 'Peeping Tom. Willy's hat and what the girls did with it. Do they snapshot those girls or is it all a fake? *Lingerie* does it. Felt for the curves inside her *deshabille*' (13: 794–6). Gerty's performance of arousal is pure masquerade, he suspects 'all a fake' – and the suspicion recalls Martha Clifford: 'It couldn't be? No, Gerty they called her. Might be false name however like my name and the address Dolphin's barn a blind' (13: 944–6). This possibility that Gerty might be Martha duly haunts 'Circe,' where both women appear to accuse Bloom of sexual perfidies: 'Leave the gentleman alone, you cheat,' The Bawd tells Gerty, 'Writing the gentleman false letters' (15: 380). Gerty and Martha are both 'cheats' insofar as their ardour is strategically feigned.

Bloom's encounter with Gerty was the nail in the coffin of *The Little Review*, which, after several warnings, was finally suppressed when serialisation reached 'Nausicaa.' The bone of contention was, primarily, Joyce's unabashed depiction of male masturbation, but the episode's consummate dissection of female heterosexuality as mannered performance casts a side-light on Jane Heap's editorial about the impending prosecution. Observing that it was driven by that 'creampuff of sentimentality,' protective concern for '[o]ur young girls,' Heap objected that '[t]he present case is rather ironical. We are being prosecuted for printing the thoughts in a young girl's mind.'[40] Heap is tongue-in-cheek: 'Nausicaa' does not attempt a psychological sketch of Gerty's inner life but instead constructs her consciousness from an often-comic palimpsest of intertextualities. The episode was, however, only a rehearsal for Molly Bloom's monologue, delivered from her bed after an afternoon of vigorous adultery with Blazes Boylan. The 'Penelope' episode is both graphically heterosexual and ebulliently performative. 'I could have been a prima donna only I married him' (18: 896), Molly ruefully remarks, summarising both her singing career and her significance as *Ulysses*'s grand finale. Like any prima donna, she has been teasingly withheld and tantalisingly trailed. In 'Calypso,' she is present first as sound – 'A sleepy soft grunt answered' (4: 56) – and later in fragments: 'an elbow on the pillow' (4: 303–4), 'large soft bubs' (4: 304–5), 'fingertips' (4: 334), 'mocking eyes' (4: 344). In 'Wandering Rocks,' she fleetingly appears as 'a plump bare generous arm' (10: 251) at a window. Otherwise, Molly only features in the thoughts and fantasies of others. In 'Circe,' she manifests in pantomime-dreamscape as 'a handsome woman in Turkish costume' (15: 297–8), with 'scarlet trousers' (15: 299), a 'white yashmak' (15: 300), 'jewelled toerings' (15: 312–13) and an attendant camel. In 'Eumaeus,' she features in the studio photograph Bloom shows to Stephen, 'a speaking likeness' which nonetheless cannot 'do justice' to 'her stage presence' (16: 1444–5, 1459). These glimpses whet the appetite for *Ulysses*'s big reveal – the *clou*, as Joyce put it, or star turn of the book.[41]

Joyce's conception of Molly as star turn sets the tone for the episode's sexual theatre. Molly recalls how carefully she staged that afternoon's encounter with Boylan: 'I gave my eyes that look with my hair a bit loose from the tumbling and my tongue between my lips up to him the savage brute' (18: 592–4). Even at the point of orgasm, she is unable to abandon self-consciousness, concerned instead 'only not to look ugly or those lines from the strain' (18: 899). Her conception of her sexuality accords with her singing career, but it also underscores Joyce's wider fascination with heterosexuality as culturally constructed rather than profoundly felt. Molly's detachment is evident from her wry asides: male genitals are dismissed as 'his two bags full and his other thing hanging down out of him or sticking up at you like a hatrack no wonder they hide it with a cabbageleaf' (18: 342–4). In contrast, she understands 'the woman is beauty of course thats admitted' (18: 559–60), slipping easily into an appreciation of others' allure. Molly calibrates the attractions of celebrated mistresses Kitty O'Shea and 'that Mrs Langtry the jersey lily' (18: 480), of an acquaintance Mrs Galbraith ('her beautys on the wane she was a lovely woman' – 18: 477) and of her own daughter, Milly ('of course shes restless knowing shes pretty with her lips so red' – 18: 1065–6). These thoughts shade imperceptibly into something more. Astride her chamber pot, Molly's speculations about Boylan's pleasure become a more satisfying caress of self-love, as she admires her own thighs: 'look how white they are the smoothest place is right there between this bit here how soft like a peach' (18: 1145–6). As Colleen Lamos suggests, the moment 'takes us beyond the impasse of debates concerning her famously "feminine" narcissism' as Molly begins to consider a distinctively queer form of pleasure: 'God I wouldnt mind being a man and get up on a lovely woman' (18: 1146–7).[42] What, in these terms, does 'being a man' mean? For Lamos, Joyce, like other male modernists, treats lesbianism as 'a more occluded secret than male homosexuality,' thus shielding Molly 'from realising the damaging implications of same-sex desire.'[43] Whether Molly realises it or not, her nostalgic longing for a long-lost friend pushes *Ulysses*'s fascination with heterosexuality's discontents to its logical conclusion.

Molly's half-resentful thoughts of 'all the pleasure those men get out of a woman' (18: 583) segue easily from Boylan to 'fathers friend Mrs Stanhope' (18: 612). Hester Stanhope was a young married woman whom Molly knew during her girlhood in Gibraltar, and her queerness is signalled by her namesake. The eighteenth-century explorer Lady Hester Stanhope famously adopted Turkish male dress of turban, trousers and slippers – like Molly herself in 'Circe' – and 'Penelope' exploits the frisson of nonconformity. Hester addresses Molly as 'my dearest Doggerina' (18: 613) and sends presents and inconsequential yet strangely charged postcards. They describe the immediate pleasures of her 'jolly warm bath' and the remembered pleasures of Molly's 'scrumptious currant scones and raspberry wafers,' ending effusively 'with love yours affly Hester x x x x x' (18: 615, 621–2). Molly's intimacy with Hester becomes a defining memory of her emotional life, as her reminiscences – 'she didn't look a bit married just like a girl' (18: 623–4) – inscribe another 'plot of female amity' which hides lesbian attachment 'in plain sight':

> I made the scones of course I had everything all to myself then a girl Hester we used to compare our hair mine was thicker than hers she showed me how to settle it at the back when I put it up and whats this else how to make a knot on a thread with the one hand we were like cousins what age was I then the night of the storm I slept in her bed she had her arms round me then we were fighting in the morning with the pillow what fun he was watching me whenever he got an opportunity. (18: 637–43)

The passage insinuates the houseless, nameless, boundary-less nature of desire between women, moving from home baking, hairdressing and manually dextrous tricks with thread to ardent night-time embraces. Hester's arms around Molly in her warm bed in the dark, the storm outside, the flirty, provocative pillow fight in the morning, together create an evocative sketch of erotic play between women – disrupted by the looming pressures of compulsory heterosexuality ('he' – Hester's husband and 'years older than her' (18: 624) – 'was watching me'). Two decades later, Molly's memories are suffused with authentic tenderness and the sadness of parting:

> she kissed me six or seven times didnt I cry yes I believe I did or near it my lips were taittering when I said goodbye she had a Gorgeous wrap of some special kind of blue colour on her for the voyage made very peculiarly to one side like and it was extremely pretty it got as dull as the devil after they went I was almost planning to run away mad out of it somewhere were never easy where we are father or aunt or marriage waiting always waiting. (18: 672–8)

Molly's sorrow at this long-ago loss elegiacally notes the inevitability of 'marriage waiting always waiting' but celebrates, nonetheless, kisses as vividly recalled as Clarissa Dalloway's remembered kiss with Sally Seton, her 'match burning in a crocus.'[44] In Homer's *Odyssey*, Penelope's domestic fidelity is symbolised by the shroud she weaves each day for her missing husband, only to defer her suitors by unravelling it secretly at night. For Joyce, this cloth of marital devotion is interwoven with Hester's '[g]orgeous wrap of some special kind of blue colour,' suggestive of secret fidelity of a very different fabric. Hester's shimmering erotic presence, as gorgeous as her shawl, remains 'of some special kind' to Molly, quietly subverting *Ulysses*'s heterosexuality.

Writing to his drinking crony Frank Budgen during the chapter's composition, Joyce described 'Penelope' as 'probably more obscene than any preceding episode' in its portrait of a 'perfectly sane full amoral fertilisable untrustworthy engaging shrewd limited prudent indifferent *Weib*.'[45] Joyce's list of adjectives is disconcertingly misogynist, but the movement from obscenity to indifference is nonetheless revealing. Behind 'obscene' content – Molly's thoughts about her body and its acts, and the bodies and acts of her male lovers – is indifference arising from her sense of heterosexual inevitability. That sense even percolates through Molly's closing recollections of Bloom's marriage proposal on Howth Head, where joyous affirmation is punctured by her 'prudent indifferent' thought 'well as well him as another' (18: 1604–5). Memories are interpolated with ghosts of other lovers: 'I was thinking of so many things he didnt know of Mulvey and Mr Stanhope and Hester' (18: 1582–3). What Bloom didn't know stands for what Molly, the 'Penelope' episode, and *Ulysses* itself can scarcely quite conceptualise. But, seven years before his conception of Molly Bloom's feelings for her lost friend, Hester, Joyce was probing the possibilities *Ulysses* never explicitly names.

Composing his only play, *Exiles*, in Trieste in the autumn of 1913, Joyce made extensive notes on his characters' inner lives. For his heroine, Bertha, he sketched two memories of girlhood intensity. The first is of 'Christmas in Galway, a moonlit Christmas eve with snow' where '[s]he thumps the piano and sits with her dark-complexioned gipsy-looking girl friend Emily Lyons on the windowsill.'[46] The second is of their parting at 'the quay of Galway harbour' where '[t]he emigrant ship is going away and Emily, her dark friend, stands on deck going out to America. They kiss and cry bitterly. But she believes that some day her friend will come back as she promises.'[47] Both memories are freighted with what Joyce terms 'a persistent and delicate sensuality' captured in 'the kisses of her friend':

> The note of regret is ever present and finds utterance at last in the tears which fill her eyes as she sees her friend go. A departure. A friend, her own youth, going away. A faint glimmer of lesbianism irradiates this mind.[48]

This 'faint glimmer of lesbianism' does not make its way so explicitly into the published work, but it leaves traces. The first memory of a Christmas-time night and two young women – one a pianist – enthralled by each another as they sit at a window seat watching the snow could be an outtake from 'The Dead.' The second, of a quayside parting, kisses and bitter tears is the seed of Molly's recollections of Hester Stanhope. It is strangely apt that shortly after writing these notes Joyce heard from Ezra Pound for the first time, with his invitation to write for *The New Freewoman*.[49] For he was already articulating a feeling and an identity which Oliver, eighteen months earlier and at the other side of Europe, had only just started to express. Like Joyce, Oliver fumbled with her terms, naming as 'chastity' what she would eventually own as lesbian selfhood. For Joyce, lesbianism was similarly inchoate, a 'faint glimmer,' but unforgettable and emotionally transformative nonetheless.

Joyce's lesbian affinities have much to do with his lesbian admirers, editors, financers and publishers. The connection, however, is not so straightforward as gratitude to those whom he acknowledged as 'my most active helpers.'[50] Indeed, 'gratitude' is not a term that can comfortably be applied to Joyce: the story of his poor treatment of Beach in particular makes painful reading. It is taken up by Alison Bechdel in the closing pages of *Fun Home* (2006), where she cites a letter from Joyce, included in the front matter of her Modern Library edition of *Ulysses*, in which he acknowledged Anderson's, Heap's and Beach's bravery. As Bechdel reminds us, Joyce nonetheless shamelessly broke his contract with Beach, publishing *Ulysses* with Random House when the ban was lifted: 'HE DID NOT OFFER TO REPAY HER FOR THE FINANCIAL SACRIFICES SHE'D MADE FOR HIS BOOK.'[51] Bechdel's reminder is salutary: Joyce treated lesbians badly, and that he treated others badly too does not excuse him. But Bechdel also reads *Ulysses* as a coming-out message between closeted gay father and lesbian daughter, and she does so by considering the emotional implications of its strikingly Sapphic publication history:

> PERHAPS IT'S JUST A COINCIDENCE THAT THESE WOMEN— ALONG WITH SYLVIA'S LOVER ADRIENNE MONNIER, WHO PUBLISHED THE FRENCH EDITION OF *ULYSSES*—WERE ALL LESBIANS. (229)

Coincidence, however, is an unsatisfactory, even disappointing explanation, and it leaves Bechdel wanting more:

> BUT I LIKE TO THINK THEY WENT TO THE MAT FOR THIS BOOK BECAUSE THEY KNEW A THING OR TWO ABOUT EROTIC TRUTH. (229)

Bechdel deserves the last word because she intuitively grasps a quality this chapter has explored. Joyce's sense of female heterosexuality as socially mandated in *Dubliners*, and as mediated or performative in *Ulysses*, presents lesbian desire as palimpsest. It is overwritten, almost erased, mistaken for or confused with something else, unrecognised – even as Oliver failed at first to recognise her own orientation as something more than an absence of desire for men. It is – perhaps necessarily, given Joyce's publication – more than a 'faint glimmer,' but a glimmer that nonetheless shines through obscurity. It would ultimately shine the brighter in *Finnegans Wake*, which, as Christy Burns has established, is rich in lesbian associations.[52] It would also become personal in the early 1930s when Joyce's daughter, Lucia, declared herself a lesbian and pursued a passionate affair with Beach's assistant, Myrsine Moschos.[53] But in *Dubliners* and in *Ulysses* in particular, Joyce's representation of women's inner emotional lives names the quality Bechdel discerns: erotic truth.

Notes

1. James Joyce, *Finnegans Wake* (London: Faber & Faber, 1939), 145: 31–2.
2. Clare Hutton has compellingly argued that Anderson and Heap's serial edition of *Ulysses* has 'a particular and indubitable authority.' Clare Hutton, *Serial Encounters: Ulysses in The Little Review* (Oxford: Oxford University Press, 2019), 16.
3. For Joyce's interest in homosexuality, see essays collected in *Quare Joyce*, ed. Joseph Valente (Ann Arbor: University of Michigan Press, 1998).
4. 'Continence and Marriage,' *The Freewoman*, 15 February 1912, 231.
5. As Lucy Bland observes, lesbianism was scarcely mentioned. Lucy Bland, 'Heterosexuality, Feminism and *The Freewoman* Journal in Early Twentieth-Century England,' *Women's History Review* 4, no. 1 (1995): 5–23.
6. Rebecca West, 'The Freewoman,' *Time and Tide*, 16 July 1926, 649.
7. 'Chastity and Normality,' *The Freewoman*, 29 February 1912, 290. For Stella Browne's role in the controversy, see Bland, 'Heterosexuality, Feminism,' 9–10.
8. *Woman Worker*, 11 August 1909, 126, quoted in Laura Schwartz, *Feminism and the Servant Problem: Class and Domestic Labour in the Women's Suffrage Movement* (Cambridge: Cambridge University Press, 2019), 76.
9. Schwartz, *Feminism and the Servant Problem*, 75–6.
10. Jane Lidderdale and Mary Nicholson, *Dear Miss Weaver: Harriet Shaw Weaver 1876–1961* (London: Faber & Faber, 1970), 47.
11. Ibid., 47.
12. Ibid., 48, 54.
13. Ibid., 53–4.
14. Richard Ellmann, *James Joyce: New and Revised Edition* (Oxford: Oxford University Press, 1982), 352.
15. *The New Freewoman*, 15 December 1913, 244. Pound's letter to Joyce was written on the same day that *The New Freewoman* published and acceded to this petition.
16. 'A Curious History,' *The Egoist*, 15 January 1914, 27.
17. Ezra Pound, *The Letters of Ezra Pound 1907–1941*, ed. D. D. Paige (London: Faber, 1962), 71. For two influential readings of the title change, see K. K. Ruthven, 'Ezra's Appropriations,' *Times Literary Supplement*, 20–6 November 1987, 1300;

and Rachel Blau DuPlessis, *The Pink Guitar: Writing as Feminist Practice* (London: Routledge, 1990), 44–5.
18. I argue elsewhere that Joyce resisted it. See Katherine Mullin, 'Joyce through the Little Magazines,' in *A Companion to James Joyce*, ed. Richard Brown (Oxford: Wiley-Blackwell, 2011), 374–85.
19. Ellmann, *James Joyce*, 353.
20. Maria Luddy, *Women and Philanthropy in Nineteenth-Century Ireland* (Cambridge: Cambridge University Press, 1995), 13.
21. James Joyce, *Dubliners*, ed. Jeri Johnson (Oxford: Oxford World's Classics, 2008), 27, 28. Subsequent references will cite page numbers in-text.
22. 'Chastity and Normality,' 290.
23. For a fuller account of *The Dead*'s discontents, see Margot Norris, 'Stifled Back Answers: The Gender Politics of Art in Joyce's "The Dead,"' *Modern Fiction Studies* 35, no. 3 (Autumn 1989): 479–503.
24. Bonnie Zimmerman, 'Lesbians Like This and That: Some Notes on Lesbian Criticism for the Nineties,' in *New Lesbian Criticism: Literary and Cultural Readings*, ed. Sally Munt (New York: Columbia University Press, 1992), 4.
25. Hannah Roche, *The Outside Thing: Modernist Lesbian Romance* (New York: Columbia University Press, 2019), 143–4.
26. Ibid., 143.
27. Instalments from *Ulysses* appeared in *The Little Review* between March 1918 and December 1920, alongside several Barnes short stories. See Hutton, *Serial Encounters*, 66–7.
28. Philip Herring, 'Djuna Barnes Remembers James Joyce,' *James Joyce Quarterly* 30, no. 1 (1992): 113–17.
29. Djuna Barnes, 'A Portrait of the Man Who is, at Present, One of the More Significant Figures in Literature,' *Vanity Fair* 18 (April 1922): 65, 104.
30. Sylvia Beach, *Shakespeare and Company* (Lincoln: University of Nebraska Press, [1959] 1991), 34.
31. 'She insisted on my accompanying her,' 'Finally, Adrienne had her way, as usual.' Ibid., 34.
32. Ellmann, *James Joyce*, 606. Joyce also paid tribute to Marsden in *Finnegans Wake*. See Thaine Stearns, 'The "Woman of No Appearance": James Joyce, Dora Marsden, and Competitive Pilfering,' *Twentieth Century Literature* 48, no. 4 (Winter 2002): 461–86.
33. Ellmann, *James Joyce*, 634; Mary T. Reynolds, 'Joyce and Miss Weaver,' *James Joyce Quarterly* 19, no. 4 (1982): 373–403.
34. Ellmann, *James Joyce*, 535–6.
35. Margaret Anderson, *My Thirty Years' War: An Autobiography* (New York: Covici-Friede, 1930), 106.
36. 'James Joyce,' *The Little Review*, 1 April 1917, 8–9.
37. 'James Joyce in The Little Review,' *The Little Review*, February 1918, back cover advertisement.
38. See Paul Vanderham, *James Joyce and Censorship: The Trials of Ulysses* (Basingstoke: Macmillan, 1998).

39. James Joyce, *Ulysses*, ed. Hans Walter Gabler (London: Bodley Head, 1993), 13: 276–8. Subsequent references will cite page numbers in-text.
40. Jane Heap, 'Art and the Law,' *The Little Review* 7, no. 3 (September–December 1920): 6.
41. 'Penelope is the *clou* of the book.' Joyce to Frank Budgen, 16 August 1921, *Letters of James Joyce*, vol. 1, ed. Stuart Gilbert (New York: Viking Press, 1957), 170. Joyce uses the term 'clou' or nail as an abbreviation of the French idiom 'le clou du spectacle' or 'the highlight of the show.'
42. Colleen Lamos, 'A Faint Glimmer of Lesbianism in Joyce,' in Valente, *Quare Joyce*, 185–200, 188.
43. Ibid., 186–7.
44. Virginia Woolf, *Mrs Dalloway*, ed. David Bradshaw (Oxford: Oxford World's Classics, 2000), 27. As Harvena Richter has established, *Mrs Dalloway* was heavily influenced by Woolf's hostile but attentive reading of *Ulysses*. See Harvena Richter, 'The *Ulysses* Connection: Clarissa Dalloway's Bloomsday,' *Studies in the Novel* 21, no. 3 (1989): 305–19. It is tempting to wonder whether this moment in Molly's monologue may, perhaps, have informed or even inspired Woolf's representation of Clarissa's memories of Sally Seton.
45. *Weib* is German for 'woman.' Joyce to Frank Budgen, 16 August 1921, *Letters* 1: 170.
46. James Joyce, *Poems* and *Exiles*, ed. J. C. C. Mays (London: Penguin, 1992), 340.
47. Ibid., 349.
48. Ibid., 350.
49. Joyce's notes for *Exiles* were dated November 1913 (ibid. 339–40); Pound's letter of introduction to Joyce was dated 15 December 1913.
50. Ellmann, *James Joyce*, 634.
51. Alison Bechdel, *Fun Home: A Family Tragicomic* (New York: Mariner Books, 2006), 230.
52. Christy Burns, 'In The Original Sinse: Gay Cliché and Verbal Transgression in *Finnegans Wake*,' in Valente, *Quare Joyce*, 201–22.
53. Carol Loeb Schloss, *Lucia Joyce: To Dance in the Wake* (London: Bloomsbury, 2003), 206, 243.

PART IV
HISTORIES AND TEMPORALITIES

10

ELIZABETHAN LOVEMAKING: COLLEGE ROMANCE AND QUEER ANACHRONISM IN EDNA ST. VINCENT MILLAY'S *THE LAMP AND THE BELL*

Sarah Parker

Edna St. Vincent Millay may at first seem an awkward fit for the term 'lesbian modernist.' Her work usually sits outside the bounds of modernism, regarded as too formal and sentimental to qualify for entry. While some critics have challenged this assessment, arguing that Millay's poetry troubles the binary between 'experimental' and 'conventional' verse, her preference for traditional forms, especially the sonnet, means she is positioned as anathema to the avant-garde.[1] Her sexual orientation is also a vexed issue. Biographers tie themselves in knots attempting to account for her so-called conversion from youthful lesbianism to mature heterosexuality.[2] Whilst her bisexuality is widely acknowledged, the fact that she had male lovers and spent the majority of her life married to Eugen Jan Boissevain, rather than forming a long-term lesbian partnership, invalidates her same-sex desire, at least in the eyes of some critics.[3] It is therefore little surprise that studies of 'lesbian modernism' tend to overlook Millay, or grant her only a bit-part role.

Challenging these assumptions, in this chapter I propose that we should consider Millay's play *The Lamp and the Bell* (1921) as an overlooked lesbian modernist work. This play, written for the Fiftieth Anniversary of Vassar College's Alumnae Association in 1921, has been almost entirely neglected by critics, including those interested in lesbian representation in the early twentieth century. This is a significant oversight given that, as I show, *The Lamp and the Bell* represents an outspoken defence of female same-sex love at a time when such 'romantic friendships' were under increased scrutiny, especially at women's colleges. Rather than writing a modern prose play to address these issues, however, Millay cloaks her controversial theme in the antiquated idiom of Renaissance verse drama, thus evading the censor by distancing her play from its immediate context. As noted, Millay's tendency towards stylistic anachronism led to her disqualification from modernism. But while it is tempting to juxtapose Millay's 'old-fashioned' form with her 'modern' content, I instead propose that the play's anachronistic queer style is in fact in keeping with its queer plot, as Millay employs 'temporal drag' to both elevate lesbian love in the present and forge connections to its historical past.[4] It is precisely Millay's anachronistic style and engagement with queer time, I suggest, that makes *The Lamp and the Bell* a lesbian modernist work.

Despite her reputation as an anti-modernist, Millay moved in recognisably modernist circles. In her early years in Greenwich Village, she was an active member of the Provincetown Players. Her play *Aria da Capo* (1921) was performed in December 1919 as part of the 'Season of Youth,' which included works by Djuna Barnes, Eugene O'Neill and Wallace Stevens. Brenda Murphy describes *Aria da Capo* as the 'best piece of non-representational theatre the Provincetown Players produced.'[5] Millay herself regarded it as 'one of the best things I've done.'[6] She was, however, decidedly less proud of *The Lamp and the Bell*, which was originally entitled *Snow White and Rose Red*. When drafting the play in 1921, she wrote to her sister Norma, expressing her concerns over what the Players – specifically Barnes – would make of it:

> I am slaving now to typewrite & ship off my Vassar play, *Snow White & Rose Red* which I have just finished [. . .] But don't let any of the *Provincetown Players* get hold of it to read. I mean this most seriously. They would hate it, & make fun of it, & old Djuna Barnes would rag you about it, hoping it would get to me.[7]

Her anxieties relate to the play's ceremonial purpose and its antiquated style:

> It's written in the first place for Vassar College, in the second place it's written to be played out of doors, as spectacularly as possible, & in a foreign country & medieval times [. . .] it's a frank shameless imitation of the Elizabethan dramas, in style, conversation & everything, & of course does not show up so darn well in comparison. – You'll think from all this that it's a bum play. You're wrong. – I expect the darned thing to make a great hit.[8]

Millay's letter implies that the play will be misunderstood if taken out of context, as it was written for a particular occasion. Composed to celebrate the founding of the Alumnae Association of Vassar College (AAVC) in 1871, *The Lamp and the Bell* was designed to showcase Vassar's performance spaces, such as the open-air amphitheatre and the Shakespeare Garden, and to include as many students and alumnae as possible in a multigenerational performance. Set in a courtly, pseudo-medieval Italy, the play required opulent historical costumes, with poetic language to match. Millay employs flexible blank verse, frequent inversions and archaisms ('nay,' ''tis,' 'aye' and so forth) in a pastiche of Elizabethan dramatic verse. The Shakespearean style of Millay's play was suited to its open-air performance, in a garden appropriately named after the Bard himself.

But crucial to the success of the play at Vassar was its theme: the enduring love between two women: Beatrice ('Rose Red') and Bianca ('Rose White'). Since the play is largely unknown today, the plot requires explication. Beatrice is the daughter of Lorenzo, the widowed King of Fiori who, at the start of the play, marries Octavia, Bianca's mother. As stepsisters, the girls become inseparable companions. They are described as more than 'just friends' – as one court lady puts it, 'I never knew a pair of lovers / More constant than those two.'[9] But their devotion is tested, as Octavia becomes suspicious of their bond, declaring, ''tis not good for two young girls / To be so much together!' (18). She arranges to separate them for six months, sending Bianca away. During this period, Beatrice falls in love with the young King Mario, visiting from a nearby kingdom. Meanwhile, her illegitimate cousin Guido schemes to marry her and secure the crown for himself. He plots with Octavia to reintroduce Bianca, in the hopes that Mario will fall in love with her instead. The scheme works, as Bianca's gentleness captures Mario's heart – as he later explains to the spurned Beatrice, 'That she should turn to me and cling to me / And let me shelter her, is the great wonder / Of the world. You stand alone. You need no shelter' (50). Having lost her two beloveds in one sweeping movement, Beatrice stoically conceals her heartbreak from the unknowing Bianca, helping her celebrate her wedding.

The women continue to be close friends until a tragic event takes place five years later: Beatrice is attacked in the woods by 'brigands' and Mario rushes to her aid. In the confusion of the fray, she fatally stabs him, mistaking him for one of her attackers. Consumed by guilt, Beatrice refuses to see the widowed Bianca and wastes away in solitude. Despite Octavia sowing seeds of doubt in her daughter's mind, Bianca visits Beatrice, demanding, 'ere I go / Tell me you do not love me' (78). After the women affirm their undying love, Beatrice confesses to Mario's murder and Bianca, appalled, flees.

Years later, Beatrice has become a benevolent queen to her subjects, but Guido still schemes to usurp her. Hearing that Bianca is on her deathbed, she rushes to go to her, but Guido stages a coup and imprisons Beatrice in a dungeon, requiring her kingdom and sexual compliance as the price of freedom. Overcome with longing for Bianca, Beatrice agrees, declaring:

> I wonder now that even for a moment
> I held myself so dear! When for her sake
> All things are little things! – This foolish body,
> This body is not I! There is no I,
> Saving the need I have to go to her! (92)

She arrives just in time, as Bianca expires ecstatically in her arms, having left a final message with her maid:

> Say to her this, Giulietta: The foot stumbles,
> The hand hath its own awkward way; the tongue
> Moves foolishly in the mouth; but in the heart
> The truth lies, – and all's well 'twixt her and me. (94)

Sealing this reconciliation, Bianca leaves her two daughters in Beatrice's charge. The play concludes with Beatrice miraculously regaining her kingdom, as Guido is murdered by a jilted lover. Finding the strength to endure, despite her loss, the play ends on a hopeful note, as Beatrice anticipates eventual reunion with Bianca:

> She is not gone from me. Oh, there be places
> Farther away than Death! She is returned
> From her long silence, and rings out above me
> Like a silver bell! – Let us go back, Fidelio,
> And gather up the fallen stones, and build us
> Another tower. (99)

The Lamp and the Bell was carefully pitched to appeal to its intended audience of over a thousand alumnae from several generations, stretching back to the class of 1883. In emphasising the enduring bond between women, Millay invokes her audience's college friendships, which in some cases became romantic relationships. An 1895 survey had revealed that out of 1,082 women who had graduated from Vassar, only 409 married; others formed same-sex partnerships or 'Boston Marriages.'[10] In making a heroic same-sex union the subject of her play, Millay honours these relationships by elevating them to Shakespearean heights. But despite its early modern setting and antiquated idiom, Millay's play also resonated with contemporary anxieties surrounding female friendships, particularly within the college atmosphere. Much as *Aria da Capo*'s pseudo-medieval allegory had covertly condemned the absurdity of the First World War, *The Lamp and the Bell* uses Elizabethan 'drag' to engage with current debates around intimate female friendships that characterised the 1910s and 1920s. In order to understand the play's intervention, we therefore need to set it in the shifting context of romantic friendships at women's colleges during this period.

From 'Smashing' to 'Crushitus': Romantic Friendships at Vassar

To imagine the heroic devotion between Beatrice and Bianca, Millay did not have to cast her mind as far back as medieval Italy. As early Millay critic Elizabeth Atkins suggests, the play has a double context: 'The kingdom of Fiori is Poughkeepsie-on-the-Hudson, and college students and faculty keep looking straight through their Italian veils.'[11] Certain lines in the play – Bianca's urging 'we must study' (8), for instance – gesture to this, forging a palimpsest between the pseudo-fictional past and the immediate present. Romantic friendships like Beatrice and Bianca's had a long history at Vassar from its founding as a women's college in the mid-nineteenth century. As Helen Lefkowitz Horowitz has shown, this culture was partly the fruit of architectural necessity. Due to a lack of space, students were often forced to share bedrooms. The design of student suites – bedrooms arranged around a parlour – created a 'private' space that was difficult for staff to monitor, resulting in a subculture of midnight feasts, pranks and bed-hopping.[12] Soon, a craze called 'smashing' developed. The 'smash' referred to an attachment forged between a senior and a junior, in which the senior adopted the role of wooer. As an article in the *Cornell Times* described it,

> When a Vassar girl takes a shine to another, she straightway enters upon a regular course of bouquet sendings, interspersed with tinted notes, mysterious packages of 'Ridley's Mixed Candies,' locks of hair perhaps, and many other tender tokens, until at last the object of her attentions is captured, the two become inseparable, and the aggressor is considered by her circle of acquaintances as – smashed.[13]

These attachments were fostered by the hierarchical structure of college life. Younger students were encouraged to admire their elders; for example, Ellen Rickert, a senior at Vassar in 1890, writes of parading in front of juniors: 'when we came out to go into Chapel, all the freshmen stood back forming admiring throngs of spectators, looking in awe at the Seniors' sweeping gowns.'[14] This scopic exchange recalls Sharon Marcus's observation that nineteenth-century women were encouraged to view the elegant, feminine woman as both (potential) self and desired other, suggesting that 'mainstream femininity was not secretly lesbian, but openly homoerotic [. . .] Victorian women were as licenced to objectify women as were Victorian men.'[15] This dynamic was particularly apparent at cross-dressed balls, where sophomores took on the 'male' role, escorting freshmen to the dance. As one Smith student describes it,

> Each soph constitutes herself a cavalier for the freshman to whom she is assigned. She sends her flowers, calls for her, fills her order of dance, introduces her partners, fetches ices and frappes between dances and takes her to supper ... Every soph sees her partner home, begs for a flower and changes orders for souvenirs, and if the freshman has taken advantage of the opportunity and has made the desired hit, there are dates for future meetings and jollifications, and a good night over the balusters, as lingering and cordial as any the freshie has left behind her.[16]

The romantic friendships fostered at women's colleges can be viewed as (in Henry Wadsworth Longfellow's phrase) 'a rehearsal in girlhood of the great drama of woman's life' – in other words, as preparation for heterosexual marriage.[17] But, as Lillian Faderman asks, what was to stop the 'rehearsal' from becoming 'the "great drama" itself?'[18] Certainly, by the end of the nineteenth century, long-term unions between women appeared increasingly viable – not least because several of Vassar's staff lived in such arrangements themselves. For example, History Professor Lucy Maynard Salmon and Adelaide Underhill, the College Librarian, lived together for over thirty years, as did Gertrude Buck and Laura Wylie, teachers in the English department. Salmon and Buck both taught Millay during her time at Vassar; several of her plays emerged from Buck's pioneering workshops.[19] These domestic 'twosomes' were no secret to Vassar students – Buck and Wylie welcomed students to their home every Thursday to play with their dogs and to 'talk about classes, politics, and life in general.'[20] These unions were proof that a same-sex relationship could indeed become the central 'drama of a woman's life' – just as such a relationship forms the central 'drama' of *The Lamp and the Bell*.

The culture of 'smashing' at Vassar was not without its detractors, however. In 1882, the committee of the Alumnae Association – the body that Millay's play eulogised – condemned 'smashes' as 'the one thing that damaged the health of the girls seriously' due to the 'pangs of unrequited attachment, desperate jealousy &c' suffered with 'as much energy as if one of them were a man.'[21] These concerns deepened in the early twentieth century, particularly after statistics revealed the low rate of marriage for women's college graduates.[22] Such findings, combined with anxieties about low birth rates and so-called race suicide – the term used by Theodore Roosevelt in his 1905 speech to the National Congress of Mothers – fuelled a conservative backlash against women's colleges, which intensified after the First World War.[23] For example, in 1921 (the year *Lamp* was performed), Vice President Calvin Coolidge accused women's colleges of communist sympathies and exhibiting 'morbid tendencies.'²⁴ This paranoia extended to the relationships cultivated at women's colleges. As sexology and Freudian psychoanalysis filtered into popular awareness, female intimacy was put under the microscope. We can observe this in an October 1913 article from *Harper's Bazar* by an anonymous 'College Graduate,' entitled 'Your Daughter: What Are Her Friendships?' The author urges parents to 'look into' their daughter's friendships, as 'crushitus' can have dire consequences: 'You would not deliberately expose your daughter to scarlet fever or diphtheria or smallpox. Regard "crushitus" as a similar disease, and do all you can to prevent it.'²⁵ The author notes that victims of 'crushitus' 'often go insane or die; many land in sanatoriums as nervous wrecks.'²⁶ The article concludes by urging parents to scrutinise their daughters' friendships as their duty to society: 'The challenge is flung at every father and mother in the land, for you are responsible for this increasing social evil.'²⁷

When we consider that this article was published during Millay's first month at Vassar, it raises the question of how far these attitudes affected her own experiences. Beginning her studies in 1913, Millay was instantly popular with her fellow students. As she wrote to her family, 'All the girls here at McGlynn's [her first-year residence], about 30, like me, I know.'²⁸ Four years older than her peers, and already a celebrated poet, Millay was an object of fascination, an admiration she was not above manipulating. She never missed an opportunity to flirt with staff and students alike, basking in the favour of Dean Ella McCaleb, for instance: 'She kissed me hello right before 'em all, to show 'em all she loved me.'²⁹ Millay particularly enjoyed the cross-dressed balls, flirting with 'Jack' (Margaret), who spied on her while dressing: 'I heard a masculine giggle and looking down saw *Jack* . . . watching me. The *best* looking boy.'³⁰ Sending photographs of a cross-dressed fellow student to Norma, Millay encourages her sister's vicarious desire: 'Isn't she *wonderful* in that picture? Couldn't you die in her arms?'³¹ For her part, Norma relished involvement in Millay's same-sex flirtations, anticipating 'all those wonderful tall girl-boys for you to abuse as suitors.'³²

As these examples suggest, Millay was open about her homoerotic attachments in her letters to family. A similar candour is seen in her letters to Arthur Hooley, editor of *The Forum*, with whom she engaged in a flirtatious correspondence. In one letter, she makes 'an observation, & not a confession' that is nonetheless revealing:

> I had not realized, until I came here, how greatly one girl's beauty & presence can disturb another's peace of mind, – still more, sometimes, her beauty & absence. – There are Anactorias here for any Sappho. – And I am glad . . . that I have never felt moved to say harsh & foolish things about an Ancient Greek philosopher or a modern English poet, whom the world has condemned & punished . . . For up here, while

some of us are thinking of the rest of us, the rest of us are thinking of you, & men like you.[33]

Millay here acknowledges the historical precedent for homoerotic desire, citing Sappho, an 'Ancient Greek philosopher' (presumably Socrates or Plato) and 'a modern English poet' – likely Oscar Wilde. And while she contrasts lesbianism and heterosexuality in her letter, for Millay herself it *was* clearly possible to think of 'you' and 'the rest of us' simultaneously: as she carried on flirtations with Hooley and other men, she also engaged in intimate friendships with women at Vassar.

Among the most serious of these was her relationship with Elaine Ralli, with whom Millay became close in her second year, describing her as 'another hockey hero, cheer-leader, rides horseback a lot, very boyish, & makes a lot of noise, not tall, but all muscle.'[34] The two became inseparable, visiting each other during the holidays in 1914–15. Their letters reveal their intimacy; Millay wrote to Ralli, 'It won't be long now until I see you. Mon ami, je ne t'oublie pas. Il ne faut pas avoir peur. Tu es encore mon enfant. Tu le sais bien. Et je t'aime. Tu le sais bien.'[35] Their intense bond came under scrutiny, however, from Millay's benefactor, Caroline B. Dow. Dow had played an instrumental role in getting Millay to Vassar, and her letter of October 1915 (written after Millay had missed meeting a friend of Dow's, due to an appointment with Elaine) alludes darkly to 'your dangers both from physical & temperamental conditions.'[36] The nature of these 'dangers' is then clarified: 'Absorbing attentions from individual students are a hindrance in spite of the pleasant things they bring. Those very things are not the best for yr. nature.'[37] Dow's letter associates this intimate friendship with corruption: 'I want you always clean, sweet & pure [. . .] I want you different from the usual type of poet who claims a freedom bordering on licence, & who thinks she can touch pitch without being soiled.'[38] The metaphor of defilement speaks volumes; Millay could not continue her relationship with Ralli without endangering her standing with Dow, who held considerable sway over her future. Millay immediately distanced herself from Elaine. In her final year, she cannily evaded accusations of an unnaturally close companionship by dividing her attentions between several friends, including Charlotte 'Charlie' Babcock, Isobel Simpson, Anne Lynch and Dorothy Coleman. But while Anne Cheney proposes that Babcock, Millay's roommate, is the model for Bianca in *Lamp* (with Millay as Beatrice), the biographical parallel is a stretch.[39] Beatrice and Bianca are more accurately described as composite figures, representing in idealised form the various relationships that Millay experienced at Vassar.

After Millay graduated in 1917, the suspicion around female friendships intensified. By the late 1920s, college friendships were policed, and could result in expulsion.[40] Wanda Fraiken Neff's novel *We Sing Diana* (1928) captures this paranoid atmosphere, riven with sexological speculation: 'Intimacies between two girls were watched with keen, distrustful eyes. Among one's classmates, one looked for the bisexual type, the masculine girl searching for a feminine counterpart, and one ridiculed their devotions.'[41] Meanwhile, theories of 'companionate' heterosexual marriage gained ground. A key proponent, Floyd Dell, used his 1930 study *Love in the Machine Age* to criticise 'the unwholesome fashionable practice of sex-segregated schools [that] brings young people into a homosexual atmosphere,' proposing a reformation of heterosexual relations 'to train young people for [. . .] living happily ever after in heterosexual mate hood.'[42] Dell was Millay's first lover when she moved to Greenwich Village, following graduation from Vassar. He describes their encounters in an unpublished memoir, applying his theories to Millay's sexual history. According to Dell, Millay insisted on 'platonic behaviour in bed' until he guessed her 'secret':

> 'You pretend you have had many love affairs – but the truth, my dear, is that you are still a virgin. You have merely had homosexual affairs with girls at college.' [. . .] I felt it was my duty to rescue her from psychological captivity.[43]

Despite claiming to have 'rescued' Millay for heterosexuality, Dell's account hints at Millay's lingering dissent, recounting discussions in which she 'defended platonic love against Freud' and frustrated his advances.[44] In a later interview, Dell grumbled that he had always suspected that Millay 'may have been fonder of women than of men.'[45] Apparently his 'cure' was not so effective after all.

THE LAMP AND THE BELL AS HEROIC LESBIAN TRAGEDY

The Lamp and the Bell shows that Dell was right to be suspicious. The play expresses Millay's continued defiance, and defence of lesbian love. While Dell regarded relationships between women as insignificant, Millay places these bonds at the heart of her play, positioning them as superior even to heterosexual marriage. The play is an artful riposte to the reactionary forces pathologising women's relationships in the early 1920s. By rendering such relationships as heroic Renaissance tragedy, Millay achieves two distinct aims. First, the historical idiom provides the safe distance necessary when representing a controversial topic. Millay was wise to 'cloak' her material, since a number of lesbian-themed plays produced in this period came under fire from the censor. For example, Sholem Asch's *God of Vengeance* (1907), performed at the Provincetown Playhouse in 1922, was subsequently pulled from the Apollo Theatre on Broadway in 1923 after less than a month and charged with obscenity. Édouard Bourdet's *The Captive* (*La Prisonnière*, 1926) faced a similar fate, with the Broadway cast arrested during a performance. Both plays are set in the present and written in a modern prose style. If Millay wanted her play to evade controversy, she realised her message would have to be carefully packaged in historical dress.

Beyond reasons of necessity, Millay's formal preference for blank verse and 'high' poetic diction also serves to elevate her same-sex love story to heroic heights. As students of Shakespeare know well, iambic pentameter is conventionally reserved for noble, tragic characters. Additionally, among the dramatic genres, tragedy has historically been regarded as the 'highest' form of art (following the theories of Plato and Aristotle). In placing the unbreakable love between two women at the centre of her play, Millay champions a lesbian heroism capable of exploding the discourses that regarded such love as insignificant, fleeting or unnatural. To further challenge these assumptions, Millay employs metaphorical language, particularly botanical imagery of flowers and trees, to emphasise the naturalness of Beatrice and Bianca's love. We first encounter them in a prelapsarian homoerotic Eden:[46]

> BEA. How beautiful it is to sit like this,
> Snow-White, – to think of much, and to say little.
>
> BIA. Ay, it is beautiful. I shall remember
> All my life long these evenings that we spent
> Sitting just here, thinking together. (12)

Their separation is foreshadowed when the jester Fidelio enters the scene, singing of waning seasons which evoke the passage from young womanhood to maturity: 'Oh, little rose-tree, bloom! / Summer is nearly over. / The dahlias bleed and the phlox is seed, / Nothing's left of the clover' (14). As Fidelio leaves, Bianca anxiously contemplates the future:

> BIA. Do you know what I am thinking, Bice?
>
> BEA. You're wondering where we'll be ten years from now,
> Or something of that nature.
>
> BIA. Ay, I was wondering
> Which would be married first, and go away,
> And would we still be friends.
>
> BEA. Oh, do you doubt it,
> Snow-White?
>
> BIA. Nay, nay, – I doubt it not, my dear, –
> But I was wondering. I am suddenly sad,
> I know not why. I do not wish to leave you
> Ever.

BEA. I know. I cannot bear
To think of parting. (15–16)

The scene concludes with Beatrice comforting Bianca like a child: 'Oh, you are tired, tired, you are very tired. / You must be rocked to sleep, and tucked in bed' (16). As Bianca later tells Octavia, Beatrice's love compensates for her mother's coldness: 'You know how I have loved her, / Since we were children. You could not be to me / What she was' (74). Octavia, pathologically unable to demonstrate maternal warmth, regards Beatrice as a rival for her daughter's affections, as seen in the early scene when Octavia refuses to admire the 'pure white' rose blooming where Beatrice and Bianca sit (18). As this instance suggests, Octavia is unwilling to participate in her daughter's innocent joys, refusing to admire the flower that represents the blossoming of Beatrice and Bianca's stainless love. Instead, she insists on viewing their relationship with suspicion, describing it as an unnatural, parasitic growth: 'They grow too much attached. They grow to feel / They cannot breathe apart. It is unhealthy' (21). Through Octavia's words, Millay channels the contemporary arguments against female intimacy, echoing the 'Your Daughter' article: 'She's older than Bianca, and I'll not have her / Putting ideas into my daughter's head!' (20). Countering these arguments, King Lorenzo takes the botanical metaphor and inverts the rhetoric of pathology, describing this youthful attachment as 'something fresh and sweet, like a young green tree' whereas ''Tis you, 'tis I, / 'Tis middle age the fungus settles on' (21). Lorenzo implies that depravity is in the eye of the (middle-aged) beholder rather than the young women themselves.

While Octavia hopes that the presence of King Mario will cause a rift between these devoted companions, their bond transcends romantic rivalry. Once again, this scenario has contemporary parallels, signalling the encroaching presence of men on campus during the late 1910s. As men increasingly participated in college dances and theatricals, the energy that had previously gone into same-sex rituals was gradually directed 'outward toward men.'[47] Such co-educational events laid the groundwork for 'companionate marriage.' However, Millay's play shows that Mario does not usurp Beatrice in Bianca's heart. When Beatrice and Mario exchange loving words passed on from Bianca, both respond with an identical phrase: 'Did she say that?' (50–1). This mirroring places their love on an equal footing. Mario admits that he was briefly 'jealous of you' (51); a jealousy reignited later, as Bianca insists on staying with Beatrice following her father's death, causing the newly wed Mario to doubt her love:

BIA. I could not leave her.

MAR. Bianca, do you love me?

> BIA. Ay, Mario!
>
> MAR. Ah, but not as I love you! (57)

In the course of the play, it becomes clear that nothing can truly threaten Beatrice and Bianca's abiding love. On Bianca's wedding day, Beatrice laments, 'They say a bride forgets her friends, – she cleaves so / To her new lord. It cannot but be true. / You will be gone from me' (47). Bianca replies with a speech invoking the play's titular images:

> BIA. Shall I forget, then, When I am old, I ever was a child?
> I tell you I shall never think of you
> Throughout my life, without such tenderness
> As breaks the heart, – and I shall think of you
> Whenever I am most happy, whenever I am
> Most sad, whenever I see a beautiful thing.
> You are a burning lamp to me, a flame
> The wind cannot blow out, and I shall hold you
> High in my hand against whatever darkness.
>
> BEA. You are to me a silver bell in a tower.
> And when it rings I know I am near home. (46–7)

The unquenchable flame and the summoning bell represent the constancy of Beatrice and Bianca's love. The burning lamp symbolises passion and Beatrice's fiery nature (she is consistently associated with the colour red, as in her nickname 'Rose Red') as well as a guiding beacon for others. Meanwhile, the tower represents the stability and shelter associated with the gentle, feminine Bianca, and the silver bell encodes the cool tones of 'Rose White.'

These speeches elevate Beatrice and Bianca's love to heroic heights. Despite the wedding being between Bianca and Mario, the exchange of vows takes place between Bianca and Beatrice. Indeed, as Cheney notes, 'The love of Beatrice and Bianca seems to overpower either woman's love for Mario.'[48] The women repeatedly prove their devotion to each other: Beatrice relinquishes Mario and is prepared to sacrifice her kingdom and her body for Bianca, while Bianca never doubts Beatrice, despite her mother's machinations. In portraying the women's devotion as lasting into maturity, Millay challenges the assumption that the homoerotic attachments of college girls could be safely dismissed as just a 'phase,' suggesting that they endure into adulthood, in spite of marriage and motherhood (in Bianca's case). Like the play itself, Beatrice and Bianca's love could therefore be said to be anachronistic, in the sense of being temporally inappropriate. Their love is finally, if belatedly, sealed in their ecstatic reunion, conveyed through stage directions rather than through dialogue: 'Beatrice enters in her riding clothes, leaps to the bed, Bianca throws her arms about her neck, and dies' (95–6). Bianca's rapturous expiration in Beatrice's arms evokes the long-standing cultural associations between orgasm and death. Their union also results in progeny, as Beatrice inherits Bianca's daughters, 'Little Snow-White' and 'Little Rose Red' – the latter of whom demands that the grieving Beatrice 'Finish the story' that her mother had begun (96). Through raising them, Beatrice has the chance to relive the story of her relationship with Bianca.

The final lines of the play also gesture to a revisionary hope in the future, as Beatrice declares her intention to 'build us / Another tower' (99). Repetition is inherent in the play's cyclical structure; Atkins describes it as 'like a symphony in which the dominant melody is associated with brief echoes of the melody that is gone and little murmurs of the one that is to come' – a circularity achieved through 'trick of the repeated phrase' such as the return of the titular metaphor in the play's final lines.[49] Through returning to this image, Millay layers past, present and future, as well as gesturing to the immediate context of the play's performance. Beatrice's vision points to present-day Vassar, which had its own tower at North Hall (later renamed Jewett House), an Elizabethan-style building with a central nine-storey tower. This building was Millay's hall of residence. Through this closing metaphor of the lamp and the bell, Millay therefore suggests that romantic friendships between women will continue to resonate throughout time, resounding into the future.

THE QUEER TIME OF THE RENAISSANCE

Having established the heroic lesbian romance plot of *The Lamp and the Bell*, and its dialogue with twentieth-century debates, the issue of form and style remains. One may reasonably ask: if Millay wanted to push back against 1920s attitudes to female intimacy, why do so in a play which was, in her own words, 'full of anachronisms [. . .] [a] shameless imitation of the Elizabethan dramas'?[50] Why does Millay employ an 'Elizabethan' style and setting for a work that aims to defend lesbian love in the present? One reason (beyond that of evading censorship) is that the Elizabethan period is particularly enabling for the imagining – or reimagining – of same-sex desire. While the Renaissance period has often been associated with homoerotic bonds between men, the era is also characterised by what Valerie Traub terms a 'Renaissance of Lesbianism.'[51] Due to a number of factors, including the translation of classical texts, the expansion of print culture, rising female literacy and the presence of a powerful female monarch on the throne, according to Traub, 'early modern England witnessed a renaissance of representations of female homoerotic desire.'[52] Such representations are found across a range of texts, from medical treatise to pornography to paintings, poetry and plays. In the latter category, authors such as Shakespeare, John Lyly, John Donne, Katherine Philips, Aphra Behn and Margaret Cavendish honour female same-sex love in their writings, celebrating female amity as noble in its constancy. For example, Shakespeare's heroines – Helena and Hermia in *A Midsummer Night's Dream*, Beatrice and Hero in *Much Ado About Nothing*, Rosalind and Celia in *As You Like It* – emphasise the insuperable nature of their bond.[53] Later in the period, Catharine Trotter's verse tragedy *Agnes de Castro* (1695) emphasises the unshakable loyalty between Agnes and Princess Constantia, with Agnes declaring as she goes to her death, 'I shall meet my Princess where I go, / And our unspotted Souls, in Bliss above, / Will know each other, and again, will love' – a passage that echoes Beatrice's anticipation of heavenly reunion with Bianca in *Lamp*.[54]

Millay was well versed in Elizabethan literature, developing her expertise during her studies at Vassar. Early critic Atkins goes so far as to describe Millay as a 'belated Elizabethan':

> I am sure that no one else in the twentieth century [. . .] has become attuned to the physical and emotional temper of that period as Millay has done. If it were not a gross sentimentalism or a denial of the inexorable rush of time to say so, one would almost aver that in her girlhood she became in spirit a veritable Elizabethan, for her plays and sonnets henceforth were to be, not mimicry of the works of Elizabethan times, but such writing as one may fancy that Drayton and Webster and Middleton and Beaumont and Fletcher might have done if they had known twentieth-century New England as well as their own time.[55]

With reference to *Lamp*, Atkins notes that its theme of intimate friendship is 'surely Elizabethan' while its plot borrows conventions from Shakespeare and other playwrights, incorporating a law court scene, a wedding scene, a play-within-a-play, and characters such as the wise fool and the plotting stepmother.[56] What Atkins overlooks, though, is the ways in which Millay's play also revises tropes from Shakespeare. As Traub and other critics note, Shakespearean plays usually shut down queer possibilities at the denouement, using heterosexual marriage to return characters to their proper gender roles. In *Lamp*, the wedding takes place in the middle of the play, and notably fails to separate Beatrice and Bianca. Their bond continues to provide the dramatic centre of the play, and the final scene is devoted to the ecstatic, if short-lived, consummation of their love.

Millay's 'Elizabethan spirit' therefore takes on markedly queer connotations when we regard the period, following Traub, as associated with female same-sex bonds. The Renaissance recurs as an especially queer time across an array of lesbian modernist works, from Bryher's essay on 'The Girl-Page in Elizabethan Literature' (1920) and her later historical novels such as *The*

Player's Boy (1953) to the early scenes of Virginia Woolf's *Orlando* (1928).[57] A biographical anecdote suggests that Millay perceived the Elizabethan era as a period associated with lesbian lovemaking. On 18 December 1933, following a poetic reading at Bryn Mawr College, Millay apparently propositioned her female host, entering her bedroom and beginning to disrobe. When the host appeared shocked, Millay declared, 'Oh, don't you like good old Elizabethan lovemaking? Oh, I like it!'[58] This seemingly throwaway remark is illuminated by the early modern contexts outlined above, building an understanding of the intimate connections between the early modern period and same-sex desire. Could it be that returning to an all-female college reminded Millay of the pleasures of 'Elizabethan lovemaking' between women? Were lesbian desire and the Elizabethan era associated in her mind, and hence the pairing of the two in *Lamp*? It is difficult to say for certain. What can be said is that Millay's play is certainly queer in its temporal anachronism. By setting her tale of same-sex love in an earlier era, conveyed in an antiquated pastiche style, Millay engages in a form of what Elizabeth Freeman calls 'temporal drag.' Expanding the term 'drag' from the specific performance of gender to a '*temporal* phenomenon,' Freeman asks, 'what is the *time* of queer performativity?'[59] For Millay, that time was the Renaissance. By clothing her play in the costume of an earlier era, Millay engages in historical drag. Her playful engagement with history invokes notions of queer time, described by Carla Freccero as 'a desire for anachronism, [. . .] queer insofar as it reads history for the pleasures of identification and desire.'[60] Rejecting linear history, queer temporality troubles 'the past-present-future march of time' and 'celebrates the queerness of nonprogressive, non-sequential time, exploring some of the radically subjective experiences of time and temporality.'[61] Millay's play engages in precisely such a project, queering temporality by animating an imagined 'history' in the present. Through conceiving the play for Vassar's anniversary, Millay layers the contemporary moment with a semi-imaginary past, brought to life via an asynchronous queer performance. This live performance, crucial to Millay's queer intervention, is the focus of the final part of this essay.

'LIVING LOVELINESS': PERFORMANCE OF THE *LAMP* AT VASSAR

The Lamp and the Bell was performed for one night only on Saturday, 18 June 1921, at nine o'clock in the evening. To mark its Fiftieth Anniversary, the Alumnae Association planned a seven-day programme of events including lectures, roundtable discussions, sports matches and musical performances. Millay's play formed a welcome centre-piece in this exhausting schedule, taking place after a 'Picnic on Sunset.' Millay was sadly not present for the performance, having recently travelled to Paris (where she would briefly join Natalie Barney's circle).[62] The festivities were attended by over 1,400 alumnae, while the multi-generational cast of the play itself was considerable, including forty-two named parts, plus additional extras for pageant scenes.⁶³ This was not the first time that Vassar had organised such a large-scale production. In October 1915, as part of the Fiftieth Anniversary of Vassar's founding, over 400 students performed *The Pageant of Athena* at the 3,500-seat open-air theatre created for this purpose. The performance was directed by Hazel Mackaye, who had overseen the closing pageant of the Woman Suffrage Procession in Washington DC in March 1913.⁶⁴ As Mary Simonson notes, such intermedial performances not only offered audiences escapism into an idealised 'Hellenic' past, they also negotiated cultural issues in the present.⁶⁵ In the case of *The Pageant of Athena*, by representing a history of learned women, the play asserted women's continuing right to education. Simonson observes that in drawing 'ancient and modern closer together with each new scene,' the *Athena* pageant 'facilitated an intermedial dialogue' between past and present.⁶⁶ This interweaving was emphasised in the finale, in which 'a mass of Vassar students' in modern dress seamlessly merged with the procession of historical personages.⁶⁷

Simonson proposes that the *Athena* pageant represented the past as a 'living legacy' which encouraged audiences to look 'both backward and forward.'⁶⁸

Figure 10.1 Margaret De Motte Brown, Beatrice (Clifford Sellers) and Bianca (Lois Duffie) in performance of *The Lamp and the Bell*, reproduced in *Vassar Quarterly* 6, no. 4 (1 August 1921), n.p.

The Lamp and the Bell functions in a similar way, offering a commentary on the present filtered through the past. Millay's experience performing in *Athena* (as the medieval poet Marie de France) likely influenced her conception of *Lamp*, in terms of both how to effectively utilise the theatrical space at Vassar and how to devise a historical spectacle with present-day resonances. Such theatrical performances were central to life at Vassar. At one point, around two-thirds of the student body belonged to Philaletheis, the college's dramatic society.[69] Millay became an active member, performing in several plays during her time at Vassar. Her most memorable role was that of the poet Marchbanks in George Bernard Shaw's *Candida* (1894). Playing this role in 1915, Millay relished the frisson generated by her cross-dressed performance; as she wrote to her family,

> It's a queer part, you know, of a boy of eighteen, a poet [. . .] I felt perfectly at home in the clothes. People told me I reminded them of their brothers the way I walked around and slung my legs over the arms of chairs [. . .] Somebody thought I was really a boy.[70]

Like Vassar's cross-dressed balls, Millay's performance allowed her to revel in masculinity, including the freedom of the clothes and the potential for female attraction. The school play features as a site of potential (if fleeting) queer possibility across various cultural representations, from Charlotte Brontë's *Villette* (1853), in which the cross-dressed Lucy Snowe flirts with Ginevra Fanshawe, to *Mädchen in Uniform* (1931, based on the 1930 play *Gestern und Heute* by Christa Winsloe), where Manuela performs in sixteenth-century male costume, before declaring her love for her teacher. Such performances allow only fleeting experimentation with alternative gender identities; roles to be donned and doffed temporarily, like the theatrical costumes themselves – but the desires unleashed, albeit temporarily, are no less powerful for that. While cross-dressed theatricals were common practice at Vassar, the contemporaneous adoption of similar practices in Paris by the likes of Natalie Barney, Renée Vivien and Colette and their circle, reveal the erotic power of historically inflected masquerade – including its potential to embody lesbian fantasy through diverse permutations of 'temporal drag.'

Like the theatrical interludes described above, the performance of *Lamp* had the potential to unleash queer possibilities resonating far beyond the play itself. The performance was joyfully received by the original Vassar audience. As Tilly, an attendee, wrote excitedly in an inscription to a print copy of the play, 'Can't you see it all? sunlit from the hill, moon over the dark trees, black clouds, a drop of rain. A setting for such a play. On came Sunday no devils! I loved it.'[71] 'Devils' is Vassar slang for depression, so Tilly implies that the performance chased away the Sunday blues. A more sober but no less positive assessment appeared in the *Vassar Quarterly* (August 1921), the only full-length review of the performance. The reviewer, Margaret Jackson Allen (class of 1901), was 'chairman of the Board of Representatives' for the Alumnae Association, as well as a 'writer of magazine articles.'[72] In her review, accompanied by a photograph of the performance (Figure 10.1), Jackson Allen emphasises the almost inexpressible pleasure that the play evoked in the audience: 'certainly no one pen can express the emotions of delight and wonder which stirred the alumnae as they watched the pageant of *The Lamp and The Bell* unfold its beauty against the background of the most beautiful night of anniversary week.'[73] She praises 'passages of vivid beauty,' drawing particular attention to the lamp and the bell speech which 'epitomizes the love of Snow White and Rose Red for each other, which being translated into college terms, means college friendship.'[74] After assessing the performance of the various actors, Jackson Allen returns to the overall effect of the play. Observing that alumnae anticipated some 'amusement [...] to relieve the strain' of their conference proceedings, they were instead deeply affected by what they witnessed:

> But at the close of the play, the alumnae were too much moved for even the conventional applause. In the usual sense they had perhaps not been 'amused' or 'entertained' at all. But they had been caught up in a vision and had seen that Vassar could produce not only intellectual power and spiritual strength but beauty, an outer beauty as well as an inner, a very living loveliness from elements of college life.[75]

Jackson Allen's review confirms that Millay's play struck its intended target. By animating her Renaissance idyll into 'living loveliness,' Millay immersed her audience in a collective 'vision.' Though the play functions as a historical pastiche and a present-day entertainment, it is also a dream of the future, anticipating a time in which the power, strength and beauty of female bonds would be acknowledged and celebrated.

Conclusion

Sadly, beyond Vassar, the backlash against female intimacy continued. The response to Millay's play shows that she was correct to be cautious about how she presented her material. When the play was published in book form by Harper and Brothers later in 1921, it was generally well received, but one reviewer demurred in the midst of his praise: 'Even the play (which is slightly disagreeable to us personally in its subject, as we do not care for Lesbianism, no matter how beautifully described), contains so much beauty that we are startled.'[76] In this case, the *Lamp*'s historical cloaking had not entirely concealed its controversial subject matter. However, Millay largely avoided opprobrium; most reviewers praised the *Lamp*'s flexible blend of Elizabethan and modern idioms. For example, one reviewer observed that the play was 'Elizabethan to the bottom yet not in the least derivative; it bubbles pure poetry.'[77]

Censorship continued to hound works that articulated same-sex desire in the later 1920s. Mostly famously, in 1928, Radclyffe Hall's *The Well of Loneliness* was banned in Britain and faced an obscenity trial in America. Millay testified in support of the novel, stating, 'To censor *The Well of Loneliness* is nonsense. To censor any book sponsored by Mr. Havelock Ellis is an offensive impertinence.'[78] In her own work, Millay remained outspoken but strategic. In 1927, she composed another play that celebrated homoerotic love, this time between two men. Set in the tenth century, *The King's Henchman* follows almost exactly the same plot as *Lamp*, portraying a tragic love triangle between King Eadgar, his devoted friend Aethelwold, and Aelfrida, the woman who sunders their bond. It was originally performed as opera (composed by Deems Taylor), and attracted wide critical acclaim, touring forty-six American cities before its final performance in 1929.

In an increasingly reactionary atmosphere, Millay republished *The Lamp and the Bell* as part of her 1927 collection *Three Plays* (alongside *Aria da Capo* and *Two Slatterns and a King*). This was a defiant move at the height of censorship – but Millay was clearly confident that her historical method would forestall criticism. We see similar strategies at work in Barnes's *Ladies Almanack* and Woolf's *Orlando* (both 1928); these works, like Millay's *The Lamp and the Bell*, can be simultaneously categorised as meditations on history, expressions of queer desire and experiments with historical pastiche.[79] In a similar manner to these celebrated modernist writers, Millay uses playful 'temporal drag' within her play not only to write about same-sex desire but to queer history itself. As this chapter has shown, Millay's pseudo-Elizabethan play catalyses a reassessment of what 'lesbian modernism' might mean and how it might manifest in unexpected forms. *The Lamp and the Bell* is a lesbian modernist work not in spite of its historical anachronism but because of its historical anachronism. The play is an intervention in the past, an act of defiance in the present, and a vision of the future.

NOTES

1. See Suzanne Clark, *Sentimental Modernism: Women Writers and the Revolution of the Word* (Bloomington: Indiana University Press, 1991); and Jo Ellen Kaiser, 'Displaced Modernism: Millay and the Triumph of Sentimentality,' in *Millay at 100: A Critical Reappraisal*, ed. Diane P. Freedman (Carbondale and Edwardville: Southern Illinois University Press, 1995), 27–40.
2. Anne Cheney, for example, attributes Millay's lesbianism to a lack of a father figure, resolved when she encountered Professor Henry Noble MacCracken at Vassar, leading to 'her conversion from lesbianism to heterosexuality.' Anne Cheney, *Millay in Greenwich Village* (Tuscaloosa: University of Alabama Press, 1975), 18.
3. Lillian Faderman, for example, describes Millay as having 'bowed to the pressure to give up exclusive lesbianism [. . .] to become at least bisexual.' Lillian Faderman,

Odd Girls and Twilight Lovers: A History of Lesbian Life in Twentieth-Century America (New York: Columbia University Press, 1991), 86.
4. For 'temporal drag,' see Elizabeth Freeman, *Time Binds: Queer Temporalities, Queer Histories* (Durham, NC: Duke University Press, 2010), 62.
5. Brenda Murphy, *Provincetown Players and The Culture of Modernity* (Cambridge: Cambridge University Press, 2005), 143–4.
6. Millay to Cora Millay, November 1919, *Letters of Edna St. Vincent Millay*, ed. Allan Ross Macdougall (Camden, ME: Down East Books, 1952), 90.
7. Millay, letter to Norma, 18 March 1921, *Letters*, 116. Millay did eventually, as feared, receive barbs from Barnes, who criticised her over-use of the exclamation 'La!' and accused her of making 'shameful interruptions of herself.' Djuna Barnes, 'Plays for Women,' *New York Tribune*, 15 October 1922, 9.
8. Millay, letter to Norma, 18 March 1921, *Letters*, 116.
9. Edna St. Vincent Millay, *The Lamp and the Bell* (New York: Harper & Brothers, 1921), 9. Subsequent references will cite page numbers in-text.
10. See Anne MacKay, 'Introduction,' in *Wolf Girls at Vassar: Lesbian and Gay Experiences 1930–1990*, ed. Anne MacKay (New York: St. Martin's Press, 1993), 1–20, 7.
11. Elizabeth Atkins, *Edna St. Vincent Millay and Her Times* (Chicago: University of Chicago Press, 1936), 37.
12. Helen Lefkowitz Horowitz, *Alma Mater: Design and Experience in the Women's Colleges from Their Nineteenth-Century Beginnings to the 1930s* (Amherst: University of Massachusetts Press, 1984), 39.
13. Quoted in ibid., 67.
14. Ellen Rickert, 2 November 1890, quoted in ibid., 150.
15. Sharon Marcus, *Between Women: Friendship, Desire, and Marriage in Victorian England* (Princeton, NJ: Princeton University Press, 2007), 3.
16. Lavinia Hart, 'A Girl's College Life,' *The Cosmopolitan* 31 (June 1901): 192, quoted in Horowitz, *Alma Mater*, 162.
17. Longfellow uses this phrase to describe the relationship between Cecilia Vaughan and her 'bosom friend' Alice Archer in his novel *Kavanagh* (Boston: Ticknor, Reed, and Fields, 1849), 39.
18. Lillian Faderman, 'Foreword,' in MacKay, *Wolf Girls*, xi–xiv, xiv.
19. Millay took Buck's 'Techniques in Drama' and was part of her pioneering Vassar Dramatic Workshop. Millay also studied Salmon's 'Periodical Literature: Its Use as Historical Material.' See Colton Johnson, 'Vincent and Vassar,' in *Vincent & Vassar: An Exhibition* (The Edna St. Vincent Millay Society and the Vassar College Library, 2017), 9–36, 25.
20. Vassar College, 'Laura Johnson Wylie,' in *Vassar Encyclopedia*, accessed 15 July 2021, http://vcencyclopedia.vassar.edu/faculty/prominent-faculty/laura-wylie.html.
21. Quoted in Horowitz, *Alma Mater*, 65.
22. A 1903 study by G. Stanley Hall and Theodate Smith showed marriage rates of Vassar alumnae were falling: 55.46 per cent of the class of 1867 were married, compared with 28.92 per cent of the 1896 class. 'Marriage and Fecundity of College Men and Women,' *Pedagogical Seminary* 10, no. 3 (1903): 309–10.

23. In his speech of 13 March 1905, Roosevelt claimed that healthy women who choose not have children deserve 'contempt as hearty as any visited upon the soldier who runs away in battle.' 'On American Motherhood,' in *The World's Famous Orations, Vol. X. America: III*, ed. William Jennings Bryan (New York: Funk and Wagnalls, 1906), accessed 20 September 2022, https://www.bartleby.com/268/10/29.html.
24. Calvin Coolidge, 'Enemies of the Republic: Are the Reds Stalking Our College Women?,' *The Delineator*, June 1921, 4–5, 66–7, 4, 5.
25. 'Your Daughter: What Are Her Friendships? By a College Graduate,' *Harper's Bazar* (October 1913), 16, 78, 78.
26. Ibid., 16.
27. Ibid., 78.
28. Millay, letter to family, c. September 1913, quoted in Nancy Milford, *Savage Beauty: The Life of Edna St. Vincent Millay* (New York: Random House, 2001), 109.
29. Ibid.
30. Millay, letter to Norma, 1 November 1913, quoted in Milford, *Savage Beauty*, 111.
31. Millay, letter to Norma, 18 November 1913, quoted in Milford, *Savage Beauty*, 111, 112.
32. Norma to Millay, 19 October 1914, quoted in Milford, *Savage Beauty*, 120.
33. Millay to Charles Vale (pseud. Arthur Hooley), 3 February 1916, quoted in Milford, *Savage Beauty*, 132.
34. Millay, letter to family, 4 November 1914, quoted in Milford, *Savage Beauty*, 118.
35. Translation: 'My friend, I do not forget you. You do not have to be afraid. You are still my child. You know that well. And I love you. You know that well.' Millay to Elaine Ralli, 25 August 1915, quoted in Milford, *Savage Beauty*, 125.
36. Dow to Millay, 31 October 1915, quoted in Milford, *Savage Beauty*, 127.
37. Ibid.
38. Ibid., 128.
39. Cheney cites letters to Charlie shortly after her marriage, such as: 'Charlie, I love you very dearly. Don't forget me entirely, just on account of that Mac Sills, – will you?' Millay to Charlotte Babcock Sills, 12 October 1919, quoted in Cheney, *Greenwich Village*, 15.
40. Barbara Miller Solomon, *In the Company of Educated Women: A History of Women and Higher Education in America* (New Haven, CT: Yale University Press, 1985), 162.
41. Wanda Fraiken Neff, *We Sing Diana* (New York: Houghton Mifflin, 1928), 199. Millay's own sister became part of this backlash. Kathleen Millay, who played Carlotta in the original performance of *Lamp*, attacked the homoeroticism of women's colleges in her novel *Against the Wall* (1929), which later became entangled in a plagiarism case with *Mädchen in Uniform* (1931), based on the play *Gestern und Heute* (1930) by Christa Winsloe.
42. Floyd Dell, *Love in the Machine Age: A Psychological Study of the Transition from Patriarchal Society* (New York: Farrar-Rinehart, 1930), 238, 364.
43. Floyd Dell, 'Not roses, roses all the way: some recollections of Edna Millay' (unpublished), quoted in Milford, *Savage Beauty*, 157.

44. Ibid., 156.
45. Floyd Dell, quoted in Emily Hahn, *Romantic Rebels: An Informal History of Bohemianism in America* (Boston: Houghton Mifflin, 1967), 241.
46. Ethel Puffer described women's colleges as 'an Adamless Eden of moral and intellectual effort.' Quoted in Patricia Ann Palmieri, *Adamless Eden: The Community of Women Faculty at Wellesley* (New Haven, CT: Yale University Press, 1995), 154.
47. Horowitz, *Alma Mater*, 285. Millay herself took advantage of these freedoms, inviting Victor Ralli, Elaine's brother, to a college dance in 1916. Milford, *Savage Beauty*, 134.
48. Cheney, *Greenwich Village*, 23.
49. Atkins, *Millay*, 41.
50. Millay to Norma, 18 March 1921, *Letters*, 116.
51. See Valerie Traub, 'The Renaissance of Lesbianism,' *GLQ* 7, no. 2 (2001): 245–63; and Valerie Traub, *The Renaissance of Lesbianism* (Cambridge: Cambridge University Press, 2002).
52. Traub, 'Renaissance of Lesbianism,' 247.
53. It is notable that Millay derives her protagonists' names from Shakespeare's *Much Ado About Nothing* and *The Taming of the Shrew*.
54. Quoted in Susan S. Lanser, '"Bedfellowes in Royaltie": Early/Modern Sapphic Representations,' in *The Cambridge Companion to Lesbian Literature*, ed. Jodie Medd (New York: Cambridge University Press, 2015), 93–106, 101.
55. Atkins, *Millay*, 49, 36.
56. Ibid., 38–9.
57. See Bryher, 'The Girl-Page in Elizabethan Literature,' *Fortnightly Review* (March 1920): 442–52. Bryher's partner H.D. also engaged with the Renaissance later in her career, meditating on Shakespeare via prose and poetry in *By Avon River* (1949).
58. Account from Elizabeth Clark (in 1974) to author, in Milford, *Savage Beauty*, 372.
59. Freeman, *Time Binds*, 62.
60. Carla Freccero, 'The Queer Time of Lesbian Literature: History and Temporality,' in Medd, *Cambridge Companion to Lesbian Literature*, 19–31, 20.
61. Ibid., 20, 22.
62. For Millay's rumoured affair with Thelma Wood during this period, see Faderman, *Odd Girls*, 86–7.
63. The original cast list records the oldest as from the class of 1883 and the youngest (playing 'Little Rose Red'), the class of 1936 (presumably jesting that she was destined for Vassar).
64. At *The Pageant of Athena*, Millay briefly met Inez Milholland, who had famously appeared on horseback during the 1913 suffrage parade. Milford, *Savage Beauty*, 127. Milholland, who died in 1916, was Eugen Jan Boissevain's first wife before Millay.
65. Mary Simonson, *Body Knowledge: Performance, Intermediality, and American Entertainment at the Turn of the Twentieth Century* (Oxford: Oxford University Press, 2013), 49.
66. Ibid., 55.

67. Ibid., 58.
68. Ibid., 59.
69. Horowitz, *Alma Mater*, 162.
70. Millay, letter to family, 8 March 1915, quoted in Milford, *Savage Beauty*, 121.
71. Inscription in copy of *The Lamp and the Bell* found on AbeBooks, accessed 26 March 2021, https://www.abebooks.co.uk/paper-collectibles/Lamp-Bell-Drama-Five-Acts-inscription/15033002142/bd.
72. See back covers of *Vassar Quarterly* 3, no. 4 (1 July 1918) and 6, no. 4 (1 August 1921).
73. Margaret Jackson Allen, 'The Lamp and the Bell,' *Vassar Quarterly* 6, no. 4 (1 August 1921): 280–2, 281.
74. Ibid., 281.
75. Ibid., 282.
76. John V. A. Weaver, 'Personally Conducted: Edna St. Vincent Millay and Charlotte Mew,' *Brooklyn N.Y. Eagle*, 20 August 1921, 8.
77. Mark Van Doren, 'Women of Wit,' *The Nation* 113 (26 October 1921): 481–2, 482.
78. Millay to Morris Ernst, 23 January 1929, quoted in Leslie A. Taylor, "I Made Up My Mind to Get It": The American Trial of *The Well of Loneliness*, New York City, 1928–1929,' *Journal of the History of Sexuality* 10, no. 2 (2001): 250–86, 268.
79. Despite disparaging Millay's play, Barnes later wrote her own pseudo-Elizabethan verse drama, *The Antiphon* (1958).

11

THE LESBIAN HERSTORY ARCHIVES AT FIFTY

Robin Hackett

In 1974, the Lesbian Herstory Archives (LHA) shelved its first documents, a complete set of *The Ladder*, in a small room off the kitchen of Joan Nestle's New York City apartment.[1] Forty-five years later, the Archives fill every crevice of a Brooklyn brownstone, the fourth floor reserved as a caretaker's residence following the founding principle that the Archives will continue to be someone's home, and without the bars to access common to research libraries and universities. Thousands of annual visitors, in person and virtual, encounter overflowing floor-to-ceiling bookshelves, rooms full of filing cabinets, tabletops covered with cardboard boxes, and a basement full of recent acquisitions.[2] Materials spill over into offsite storage units, temperature and moisture controlled, and electronic clouds full of digitised sound and image recordings. Readers, academic and casual, from across town and across continents, use the Archives to access the largest collection of lesbiana in the world, including thousands of books, periodicals, pulp novels of the 1950s housed on shelves labelled 'survival literature,' newspaper clippings, published articles, essays by college students, the papers of well-known poets including Audre Lorde and Adrienne Rich, as well as the papers of a great many more lesbians who may have lived obscurely, but whose photos and letters, T-shirts and posters, shoes and music, banners and buttons have been solicited, acquired, appreciated, catalogued and preserved by multiple generations of volunteers who call themselves archivettes, and who are trained by those who came before them in the unique archival principles of the LHA.[3]

Arguably, the most unusual thing about this highly unusual archive is its continuing existence and growth through the neoliberal 1980s and 1990s, and into the queer theoretical turn – years during which lesbianism is often considered *passé* and the vast majority of lesbian and feminist organisations that were started in the 1970s, from bookstores, to presses, to health collectives, have collapsed.[4] The continuing existence and growth of the LHA can be understood, in part, as a function of material conditions. More compellingly, and more germane to the questions about the continuing relevance of lesbian modernism posed by this collection, the sustainability of the LHA provides an aspirational model for a transformed public operating from a politics of accountability, reparations, kinship and love, and resistant to what Achille Mbembe calls necropolitics – a feature of colonialism and modernity alike – in which a continually shifting demographic of people, often brown, black, indigenous and/or queer, are cast as waste, and thus properly dead.[5] Begun in the 1970s, the LHA, I argue, is a descendant of early twentieth-century lesbian modernism. It is, as well, productively anti-modern in its resistance to necropolitics, and in its resonance with Donna Haraway's anti-modern Chthulucene – an epoch in which tentacular thinking across time and species serves the making of kinship, indifferently horrific and joyful, but antidotal to death-distributing hierarchies.[6] With the substantial caveat that the LHA does not focus on cross-species kinship, there is something of Haraway's compost-like Chthulucene in the warm, tessellated loam that is 484 Fourteenth Street in Brooklyn, New York.

Material

Among the great variety and volume of holdings are all of the Archives' own newsletters, including nineteen print versions produced irregularly between 1975 and 2004, and an up-to-date web presence.[7] Notwithstanding the already overflowing building, every newsletter and the website invite readers to donate the matter of their lives to the LHA – to preserve old love letters and photographs the broken-hearted might be inclined to throw away, the closeted or the indifferent to destroy, or the incredulous to ignore. It is indeed hard to believe that the newest generation of archivettes want more ordinary stuff from ordinary people, but continuous calls for donations clarify that they do. In defiance of the obituary phrase 'no known survivors,' understood as a 'euphemism for the death of a lesbian,' the early coordinators intended the LHA, and the community it serves, to be one another's survivors. The title of Megan Rossman's award-winning short documentary *Love Letter Rescue Squad* commemorates the fact that among the items in the collection are documents of lesbian lives otherwise destined for the trash, including material retrieved from the kerb of a Greenwich Village street where it had been left for the garbage collectors.[8] This rescued letter, the subject of LHA legend, was saved first by a gay man who inadvertently picked it up with some file folders he offered to the LHA for reuse. In one folder was a single, forgotten love letter written by a woman who had lived in the nineteenth century. On her death, the family donated most of her papers to Smith College, threw out the love letters, and put what they thought were empty folders out with the trash. The archivists found the letter, reunited the original with the rest of the woman's papers at Smith, and recount the story of the rescue in order to illustrate both the importance of the Archives' mission and the community-based, scrappy and collective efforts to resource the fledgling organisation.[9]

Also rescued and housed in the LHA are diaries willed to the LHA by Marge McDonald, who spent her youth in the Midwest lonely and unhappy, but felt transformed by learning of the Archives' existence. She lived a closeted life, but the LHA and the broader gay liberation movement of the 1970s gave her a point of reference. She originally wrote her diaries in a tiny hand to avoid discovery, but later retyped them so that when they came to the Archives they would be easy to read. The lawyer handling her estate called the LHA to report that if nobody picked up the materials by the following day, the family, distraught over the discovery of their relative's lesbianism at the reading of the will, would have taken them to the dump. Archivists enlisted the help of the Women's Studies department of a local university to find a lesbian with a truck who could go immediately to the site, and Deb Edel, Joan Nestle and Nestle's then lover Eileen set out from New York by car to complete the rescue.[10] Edel also describes jumping into action in response to a phone call from a woman threatening to destroy photos of her soon-to-be ex-lover if no one showed up quickly to rescue them.[11] Among the Archives' essential functions is to be a repository for the documents of lives and loves that patriarchal families cannot be relied on to name or claim, and that lesbians ourselves do not always choose, or think, to preserve.

The focus on print matter in the LHA collection reflects the political and aesthetic convictions both of the era during which the Archives were begun and of earlier lesbian modernism, including a belief in print as an essential feature of feminist movements and lesbian existence. The women's movements of the twentieth century involved books as centrally as they did bodies. The life trajectory of print matter is not as spectacular as sexual freedom, reproductive justice or gender-based violence. But the centrality of books to feminist movements is a consistent refrain in feminist scholarship and is described in detail in the small subfield, feminist book history.[12] Print matter, from books to newsletters to fliers, was a mechanism for helping individuals understand themselves and their experiences as part of a collective, as well as for facilitating collective action. Rob Nixon's discussion of fiction in *Slow Violence and the Environmentalism of the Poor* clarifies the particular importance of fiction to building community in the context of enduring cultures of misogyny and anti-lesbian hostility: when violence is slow, rather than spectacular, fiction writers can make violence seen.

Nixon's focus is on slow violence in the form of environmental degradation, but his insight helps explain the importance of fiction to strains of feminism and lesbian culture formation that address generational and institutional violence.[13]

The importance of novels to lesbian survival, in particular, is evident in the LHA's use of the curatorial phrase 'survival literature' to catalogue and shelve the pulp novels that were 'often the only depictions of lesbian life and sex available from the 1930s to the 1960s.'[14] Such novels, cheap and sometimes available in grocery stores, enabled lesbians to develop a sense of collectivity even as they were personally closeted or isolated. Radclyffe Hall's *The Well of Loneliness* (1928), important to both lesbian and trans histories, is the subject of a poignant LHA anecdote illustrating its literally lifesaving power.[15] At an LHA event, Joan Nestle recounts, an elderly Jewish survivor of a Nazi death camp credited Hall's novel with saving her life: having read the novel as a teen, before being arrested, made her want to live long enough to kiss a woman.[16] That this story was originally told at an LHA event in the 1980s, and has since become part of LHA mythology, points to the fact that if print matter has been important to lesbian survival, the collection of print matter into travelling exhibits curated by the LHA serves to amplify that effect. The place of the anecdote in LHA lore points, as well, to the intersecting and, importantly, also distinct trans and lesbian histories and literatures archived at the LHA.

Money mattered, too, of course. In this regard, the founders – Sahli Cavallaro, Deborah Edel, Joan Nestle, Pamela Oline and Julia Stanley – were both careful and lucky. Nestle and Edel explain that they did the work of collecting and exhibiting materials before they solicited funds from the community they served, thus earning credibility among potential donors.[17] The only reference to money in early issues of the *Newsletter* is not a request for donations to the Archives but rather a call for readers to spend money subscribing to lesbian publications, accompanied by a list of titles and addresses enabling readers to do so. Over time, and especially during the push to raise a building fund, requests for funding for the LHA became a regular feature of the newsletter. But archival work continued to be the priority: overwhelming any focus on solicitations, the newsletters feature bibliographies of materials related to lesbian lives; 'in *memoriam*' pages; letters chronicling the experiences of archivists who carried LHA exhibits around the country; reports about 'At Home in the Archives' events; histories of lesbian communities; transcripts of materials gathered by researchers; announcements; thank yous; and the ever present request for more materials from the everyday lives of ordinary lesbians.

The founders' relative wealth also contributed to the sustainability of the Archives. While the resources of the Archives early on were extremely modest, the founders had jobs and education in an era in which white women in particular were reaping benefits from affirmative action. The founders tithed money from paid work. They had hours to spend as volunteers. Nestle has written about her working class and poor childhood. But she had spare room in a New York City apartment, and the rent she paid covered initial overhead costs for space and electricity. Dedicated volunteers contributed, and have continued to contribute, hours and years of their labour. Visitors dropped contributions into a jar, which still rests prominently near the entrance paired with a sign over the photocopier in the kitchen requesting that users deposit twenty-five cents per copy in the jar, 'more if, less if.'[18] Readers of the *Newsletter* sent donations small and large, including one from a donor who expressed a desire to help greater than the poverty which limited her contribution to a couple of postage stamps. Community members organised parties and dances on behalf of the Archives. Musicians donated proceeds from concerts. Lesbians and gay men, including victims of AIDS, who had often worked with lesbians in ACT-UP, remembered the Archives in their wills.[19]

This combination of material factors – the importance of print matter to feminist politics, the founders' primary commitment to the services they promised, and their means to cover modest and gradually increasing operating costs – contributed to a continuously solvent and expanding institution. The Archives incorporated as a nonprofit in 1979, making donations tax deductible. The *Newsletter* listed expenses and income for the first time in 1984: annual fixed costs were $822; acid-free archival materials and an overhaul of the copier amounted to another several hundred. Also in the 1984 newsletter, the archivists announced that they had won a few small grants and planned to apply for more. Twenty years later, in the spring 2004 issue, three years of financial reports list annual expenses between $50,000 and $60,000, and income ranging between $27,000 and $91,000. By this time, as well, the Archives had moved from its original location to the Brooklyn brownstone bought for $303,000 in 1991, and paid off in full for $451,000, including the price of renovations, four years later.

Currently, the Archives have an updated website featuring a visual tour of the building, a calendar of events and drop-in hours, including virtual and Zoom events during the Covid-19 pandemic, instructions about how to use the Archives, a brief history, descriptions of travelling exhibits and information about internships. There are links, as well, to primary archival material, including all the newsletters, dozens of photographs, and audio and video recordings. In social and traditional media, the Archives have a robust presence. Blog, Instagram and Facebook posts announce upcoming events, including story hours, public tours, arts workshops, celebrity readings and seminars. The fall 2020 issue of *Sinister Wisdom* commemorates the forty-fifth birthday of the Archives. Subtitled *Forty-Five Years: A Tribute to the Lesbian Herstory Archives*, the issue collects nearly 200 pages of loving and grateful testimony for the life-affirming, lifesaving and sanity-serving function of the Archives.[20] Contributors, including founders, read from the collection at a fall 2020 Zoom event attended by hundreds. A February 2021 blog post announced that the LHA had won a $90,000 Mellon Foundation grant.

The importance of material factors is not, however, the only takeaway from the ongoing success of the Archives through a time when so many similarly motivated, and similarly resourced, organisations failed. More significant, I would argue, is that the archival principles of the LHA provide a model for the development of a public prepared for the ongoing practice of advancing queer kinship – a kinship that crosses time and place, that is cyborgian in its relation to matter, and that is inclusive of the most abject among us.[21] The lesbian modernism of the LHA inherits community-making impulses, a relation to print, as well as specific documents and histories, from the lesbian modernism of the early twentieth century. It also exists despite the fact that many white lesbian modernists, such as Radclyffe Hall and Virginia Woolf, with outsized roles as representatives of the field, work with broad definitions of 'outsiderism' that express racist, antisemitic and/or class elitism.

Necropolitical

In his discussion of necropolitics, Achille Mbembe argues that it is a feature of late modern sovereignty to create brown and black people as classes properly dead. Foucault's notion of biopower – the expression of sovereignty as the capacity to decide who lives and who dies – Mbembe writes, 'is insufficient to account for contemporary forms of the subjugation of life to the power of death' (92). Instead, necropolitics, or necropower, accounts

> for the various ways in which, in our contemporary world, weapons are deployed in the interest of maximally destroying persons and creating *death-worlds*, that is, new and unique forms of social existence in which vast populations are subjected to living conditions that confer upon them the status of the living dead. (92)

Using examples from Nazi Germany, the Israel–Palestine conflict, Apartheid South Africa and US plantation slavery, Mbembe elaborates ways in which the properly dead are projections of colonialists' fears of a return on their own violence; the properly dead exist, as well, with pasts and futures erased, including, in settler colonialism, from the future of the modern state, romanticised as the good life based in reason and autonomy (67). Necropolitical spaces of late modernity, real and metaphorical, are variously filled with indigenous people, descendants of formerly enslaved people, terrorists, criminals, Jews, Muslims and queers. Moreover, necropolitical space is routinely populated anew with shifting, disproportionately brown and black demographics of people. The category of properly dead, rather than any fixed demographic, is the constant, and the constantly murderous, force of the biopolitical state.

Museums, as they are commonly organised, are more complicit than resistant to necropower. 'The museum,' Mbembe writes, 'has not always been an unconditional place of reception for the multiple faces of humanity taken in its unity. On the contrary [. . .] the museum has been a powerful device of separation,' with the primary principle of curation being

> the conviction that because different forms of humanities have produced different objects and different forms of culture, these objects and forms of culture ought to be placed and exhibited in distinct places and assigned different and unequal symbolic statuses. The slave's entry into such a museum would doubly hallow the spirit of apartheid that lies at the source of this cult of difference, hierarchy, and inequality. (171)

By contrast, enslaved Africans, wherever they have happened to be, never stopped 'the Sisyphus-like effort to resist being turned into waste' in 'producing symbols and rituals, languages, memory, and meaning – and therefore the substance necessary to sustain life' (159). Nor did they stop 'the interminable labor of caring for and repairing that which has been broken' (159). If the museum is a site of further damage, and not a site of repair, however, the archive, as Mbembe describes it, has potential. Digging into archives is risky, he says. One has to go in as if through cracks and fissures, in order

> to create a memory by obstinately fixing shadows rather than real events, or rather historical events submerged in the force of shadow. Often it has been necessary to outline, on preexisting traces, our own silhouette, to grasp for ourselves the contours of the shadow and to try to see ourselves from the shadow, as shadow. (173)

Mbembe's insistence that resistance to necropolitical violence exists in the recovery of shadows, and from shadows, who and what is deemed waste might well be a description of the aspirations of the LHA.

Theorists including C. Heike Schotten, Lee Edelman, José Muñoz, Jasbir Puar and Ann Cvetkovich have built, from Mbembe's characterisation of necropolitics, more explicitly queer analyses.[22] They argue for queer politics that can be understood, variously, as entreaties to embrace terrorism (Schotten), to celebrate the death drive (Edelman), and to understand the utopian futurism of queer performance (Muñoz). Puar describes assemblages of matter and affect in order to clarify the processes by which the state casts brown people as terrorists, and thus among the properly dead. Puar also clarifies the failures of homonormative inclusion: making space at the table for some, at the cost of reiterating necropolitical space of victimisation for others, is not effective resistance to necropolitics. By contrast, according to Cvetkovich, archives *do* resist necropolitics. The impulse to archive is itself a response to the trauma of death, and collections such as the LHA that include the matter of everyday life archive trauma most fully. Moreover, the LHA archives both material objects and feelings, including cross-generational and collective traumas. Importantly, the LHA depathologises the trauma it archives, building collectivity based on affect rather than, for instance, as is more conventional, on national or ethnic origin, or heterosexual reproduction.[23]

Mbembe is one of many scholars who see modernism as complicit with death-dealing forces. 'Modernity,' he writes, 'is at the origin of multiple concepts of sovereignty and thus also of the biopolitical' (67). In late modernity, 'the ultimate expression of sovereignty is the production of general norms by a body [. . .] comprising free and equal individuals' operating on reason, and engaged in the twofold process of self-institution and self-limitation' (67). It is a particular feature of late modernity that sovereignty is expressed as 'the generalized instrumentalization of human existence and the material destruction of human bodies and populations' (68). Similarly, Donna Haraway criticises modernism in the same terms she uses to criticise the Anthropocene. Environmentalists use 'Anthropocene' to point to human-caused environmental change. But for Haraway, hope for the planet, and for all species on it, requires turning away equally from human and future centredness towards the Chthulucene, an epoch she compares, euphorically, to compost. The Chthulucene is characterised by tentacular thinking that facilitates kinship, both banal and aspirational, across species and times, rejecting alike doomsday and hopeful future thinking.

In contrast to Mbembe and Haraway, Susan Stanford Friedman is not explicitly anti-modern. But her expansion of modernism and modernity removes from it any whiff of modern/tradition hierarchal binary. After decades during which literary modernism was defined by the men of 1914 and their 1922 publications, and subsequent decades during which scholars stretched the boundaries of modernism to include multiple modernisms, including lesbian modernism, Friedman takes modernism planetary, arguing that multiple – including past and future – modernisms are the aesthetic productions that respond to periods of cataclysmic change across both time and space, thus separating notions of modernism and modernity not only from the Euro-American early twentieth century but also from the common hierarchical binary of 'the west' versus 'the rest.'[24] Her planetary modernism accounts for the fact that people migrate and flee ongoingly; we are captured and expelled; we reattach ourselves to soil and make new archives of legacy and belonging, including national belonging. Friedman's thinking about modernism shares something with Haraway's anti-modern tentacular thinking. Moreover, it follows from Friedman's recursive and planetary view of modernism that there are multiple lesbian modernisms, including a lesbian modernism that responds to the civil rights movements of the 1970s, and hence to the white supremacy and other exclusionary features of lesbian and queer modernisms from which it grew.

Taken together, Friedman, Mbembe, Haraway, and the queer scholars who have built on Mbembe's work underscore both the significance of the Lesbian Herstory Archives and the role of lesbian modernity, as expressed by the LHA, as an aspirational model for an ideal public, one that is resistant to the threat of becoming waste, as well as to the more enduring, recursive and capacious violence of the necropolitical category itself. The operations of the LHA involve archivettes, coordinators and users of the Archives all in making kinship from and with material literally retrieved from the garbage.

Anti-colonial resistance to becoming waste is among the primary inspirations of LHA founder Nestle. In a 1977 letter to Judith Schwarz, who joined the LHA coordinating committee shortly after this exchange, Nestle writes:

> I am a thirty-seven year old lesbian who came out around 1960. I led two separate lives for many years. My life changed very much with the changes in the lesbian community in NY; I participated in early gay rights demonstrations, joined CR groups, became a feminist. It was a long journey from self-hatred. For the last eleven years, I have been teaching third world literature to students who have experienced colonialism first hand. Two years ago, I was reading a work by Albert Memmi called *The Colonizer and the Colonized* and as I read it, changing the pronouns to 'she' and 'her,' a connection started growing. 'We should add that [she] draws less and less from her past. The colonizer never even recognized that [she] had one, everyone knows that the commoner whose origins are unknown has no history. Let us ask the colonized [herself]: who are her folk heroes? Her greatest popular leaders? Her sages? At most she will be able to give us a few names, in complete disorder, and fewer and fewer as on goes down the generations. *The colonized seems condemned to lose her memory.*'
>
> I see what we are trying to do as a refusal to be kicked out of time again, as a reclaiming as a cherishing of ourselves that will create generational connection.[25]

It is the ongoing work of the LHA to defy necropolitical forces: to remove specific items relative to lesbian history from the trash, and build from those items a collective history; to claim memories; to insist on a past as an essential part of the process of having a future. Nestle's letter is built upon a comparison between lesbians and colonised people – a comparison that resonates problematically across the span of white-authored feminism beginning with Mary Wollstonecraft's comparisons between enslaved people and wives.[26] Nestle's comparison between colonised people and lesbians is, as well, however, evidence of the ways in which civil rights activists of the 1960s and 1970s took inspiration and ideologies from one another, and from pan-African independence movements.

Nestle's use of 'ourselves' in her letter to Schwartz also reflects foundational confidence in identity politics, as does the initial 1975 newsletter, addressed 'Dear Sisters.' This newsletter is worth quoting at length as it emphasises the way in which collectivity multiply shapes the origin story of the LHA. The five founders introduce themselves thusly:

> We are a group of women who met initially at the first conference of the Gay Academic Union in the Fall of 1973. Some of us formed a C-R [Consciousness Raising] group, and, as we grew closer to each other, we began to focus on our need to collect and preserve our own voices, the voices of our Lesbian community. As our contribution to our community, we decided to undertake the collecting, preserving, and making available to our sisters all the prints of our existence. We undertook the Archives, not as a short-term project, but as a commitment to rediscovering our past, controlling our present, and speaking to our future. We seek to preserve for the future all expression of our identity—written, spoken, drawn, filmed, photographed, recorded.
>
> We are just in the beginning stages. A lot of material is coming in and we are in the process of sorting and cataloging it. This is our first newsletter. We hope that the Archives will serve as a center for all women who want to get a sense of their Lesbian Herstory, through tangible expression of the lives we have lived. Our collection is small but growing, and we will do our best to insure that it will never be misused. For us, there is excitement and joy in sharing the records of our lives, and our Archives will be as living as the material we can collect and you can send us. We want to encompass the happenings of the whole Lesbian community, and for this we need your help. Future newsletters will contain listings of our holdings as the cataloging and sorting and collecting progresses, and suggested topics for research as we become aware of them.[27]

This newsletter, mailed with an insert clarifying the structure and purpose of the fledgling organisation, reflects confidence in a knowable *us* – not just the *us* who broke off from the Gay Academic Union but the *us* the founders intend to serve: *our* lesbian community, *our* lesbian expressions, and *our* future.

Such confidence in a knowable community of lesbians has been effectively and meaningfully challenged by scholars of intersectionality and queer studies.[28] But Jennifer Nash and Elena Gambino, among others, illustrate the ways in which the dismissal of lesbian feminism as an essentialist stance is less a matter of accuracy than it is a backward-looking characterisation that both ignores the foundational importance of black women to feminist and queer theories and inaccurately understands the public nature of lesbian identity politics in circulation in the 1970s and 1980s. Nash describes black feminist traditions of the 1970s and 1980s as love politics, a strategy for constructing political communities that takes intragroup difference around sexuality and class, for instance, as foundational, and avoids the pitfalls of essentialism.[29] Elena Gambino describes lesbian feminism of the period as a commitment to an intentionally built public founded on the principles of listening, accountability and repair.[30] Such scholarship on black feminist and lesbian feminist politics enables a more nuanced understanding of feminist efforts of the 1970s and 1980s to usher in a public with the capacity to advance not merely humanist aspirations for an inclusive democracy but, more radically, a depathologising and affective (rather than essentialist) assemblage. Work by Nash and Gambino clarifies that the impulse behind the reference to *we* and *us* in the initial newsletter of the LHA is less referential than it is agential: as practised in the 1970s and 1980s, lesbian feminism was an effort to usher in a public based on lesbian expression, to assert lesbian existence, and, importantly, to address and repair intragroup inequities based on race, class and gender. Conversely, the essentialism commonly attributed to lesbian feminism, as well as the association of black women in particular with identity politics are products of the queer theoretical turn that serve to produce *queer*ness as the ultimate politics of freed desire, resulting in the loss of lesbian and black feminist politics of repair and accountability. Related to lesbian modernism of the early twentieth century, there is, here, a model for kinship that addresses, rather than glosses over, the white supremacy often evident in individual lesbian and queer modernist authors, as well as in the retroactive creation of the field of lesbian modernism.

Moreover, the principle of working for a 'whole community' continued to develop meaning as the LHA grew and flourished from the early seventies until now. Inclusiveness as practised by the LHA is a continuously renewed practice of accountability and reparations. For work meetings beginning early in the history of the LHA, founders agreed to put aside even private aversions: hostile ex-lovers could refuse to share any space but the Archives. They collected materials from the 'whole lesbian community,' by which they meant that the materials gathered and the people involved with the Archives reflected intragroup difference as fully as the founders and later coordinators knew, at every turn, how to accomplish. Lesbian feminists are part of that whole community. So are sex workers, participants in S/M sexuality and members of butch/femme cultures. When women's organisations fractured, in the 1970s and 1980s, around analyses of racism and intragroup difference, the LHA redoubled efforts at inclusiveness that had been central from the beginning. Porn wars raged in the 1980s but did not limit what was collected or exhibited. Both Edel and Nestle repeat a story of Nestle having answered 'yes' when asked if the materials of even a lesbian Nazi would be included in the Archives.[31] Inclusiveness was counted as evidence of progress for Nestle and Edel, who commented that the movement for lesbian rights had been successful enough that the LHA did not need to serve an ambassadorial function, or as they put it, be a 'role model archives,' and was thus free to recognise the full diversity of lesbian communities, equitably serving not only those most stigmatised in the non-lesbian world but also the most hated within it.[32]

Nor were Nestle's comments about including hateful lesbians hypothetical. During the queer theoretical turn, Nestle condemns lesbian-feminist critiques of pornography, butch-femme gender expression and S/M sexuality in the strongest possible terms as fascist.[33] She also compares efforts to censor pornography to McCarthyism, the repressive effects of which she has first-hand knowledge.[34] But she never wavers in her insistence that wholly inclusive archival practices are necessary. Indeed, the LHA includes the papers of McCarthy-era FBI informant Angela Calomiris, who testified for the prosecution at the 1949 Smith Act trial of the leaders of the American Communist Party, and who had a reputation in Greenwich Village for having turned in lesbians to the police and to the FBI.[35]

Moreover, the Archives' principles of collection were, from the beginning, based on an understanding that inclusive politics are not a matter of morality; they are a product of the fact that there are structural, conceptual and historical similarities between sexual deviance, gender deviance and racial deviance: all challenge heteropatriarchal logics of cultural reproduction. The racial motives of heteropatriarchal sexual proscriptions are well theorised. As Cvetkovich puts it,

> there is a structural similarity between interracial and homosexual coupling, both of which can be constructed as queer forms of cultural reproductions. The desire for 'natural' reproduction can be understood as a way of refusing the trauma of cultural dislocation through a fantasy of uninterrupted lineage.[36]

Lesbian culture, as represented by LHA, is a product of affect and affiliation that are neither biological nor national.

Inclusion is also an ever-receding aspirational goal for the LHA. We do not know, now, who we will be in the future, as the evolution of Nestle's own thinking about trans exclusions illustrates. Of working in the Archives with a trans lesbian named Chelsea, Nestle writes:

> I responded to Chelsea's concerns about how best to serve a growing movement for liberation with memories of some of my own struggles with the early spokeswomen of the lesbian-feminist movement, my anger at their disdain for the bar community that had given me my first lessons

in queer defiance, my fears about the exclusions deemed necessary when a political passion calls for a unified front. [. . .] If we had done things differently as lesbian-feminist women, as a gay liberation movement in the thirty years since Stonewall, Chelsea and her comrades would not have to be fighting for their most basic rights in the 1990s. But we had been so sure then that we knew who was a 'woman' and who a 'man,' what gender meant and what it did not, what embarrassed us and what made us feel, in our own peculiar way, at home. It is one of the complex ironies of the liberation movements that often the passion of their certainties creates the need for future, more inclusive visions of emancipation.[37]

The historical mission of the Archives asserts lesbian history and lesbian future to counter the now of lesbian erasure.[38] In doing so, the Archives reference a knowable 'We,' utopian and universal and problematic. But the LHA also stands with terrorists, or, as Nestle puts it, the 'most stigmatized among us' – whoever it is occupying that space in any given moment. There is no one the Archives will abject in exchange for a place in the biopolitical sphere; to do so would be to participate in what Puar would criticise as 'homonormative' politics, in which some lesbians are recuperated for life at the expense of someone else being cast as properly dead.[39] Resistance to the ongoing necropolitical process of turning some into waste is literalised in the Archives' collection itself: it includes the garbage, the detritus of lesbian past and present, as a condition for lesbian future. The history, policy and practices of the Archives amounts to the assertion that we stand together as garbage, in kinship with garbage, in pleasure, and claims these practices as resilient and life affirming.

Speaking of Nazis

As I write this in April 2021, federal and state police in Washington DC are using social media to identify individual members of white supremacist mobs that broke into the Capitol buildings on 6 January 2021 with the goal of preventing the certification of the election of Joe Biden and Kamala Harris as President and Vice President of the United States. Attackers displayed confederate and Nazi symbols, directed racial epithets at people guarding the Capitol, and erected gallows on the grounds. The mob violence resulted in deaths, damage, injuries and terror. However, as satisfying as it would be to see white supremacists punished, Mbembe and others would caution us against casting even Nazis into the class properly dead. To be clear, I am not talking about forgiveness, and nor are Edel or Nestle being forgiving or friendly when they insist that even the materials of a lesbian Nazi belong in the Archives. Inclusion does not necessitate forgiveness.

But the current resurgence of white supremacy surprised many in the US who did not know of its virulence and continuity specifically because US white supremacists are repeatedly removed from their place in our collective archive. Even if efforts to cast them into necropolitical space in the current crisis succeed – by designating them terrorists and criminals and jailing them – such successes are also motives for them to reconvene: Mbembe and others remind us that necropolitical force is never totalising. The example of the LHA provides, in place of necropolitics, an imperfect model for ushering in a modern public. Scholars of the history of the LHA, and the logics of its founding, are well suited to lead in eradicating white supremacy by refusing aspects of social movements that also refill the category of the properly dead.

The existence of fascists and informants among us notwithstanding, the fact that a lesbian archive can model inclusive modernity and the fulfilment of enlightenment promises (however much we might also want to critique the way those principles are deployed) is not a coincidence. Sexual deviance, gender deviance and racial deviance similarly defy blood and soil logics of cultural reproduction and belonging. An archive of such deviance, even as it produces a collectivity, defeats the tribal logics of white identity in which processes of cultural reproduction and uninterrupted lineage are consistently sexualised.

Fittingly, and hopefully, then, in this time of the visible rise in white supremacist activism, there is also a surge of interest in feminism and feminist politics of the 1970s and 1980s. In 2018, *Publisher's Weekly* reporter Claire Kirch describes what was dubbed a 'Trump bump' at Charis Books & More in Atlanta; the number of feminist bookstores in the US dipped from a high of more than a hundred during the 1980s and 1990s, to below ten in the 2010s; but after the 2016 election, new stores opened, and existing stores saw an uptick in sales, walk-in customers, and attendance at book talks and discussion groups.[40] The January 2017 women's march on Washington DC was repeated in towns and cities across the nation. Miriam Webster listed 'feminism' as the 2017 word of the year. Also in 2017, the National Women's Studies Association conference commemorated the fortieth anniversary of the publication of the Combahee River Collective Statement. Conference presentations emphasised links between Black Lives Matter activism and the aims of the Combahee River Collective, and conference-goers noted the resurgence of interest in feminist politics and tactics of the 1970s and 1980s. Covid-era shutdowns have put downward pressure on all public activities, and are an occasion for backlash against feminist and antiracist progress in particular.[41] But there is ongoing media coverage of sexist and racist harassment and violence. And notwithstanding the Covid-19 shutdowns, the election of Kamala Harris has been accompanied by an upsurge in demand for 'new titles focused on women's and girl's empowerment, feminism, and the connection between those issues and the distinct problems faced by women of color.'[42] Preparing ourselves to advance equity into the future – through the aftermath of the Capitol riots, beyond whatever post-Covid backlash we face, as well as through cycles of progress and heteropatriarchal retrenchment that are to come – is a matter of understanding all the forces, intellectual and material, that contributed to the unique survival of the Archives, and of recognising the LHA as a sustainable model for modernity that is not dependent on continuously vacating and reconstituting a class of properly dead.

Notes

1. *The Ladder* was the newsletter of the Daughters of Bilitis, a homophile organisation active 1955–95.
2. The LHA website includes a photographic tour of the rooms of the Archives.
3. Materials are arranged alphabetically by first name of the donor into special collections, and/or separated into components and cross-referenced. For instance, novels are shelved with other novels, T-shirts are collected and exhibited together, and mixed genre materials from specific organisations are filed under the names of those organisations. There are also 'lesbian and . . .' subject files, as well as periodical files.
4. There are notable surviving organisations, in addition to the LHA, including The Feminist Press in New York, and the Boston Women's Health Book Collective.
5. Achille Mbembe, *Necropolitics* (Durham, NC: Duke University Press, 2019). Subsequent references will cite page numbers in-text.
6. Donna J. Haraway, *Staying with the Trouble: Making Kin in the Chthulucene* (Durham, NC and London: Duke University Press, 2016).
7. In 2021, there is an up-to-date website, and a robust social media presence announcing regular online events. See https://lesbianherstoryarchives.org.
8. *Love Letter Rescue Squad*, directed by Megan Rossman (Vimeo, 2016), 6 min., 49 sec., accessed 20 September 2022, https://vimeo.com/ondemand/girlsonfilm3/280536513. The film won the best student documentary award in Cannes, 2017.
9. See Deborah Edel, Joan Nestle and Judith Schwarz, Interview, *Lesbian Herstory Archives AudioVisual Collections*, accessed 28 March 2022, http://herstories.prattinfoschool.nyc/omeka/items/show/416.
10. Flavia Rando, Interview with author, telephone, 3 February 2021.
11. *The Archivettes*, directed by Megan Rossman (Women Make Movies, 2019), 1 hr., 1 min., accessed 20 September 2022, https://vimeo.com/ondemand/thearchivettes0?utm_source=email&utm_medium=vod-receipt-201602&utm_campaign=29546.
12. Kathryn Tracy Adams, 'Paper Lesbians: Alternative Publishing and the Politics of Lesbian Representation in the United States, 1950–1990' (PhD diss., University of Texas at Austin, 1994); Jaime Harker and Cecilia Konchar Farr, *This Book Is an Action: Feminist Print Culture and Activist Aesthetics* (Urbana: University of Illinois Press, 2016); Kristen Hogan, *The Feminist Bookstore Movement: Lesbian Antiracism and Feminist Accountability* (Durham, NC: Duke University Press, 2016); Simone Murray, *Mixed Media: Feminist Presses and Publishing Politics* (London: Pluto Press, 2004).
13. Rob Nixon, *Slow Violence and the Environmentalism of the Poor* (Cambridge, MA: Harvard University Press, 2011).

14. Emma Levesque-Schaefer, 'Books and Monographs,' in Lesbian Herstory Archives, n.d., accessed 20 September 2022, https://lesbianherstoryarchives.org/collections/books-monographs/.
15. For a discussion of *The Well* as early trans novel, see, for instance, Melanie A. Taylor, '"The Masculine Soul Heaving in the Female Bosom": Theories of Inversion and *The Well of Loneliness*,' *Journal of Gender Studies* 7, no. 3 (November 1998): 287–96.
16. Joan Nestle, 'The Bodies I Have Lived With: Keynote for 18th Lesbian Lives Conference, Brighton, England, 2011,' *Journal of Lesbian Studies* 17, no. 3–4 (1 July 2013): 215–39. See also, Paulina Pająk, 'Echo Texts: Woolf, Krzywicka, and *The Well of Loneliness*,' *Woolf Studies Annual* 24 (2018): 11–34.
17. Edel, Nestle, Schwarz, Interview.
18. More if you can, less if you can't. Sliding scale fees reflect the LHA's foundational commitment to equitable access, a commitment so common to feminist organisations of the 1970s and 1980s that it can be invoked in half phrases.
19. For a detailed history of coalitions in Act-Up, see Sarah Schulman, *Let the Record Show: A Political History of Act Up New York, 1987–1993* (New York: Farrar, Straus and Giroux, 2021).
20. Elvis Bakaitis, Shawn(ta) Smith-Cruz and Red Washburn, eds, *Sinister Wisdom 118: Forty-Five Years / A Tribute to the Lesbian Herstory Archives* (Fall 2020).
21. I use 'cyborg' as theorised in Donna J. Haraway, 'A Cyborg Manifesto,' in *Manifestly Haraway* (Minneapolis: University of Minnesota Press, 2016).
22. C. Heike Schotten, *Queer Terror: Life, Death, and Desire in the Settler Colony* (New York: Columbia University Press, 2018); Lee Edelman, *No Future: Queer Theory and the Death Drive* (Durham, NC: Duke University Press, 2004); José Esteban Muñoz, *Cruising Utopia: The Then and There of Queer Futurity* (New York: New York University Press, 2009); Jasbir K. Puar, *Terrorist Assemblages: Homonationalism in Queer Times* (Durham, NC: Duke University Press, 2017); Ann Cvetkovich, *An Archive of Feelings: Trauma, Sexuality, and Lesbian Public Cultures* (Durham, NC: Duke University Press, 2003). See also Jin Haritaworn, Adi Kuntsman and Silvia Posocco, eds, *Queer Necropolitics* (Abingdon: Routledge, 2014).
23. Cvetkovich, *Archive of Feelings*, 121–2. The traumas of AIDS victims and caregivers figure prominently in Cvetkovich's analysis, as many of the lesbians involved with the LHA also gave care to AIDS victims and worked together with gay men in Act-Up.
24. Susan Stanford Friedman, *Planetary Modernisms: Provocations on Modernity across Time* (New York: Columbia University Press, 2015).
25. Joan Nestle, 'Newsletter 6,' *Lesbian Herstory Archives* (27 November 1977): 1–26, 11 (Nestle's emphasis). Nestle does not give a citation for Memmi in her letter. But she is quoting an English translation she notes having read in 1975, which might be either the first English translation, Albert Memmi, *The Colonizer and the Colonized* (New York: Orion Press, 1965), or Albert Memmi, *The Colonizer and the Colonized* (London: Souvenir Press, 1974). The passage quoted is on pages 146–7 of the latter.
26. Mary Wollstonecraft, *A Vindication of the Rights of Woman: A Norton Critical Edition*, ed. Deidre Shauna Lynch, 3rd ed. (New York: W. W. Norton, 2009), 7, 27.
27. 'Newsletter no.1,' *Lesbian Herstory Archive*s (June 1975): 1. In its entirety, including the insert, a few short notices about research projects under way, and a bibliography

of 'Serial Media with Lesbian Content,' the first newsletter is seven pages long, with the twenty-two-item bibliography taking up most of the space.
28. Feminist scholars, as well as scholars in sexuality, race and ethnic studies, have meaningfully and repeatedly tested the limits of identity politics. Sojourner Truth's 'Ain't I a Woman' speech in 1851 points out that womanhood does not mean similarly across racial difference. Audre Lorde and black feminists in the women's liberation era exposed the ways in which poverty, citizenship, gender and colour, among other nodes of identification, additively limit access to education, resources and health. Kimberlé Crenshaw coined the term 'intersectionality' in 1989 to talk about these interworkings of race, gender, sexuality and class. In the early 1990s, inspired in part by the history of activists including lesbians and LHA founders who worked in HIV and AIDS prevention education, queer scholars intervened in social justice advocacy by exposing the histories of sex, race and gender, among other concepts through which people understand themselves and their affiliations.
29. Jennifer Nash, 'Practicing Love: Black Feminism, Love-Politics, and Post-Intersectionality,' *Meridians* 11 (31 December 2011): 1–24.
30. Elena Gambino, '"Presence in Our Own Land": Second Wave Feminism and the Lesbian Body Politic' (PhD diss., University of Minnesota, 2019), ProQuest (22618553).
31. Edel, Nestle, Schwarz, Interview.
32. Ibid.
33. See Joan Nestle, 'The Politics of Thinking' and 'Lesbian Sex and Surveillance,' in *A Fragile Union: New and Selected Writings* (San Francisco: Cleis Press, 2018), 89–96, 115–25.
34. Joan Nestle, 'My History with Censorship,' in *A Restricted Country* (San Francisco: Cleis Press, 2018), 140–6.
35. Lisa E. Davis, *Undercover Girl: The Lesbian Informant Who Helped the FBI Bring Down the Communist Party* (Watertown, MA: Charlesbridge Publishing, 2017).
36. Cvetkovich, *Archive of Feelings*, 122.
37. Joan Nestle, 'On Rereading Esther's Story,' in *Fragile Union*, 110.
38. For an early and thorough analysis of lesbian erasure, see Adrienne Rich, 'Compulsory Heterosexuality and Lesbian Existence,' *Signs: Journal of Women in Culture and Society* 5, no. 4 (1980): 631–60.
39. Puar, *Terrorist Assemblages*.
40. Claire Kirch, 'Trump Presidency Reinvigorates Feminist Bookstores,' *Publishers Weekly*, 9 March 2018, accessed 20 Septeber 2022, https://www.publishersweekly.com/pw/by-topic/industry-news/bookselling/article/76289-trump-presidency-reinvigorates-feminist-bookstores.html.
41. 'NWSA Presidential Statement on COVID-19,' National Women's Studies Association, 16 March 2020, accessed 20 September 2022, https://www.nwsa.org/news/494121/NWSA-Presidential-Statement-on-COVID-19.htm.
42. Diane Patrick and Calvin Reid, 'Is Women's Empowerment Coming to Publishing?,' *Publishers Weekly*, 29 January 2021, accessed 20 September 2022, https://www.publishersweekly.com/pw/by-topic/industry-news/publisher-news/article/85436-is-women-s-empowerment-coming-to-publishing.html.

12

HIDDEN IN PLAIN SIGHT: THE RECONSTRUCTION OF LESBIAN MODERNIST SEXUAL HISTORIES

Jo Winning

The recuperation of lesbian modernism as a set of aesthetic experiments within literature, the visual arts and architecture, and as a catalogue of instances of cultural production, has constituted a body of work, and set of critical interventions, undertaken by feminist, lesbian and queer scholars since the late 1980s. This work has been necessary, restorative and often challenging. Prising open the definition of modernism to reveal the hidden and the neglected practitioners on the 'periphery' of this explosive and canonised period has focused on the pressures that including lesbian, queer and dissident sexual identities and desires brings to bear upon the very nature of 'modernism.' Alongside this recuperative work on the textual, visual and material products that the lesbian modernists (if we *may* describe them in this way) created, the urge to recover life stories and biographical narratives of lived dissidence has run alongside the interpretation of art objects. Now at a substantial historical remove of over thirty years, what happens if we return to the foundational work of Gillian Hanscombe, Virginia Smyers and Shari Benstock, and ask how we might now regard the critical readings of the period that entangled lived experience with the will to aesthetic experimentation and posited the model of 'writing for their lives' as a persuasive paradigm for understanding embodied modernist practice?[1]

Shari Benstock's aim, in her major excavation of Paris as a site of female modernist cultural production *Women of the Left Bank*, was to '[emphasise] the *differences* of Modernist women's experiences in both history and literature' and to '[trace] differences between and within literary practices and lived circumstances in this period, choosing as one – among many – of its determining factors the difference of gender.'[2] Whilst Benstock is focused principally on gender, she is also alert to sexual identity and its imbrication in the radical aesthetic agendas of many female modernists. Lesbian modernists, she writes, are far freer than those heterosexual female modernists whose creative labour is often occluded by that of their male counterparts: 'it is not accidental, I think, that the powerful communities of women artists were established by lesbians or that heterosexual women Modernists remained in the shadows of their male colleagues – men who were husbands, lovers, or literary supervisors.'[3] The issue of sexual identity provides a fundamental challenge to received versions of modernism that have dominated across the earlier decades of the twentieth century. Presenting the apparent freedoms of lesbian practitioners when compared with their heterosexual peers is so striking to Benstock that she believes it reveals 'the cracks and divisions of the Modernist façade, exposing the ways in which individual contributions to this eclectic movement have been effaced in the effort to render Modernism monolithic.'[4] This, then, is the first notable function of the concept of a *lesbian* modernism: its ability to reveal the reality of modernism's multiple versions.

The strong emphasis on modes of living, intimacy and creativity is evident too in the work of Gillian Hanscombe and Virginia L. Smyers, whose *Writing for Their Lives: The Modernist Women, 1910–1940* traverses American and British literary and cultural landscapes to uncover the occluded lives and works of female modernism. In her Preface, Smyers writes that '[l]ives, the details of lives, what a person looked like, wore, ate, felt like, loved – have become almost obsessions with me.'[5] In the course of recuperating biographical narratives, Smyers, like Benstock, unearths the seeming link between sexuality and creativity:

> They all seemed to write to each other, or about each other. They introduced one to the other. They sometimes fell in love with each other or with each other's partners [. . .]. None of them seemed to live conventionally: some were lesbian, some were bisexual, some promiscuous, some seemingly asexual.[6]

Smyers's collaborator, the Australian scholar Gillian Hanscombe, who had been working on the 'forgotten' modernist Dorothy Richardson since the late 1970s, remarks, as they uncover the forgotten female network of writers, editors, artists and patrons at the heart of modernist cultural production, that 'it's another Bloomsbury.'[7] In her Preface, she argues that she is less concerned with biographical detail than with 'the nature of that network, and what it might reveal about the modern breaking down of boundaries between "art" and "life" which became known in literary history as modernism.'[8] Like Benstock,

Hanscombe too understands that the recovery of these female practitioners and their creative practices brings pressure to bear on received conceptions of canonical modernism.

What is particularly noteworthy, however, as we revisit these crucial recuperative interventions in the telling of the history of modernism in the 1980s, is Hanscombe's astute, and indeed reflexive, description of her own critical practice:

> In many ways I have fallen prey to that most a-historical of orientations during the preparation of this book: that is, the imagining of these writers as if they had not lived more than half a century ago, but as if they were still around, since – for me – so much of what interests me about them still seems both current and futuristic.[9]

As a lesbian feminist scholar, Hanscombe expresses a profound affective investment in this recalibration of the relationship between radical modes of living and aesthetic and literary experimentation: 'What I want to persuade you that how these women lived-what-they-wrote or wrote-what-they-lived is part of the jigsaw of women's cultural tradition and part, too, of the conditions we still write from today.'[10] For Hanscombe, this work of recovery provides a template for contemporary lives. This, then, is to acknowledge the second notable function of the concept of lesbian modernism, which is the way it speaks to, and of, the present moment in which it is described. As the field of critical study of the sexuality in, and of, modernism has burgeoned through the 1990s and into the first decades of the twenty-first century, other critical terms have emerged. To capture the enmeshment of aesthetic and material practices, and attending to the terminology used by some modernist practitioners themselves (perhaps most notably Natalie Barney, Virginia Woolf and H.D.), scholars such as Diana Collecott and Laura Doan have deployed the term 'Sapphic modernism.'[11] More recently, embracing principles of inclusivity but also undecidability, scholars have coined the term 'Queer modernism,' assertively drawing upon what Eve Kosofsky Sedgwick describes as the 'open mesh of possibilities, gaps, overlaps, dissonances and resonances' embedded and embodied within the paradigm of queerness and its textualities, as a way of describing sexually dissident modernism.[12] As I have argued previously, '[t]he body of criticism that has grown up out of the eventual recognition and recuperation of sexual dissidence within modernism has had to acknowledge its own contemporariness, its situatedness within its own cultural moment.'[13] The question of investment is evidenced in one of the most recent iterations of the concept of lesbian modernism, Diana Souhami's *No Modernism Without Lesbians*, published in 2020. The biographer of a sizable clutch of lesbian modernists, including Gluck, Gertrude Stein, Natalie Barney and Romaine

Brooks, Souhami confidently asserts that 'modernism would not have taken the shape it did without the lesbians who gravitated to Paris.'[14] Souhami has little truck with the complexities of either the historical accuracy of using the term 'lesbian' or the contemporary nuancing of sexual and gender identities:

> I call them all lesbians, but the words lesbian, dyke and daisy were not much used by them. [...] I duck the initialism of the present age: the LGBTQIA, the QUILTBAG (queer or questioning, undecided, intersex, lesbian, trans, bisexual, asexual or allied, gay or genderqueer) plus the +. [...] There are but twenty-six letters in the Roman alphabet and life is short.[15]

Souhami's dismissal of any engagement with terms other than 'lesbian,' in usage either *then* in the early twentieth century or *now* in our contemporary twenty-first-century context when terms are in such flux, forecloses any nuanced discussion of the complexity of identity and identification. By contrast, what Hanscombe and Smyers's framing of their use of terms such as 'lesbian' and their reading of the lives and works of these practitioners through their own lived experience and political beliefs bring into the discussion are our *own* practices as researchers into literary networks, our embodied, felt actions of research, investigation and interpretation as we attempt to reconfigure the map of a life, a literary work, an act – or acts – of collaboration and their places within the modernist network. This is important since both the concept of lesbian modernism and the terminology we use to construct it actually derive from *our* frames of reference, not those of the practitioners we read and research. In the next section, I consider the need for a reflexive research practice in which the affective processes of researching lesbian modernism are conceptualised and kept in view.

Reflexive Research Practice and Lesbian Modernism: Listening to the Ghost Notes

The material practice of music provides us with a useful metaphor: the ghost note. In music, a ghost note is a musical note with a rhythmic value, but no discernible pitch when played. There are various ways of recording a ghost note in musical notation, for example written in parentheses around the note head. On stringed instruments, the ghost note is played by sounding a muted string, so that it is percussive rather than pitched. On drums, ghost notes are played very softly in between the main notes and most commonly on the snare. Bass players will often use ghost notes for intensifying rhythm. In singing, ghost notes are most commonly words that are spoken in rhythm rather than sung.

The compelling thing about ghost notes is what they do to us as both musicians and listeners. The effect of the ghost note is to draw us in. Ghost notes pull at our ears and our bodies and our interest. They intensify the experience of rhythm even where they do not fully articulate it. Absence – or partial absence – is the very thing that connotes presence for us. The figure of the ghost is the manifestation of loss and also of return. Mostly of course, unless one is the musician who is playing them, ghost notes are things which do their work on us without our conscious awareness; unless one is listening very carefully, we do not hear them. Or perhaps we might say, if the music is to have the most profound effect on us, it is better if we are simply listening and not hearing.

This binary opposition between hearing and listening can be drawn out through the work of the French philosopher Jean-Luc Nancy. At the outset of his book *Listening*, Nancy issues a provocation to the discipline of philosophy: he asks, 'Is listening something of which philosophy is capable?'[16] In other words, Nancy asks, can philosophy throw off its compulsion to assume prior knowledge, even as it approaches experience and interpretation, and can it open itself to a position of unknowingness? Nancy writes, 'Isn't the philosopher someone who always hears (and hears everything), but who cannot listen, or who, more precisely, neutralizes listening within himself, so that he can philosophize?'[17] Nancy draws the distinction between *hearing* – in French, *entendre* – and *listening* – in French, *écouter*. *Entendre* means 'to hear' but it 'also means *comprendre*, "to understand," as if "hearing" were above all "hearing say" (rather than "hearing sound"), [. . .] regardless of whether the sound perceived was a word or not.'[18] By contrast, in relation to *écouter*, Nancy asks:

> What secret is at stake when one truly *listens*, that is, when one tries to capture or surprise the sonority rather than the message? **What secret is yielded – hence also made public – when we listen to a voice, an instrument, or a sound just for itself?** And the other, indissociable aspect will be: what does *to be* listening, *to be* all ears, as one would say 'to be in the world,' mean? What does it mean to exist according to listening, for it and through it, what part of experience and truth is put into play? What is at play in listening, what resonates in it, what is the tone of listening or its timbre? Is even listening itself sonorous?[19]

Listening describes an act in which one is open to *receiving*. What is of real interest in Nancy's formulation is the concept of the secret which reveals itself to the one who listens to *sound* rather than *meaning*. The resonance of this formulation deepens as it develops into a discussion about subjectivity – the observation that listening becomes a way of being as well as an act of using the aural senses. True listening, according to Nancy, is 'always to be on the edge of meaning, or in an edgy meaning of extremity, and as if the sound were precisely nothing else than this edge, this fringe, this margin [. . .].'[20] To be sure, according to Nancy, listening is not easy for the subject accustomed to feeling she knows the truth before she hears it, or as she hears it. Listening therefore requires a tolerance of uncertainty, of ambiguity, a preparedness to not *know* from the outset. We might slice this issue in a similar way through the frame of Roland Barthes's account of listening: '*Hearing* is a physiological phenomenon; *listening* is a psychological act.'[21] If listening is a psychological act, the listener's psyche, identity, memory, projections, repudiations come into the frame. One's ability to listen depends upon who one is, how one functions, where one is located.

Let me stitch this back into my main discussion about reflexive research into lesbian modernism by rephrasing Nancy:

> Isn't the *researcher* someone who always hears (and hears everything), but who cannot listen, or who, more precisely, neutralises listening within herself, so that she can *research*? Do we *neutralise* listening in ourselves as we contemplate the networks of modernism?

To what extent has the unearthing and conceptualising of lesbian modernism required the individual researcher to listen to ghost notes, instead of hearing the reiteration of versions of history and human behaviour and cultural production that resemble dominant culture? In this regard, my use of the concept of the ghost note constitutes an interesting parallel with Terry Castle's iconic and influential term 'the apparitional lesbian.' As Castle notes in relation to the visual vocabularies of twentieth-century film, '[t]he lesbian remains a kind of "ghost effect" in the cinema world of modern life: elusive, vaporous, difficult to spot – even when she is there, in plain view, mortal and magnificent, at the center of the screen.'[22] Castle describes the necessary 'task of refocusing' undertaken in interpretive work by the critic that will give the ghostly, occluded figure of the lesbian fleshly form.[23] Similarly, I would argue that in the many instances of the biographical and literary interpretations undertaken in work on lesbian modernism, the listening researcher must learn to recognise the pull of the ghost notes, the blips, glitches and disturbances of the dominant narratives of modernism, since it is these that constitute the first traces of the sexual and literary dissidence defined as lesbian modernism.

As a lesbian modernist scholar, whose work in the field began with Dorothy Richardson, I have continued to be drawn in my encounter with both her literary oeuvre and her life story by the ghost note of dissident sexuality. Its rhythm has been insistent, syncopating my responses to the archival materials of letters, manuscripts and photographs, as well as my critical reading of certain of the novels in the *Pilgrimage* series. The recentralisation of Richardson within the field of modernist critical studies has most recently been advanced by the Dorothy Richardson Scholarly Editions Project, in which Richardson's life-work *Pilgrimage* is being produced in a new eight-volume critical edition, and her extensive correspondence is being published in a first full three-volume annotated collection.[24] Archival work on the Project has uncovered not only new textual materials but also narratives of lived experience and familial intervention into both the publication of Richardson's final novel *March Moonlight* and biographical accounts of her life. These findings require astute critical analysis and revisions of what we understand as the relationship between textual production and sexual history, and also have bearing upon our critical understanding of what lesbian modernism might mean in relation to Richardson.

'Relaunching Richardson': Lesbian Modernism *avant la lettre*

Richardson's archive is extensive, spread across continents in university and library holdings in the US and the UK.[25] Whilst few full manuscripts remain from the *Pilgrimage* series, there are voluminous amounts of Richardson's letters, essays and photographs, as well as critical writings about her work. Amongst the writings on Richardson, prominent figures such as John Cowper Powys and Horace Gregory have received previous scholarly attention. However, one of the connected holdings in the Harry Ransom Center, University of Texas at Austin, contains a notebook and papers about Richardson, written by the little-known mid-twentieth-century writer Kay Dick. We understand lesbian modernism as a relatively recent critical term and the recuperative work of the 1980s as the first real engagement with sexual dissidence within modernism. Yet Dick's mid-twentieth-century engagement with *Pilgrimage*, and her committed endeavour to produce critical work that acknowledges and theorises the foundational theme of same-sex desire and sexuality in Richardson's work and life, demonstrates the strength of what I am calling the ghost note of sexual dissidence. It also evidences that an understanding of enmeshment of sexuality and modernist creativity was formulated relatively soon after the end of the modernist period.

Born in London in 1915, educated in Geneva, Dick finally settled in the literary networks of London, working as an influential editor for P.S. King & Son and writing articles for the *New Statesman*.[26] Dick was involved in a twenty-year relationship with the novelist Kathleen Farrell, and was open about her sexual identity. Kay is diminished and dismissed by Michael De-la-Noy, in the obituary he writes for her in *The Guardian*, as being '[f]or many years [. . .] at the centre of literary intrigue and gossip. She expended far more energy in pursuing personal vendettas and romantic lesbian friendships than in writing books.'[27] The recent republication of her radical dystopian novel *They* (1977) has prompted a revision of Dick's literary status. Sam Knight notes:

> During the Second World War, at the age of twenty-six, Dick had been the first female director of a British publishing house. Under a pseudonym, she edited *The Windmill*, a literary magazine, where she commissioned

work from George Orwell. (Orwell inscribed her copy of *Animal Farm*: 'Kay—To make it and me acceptable.') Dick was bohemian and fully on the scene. She wore a monocle, used a long cigarette holder, and kept her short hair in a permanent wave.[28]

In 1956, Dick read Richardson's *Pilgrimage* for the first time, prompted by references to her work in American scholar Leon Edel's critical work *The Psychological Novel: 1900–1950*.[29] Dick was so compelled by the novel-sequence that she started immediately on her own critical interpretation, making a series of notes about the novels which attempted to trace their main themes and method of construction. Reading the third novel, *Honeycomb*, Dick notes Richardson's coverage of 'the "Wilde" scandal' (meaning the trial of Oscar Wilde in 1895); she maps the events onto Richardson's own life, working out that she is in her twenties at the time Wilde was prosecuted.[30] She finds 'the "hint" of homosexual love' in the novel. In her notes on the fourth novel, *The Tunnel*, Dick pays close attention to modernist form, noting it to be 'more "ambitious" as a novel' and 'more fitted to the "str[eam] of consc[iousness]" label.'[31] By the fifth novel, *Interim*, Dick is engrossed and asking questions about Richardson's representation (or lack of it) of sexuality: 'What is lacking in DR? The basic lack? She lacks the passion of love – the backdrop of its absolute necessity even if her Miriam doesn't experience sex.'[32] Later, it would appear that Dick hears a particularly striking ghost note in the tenth novel of the series *Dawn's Left Hand*, writing that 'this is the 1st important revelatory novel.'[33] She is particularly drawn to what she reads as its lesbian subtext: 'DR didn't dare show sexual love between M and Amabel – she was quite "daring" in the sleeping with love together and the obvious sense of <u>real</u> satisfaction as contrast with sex with Hypo.'[34] This concept of authorial 'daring' is surely profound in 1956, in a mid-century context in which the prevailing homophobia within British culture might be epitomised by the brutal treatment of the mathematician and computer scientist Alan Turing, who died by suicide in 1954 after enforced chemical castration in the wake of being charged with 'gross indecency.'[35] Determined to reintroduce Richardson to the reading public, Dick conceives to write a critical book which explores Richardson's writing practice in *Pilgrimage*. In May of 1956 she approaches J. M. Dent & Sons, Richardson's British publisher, trying to locate her whereabouts. Despite an initially positive response, it very quickly appears that Richardson is a lost object, even to the editors at Dent. A. J. Hoppé replies to Dick's enquiry saying:

> I am so sorry to have misinformed you about Dorothy Richardson. As a matter of fact we have heard nothing of her since her affairs passed, under Power of Attorney, into the hands of a gentleman who is our only contact with her.[36]

This 'gentleman' is Philip Batchelor, Richardson's nephew. Richardson, it transpires, is still alive in 1956, sequestered in a nursing home in Beckenham in Kent, where she has been placed apparently against her will by Batchelor and her sister-in-law, Rose Odle. Rose Odle had married Edwin Odle, the brother of Alan Odle, with whom Richardson had formed a late marriage.

Dick, undaunted, persists and writes back to Hoppé with the extent of her plans to 'relaunch' Richardson; she plans, alongside her critical book, readings from *Pilgrimage* for the BBC and a British Council pamphlet. With great vigour she remarks, 'I am getting really going in this quest for D.R.'[37] Here, it is notable that Dick demonstrates the same strong affective pull to recover Richardson's work and life that we see repeated in the recuperative archival work undertaken by later twentieth-century scholars such as Hanscombe and Smyers.

By early June, Dick has managed to make contact with Rose Odle and later in June, Dick, accompanied by her partner, Farrell, makes several trips to see Odle at her home in Biggin Hill in Kent. They record their experience of these meetings in a notebook (Figure 12.1).

The notebook's narrative reads like a ghost story. It is a work with two voices, written in a mix of Dick's and Farrell's handwriting, with each dated

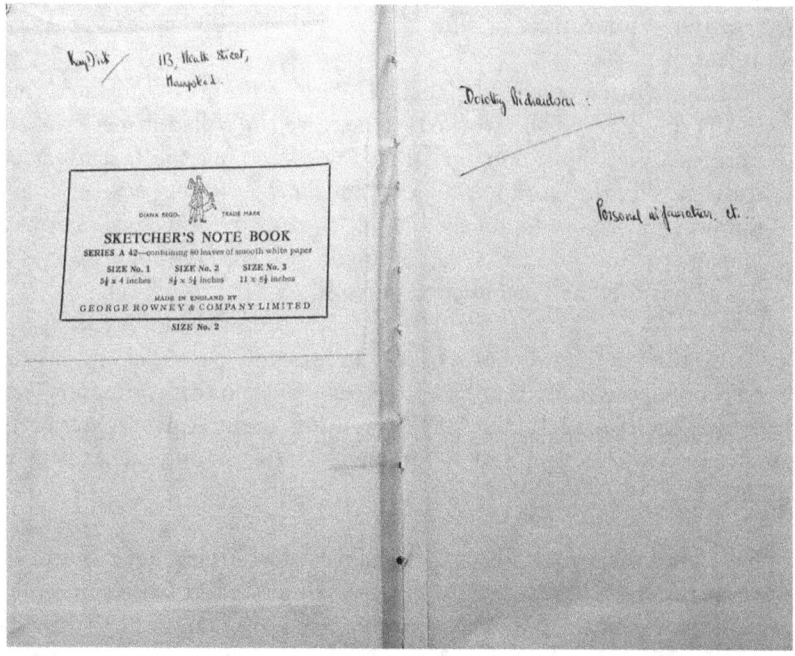

Figure 12.1 Kay Dick's 'Dorothy Richardson' notebook, Series I Works, Kay Dick Papers, Harry Ransom Center, University of Texas at Austin

encounter with Odle written up by one of them. Richardson, aged eighty-four, is resident nine miles away from Odle's house in a nursing home in Beckenham, Kent. Odle herself is living down a relatively remote country lane. The notebook details how Dick and Farrell's repeated requests to meet with Richardson are blocked by Odle, who moves between describing Richardson as on the one hand near death, and on the other as being mobile and communicating. Dick notes that 'Rose has a miscellaneous assortment of D.R. papers i.e. odds & ends of biographical notes, letters, cuttings, photographs, books, MSS & periodicals which contain D.R's freelance journalism. She refuses to let these papers go out of her possession.'[38] Dick and Farrell realise that one of the things Odle is hiding amongst these papers is an unpublished manuscript – the unfinished text of *March Moonlight*, the thirteenth novel of the *Pilgrimage* series. In 1956, all that existed of this novel in the public domain were three draft sections of the novel, titled only 'Work in Progress,' which had been published in 1946 in Bryher's magazine *Life and Letters*.[39] Farrell notes:

> R.O. says she saw some of *March Moonlight* when it was being 'written' & thought it 'confused' – when Kay suggests it might be published, as an unfinished work, R.O. said it would be of no interest to anybody and did not want to pursue the subject.
>
> I think, but cannot be sure, there are about 200 pages of typescript – at least.
>
> R.O. has it in envelope labelled Work in Progress and said 'you see this is the last mss she worked on because she called it merely work in progress.' But on looking at DMR's notes I think she first intended to use this as a title 'work in progress' not *March Moonlight* – so far as one knows it may even be finished (some of the novels were short ones) or almost so. One wonders whether anyone except possibly R.O. has read it – or has even had a chance to do so.[40]

The couple's tone in the notebook grows increasingly paranoid and disturbed as they become convinced that Odle is keeping Richardson's literary effects hidden away in locked bookcases, preventing unpublished material from entering the public domain and suppressing 'truths' about Richardson from emerging:

> Even bookcases R.O. keeps locked up as she 'got her keys' out to show us something – but never I think, showed it. So it is obvious that the few parcels of stuff she did produce were sorted out as most likely to inflame much curiosity and she was determined that we should not be able to lay our hands on anything she did not want us to see. In an isolated place like that and living the kind of odd existence she does, it is most unlikely

that she would in the usual way keep bookcases locked up. Whole atmosphere <u>very</u> strange.[41]

The couple never gain access to the manuscript of *March Moonlight*. Odle refuses to let them see it. If we think about both the biographical and literary processes of relaunching Richardson at this point in the 1950s, we might argue that Rose Odle functions as a block, a stop, a silencing. A strained communication continues between the couple and Odle in which there is a kind of cat-and-mouse game in which Odle promises to show material or provide new information, but never fulfils these promises. The remainder of 1956 passes in letters between Dick and Odle, and there is a kind of fantasy enacted in which Odle ostensibly confers upon Dick the right to be the one to reinstate Richardson within the literary landscape. Hanging over this correspondence is Richardson's slow progress towards death, which finally happens the next summer on 17 June 1957. At the point of Richardson's death, when Odle discovers that she has been made literary executor, the tone of her letters to Dick rapidly changes. On 23 July 1957, she writes:

> Dear Kay Dick,
> I want to explain to you my rather brief note sent to you recently.
> As I made clear at the time when you made copies of letters and MSS. concerning D. M. Richardson, I had not yet the right to give permission for publication of any of this matter.
> Seeing that you were then hopeful of an Article in 'Encounter' I thought this would help you to get the atmosphere, and as you were so interested in D. M. Richardson I gave all the help I could.
> Now that it has been confirmed in D. M. Richardson's Will that I am her Literary Executor, I have had to make definite decisions about the use of this material. Therefore, I cannot agree to any letters or other matter shown to you or copied by you, being published.
> [. . .]
> Yours sincerely,
> Rose I. Odle[42]

Dick replies assertively, and indeed defensively, as soon as she receives this letter:

> Dear Mrs. Odle,
> This is to acknowledge your letter of July the 23rd. There appears to be some misapprehension on your part, because I have made no copies of any Dorothy Richardson letters or manuscripts, having, in fact, hardly seen many and having had no opportunity of studying those which you did show me.

You will no doubt recall that when you showed me a large box of miscellaneous articles, review cuttings, photographs, notes, etc., concerning Dorothy Richardson and invited me to make copies there and then I told you I would much prefer to study these at leisure.

[. . .]

I am pleased to hear that a collection of Dorothy Richardson's letters are being prepared for publication. This will help all future critical appreciations of her work. I gather that Miss Stella Martin Curry [sic] is editing this, or is it with you?[43] I shall much look forward to reading the published volume.

[. . .]

Yours sincerely,[44]

In an immediate reply, Odle delivers her fateful blow of foreclosing Dick's determination to reintroduce Richardson's 'daring' lesbian literary experimentation to literary culture:

Dear Kay Dick

Thank you for your letter. No, of course not S. M. Curry [sic]. I consulted her on quite another matter to do with plays, as she has written them. No, it is a writer and critic famous for the work he has done on writers and novels; I felt it only fair to D's memory to accept the offer of a man whose reputation will place her among the classical writers.

Otherwise I would not have gone back on an implied intention. The book will not be begun until 2 years time. Meanwhile I am to collect material. What was to have been a critical work is (in view of the fresh material that has come to hand, revealing so much more of the essential D.M.R.) is to become also a biography; either including the letters, or possibly these may make a separate volume.

Indeed I feel your interest in D.M.R.'s work to be so genuine that it is as much as I can do not to show you this fresh material. But the author in question will not touch the biography unless he has access to unpublished matter. So that I am anxious, for the sake of D's niche in the future that any particular, or intimate matter you copied, whether of a dramatic or very 'newsy' value, should not be out prematurely.

[. . .]

Yours sincerely,
Rose I. Odle

Various factors appear to be at play in Odle's initial dalliance with Dick and Farrell: status, power, gender, and ultimately sexual identity. Odle tantalises with the promise of 'fresh material' that will reveal more about Richardson, but there is another male writer and critic whose own reputation will do more to enhance Richardson's own. The man whom Odle refuses to name in the brush-off letter to Dick, and to whom she commits to give full access to Richardson's papers, somewhat ironically, given the fact that his critical work was Dick's first exposure to Dorothy Richardson, was Leon Edel. Identifying exactly what the 'fresh material' was, with the benefit of hindsight and seventy years' more research into Richardson's estate, it is likely that Odle was offering Edel access to the bundle she describes as *Work in Progress*, likely the draft materials of *March Moonlight*, and also letters between Richardson and Veronica Grad, the real-life equivalent of the character of Amabel in the *Pilgrimage* series, with whom Richardson had a long and complicated romantic, and likely sexual, relationship.[45]

'Finesse the lesbian theme': Acts of Biographical Burying

Leon Edel's principal reputation was as a Henry James scholar. He produced a five-volume *Henry James: A Biography*, which was published between 1953 and 1972. As well as a practitioner, Edel was also a theorist of biographical technique. Summarising his theory of biographical practice, one might say that he believed in the imbrication of the biographer with the biographical subject, the need for the biographer to produce his own psychologically inflected account of the life:

> The great and important biographies [. . .] derive from feelings akin to love and are written because the biographer feels a need to explore the given life regardless of publisher interest and possible success. Since we are focusing on biography as an art, let me put it this way: biography for better or worse is an involvement with another person; if the biographer forms an attachment or is 'hooked', the affair can last for years. It acquires, at any rate, a history of its own, a very complex history.[46]

Edel's notion of 'a very complex history' is, to put it bluntly, an understatement. As Michael Anesko notes, Edel described other scholars working on James as 'trespassers' on his territory.[47] Anesko details the way in which the 'restrictions concerning the use and publication of the James papers were lifted' only after the last volume of Edel's biography of James was published.[48]

Edel did not, in fact, go on to write the definitive text on Richardson; that task fell to his PhD student Gloria Glikin Fromm, who goes on, a decade later in the 1960s, to become embroiled with Rose Odle again. Fromm, like Dick, endures another cat-and-mouse game in which the ghost note of lesbian sexuality plays over and over again. In 1970, counselling Fromm about the difficulties of the block posed by Odle, Edel writes:

> Stop <u>stewing</u> in your old power-struggle with Rose – stop using it as a deterrent to finishing the book. Simply <u>finish the book</u>. That is the main

> thing: whether there is more material or not – whether she will try to blast you or not – get the thing done, as quickly as you can. One never can know everything: you know enough – *and you can certainly finesse the lesbian theme as I did the Andersen story*. This is all I can answer. The book can stand up – and you can take your chances.[49]

What Edel does with 'the Andersen story' in his Henry James biography is to write out, to obscure, the intimate relationship between James and the Norwegian-American sculptor Hendrik Christian Andersen.[50] And, indeed, what Fromm does in the biography that she finally published in 1977 is to provide a mixture of obfuscation and conjecture about the complex web of love, desire and repudiation that underpins the relationship between Richardson and Veronica Grad:

> Veronica stayed with Dorothy through that night; and in trying to comfort her, Dorothy grasped the full extent of her extravagant feelings: Veronica was convinced not merely that there was a special sympathy between her and Dorothy, but that they were two halves of a single whole. Dorothy understood at last that Veronica wanted to share her life, to experience *everything* in common.[51]

With the somewhat oblique reference to Plato's *Symposium*, and the Platonic model of lovers as two halves of a whole, and the coy use of the italicised 'everything,' Fromm indeed 'finesses' the lesbian 'theme' in Richardson's biography, obscuring it sufficiently that it disappears beneath a more legible narrative of heterosexuality, seemingly secured by Richardson's relationships with H. G. Wells and Benjamin Grad and her eventual late marriage to Alan Odle. What Dick might have done with the materials, how she might have listened, understood and represented Richardson's lesbian modernism, will never be known.

The Fate of *March Moonlight*

The final novel of the *Pilgrimage* series, *March Moonlight*, unpublished and most likely unfinished at the time of Richardson's death in 1957, is one of the most important texts when it comes to Richardson's lesbian modernism. As I have previously written, alongside the typescript manuscript that was eventually placed in the Beinecke Rare Book and Manuscript Library at Yale, there are some handwritten manuscript fragments that differ from the typescript and show heavy revisions and the censoring out of an explicit story of lesbian desire.[52] In the light of this archival research, and the (as it transpires correct) suspicions of Dick and Farrell, it is clear that Odle was aware of the literary, and more importantly financial, capital that was in her possession with the manuscript draft of *March Moonlight*. In amongst these torsions and derailments of material and the ghost note of sexual identity, what happened to the manuscript that Odle held in her locked bookcases in Biggin Hill? For one thing, the provenance of the carbon copy of the 161-page typescript manuscript is not clear, and there is no full autograph manuscript against which to compare it. All that remains in Richardson's hand are fragments. In this regard a strong ghost note sounds here about censorship, and Odle's possible intervention in the shape of the text.

From the early 1960s, in addition to her communications with Edel about the publication of letters, a biography and this final instalment of the *Pilgrimage* series, Odle was in touch with the American poet and critic Horace Gregory. Gregory, who had corresponded with Richardson in the 1930s, was keen to write a book about Richardson and her work, a plan that was strongly encouraged by Odle for the way in which it would raise Richardson's profile and her literary stock in the marketplace. Gregory's first thought is a biography, and he and Odle correspond about Richardson's letters and personal papers. The theme of sexual identity is revealed and then foreclosed in a letter Odle writes to Gregory in 1964:

> Something else re D has turned up. I told you 'Amabel' (Vera Grad – who married Benjamin ie. Michael) rang me up full of hatred, alternately with adoration, the day of D's death, and asked for her wedding ring, which she now has. The son, David, kept as resolutely apart on the two occasions when they came to see me at 13. Hillside.
>
> Before I left London: a man rang me up and said he knew Miss Natalie Barney, now 87, and living in Paris, knew D.M.R. She had written a book 'Sexual Variations in Women' and gave D.M.R. as an example of a lesbian. I so disliked the tone of the man, the whole idea, that I did not follow this up. But it might explain the reluctance of 'Amabel's' son to let her talk to me, and their attitude of withholding any information as they thought the private life of authors was not for publication.
>
> My own attitude is that there may have been a passing phase with D. – it may have made her afraid of women later, but I think more as rivals, where literature and men were concerned, than in any intimate relationship. The importance of all sorts of sex relationship has been over-emphasised so much in our time. Much of what I tell you, is for you to know, not necessarily to impart. That is for your judgement. I am certain that from the time I knew her – 1917 there was no such lesbian tendency.[53]

Letters from Odle to Gregory also show that, as she had done with Edel, the promise of the unpublished manuscript of the final novel of *Pilgrimage* is a bargaining chip:

> Re <u>Moonlight</u>. Dent's have told me they would consider a volume of miscellanea, letters, stories, articles on D. How about such, to include

> 'Moonlight.' Have you, or Edel, a bright student [. . .] who might start now to prepare such??? [. . .] I watched 'Moonlight' collect dust on her table for some years. Untouched.[54]

For his part, Gregory wanted to release the unpublished material from *Pilgrimage* at the same time as his proposed book. Serendipitously, Gregory's son, Patrick Gregory, was working for Alfred A. Knopf, Richardson's American publisher. In a cryptic postscript to a memo sent between senior members of the editorial team at Knopf, about the potential reprint of the *Pilgrimage* series in a collected edition, reference is made to the hidden history of *Pilgrimage* and the location of 'the manuscript of the concluding section' (Figure 12.2).[55]

March Moonlight was incorporated into the four-volume collected edition of *Pilgrimage* that was published in 1967 by J. M. Dent & Sons in the UK and Alfred A. Knopf in the US. It was timed to hit the literary marketplace at the same time as Gregory's *Dorothy Richardson: An Adventure in Self-Discovery*, which was framed as 'a brilliant examination' of Richardson's life and work that was based on unique access to 'private papers and correspondences,' as well as 'the recent discovery of the unpublished manuscript of the final section of *Pilgrimage*' which 'enables the reader for the first time to view Miss Richardson's work as a complete cycle.'[56] Gregory's book was dedicated to Rose Odle.

Hidden in Plain Sight

Dick's experience with the ghost note of sexual dissidence she listens to in the work and life of Richardson, her frustrating encounter between 1956 and 1957 with Odle, and her lived experience of how lesbian sexuality can be rendered an object hidden in plain sight may never have made it into a critical work on lesbian modernism (should she have chosen to use the later term), but it may well have found its way symbolically into her own fiction. In 1984, Dick publishes *The Shelf*, a remarkable novel in which a clandestine lesbian relationship is finally revealed through letters that have remained sequestered away until their author dies. To quote the synopsis of the novel in its back matter:

> 'The shelf' is a repository in the coroner's office where Cassandra's letters to Anne had first been lodged – as well as that other, unposted letter found in Anne's handbag. It was all so long ago – back in the 1960s – but Cass has not been able to forget the passion Anne engendered in her, their brief affair, and the mystery that ended it.[57]

The frame of the novel itself is a confessional letter Cass writes to her friend Francis many years after the affair. The resolution of the retold story – after Anne's suicide – is the restitution of these intimate letters, including the love letter-cum-suicide note that Anne writes Cass, into Cass's own hands. Narrative

ALFRED A. KNOPF, Inc., 501 Madison Avenue, N.Y.C. 22

DATE: 10/19/65

MEMO TO: Mr. Koshland

FROM: Mr. Lowry

I have just been informed by a usually reliable source that we are going to republish by means of sheet import from Dent PILGRIMAGE by Dorothy Richardson. Do you think that there is any way that I could in the future be informed of these decisions before they become firm?

It would seem to make little sense to arrange for a sheet import deal before canvassing the subsidiary rights situation. Is it too late to second-guess you on this?

TL:jp

P.S. I think it would be well were you to quiz Pat Gregory about his special knowledge that PILGRIMAGE was never finished and that he knows somebody who has the manuscript of the concluding section (mentioning, of course, no names).

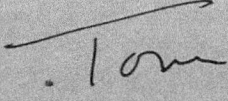

Figure 12.2 Thomas Lowry's editorial memo to William A. Koshland about the 'March Moonlight' manuscript

closure is thus achieved when these intimate written objects are returned to their rightful owner. The letters are given to Cass by the Coroner's Office police officer who has investigated Anne's death. The police officer's actions in *The Shelf* might be read as a symbolic intervention of the forces of justice and authority into the writing – and righting – of history. Critically, we might understand the novel is a material attempt to redress the familial and socio-cultural power structures that defeated Dick.

The Dick materials cast yet more new light on the apparent 'conundrum' of the sexualities embedded and narrated in the *Pilgrimage* series, but in addition, and in a way that moves beyond the specificity of Richardson's oeuvre, they call into question the willed *mis*reading of biographers, critics and scholars that has often reduced dissident sexuality to something hidden in plain sight. There is a politics of visibility here. Dick's thwarted quest to 'relaunch' Richardson in the 1950s has a strong valency in our current moment, as sexual desires, gendered identities and liveable lives, and the terms we choose to use to describe them, swirl potently in cultural, political and academic discourse. Using the example of this recent archival scholarship as a test case, I would argue that we need to retain a notion of lesbian modernism in play, for all its provisionality and its multiple iterations within modernist critical studies, for what it keeps open, and what it continues to challenge.

NOTES

1. See Gillian Hanscombe and Virginia L. Smyers, *Writing for Their Lives: The Modernist Women, 1910–1940* (London: The Women's Press, 1987).
2. Shari Benstock, 'Preface,' in *Women of the Left Bank: Paris, 1900–1940* (London: Virago, 1987), n.p. (emphasis in the original).
3. Ibid.
4. Ibid.
5. Virginia L. Smyers, 'Preface II,' in Hanscombe and Smyers, *Writing for Their Lives*, xvi–xviii, xvi.
6. Ibid., xvii.
7. Gillian Hanscombe, 'Preface I,' in Hanscombe and Smyers, *Writing for Their Lives*, xiii–xv, xiv.
8. Ibid., xiv.
9. Ibid., xiv–xv.
10. Ibid., xv.
11. See, amongst other titles, Diana Collecott, *H.D. and Sapphic Modernism 1910–1950* (Cambridge: Cambridge University Press, 1999); Laura Doan, *Fashioning Sapphism: The Origins of a Modern English Lesbian Culture* (New York: Columbia University Press, 2001); and Laura Doan and Jane Garrity, eds, *Sapphic Modernities: Sexuality, Women and National Culture* (Basingstoke: Palgrave Macmillan, 2006).
12. Eve Kosofsky Sedgwick, *Tendencies* (Durham, NC: Duke University Press, 1993), 8. For queer modernism, see, amongst other titles, Robert L. Caserio, 'Queer Modernism,' in *The Oxford Handbook of Modernisms*, ed. Peter Brooker, Andrzej

Gąsiorek, Deborah Longworth and Andrew Thacker (Oxford: Oxford University Press, 2010), 199–217; and Penny Farfan, *Performing Queer Modernism* (Oxford: Oxford University Press, 2017).
13. Joanne Winning, 'Lesbian Sexuality in the Story of Modernism,' in Brooker et al., *Oxford Handbook of Modernisms*, 218–34, 234.
14. Diana Souhami, *No Modernism Without Lesbians* (London: Head of Zeus, 2020), 20.
15. Ibid., 14–15.
16. Jean-Luc Nancy, *Listening* (New York: Fordham University Press, 2007), 1.
17. Ibid.
18. Ibid., 6.
19. Ibid., 5 (emphasis mine).
20. Ibid., 7.
21. Roland Barthes, 'Listening,' in *The Responsibility of Forms* (Berkeley: University of California Press, 1991), 245.
22. Terry Castle, *The Apparitional Lesbian: Female Homosexuality and Modern Culture* (New York: Columbia University Press, 1993), 2.
23. Ibid., 3.
24. See 'Dorothy Richardson Scholarly Editions Project,' Dorothy Richardson Website, accessed 2 August 2022, https://www.keele.ac.uk/drsep/.
25. Dorothy Richardson's main archives are held at: Beinecke Rare Book & Manuscript Library; Harry Ransom Center, University of Texas at Austin; New York Public Library; McFarlin Library, University of Tulsa; and the British Library.
26. See 'Kay Dick,' Curtis Brown Group, accessed 2 August 2022, https://www.curtisbrown.co.uk/client/kay-dick.
27. Michael De-la-Noy, 'Kay Dick,' *The Guardian*, 24 October 2001.
28. Sam Knight, 'Rediscovering a Lost Dystopia and Its Prescient Author,' *The New Yorker*, 2 February 2022, accessed 8 April 2022, https://www.newyorker.com/news/letter-from-the-uk/rediscovering-a-lost-dystopia-and-its-radical-author. See Kay Dick, *They* [Foreword by Carmen Maria Machado] (London: Faber & Faber, 2022).
29. See Leon Edel, *The Psychological Novel: 1900–1950* (London: Rupert Hart-Davies, 1955).
30. Autograph notes, n.p. Kay Dick Papers, Series I Works, Harry Ransom Center, University of Texas at Austin.
31. Ibid.
32. Ibid.
33. Ibid.
34. Ibid.
35. See Andrew Hodges, *Alan Turing: An Enigma* (London: Vintage, 2014).
36. A. J. Hoppé to Kay Dick, typescript letter dated 16 May 1956. Kay Dick Papers, Series II Correspondence, Harry Ransom Center, University of Texas at Austin.
37. Kay Dick to A. J. Hoppé, typescript copy of letter dated 7 June 1956. Kay Dick Papers, Series II Correspondence, Harry Ransom Center, University of Texas at Austin.
38. Kay Dick and Kathleen Farrell, 'Dorothy Richardson' notebook, Kay Dick Papers, Series I Works, Harry Ransom Center, University of Texas at Austin, 4.

39. See Dorothy Richardson, 'Work in Progress,' *Life and Letters* 49 (April 1946): 20–44; 'Work in Progress,' *Life and Letters* 49 (May 1946): 99–114; and 'Work in Progress,' *Life and Letters* 51 (November 1946): 79–88.
40. Kay Dick and Kathleen Farrell, 'Dorothy Richardson' notebook, Kay Dick Papers, Series I Works, Harry Ransom Center, University of Texas at Austin, 34.
41. Ibid., 35.
42. Rose Odle to Kay Dick, typescript letter dated 23 July 1957. Kay Dick Papers, Series II Correspondence, Harry Ransom Center, University of Texas at Austin.
43. Stella Martin Currey (1907–94) was a British/South African writer, who wrote fiction, plays for radio and television, and short stories. Her most famous text is *One Woman's Year*, first published in 1953 and still in print with Persephone Books.
44. Kay Dick to Rose Odle, typescript copy of letter dated 24 July 1957. Kay Dick Papers, Series II Correspondence, Harry Ransom Center, University of Texas at Austin.
45. For further discussion of the complicated relationship between Dorothy Richardson and Veronica Grad, see Gillian E. Hanscombe, *The Art of Life: Dorothy Richardson and the Development of Feminist Consciousness* (London: Peter Owen, 1983); Joanne Winning, *The Pilgrimage of Dorothy Richardson* (Madison: University of Wisconsin Press, 2000); and 'Chronology,' in *The Oxford Edition of the Works of Dorothy Richardson, Volume IV*, ed. Scott McCracken (Oxford: Oxford University Press, 2020), xxi–xxxviii.
46. Leon Edel, 'The Art of Biography,' *Paris Review* no. 98 (Winter 1985), accessed 28 May 2022, https://www.theparisreview.org/interviews/2844/the-art-of-biography-no-1-leon-edel.
47. Michael Anesko, *Monopolizing the Master: Henry James and the Politics of Modern Literary Scholarship* (Stanford, CA: Stanford University Press, 2012), xiii.
48. Ibid.
49. Leon Edel to Gloria Glikin [Fromm], autograph letter dated 2 August 1970. Gloria G. Fromm Papers, Harry Ransom Center, University of Texas at Austin (emphasis mine).
50. For a full account of Edel's attempts to control access to letters and to manipulate the representation of the James–Andersen relationship, see Michael Anesco, 'The Legend of the Bastard,' in *Monopolizing the Master*, 158–92.
51. Gloria G. Fromm, *Dorothy Richardson: A Biography* (Athens and London: University of Georgia Press, 1994), 54.
52. See Winning, *Pilgrimage*.
53. Rose Odle to Horace Gregory, autograph letter dated 10 November 1964. Series I Correspondence, Dorothy Richardson Collection, Beinecke Rare Book and Manuscript Library, Yale University.
54. Rose Odle to Horace Gregory, autograph letter, n.d., Series I Correspondence, Dorothy Richardson Collection, Beinecke Rare Book and Manuscript Library, Yale University.
55. Typescript memo, Thomas Lowry to William A. Koshland, Alfred A. Knopf, Inc. Records, Harry Ransom Center, University of Texas at Austin.
56. Front matter, in Horace Gregory, *Dorothy Richardson: An Adventure in Self-Discovery* (New York: Holt, Rinehart and Winston, 1967).
57. Back matter, in Kay Dick, *The Shelf* (London: Gay Men's Press, 1984).

INDEX

Ackland, Valentine, 34
Alcott, Louisa May, 171
anachronism, 20, 34, 36, 91, 225–6, 236–7, 239, 243; *see also* queer theory/studies, queer temporalities
Ancient Greece, 7–9, 67, 69, 147, 231–2; *see also* homosexuality (male) and Hellenism; Sappho
Andersen, Hendrik Christian, 278
Anderson, Margaret, 34, 167, 204, 211–12, 218
My Thirty Years' War (1930), 167
antiracism, 13, 261
Antoinette, Marie, 101, 106–7
art history, feminist approaches to, 16, 17, 124–5, 136
asceticism, 18, 57–8, 65–9, 75n53
asexuality, 41, 62, 70, 75n41, 75n42, 157, 266, 268
Atwood, Tony, 57, 60, 71, 72n7, 77n74
autobiography, 14, 20, 38, 58, 61, 70–1, 74n36, 80, 93n6, 102, 117n23, 165–74

Balzac, Honoré de, 8, 83, 85
Barnacle, Nora, 211

Barnes, Djuna, 15, 38–40, 41, 134, 167, 226, 247n79
and Edna St. Vincent Millay, 226, 244n7
and James Joyce, 209–10
Ladies Almanack (1928), 6–7, 9, 11, 26n59, 38, 39, 41, 84, 166, 212, 243
Nightwood (1936), 3, 26n59, 39
'Paprika Johnson' (1915), 209
Barney, Natalie Clifford, 7, 18–19, 27n76, 34, 38, 39, 78–96, 126, 140n36, 166, 239, 241, 267, 279
and Honoré de Balzac's *Séraphîta* (1834), 83, 85
and influence of the Bible and Christian spirituality, 81, 83–6, 88
and John Milton's *Paradise Lost* (1667), 83, 87–8, 95n31
The One Who Is Legion or A.D.'s Afterlife (1930), 7, 18–19, 78–96; and publishing of, 81, 93n9
and Radclyffe Hall's *The Well of Loneliness* (1928), 7, 85, 184
and sexology, 79, 80, 83, 85, 86
Barrett Browning, Elizabeth, 9, 166

285

INDEX

Batten, Mabel ('Ladye'), 176, 177
Baty, Thomas *see* Clyde, Irene
Baudelaire, Charles, 8, 96n16
BBC, the, 99, 273
Beach, Sylvia, 34, 38, 134, 165, 167, 204
   and James Joyce, 210–12, 218–19
   and Shakespeare and Company, 204
Bechdel, Alison, 218–19
   Fun Home (2006), 218–19
Bell, Quentin, 41
Bell, Vanessa, 124, 174
Benstock, Shari, 43–4, 81–2, 126, 265–6
Bentley, Gladys, 13–14, 26–7n72
Bernstein, Henri, 173
Bible, the, 65, 80–1, 83–5, 88, 147–8, 152–3, 157, 234, 246n46
bildungsroman, 57, 67
biography, 9, 18, 19, 20, 36, 41, 42, 52n34, 61, 68, 76n68, 100–19, 127, 165–8, 173–80, 190, 197, 206, 225, 232, 239, 265–7, 270–9, 282
bisexuality, 2, 3, 4, 7, 13, 36, 60, 61, 114, 120, 130, 135–6, 152–7, 225, 233, 243n3, 266, 268
Black artistic movements, 7, 11–15; *see also* antiracism; Black cultures and representation; feminism, Black feminism
Black cultures and representation, 9, 11–15, 26n72, 35, 249, 253, 257–8, 261, 264n28; *see also* antiracism; Black artistic movements; feminism, Black feminism
blindness, 146–62; *see also* disability
Bloomsbury, 41, 266
Borderline (1930), 12–13
Boston Marriages, 228; *see also* romantic friendships
Bourdet, Édouard, *La Prisonnière* [*The Captive*], 134, 233–4
British Society for the Study of Sex Psychology, 205; *see also* sexology
Brooks, Romaine, 38, 124, 125–6, 140n36, 150, 166, 267–8
Browne, Stella, 205
Bryher, 12–13, 14, 34, 58, 199, 238–9, 274
Burdekin, Katharine, 16, 17, 101, 106–7, 118n39

Bush, George W., 34
Bussy, Dorothy (Dorothy Strachey), *Olivia* (1949), 184

Cahun, Claude, 126, 134, 167
   Aveux non avenus (*Disavowals, or Cancelled Confessions*) (1930), 167
Canada, 33, 34, 156
Cape, Jonathan, 10
Carpenter, Edward, 23n28, 95n28, 153, 205
Castle, Terry, 122, 149, 270
   The Apparitional Lesbian, 122
Cather, Willa, 58, 100
Catholicism, 6, 57, 65–7, 69, 76n68, 127, 140n36, 146, 179
Cavalaro, Sahli, 251
celibacy, 18, 57–8, 62–5, 68–70, 75n41, 75n42
censorship, 9–11, 12, 13, 17, 26n59, 33, 60, 134–5, 144n83, 144n84, 157, 179–80, 204, 226, 233, 237, 243, 259, 278–9; *see also* Hall, Radclyffe; Joyce, James; obscenity; pornography
Chaplin, Charlie, 171
cisgender, 3, 4, 6, 19, 47, 59, 60, 145, 146, 159
cisnormativity, 5, 19, 57, 65
class, 9, 11–14, 21, 24n38, 38–42, 57, 58, 63, 127–8, 133, 147–50, 155–6, 252, 253, 258, 264n28
Cline, Sally, 166, 175, 176, 177
clothing, 108, 110, 111–13, 118n41, 127–9, 212, 216, 230–1, 240, 241; *see also* crossdressing
Clyde, Irene, 6, 23n25, 194–5
Colette, 38, 123, 138n9, 241
collaboration, 8, 14, 20, 21, 114, 167, 168, 171, 174, 185–90, 196, 198, 266, 268
Cook, Blanche Wiesen, 40–3, 44, 45, 53n48
Coward, Noël, *Private Lives* (1930), 149
Craig, Edith, 56–7, 60–1, 68, 71, 199
Craig, Edward Gordon, 57
crossdressing, 56–7, 72n11, 196, 212, 216, 230–1, 238–9, 241; *see also* clothing

Cult of the Clitoris *see* Pemberton Billing trial
Cunard, Nancy, 190

D'Annunzio, Gabriele, 129, 140n36, 176
Dellamora, Richard, 150, 159, 161n40
Dent, J. M. & Sons, 272, 278, 280
Detloff, Madelyn, 34, 47–8
Dick, Kay, 271–82
  The Shelf (1984), 280–1
  They (1977), 271
Dickens, Charles, 171
Dickinson, Emily, 9
disability, 146–7, 150–1, 155, 158; *see also* blindness
Doan, Laura, 6, 11, 37, 73n16, 153, 154, 155, 267
D'Ora, Madame (Dora Kallmus), 127, 129, 130
Douglas, Lord Alfred, 7
Douglas, James, 10
Dunye, Cheryl, *Watermelon Woman, The* (1996), 15

Edel, Deborah, 250, 251, 258–9, 260
Edel, Leon, 272, 277–80
Edelman, Lee, 254
Egoist, The and *Egoist,* 15, 204, 206–7, 211
Eliot, T. S., 18, 26n59
Ellis, Edith *see* Lees, Edith
Ellis, Havelock, 5, 10, 61, 63, 134, 153–4, 167, 243
  Sexual Inversion (1897), 5, 61
Endymion, 69

Faderman, Lillian, 4, 230, 243n3
fascism/Sapphic fascism, 16, 17, 24n38, 47, 140n36, 176, 259, 261
fashion *see* clothing; crossdressing
feminism, 2, 3, 6, 7, 14, 20, 21, 22n8, 33–8, 40–9, 56–60, 63–5, 69, 71, 72, 102, 124–5, 136, 159, 183–99, 205, 207, 208, 249–52, 256, 257–8, 259, 260, 261–2, 265, 267
  and art history, 124–5, 136
  Black feminism, 35, 257–8, 264n28
  white feminism, 55n79
feminist modernism, 16, 21, 32, 34, 41–3, 44–9, 56–77

Field, Michael (Katharine Bradley and Edith Cooper), 8
Field, Ruth Fuller (Mary Casal), *The Stone Wall* (1930), 167
First World War, 127, 148–9, 150, 152–3, 155, 159, 177, 229, 230
  American Fund for the French Wounded, 173
Fox-Pitt, St George Lane, 177
Frederics, Diana, *Diana: A Strange Autobiography* (1939), 167, 181n14
Freewoman, The and *The New Freewoman,* 190, 193–6, 204–7, 211, 218, 219n15; *see also* Marsden, Dora
Freud, Sigmund, 95n28, 110, 147, 231, 233
  and Oedipus, 147
friendship, 18, 57, 67–70, 77n69, 107, 179, 209, 217, 227–33; *see also* romantic friendships
Fromm, Gloria Glikin, 277–8

Gawthorpe, Mary, 205
gendered gaze, 19, 136, 192
Gluck, 123, 130, 138n9, 267
Goldsmith, Margaret, 9, 14, 15, 18, 19, 99–119
  Belated Adventure (1929), 100
  Christina of Sweden: A Psychological Biography (1933), 101, 103–4, 106, 108, 109–11, 112, 115
  Ein Fremder in Paris: Roman [*A Stranger in Paris: A Novel*] (1930), 100
  Frederick the Great (1929), 101
  Patience Geht Vorüber: Ein Roman [*Patience Passes By: A Novel*] (1931), 100
  relationship with Vita Sackville-West, 99–100
  Sappho: A Psychological Reconstruction of Her Life (1936), 9, 101, 103–6, 108
  Venus in Scorpio: A Romance of Versailles, 1770–1793 (1940), 101, 106–7
  Women and the Future (1946), 101
  Women at War (1943), 101, 113

Gore-Booth, Eva, 6, 15, 20, 183–203, 206
   and Constance Markievicz, 186–8, 191, 192, 193
   and Esther Roper, 6, 183–90, 194–6, 206
   and *Urania*, 6, 15, 23n28, 183, 186, 194–8
   and W. B. Yeats, 187, 192–3
   'Women's Rights' (poem in *The Egyptian Pillar*) (1907), 186, 191–3
Grad, Benjamin, 278
Grad, Veronica, 277–9
Gregory, Horace, 271, 279–80
   Dorothy Richardson: An Adventure in Self-Discovery (1967), 280
Grimm's fairy tales, 171
Guardian, The, 271

H.D. (Hilda Doolittle), 8–9, 12–13, 34, 199, 246n57, 267
Hackett, Robin, 2, 9, 12, 14, 17, 20, 36, 248–64; *see also* primitivism
Halberstam, Jack, 5, 58–9, 134
Hall, Radclyffe, 4, 6–7, 9–12, 16, 20, 23n21, 23n24, 38, 42, 58, 76n68, 85, 145–62, 167, 174–80, 212, 253
   and 1920 slander trial, 177
   Adam's Breed (1926), 146, 155–9, 177
   and bisexuality, 152–5, 156
   'The Blind Ploughman' (1913), 146–8, 150, 159
   and Catholicism, 155–9, 179
   and censorship, 10–11, 16–17, 33, 179–80, 243
   and class, 12, 147, 148–50, 155–6, 253
   and creative reproduction, 167, 199
   and disability, 145–6, 155
   experience of sexual abuse, 178
   and fascism, 176
   The Forge (1924), 146, 148–52
   friendship with Christopher St. John, 60
   and gender nonconformity, 60, 178
   'Ghosts' (undated), 147, 161n25
   and heterosexuality, 19, 145–6, 149–50, 154–5, 158–9
   involvement in the Society for Psychical Research, 177
   and literary experimentation, 145–6, 157, 159
   and male sexuality, 19, 145–62
   The Master of the House (1932), 146, 155–9, 177
   and racism, 11–14, 176
   relationship with Una Troubridge, 20, 166, 174–80
   Songs of Three Counties and Other Poems (1913), 147, 149
   Una Troubridge's *The Life and Death of Radclyffe Hall* (1961), 166, 174–80
   The Unlit Lamp (1924), 150, 152
   The Well of Loneliness (1928), 5–7, 9–14, 16–17, 26n60, 33, 41, 42, 53n52, 60, 67–8, 85, 110, 145–6, 147, 150, 152–5, 158, 159, 161n38, 166, 167, 177, 178, 179–80, 184, 196–7, 243, 251
Hamilton, Cicely, *A Pageant of Great Women* (1909), 56
Hanscombe, Gillian, 43, 265, 266–8, 273
Haraway, Donna, and Chthulucene, 249, 255–6
Harlem Renaissance, 12–13
Harris, Bertha, 14, 38–41, 42–3
Hartman, Saidiya, 13–14, 35
Heap, Jane, 34, 167, 204, 211–12, 214, 218
heterosexuality, 4–5, 12–13, 14, 19, 130, 133, 134–6, 145–6, 149, 151–9, 172, 205, 208, 209, 211–9, 233, 266
Hirschfeld, Magnus, 95n28, 134
history or historical writing, 104–5
Hitler, Adolf, 176
Homer, *Odyssey*, 217
homosexuality (male), 10, 67, 146–51, 154, 155–7, 215, 237, 243
   and Hellenism, 7–8

intersectionality, 14, 48, 257, 264n28; *see also* feminism, Black feminism; race
Inversions, 135

Jacob, Mickie (Naomi), 179
James, Henry, 277–8

Jardine, Grace, 205
Joan of Arc, 56, 101, 103, 106
Joyce, James, 4, 10, 15, 20, 174, 204–21
 and censorship, 204, 206, 211–12, 214
 Dubliners (1914), 204, 206–10, 212, 219
 Exiles (1918), 217–18
 Finnegans Wake (1939), 204, 219, 220n32
 Lucia Joyce, 219
 A Portrait of the Artist as a Young Man (1914), 204, 206–7, 211
 Ulysses (1922), 10, 20, 33, 204, 209, 210, 211–19, 220n27, 221n44

Knopf, Alfred A., 280–1
Krafft-Ebing, Richard von, 95n28, 134, 152

Ladder, The (newsletter of the Daughters of Bilitis), 248, 262n1
Larsen, Nella, *Passing* (1929), 7, 24n34
Lawrence, D. H., *Lady Chatterley's Lover* (1928), 10
Lawrence, Margaret, 100, 156
Lees, Edith (Edith Ellis), 206
Lehman, John, 41
Leonard, Gladys Osborne, 177
Lesbian Herstory Archives (LHA), 14, 17, 18, 20, 248–64
 and Adrienne Rich, 248
 and Audre Lorde, 248
 and finances, 249, 251–3
 and inclusion, 258–60
 and inclusion of trans women, 259–60
 and lesbian modernism, 249, 250, 253
 and Megan Rossman's *Love Letter Rescue Squad* (2016), 249
 Newsletter, 249, 250, 251, 252, 255, 257, 258, 263–4, 261–2n27
 and pornography, 258, 259
 and Radclyffe Hall's *The Well of Loneliness* (1928), 251
 and *Sinister Wisdom*, 252
 see also Haraway, Donna, and Chthulucene; necropolitics; Nestle, Joan
lesbian modernism
 and 1928, 6, 9–10, 41, 166
 affective responses to, 1, 20, 31–55, 70–1, 268–71, 273
 and antisemitism, 253
 defining lesbian modernism, 1–5, 31–55, 58–61, 91–2, 265–77, 282
 development as scholarly field, 38–55, 267–8, 271
 and late modernism, 168
 and male sexuality, 145–62
 and male writers, 4, 204–21
 and Sapphic modernism, 6, 19, 24n38, 25n42, 32, 36, 40, 44, 267
 term coined by Minow, Makiko, 2, 36
 see also Black artistic movements; fascism/Sapphic fascism; feminist modernism; queer modernism; trans modernism
Life and Letters, 274
Little Review, The, 167, 204, 209, 211, 214
Locke, Alain, 13
Lorde, Audre, 42, 48, 248, 264n28
Louÿs, Pierre, *Les chansons de Bilitis* (1894), 36, 105, 143n68, 143n76
Lowell, Amy, 9
Loy, Mina, 193–4, 195
Lydis, Mariette, 120–44
 bisexuality, 120, 130, 135–6
 compared to Sappho, 120
 contemporary critical reception, 123–4
 Lesbiennes (1926), 120–2, 125, 127, 131–7, 139n30, 144n86
 and Paris, 120, 122, 125, 130–7, 140n36, 141n50
 representations of, 123, 127–30

Mackenzie, Compton, *Extraordinary Women* (1928), 9, 10, 53n48
Markievicz, Constance, 186–8, 191, 192, 193; *see also* Gore-Booth, Eva
Marsden, Dora, 34, 189, 193–4, 195, 204–6, 211, 212, 220n32
masculinity, 3, 4, 5, 13, 18, 19, 56–77, 145–62; *see also* trans masculinity
Matheson, Hilda, 99, 111
Mbembe, Achille *see* necropolitics
middlebrow, 17, 145–6, 159
Miles, Eustace, 206

Millay, Edna St. Vincent, 4, 14, 15, 17, 18, 20, 225–47
  and anachronism, 20, 225–6, 236, 239, 243
  Aria da Capo (1920), 226, 228–9, 243
  defence of *The Well of Loneliness* (1928), 243
  and Djuna Barnes, 226, 243, 244n7
  The King's Henchman (1926), 243
  The Lamp and the Bell (1921), 4, 17, 18, 20, 225–9, 233–7, 239–43
  and Provincetown Players, 226
  and the Renaissance/Elizabethan literature, 237–8
  at Vassar, 229–33, 239–42
Minow, Makiko, 2, 36, 43–4
modernism
  and art history, 124–5
  and family/kinship networks, 183–90
  focus on the experimental, 15–18, 125
  see also lesbian modernism; feminist modernism; late modernism; queer modernism; trans modernism
Monnier, Adrienne, 134, 167, 204, 210–11, 212, 218
  and Shakespeare and Company, 204, 210
Moore, Marianne, 193
Moschos, Myrsine, 219
music, 14, 210, 248, 268–9
Mussolini, Benito, 176

Nancy, Jean-Luc, 269–70
nation, 27n76, 129, 149, 187, 208, 255, 259, 261,
Neff, Wanda Fraiken, *We Sing Diana* (1928), 232–3
necropolitics, 249, 253–60, 261
Nestle, Joan, 14, 248, 250–2, 256–7, 258–60, 263n25
New Statesman, 271
New Woman, 129–30
New York, 38, 40
  Gertrude Stein and Alice B. Toklas in, 169
  and the Lesbian Herstory Archives, 20, 248–50, 252,
  and publication of *The Little Review*, 204, 211–12

Nicholson, Harold, 101
Nicholson, Nigel, 41
non-binary, 60, 72n9
Nugent, Richard Bruce, 13

obscenity, 8, 9, 10, 33, 132, 135, 137, 179, 211, 217, 233, 243; *see also* pornography
Odle, Alan, 273, 278
Odle, Edwin, 273
Odle, Rose, 273–80
Oline, Pamela, 251
Oliver, Kathlyn, 204–5, 207–8, 212, 218–19
Orwell, George, 272
Oxford, The University of, 1, 57, 66

Pankhurst family, 185, 189–90, 193, 195
Paris
  Alice B. Toklas in, 170, 171, 172–3
  art market, 131, 136, 137n4
  brothels and prostitution, 131–3, 142n64, 143n72
  Djuna Barnes in, 38, 39–40
  Edna St. Vincent Millay in, 239
  lesbian/queer subcultures, 7, 21, 38, 39–40, 42, 43, 92n1, 115, 133–4, 154–5, 160n3, 241, 265, 268
  and modernism, 39–40, 42, 125, 265–6, 268
  represented in *The One Who is Legion* (1930), 84, 93n6
  represented in *The Well of Loneliness* (1928), 154–5, 160n3, 161n36, 184
  Sylvia Beach in, 204, 210
  see also Lydis, Mariette
Pater, Walter, 8
Pemberton Billing trial (1918), 11
Picasso, Pablo, 172–3
Pioneer Players, 57
Plato, 7, 172, 232, 233, 234, 278
Platonic love *see* homosexuality (male); Wilde, Oscar
POOL film group, 12–13
pornography, 123, 132, 134, 137, 237, 258–9; *see also* obscenity
Pound, Ezra, 206–7, 218, 219n15, 221n49

Powys, John Cowper, 271
primitivism
  and modernism, 9, 12–13
  Sapphic primitivism (Robin Hackett), 2, 9, 36
Prosser, Jay, 5, 58, 72n11
psychoanalysis, 17, 107, 110, 138n9, 147, 178, 231; see also Freud, Sigmund

queer modernism and lesbian modernism, 1–3, 5, 12, 13, 19, 21, 24n38, 32, 34, 35, 43, 46, 47–9, 267
queer theory/studies, 33–4, 46, 47, 267
  queer temporalities, 36, 37, 42
  see also anachronism

race see antiracism; Black artistic movements; feminism; whiteness; necropolitics
Raitt, Suzanne, 36–7, 39, 40, 52n33
Ray, Man, 123
religion see Catholicism
Renaissance period, 7, 226, 233, 237–9
Rhondda, Lady (Margaret Haig Thomas), 100
Rich, Adrienne, 134, 248
Richardson, Dorothy, 2, 14, 15, 17, 20–1, 190, 266–84
  archive, 271, 274, 278–80
  correspondence, 270–1, 280
  engagement with Oscar Wilde's work, 272
  later life, 272–4
  marriage to Alan Odle, 273, 278
  Pilgrimage (1915–1938), 17, 270–1, 272, 273, 274, 279, 282; *March Moonlight* (1967), 271, 274–5, 277, 278–80
  relationship with Veronica Grad, 278
  Richardson Scholarly Editions Project, 20, 270–1
Robeson, Paul, 12–13
Robeson, Eslanda, 12–13
romantic friendships, 4, 69, 225, 228, 229–33, 237; see also Vassar
Roper, Esther, 6, 183–90, 194–6, 206
Rubin, Gayle, 39–41, 43
Rye, 60

Sackville-West, Vita, 7, 18, 19, 25n42, 26n60, 34, 36, 41, 45, 60, 71, 76n68, 99–119, 166
  Aphra Behn: The Incomparable Astrea (1927), 101, 103, 104
  The Diary of Lady Anne Clifford (1923), 101
  The Eagle and the Dove (1943), 111
  and masculinity, 119n57, 108–14
  Pepita (1937), 101, 104–5, 114–16
  relationship with Christopher St. John, 60, 71
  relationship with Margaret Goldsmith, 99–100
  relationship with Virginia Woolf, 25n42, 41, 45, 60, 99, 101, 166
  Saint Joan of Arc (1936), 101, 103, 104, 105, 106, 108–9, 110, 112, 114
  The Women's Land Army (1944), 101, 111–13, 114
Saint John the Baptist, 65–6, 156, 161n40
Saint Clare, 151
Saint Francis of Assisi, 151, 158
St. John, Christopher, 4, 15, 18, 56–77
  and Catholicism, 65, 66–7, 69
  The Crimson Weed (1900), 72n8
  engagement with Oscar Wilde's work, 65–7
  friendship with Radclyffe Hall and Una Troubridge, 60
  Hungerheart: The Story of a Soul (1915), 56–77
  relationship with Edith Craig and Tony Atwood, 57, 60, 61, 68, 71
  relationship with Vita Sackville-West, 60, 71
  and suffrage movement, 56–7, 63
  and trans masculinity, 56–77
Sapphic modernism; see fascism/Sapphic fascism; lesbian modernism; Sappho
Sappho, 8–9, 24n38, 25n42, 39, 51n23, 56, 94n16, 94n19, 130, 131, 141n48, 188, 197, 231–2; see also Goldsmith, Margaret; Lydis, Mariette
Schwob, Marcel, 167
Second World War, 111, 271
self-publishing, 131, 132

INDEX

sexology, 5–7, 17, 24n38, 58, 59, 61–5, 79, 80, 83, 85, 109, 119n45, 126, 132, 134, 167, 184, 196–7, 231, 232
   and British Society for the Study of Sex Psychology, 205
   and sexual inversion, 5–6, 7, 11–12, 16, 23n21, 61–2, 109, 79, 80, 86, 95n28, 109, 134, 145, 147, 152–4, 156, 159n1, 161n38, 161n40, 178, 184, 196
   and Uranianism, 7, 23n28, 153, 197, 205
   see also Ellis, Havelock; Hirschfeld, Magnus; Krafft-Ebing, Richard von
Shakespeare, William, 8, 57, 71, 77n74, 227, 228, 234, 238, 246n57
Shakespeare and Company, 204, 210; *see also* Beach, Sylvia; Monnier, Adrienne
Sissinghurst Castle, 60
Six Point Group, 100
Smallhythe Place, 57, 60, 71, 77n74
Smyers, Virginia L., 2, 43, 265, 266, 268, 273
Society for Psychical Research, 177
Souhami, Diana, 166, 175, 177, 267–8
Souline, Evguenia, 23n21, 167, 175, 176–7, 179
spirituality, 57, 67–8, 147, 188; *see also* Catholicism; theosophy
Stanhope, Lady Hester, 216
Stanley, Julia, 251
Stein, Gertrude, 15, 17, 20, 34, 36, 38, 39, 42, 44, 58, 76n60, 140n36, 165–74, 178, 180, 182n48, 184, 267
   The Autobiography of Alice B. Toklas (1933), 38, 166, 167, 168–70, 171, 174
   and creative reproduction, 167
   Everybody's Autobiography (1937), 169, 170, 172, 174
   The Making of Americans (1925), 172
   'Melanctha' and *Three Lives* (1909), 174
   and relationship with Alice B. Toklas, 42, 165–82
   Wars I Have Seen (1945), 174
Strachey, Dorothy *see* Bussy, Dorothy

Strachey, Lytton, 102, 116
Strachey family, 189–90
Stryker, Susan, 59, 60, 71
suffrage movement, 56–7, 63, 240, 188, 189, 190–4
suffragette movement, 63, 100, 115, 190, 206
Swinburne, Algernon Charles, 8
Symonds, John Addington, 8, 61
   Sexual Inversion (1897), 61

Terry, Ellen, 57, 68, 72n8, 77n74
Thackeray, William Makepeace, *Vanity Fair* (1848), 171
theosophy, 6, 17, 194
Toklas, Alice B., 15, 17, 20, 34, 38, 42, 165–74, 175, 176, 177, 178, 180
   The Alice B. Toklas Cook Book (1954), 168, 181n23
   editing of Stein's work, 168
   relationship with Gertrude Stein, 42, 165–74, 180
   and unreliable narration, 171
   What Is Remembered (1963), 165–6, 168–74, 176, 180
Townsend Warner, Sylvia, 9, 16, 36, 76n68
trans, 1, 6, 15, 32, 36, 57, 59, 60, 61, 65, 68, 69, 119n45, 159, 196, 251, 259, 268; *see also* non-binary; trans femininity; trans masculinity; trans modernism; trans studies
trans femininity, 3, 6, 58, 73n14
trans masculinity, 3, 4, 5, 18, 56–77, 109, 119n45
trans modernism, 3, 4, 5–6, 6–7, 18, 21, 23n24, 24n38, 56–77
trans studies, 3, 4, 47, 57, 58, 59, 60, 72
Traub, Valerie, 7, 237–8
Troubridge, Admiral Sir Ernest Charles Thomas, 175
Troubridge, Una, 12, 20, 38, 60, 150, 166–8, 174–80
   1920 slander trial, 177
   and Catholicism, 179
   editing of Radclyffe Hall's work, 176–7
   and fascism, 176
   involvement in the Society for Psychical Research, 177

The Life and Death of Radclyffe Hall (1961), 166, 174–80
  relationship with Radclyffe Hall, 20, 166–8, 174–80
  and unreliability narration, 166, 175–6, 177–9
  work as sculptor and translator, 166
Turing, Alan, 272
Tynan, Katharine, 186, 197

Urania, 6, 15, 183, 186, 194–8
Uranianism *see* sexology

Vanity Fair, 210
Vassar, 17, 20, 225–47
  culture of romantic friendships ('crushing', 'smashing'), 225, 229–33
  performance of *The Lamp and the Bell* (Millay, 1921), 20, 227–9, 230, 239–42
Vaux, Marc, 121–3, 126, 127, 128, 134, 137n4
Vauxcelles, Louis, 124
Vivien, Renée, 8, 34, 38, 39, 241
Von Reinhold, Shola, *LOTE* (2020), 15

Warner, Sylvia Townsend, 9, 16, 36, 198–9
Weaver, Harriet, 34, 204, 206, 211, 212
  and Egoist Press, 204
Wells, H. G., 278
West, Rebecca, 190, 205, 206
whiteness, 9, 11–14, 21, 34, 43, 47, 48, 49, 50n12, 55n79, 58, 63, 251, 256, 258, 260–1

White, Max, 171, 172
Whitman, Walt, 8
Wilde, Dolly, 93n9
Wilde, Oscar, 7–8, 65–7, 75n56, 75n57, 158–9, 232, 272
  De Profundis (1905), 66
  Salomé: A Tragedy in One Act (1894), 11, 65–6
Winning, Jo, 2, 15, 17, 20–1, 27–8n85, 126, 265–84
Woman Worker, The, 205
Women Writers' Suffrage League, 57
Wood, Thelma, 246n62
Woolf, Virginia, 9, 14, 15, 25n42, 35, 41–2, 43, 44, 45, 54n73, 60, 99, 100, 101, 102, 157, 167, 174, 190, 253, 267
  A Room of One's Own (1929), 184–5, 190, 195
  Flush: A Biography (1933), 102, 166
  Mrs Dalloway (1925), 216–17; influence of *Ulysses* on, 221n44
  'The New Biography' (1927), 166
  Orlando: A Biography (1928), 6–7, 10, 11, 17, 25n49, 41, 45, 60, 102, 112, 166, 239, 243
  on *The Well of Loneliness* (1928), 26n60
  'A Woman's College from Outside' (1926), 197–8

Yeats, W. B., 186–7, 191–3, 206
  'The Stolen Child' (1886), 186, 192–3

Zimmerman, Bonnie, 3, 45

EU representative:
Easy Access System Europe
Mustamäe tee 50, 10621 Tallinn, Estonia
Gpsr.requests@easproject.com

www.ingramcontent.com/pod-product-compliance
Lightning Source LLC
Chambersburg PA
CBHW050207240426
43671CB00013B/2246